SOLIDARITY AND SUFFERING

SUNY Series,
Religion and American Public Life

William D. Dean, editor

SOLIDARITY AND SUFFERING
Toward a Politics of Relationality

Douglas Sturm

STATE UNIVERSITY OF NEW YORK PRESS

Production by Ruth Fisher
Marketing by Patrick Durocher

Published by
State University of New York Press, Albany

©1998 State University of New York

For information, address State University of New York Press,
State University Plaza, Albany, NY 12246

Library of Congress Cataloging-in-Publication Data

Sturm, Douglas
      Solidarity and suffering : toward a politics of relationality /
Douglas Sturm.
            p.   cm. — (SUNY series, religion and American public life)
      Includes index.
            ISBN 0–7914–3869–4 (alk. paper). — ISBN 0–7914–3870–8 (pbk. :
alk. paper)
            1. Social justice.   2. Solidarity.   3. Religion and politics.
      4. Religion and social problems.   I. Title.   II. Series
      HM216.S795   1998
      303.3'72—dc21   97–45207
                                                                                CIP

10 9 8 7 6 5 4 3 2 1

CONTENTS

ACKNOWLEDGMENTS

Many of the chapters in this text are revisions of essays that have appeared elsewhere in various journals and books. Permission has graciously been granted by the publishers of those essays—as listed below—for their use in this new context.

"A Prospective View of the Bill of Rights: Toward a New Constitutionalism," *Journal for Peace and Justice Studies*, vol. 5, no. 1, 1993, pp. 1–14.

"Property: A Relational Perspective," *Journal of Law and Religion*, vol. IV, no. 2, 1986, pp. 353–404.

"A Vision of Justice as Solidarity," *Journal of Law and Religion*, vol. XIII, no. 1, 1997.

"On the Suffering and Rights of Children: Toward a Theology of Childhood Liberation," *Cross Currents*, vol. 42, no. 2, 1992, pp. 149–73.

"The Idea of Human Rights: A Communitarian Perspective," *Process Studies*, vol. 23, nos. 3 & 4, 1994, pp. 238–55.

"The Socialist Vision Revisited," *Creative Transformation*, vol. 3, no. 4, 1994, pp. 1, 3–6.

"Criminality and Community," *Creative Transformation*, vol. 4, no. 2, 1995, pp. 18–21.

"Affirmative Action and the Deprivations of Racism," *Creative Transformation*, vol. 4, no. 4, 1995, pp. 17–20.

"Property: A Relational Perspective," *Economic Life: Process Interpretations and Critical Responses*, edited by W. Widick Schroeder and Franklin I. Gamwell (Chicago: Center for the Scientific Study of Religion, 1988), pp. 29–77.

"Democratic Theory and Corporate Governance," *International Journal of Value-Based Management*, vol. I, no. 1, 1988, pp. 93–111.

"The Socialist Vision Revisited," *Religious Socialism*, vol. 19, no. 5, 1995, pp. 3–5, 10.

"Religion as Critique and the Critique of Religion: The Problem of the Self in the Modern World," *Religion: Journal of the KSR*, vol. 27, no. 2, March 1990, pp. 1–7.

"Crossing the Boundaries: On the Idea of Interreligious Dialogue and the Political Question," *Journal of Ecumenical Studies*, vol. 30, no. 1, Winter 1993, pp. 1–19.

"Wisdom and Compassion: The Deeper Dimensions of Understanding," *Bucknell World*, vol. 23, no. 3, May 1995, pp. 6–7.

"Faith, Ecology, and the Demands of Social Justice," *Religious Experience and Ecological Responsibility*, edited by Donald A. Crosby and Charley D. Hardwick (New York: Peter Lang Publishers, 1996), pp. 287–313.

Long before they were published in any form, the thoughts and ideas expressed through these pages were refined and reformed as a result of many, many discussions with colleagues and students, friends and strangers in diverse venues: Bucknell University, University of Tennessee, St. Andrew's University, American Academy of Religion, Hamline University School of Law, University of Kansas, Norman Thomas Society, Society of Christian Ethics, University of Chicago— and sometimes in airplanes, on the streets, at coffee houses, and during interminable meetings of NGOs. Not everyone with whom I have shared my reflections and yearnings has been sympathetic with my perspective, but all have treated me with the kind of respect that every member of the community of life deserves. For that I am most grateful, but shall remain unsatisfied until that respect and all that it entails shape every one of our relationships everywhere and at all times. I am most appreciative, however, for my immediate family—my wife, Margie Jean Anderson Sturm, and my sons, Hans and Rolf—whose sensitivities about the dynamics of solidarity and suffering have been consistently supportive of my endeavors even where those endeavors have detracted from our time together. We have, nevertheless, been constantly together in our commitment to that cause whose name is justice and whose ultimate quality is love.

1

Prelude:
Toward a Politics of Relationality

> Let justice roll down like waters and
> righteousness like an ever-flowing stream.
> —*Amos 5:24*

> Existence in most instances
> is sustained by a perilously slight
> margin of sensitivity.
> —*Bernard E. Meland*[1]

ON THE VERGE OF A NEW CENTURY:
A QUESTION OF OUR FUTURE

We are at this moment on the verge of a new century. In one sense, the timing—passing from the twentieth to the twenty-first century—is but an arbitrary point of measurement, a convenience designed to measure the passage of years. But, in a more profound sense, the timing is fraught with deep significance.

In our move into the new century, we are confronted with a massive decision about the character and quality of our common life. The future, we must understand, is not predetermined. What the new century will be is not prescribed. What it will be is up to us. Within the configuration of constraints we are bequeathed by our past, our future is an open possibility. Many peoples, aware of that open possibility, are clamoring for radical change in our forms of interaction domestically and internationally on the supposition that we have it within our powers to create a new time and a new way of life—in some fashion, we like to think, an advance on the present. From many angles and in many venues, struggles are underway about social and cultural reconstruction. And, as all the parties to those struggles are aware, the stakes are high.

In this context, the question we are compelled to ask—of ourselves and of each other—is two-sided. It is political and it is religious. On its politi-

1

cal side, the question, most simply put, is: How shall we live our lives together? On its religious side, the question, cast most directly, is: Who are we? What is our place and our destiny in the world? These two sides of the question are, I would insist, caught up with each other. They cannot, in the final analysis, be separated, although each addresses its own dimension of the matter. The question in both of its forms is, at this moment, urgent.

To be sure, if we are even minimally aware of all the repercussions and reticulations of our everyday lives, we know that we are constantly providing some sort of response to that two-sided question. The shape of our future and the meaning of our lives is ever being determined afresh by how we conceive ourselves and how we interact with each other, even if all we do is to reproduce the routine forms of thought and interaction we have inherited. That is so often—too often—the path of greatest ease even when we find that path somewhat uncomfortable. Yet these everyday determinations are far from humdrum. At particularly eventful moments, we can discern their import with stark clarity, sometimes with frightful clarity, especially when we are brought to awaken from our slumbers and to realize the depth and extent of suffering that results from what appear to be ordinary routines.

Consider, in this light, some of the major political eruptions of the twentieth century. During that period, we have been confronted with a range of massive drives to capture the minds and energies of people that have, in time, exploded in devastating violence—fascism, state socialism, apartheid, religious authoritarianism, neocolonialism, military dictatorship. All of these movements have tended to proclaim commitment to high principle. All of them, at least for a time, became settled (and respected) ways of life somewhere in the world. Yet all of them have threatened whole classes of humans with subjugation if not annihilation—and were often, sad to say, true to their word. Other forms of political contention have appeared more benign, even joining in common battle against the extremes, but oftentimes conniving to conceal, while seeking to suppress, important revolutionary struggles against them by dissenting groups—associated by race, class, gender, ethnic heritage, or nationalist identity—each of them (those in dissent) seeking liberation from the oppressive rule of established powers.

Sometimes, in the United States, we tend to consider these eruptions and struggles as merely momentary aberrations, exceptional cases, not unimportant, but to be gotten over as quickly as possible in order to return to business as usual. Moreover, we suspect that "politics" in its ordinary course is no more than a tiresome struggle over who gets what, when, where, and how—a jockeying for privilege and power, an effort to shift the burdens of our common endeavors onto others and to gain more benefits for ourselves. That's certainly one way to read the political process.

But that way of reading the political process is superficial if not deceptive. It skims the surface of what is more profoundly at stake in the public forum. The deeper concern of the public forum—even when the question of distribution (who gets what, when, and how much) is the immediate item on the agenda—is the shape and extent of our togetherness (that's the political side of the question posed above). And how we address that concern depends on how we construe our identity and our destiny (that's the religious side of the question posed above). That is, the struggles that transpire in the public forum are never merely over how to allocate the benefits and burdens of a social system even though that may be their immediate manifestation. They are, if you will, struggles over our soul. They are struggles over how we understand ourselves, our relationships with each other, our place in the world, our responsibility to the future, our participation in the whole ongoing community of life. The question of distribution, that is, is inextricably linked to the question of ontology (who are we, what is the shape of our relationship with each other, what is the character of our destiny?).

At the moment, the public forum in the United States is alive with contending perspectives on these questions, each promoting its own way of approaching the future, each delineating some way of comprehending our identity and our destiny, each with a vision of what the new century should be. That is the context in the midst of which I have initiated this move toward a politics of relationality. In a sense, of course, this proposal for a politics of relationality simply adds one more voice to the public forum. But I am convinced that it is more than simply one more voice. I am convinced that, given the current circumstances of the community of life, a politics of relationality is more sensible, more adequate, more responsive to those circumstances than are the alternatives.

We are, in my judgment, living at a time of crisis—a time at which the health (if not the survival) of the entire community of life, human and nonhuman, is at risk. We need to shape our political and our religious commitments in response to that condition with the objective of reorienting our lives and transforming our institutions in a way that contributes to the vibrancy and vigor of the whole community and each of its members. We must address the ecological crisis where untold numbers of species are rapidly becoming extinct. We must address the social crisis where forgotten and marginalized peoples are suffering under conditions of neglect and oppression. We must address the economic crisis where circumstances of absolute poverty keep one-fifth of the world's population in misery. We must address the political crisis where violence tends to reign supreme and freedoms are severely curtailed. But we can address this manifold crisis adequately, I believe, only if we can come to understand ourselves as denizens of a vast and variegated community of life—denizens whose well-being as selves is intimately intertwined with the well-being of all. That is a central understanding of the politics of relationality and sets it apart from other voices currently dominant in the American public forum.

Among those voices, a *politics of welfare* played a prominent role for over fifty years in the twentieth century.[2] The politics of welfare, epitomized in the New Deal, emerged as an effort to mitigate the dysfunctional effects of the burgeoning growth of a highly concentrated corporative industrialism initiated during the turn from the nineteenth century to the twentieth century. The New Deal's programs—intended to stabilize the economy, to develop a social insurance program for the needy, to provide employment for the able-bodied, and to protect the vulnerable from exploitation by those in control of the productive process—were inspired by a principle of equality. From the standpoint of a politics of welfare, as civilization advances, no one should be deprived of the benefits of the social system; no one should be left out; each and every citizen holds equal rights in the distribution of the basic powers and privileges of the political and economic order. But, in large part, the politics of welfare has not been transformative. It is designed primarily as remedial. Its overarching concern is to sustain the dominant system of corporate industrialism, although to spread its benefits more evenly across the citizenry.

However, with the Reagan Revolution, the politics of welfare collided with a *politics of liberty* (whether under the banner of neoconservatism or libertarianism).[3] The politics of liberty, resting on a principle of desert, launched a wholesale attack on the redistributive policies of the welfare state as, in effect, a form of illegal if not immoral confiscation. Appealing to traditional rights of the classical liberal tradition—rights of private ownership and of voluntary exchange—its stated intent was to delimit the functions of government. The basic purpose of government, from this perspective, is fundamentally if not solely protective: hence the need for an indomitable military force and a vigorous program of law and order. Otherwise, individuals—either alone or in corporate associations—are to be left to live their lives as they wish, to use their fortunes as they see fit, and to dispose of resources they possess without constraint. Whatever responsibilities individuals (or corporations) may have to others (aside from respecting their inalienable rights) must be undertaken voluntarily. Given the politics of liberty, the use of coercive power to enforce such responsibilities, however important those responsibilities might be, is simply improper.

During that same period of time, groups from somewhat different traditions raised serious questions about both the politics of welfare and the politics of liberty. Those forms of politics, while attending, each in its own way, to the important issue of how the burdens and benefits of the social process are to be distributed, are, it was claimed, utterly neglectful of a more profound issue of social morality, namely, what, within the ethos of a people, enables it to cohere, to collaborate, to sustain its basic traditions and institutions? Out of concern for this issue arose a *politics of community* with its primary focus on virtue—the kinds of moral and political virtue that constitute the character and continuity of a people. Where concerns for liberty and equality may, with appreciably different results, honor our individuality (therefore our separateness), they both overlook the vital human quality of sociability (therefore our connectedness). In some versions, the politics of community promotes the particular virtues and principles of a traditional religious heritage (e.g., the Christian Coalition).[4] In other versions, it takes a more latitudinarian position, stressing the republican values of respect, tolerance, mutuality, caring (e.g., communitarianism).[5]

Not all peoples in the American public forum, however, are attracted to the seeming magnanimity of communitarianism or to the high principles of either the politics of welfare or the politics of liberty. All these forms of politics are discerned as deceptive, favoring, despite their claims to the contrary, the wealthy and powerful, the privileged, the dominant class of the social system. The alternative is a *politics of difference,* a multicultural politics, generated by the sufferings of communities of people subordinated and marginalized by the mainstream, communities whose needs and values are ignored (or distorted through cooptation) by the major institutions of the United States.[6] In supporting a politics of difference, various communities of color, gays and lesbians, immigrants from once colonized lands (formerly designated

"Third World" countries), feminist and womanist groups are concerned not merely to preserve the values and sensibilities of their respective traditions of experience. Their intent is far more radical than that. They are engaged in a fundamental critique of the presuppositions and import of corporate capitalism. They resist seemingly well-intentioned efforts to assimilate them into the prevailing system out of their commitment to a style of life in which economic values are subordinated to other, more humane values and the cultural imperialism of mainstream America is eschewed.

Equally critical of dominant institutions with their overweening drive toward economic growth and their propensity to measure all things as an economic resource is a *politics of ecology*, which—in its more extreme forms—is yet a minor voice in the American public forum, although it manifests a proper concern for the place and role of the human species within the biosphere.[7] From a genuinely ecological perspective, humans are forced to reassess their identity and their responsibility to the entire community of life. While in comparison with other species, we have our own genius, our interests and desires should not, from this angle, run rough-shod over other forms of life. Rather we should, through our institutional policies and practices, promote the sustainability of those ecosystems of which we are a part and which are composed of a delicate balance among diverse kinds of living and nonliving entities. From this standpoint, we are in desperate need of radically reconstructing the way we think about ourselves and the way in which we live our lives.

Each of these forms of politics in the American public forum, in my judgment, has some merit in the sense that each, at its best, bears witness to a moral principle worthy of serious consideration:

- politics of welfare: respect for the *dignity* of all agents in the community;
- politics of liberty: deference to the *subjectivity* of each agent in the community;
- politics of community: the need for *empathy* among all members of the community;
- politics of difference: the importance of *diversity* within the community;
- politics of ecology: the *inclusiveness* of all forms of life within the community.

But none of these forms of politics, by itself, seems adequate as a response to the crisis that confronts us. Each of them, in fact, by itself, demonstrates severe limitations in comprehending the depth and character of the crisis that typifies our moment in the world's history. In that context, I am proposing a politics of relationality as a possibility that incorporates all of these principles, but in a reconfiguration that stretches beyond them and constructs a cogent possibility for our transition into the twenty-first century. At the heart of the politics of relationality is a principle of justice as solidarity.

JUSTICE AS SOLIDARITY

In times such as these, if we are cognizant—and honest—about the circumstances that make up our common life, we must admit to the thick interdependency of our lives. We cannot be what we are, we cannot do what we do, we cannot accomplish what we accomplish apart from one another. Perhaps more than we can ever fully discern, our lives are but expressions, albeit creative expressions, of a communal matrix that sustains us, inspires us, and constitutes the origin of our dreams and yearnings, our obligations and our rights. We are members of each other. We belong together. That is the source of our joy in life, although that is, as well, the source of the tragedies of life, the dark side of our history, which, on all too many occasions, makes us shudder and anxious about our destiny.

I do not mean this comment, please understand, as sheer sentimentality. It is, instead, both a political affirmation and a religious declaration, and, as such, it provides an opening for reflection on a major theme of the politics of relationality—the principle of justice as solidarity. I shall explain what I mean by justice as solidarity under the headings of four subthemes: alienation, relationality, otherness, and spirituality.

As an entrée to this reflection, I would call upon a well-known declamation of the ancient Hebrew prophet, Amos: "I hate, I despise your feasts, and I take no delight in your solemn assemblies. . . . But let justice roll down like waters, and righteousness like an ever-flowing stream."[8] On the face of it, that declamation was a rather harsh commentary on the customary solemnity of temples and courts with all their ceremonial falderal. But, more profoundly, we should recall that Amos was addressing a society riven with divisions: between rich and poor, rulers and subjects, priests and people, elite and needy. The covenant of justice, a covenant of brotherhood and sisterhood had been broken. Suffering was rampant. The powerful and affluent were unresponsive. Amos, speaking the voice of the covenantal God, was, in these words, calling the people to repentance—to a radical transformation in their ways of understanding and in their social and political practices. Justice, expressive of the mind of God, was a judgment against the perversities of the day and a vision of possibilities for tomorrow. The concept of justice in Amos, while not without distributive connotations (who gets what and how much), was, more accurately, indicative of the quality of a vibrant community, a community whose energies are directed to the welfare of all its members, a community through which the life of each and all might be continuously nourished, from birth to death. That's the import of solidarity. Justice as solidarity is a synonym for the covenantal community.

Against that backdrop, consider four subthemes that bear on the meaning of justice as solidarity.

First, alienation. We are living in a time of intense suffering. In large part, that suffering is a consequence, directly or indirectly, of patterns of human interaction. By suffering, I mean not so much discomfort (a subjective feeling) as deprivation (an objective condition). We suffer when deprived of that range of possibilities that makes up a vibrant community.

To be so deprived is a function of prevailing forms of symbiosis. Those deprived, even those living under the most dire of circumstances, are still, in their suffering, participants in the human community. That is why I use the term *alienation*. Alienation is a negative form of belonging. Alienation is not so much the separation of person from person or group from group as a form of interaction through which a people is constrained, by the seeming necessities of the case, to act against their own good, albeit to the seeming advantage and under the hegemonic control of another people.

Instances are not hard to come by: women whose lives are largely determined by the predominance of patriarchal social forms; blacks forced to live and to work in the bowels of racist institutional structures; workers whose livelihood is configured by the dictation of economic powers beyond their grasp. We should add, in this era of emergent ecological consciousness, the whole sphere of animality and vegetation which has become so extensively governed and exploited by the prescriptions of human interest.

Structures of alienation are pervasive throughout the world, even, ironically enough, coopting valiant efforts to modify or to transform them. In developing his controversial thesis about the "permanence of racism" in the United States, Derrick Bell observes: "Black people will never gain full equality in this country. Even those herculean efforts we hail as successful will produce no more than temporary 'peaks of progress,' short-lived victories that slide into irrelevance as racial patterns adapt in ways that maintain white dominance."[9]

However, the irony deepens, for, I would maintain, the deprivations of alienation are visited on all its parties, dominant and subordinate. That is the burden of James Baldwin's advice to his young nephew—that he, as a black, must, despite impulses to the contrary, accept white people, even with love, because, he insists, these "people have no other hope. They are, in effect, still trapped in a history which they do not understand; and until they understand it, they cannot be released from it." These white people, he admonished, are your own brothers and sisters, your lost, younger brothers and sisters, and we must, out of love, force them "to see themselves as they are, to cease fleeing from reality, and begin to change it. For this is your home, my friend, do not be driven from it."[10]

I do not mean, by citing Baldwin's advice, to suggest that the full task of struggling against the structures of alienation falls to the primary victims; but I do mean to propose that primary victims have a wisdom about our condition that others require for their own enlightenment and that, from the perspective of our profoundest good, we are all victimized by these structures. Whether alienation is present in the fury of military action, the dynamics of corporate capitalism, or the seductive powers of mass media, we are—as primary victims discern with greater lucidity than the rest of us—all caught up in a system devoid of the quality of solidarity, save in rare, but precious, moments of disclosure, moments revelatory of an alternative possibility.

Second subtheme: relationality. Underlying the sociology of alienation is an ontology of relationality, by which I mean that each of us, even in our uniqueness, is a living distillation of generations of interaction. We are social beings whose individuality can be comprehended only contextually. Our identity, while bearing the stamp of our own agency, is nonetheless contingent on an organic inheritance the full depths of which we cannot pretend to comprehend fully. The more each of us pursues what makes us what we are, the more we are led into all the nooks and crannies of the whole community of life across the millennia.

In stressing our dependency on that nexus of relationships that constitutes our matrix and that is part and parcel of our very selves, I do not mean to detract from our creativity. What each of us feels, what each of us thinks, what each of us does makes a difference in the world. We are born of a past, but we are progenitors of a future. There is, in short, a constant interplay between our selves as creative agents and the world as an inheritance bequeathed to each tomorrow. The quality of that interplay is the subject of all normative discourse, including moral reflection, political thought, and jurisprudence.

In the case of Anglo-American jurisprudence, engaged nowadays in a multivoiced and serious contention over the meaning and character of law, I would, for purposes of this exercise, contrast two possibilities, each constructed on its own ontological understanding: a jurisprudence of individuality and a jurisprudence of solidarity. The former, a jurisprudence of individuality, is concentrated on the basic norm: preserve autonomy! The latter, a jurisprudence of solidarity, is focused on an alternative basic norm: enhance community! In their contrast to the prevailing world situation, both are revolutionary in import, that is, both run contrary to the prevailing practice of law.

The former is exemplified in Richard A. Epstein's recent proposal of six "simple rules for a complex world"[11] which, he claims, extracts the genius of the common law. The foundational rule of the set—individual self-ownership—as it expands, developing its implications, gives rise to three correlative rules—of property ("you take what you can get"), contract ("voluntary exchange"), and torts ("keep off"). Understanding the need, now and then, to encroach on each other's sphere of life, Epstein attaches a two-sided secondary rule, summarized as "take and pay," that is, under conditions of necessity, it is not always inappropriate to consume another's property, but in such cases just compensation is requisite.

The model is elegant in its simplicity, but seems utterly lacking in reality in its failure to comprehend the dynamics of alienation. Its ultimate flaw is ontological. In its drive to preserve autonomy and therewith to promote the market as the most efficient means for the resolution of social problems, it ignores our essential connectedness with the community of life. It is narrowly anthropocentric, neglectful of the deep ecology of our living circumstance, and it is unrelentingly individualistic, neglectful of the interactive character of culture and history.

As an alternative perspective on who we are, how we live, and what we might do to better shape our common life, consider Carol Gould's version of a feminist ontology, summarized in these words:

> although it is only individual human beings that exercise agency and not institutions or society as a whole, yet these individuals are social beings who act in and through their social relations. They engage in joint or common agency in which they seek to realize common goals; or, in pursuit of their individual goals, they require the respect, recognition, or forbearance of others, and their individual acts bear on others in various ways. When individuals act with respect to each other, their relations take the form either of domination and subordination or of reciprocity.[12]

Gould's is an ontology of relationality, giving rise to an understanding of history as a dialectic between alienation and solidarity. The vision she has articulated provides a firm foundation for a jurisprudence of solidarity in which the driving passion of law is not so much to protect the individual against trespass as it is to create a quality of social interaction conducive to the flourishing of a vibrant community of life across the world. That, I would propose, is the profoundest aim of justice.

Third subtheme: otherness. At this point, we must be cautious. I have been unfolding the meaning of justice as solidarity. I have been promoting that principle as a quality that should permeate the structures of our common life. I have affirmed that justice so understood should be the driving passion of our normative discourse. But the demands of solidarity might seem, on initial consideration, to smack of conformism, requiring each and every member of the community to assume the same character, to adopt the same style of life, to look and to act alike. Can justice as solidarity take account of eccentricity, difference, otherness, alterity? I would like to think so.

Consider, in this connection Patricia Cain's critique of prevailing forms of feminist jurisprudence. Feminist jurisprudence, she declares, is singularized by its attention to the peculiarities of female experience—the joys and sorrows, the questions, the needs, the limitations, the deprivations of that experience. But whose experience counts? She charges that "current feminist legal theory is deficient and impoverished because it has not paid sufficient attention to the real life experiences of women who do not speak the 'dominant discourse.'"[13] Feminist legal theory, while properly serving as a critique of the blinders that constrain traditional forms of law, must itself be subjected to critique, to a kind of self-critique; it must guard against assuming that female experience is uniform; it must, for instance, as Cain insists, become open to the lesbian possibility. "Feminist legal theory must recognize differences in order to avoid reinforcing lesbian invisibility or marginality."[14]

In sum, the lesbian, too, if I may put it this way, has place in the community—that place must be recognized and respected within the structures of the community, that voice must be heard, that way of living out one's destiny must be honored. That is how I would construe—admittedly for my own purposes—the ancient precept: "You shall not wrong or oppress a stranger, for you were strangers in the land of Egypt."[15] The covenantal community embraces the stranger. It greets the stranger as companion, understanding that the other, however strange or familiar, belongs to the circle of life. Whether ordinary or extraordinary, mainstream or sidestream, we are all participants in the common adventure of life and must be regarded as such. Each, in our uniqueness, has something to contribute to that adventure.

That is the spirit that underlies Henry James Young's "theology of social pluralism," an instructive effort to demonstrate the compatibility of a relational ontology with the African American experience.

> Within a pluralistic society the goal is to discover ways of allowing self-actualization in the context of relationality. This requires an open system rather than a closed one. . . . For individuals in society to relate successfully to others they have to be open and vulnerable. And Whitehead's notion of interdependence, which is primary in his notion of the self, suggests that while maintaining a sense of openness to other ethnic social groups, one should also adhere to one's own unique ethnic tradition.[16]

As Young intimates in his concept of social pluralism, within the orbit of justice as solidarity, there is a normative boundary to otherness, but a boundary that is fluid, a boundary whose precise delineations are always open to renegotiation. The boundary emanates from the burden of reciprocity: as one demands respect from others, so one ought show respect for others. In our differences, we must not forget our togetherness. In this sense, an ethics of rights and an ethics of care are conjoined by a principle of complementarity and, in their conjunction, both are necessary ingredients of any effective politics of difference.

Final subtheme: spirituality. The vision of justice as solidarity in the construction I am proposing rests, ultimately, on an affirmation of the reality of spirit as a dimension of all existence. I am here following the lead of Bernard E. Meland, a radical empiricist theologian out of the tradition of process thought, who defines spirit in the following way:

> Spirit connotes a depth of sensitivity that forms the matrix of relations in which all life is cast. This depth of sensitivity is not so much known as lived in. It is a kind of womb or matrix out of which the waking life of individual persons emerges and in which individuals participate, knowingly or unknowingly, as living creatures. We may say that spirit is a quality of being which arises out of a particular depth of sensitivity in relations. It is, in other words, a goodness in relationships.[17]

In affirming the reality of spirit so understood, I do not mean to identify all forms of sociality with spirit. The bulk of our ordinary interactions is conducted devoid of any explicit attention to the dimension of spirit at all. These interactions have, instead, a utilitarian cast; they are, as we tend to say, of a practical nature. They enable us to cope with the immediate needs of survival. They call upon an everyday wisdom, much of which is passed on by word of mouth, and they conform to routine expectations. In itself, the utilitarian orientation is benign and may even be necessary to fulfill some of the more immediate needs of life. After all, garbage must be collected, clothes must be cleaned, houses must be constructed, food must be prepared, resources must be transported.

However, the utilitarian orientation, whether manifested in the grubbiness of everyday chores or in the seemingly sophisticated manipulations of corporate capitalism, has an almost irresistible tendency to become all-consuming, and to set itself up as the sole mark of progress and success. When that happens, the results are often disastrous, ranging from indifference and neglect (as in the treatment of the homeless or of school children in the inner city) to hostility and oppression (as in the formation of sweatshops or efforts to undercut labor unions), resulting in the formation of massive structures of alienation—all justified as long as "the job gets done" and gets done "efficiently."

We know better, I would like to think, than to allow this tendency, however powerful its presence, to coopt our personal relationships and our institutional forms. We know better because of those moments when we are visited with an intimation of the reality of spirit—when, however fleetingly, we become aware of the uncalculated goodness inherent in the depth of sensitivity on which each of us is so dependent for our ultimate sanity and from which we obtain a presentment of authentic value. An intensified awareness of this matrix of sensitivity would mean, in its effects on us, the deepening and extending of our own sensitivity to life in all its forms and manifestations—to its joys and sorrows, its heights and its limitations. It would move us from the crude realism of aggressive competitiveness toward the more genuine realism of creative intercommunication.

Appreciative consciousness is Meland's language to indicate that orientation of mind which, provoked by wonder, makes for maximal openness to the rich fullness of events and respect for the possibilities of growth resident in those events. In the interaction of life with life, appreciative consciousness is marked by receptivity to the other, rapport with the other, and release of energies toward the creation of new forms of interaction with the other—all with the aim of enabling that inclusive community in which self and other are participants to flourish. With appreciative consciousness, one discerns structures of alienation for what they are and is empowered to stretch beyond those structures toward the formation of new lines of relationship, moving us all, in however minimal a way, in the direction of justice as solidarity. Appreciative consciousness, in this sense, is an exercise in spirituality—born of an awareness that, with our differences, we belong together; nurtured in its openness to our communal ground; and given force as we press toward the transformation of our common life, overcoming structures of alienation and sensitizing us all to the lives of each other.

On one level, I am not at all sanguine about the prospects of this vision of justice as solidarity in our current context. The forces that militate against it seem to predominate at this point in our history. On another level, I am convinced that, in the final analysis, the community of life is contingent, for its survival and its sustenance, on justice as solidarity. Without its presence among us, we simply could not continue to be. That surely is the point of Meland's plaint—that "existence in most instances is sustained by a perilously slight margin of sensitivity." But, wonder of all wonders, it is so sustained. Perhaps at times all we can do in our pursuit of a politics of relationality is to resist any further erosion of that margin. If nothing else, that in itself is a vocation worthy of our commitment. At the same time such a holding action should not deter us from the more revolutionary impulse that inheres in the vision of justice as solidarity, at least as I intend it.

AGENDA

The ontology of relationality, presented above as the second subtheme of justice as solidarity, is the basic supposition informing all the chapters that follow. From that perspective, I am making a case for a politics of relationality—a form of action in which the quality of our connectedness with each other is of eminent importance, more so than the kinds of goods and benefits that accrue to each of us in our separateness from each other. A politics of relationality is a form of communitarian theory, but, in the version I am delineating, of a sort that is not reluctant to call on the agency of government to engage actively and vigorously throughout our social and economic associations to promote justice as solidarity. Communitarianism nowadays is often called upon to promote a kind of social conservatism and political localism. But I intend a communitarianism that is consistent with a robust pluralism and an inclusive public forum whose aim is the conjunctive participation of us all in a unity of adventure.

In Part I, I am proposing a reinterpretation of the idea of human rights, contrasting it with the more individualist interpretation customary in traditional liberalism and illustrating its import by attention to the controversial issues of the rights of children and affirmative action.

In Part II, I focus on the character of economic relations, developing a reinterpretation of the meaning of property and suggesting the need to incorporate the principles of strong democracy into the structure of corporate governance. Following through on the implications of a relational approach to economic theory, I present a brief defense of the democratic socialist vision despite the wide-spread claim that socialism as an option is dead.

The chapters in Part III are devoted to the problematique of religion within contemporary culture, acknowledging the need for a radical critique of religious thought and practice and dealing directly with the matter of religious pluralism and the effects of that pluralism on our common life. Moreover, I argue, somewhat audaciously, that, at its profoundest (religious) level, understanding—the kind of understanding we should be promoting in all our educational institutions—is conjoined with compassion and a drive for justice, providing therewith a point from which a critique of traditional religion is possible.

Part IV stems from an acknowledgment that, under current conditions, we confront—almost overwhelmingly—a politics of annihilation and we must seek a means of approaching serious social conflict in more constructive ways than we have tended to in the past. I suggest that that is a task intrinsic to the mission of higher education and I call upon the tradition of nonviolence as an alternative mode of confronting oppositional forces, domestically and internationally.

In Part V, I make explicit the need to broaden the politics of relationality to include the whole biosphere, drawing together the concerns of both deep ecology and social ecology. I conclude with a note on the conjunction between the ecological principle and koinonology, the kind of moral reflection that, I suggest, should be paramount in our practical life as we move into a new century.

All the chapters that follow are inspired by the Johannine sentiment that is too often limited to close intimate relations but that, I would assert, is equally applicable to the political structures that sustain our lives:

> Beloved, let us love one another; for love is of God, and those who love are born of God and know God. Those who do not love do not know God; for God is love. (I John 4:7)

That religious sentiment, as I explicate it throughout this text, is conveyed through the philosophical principle of internal relations (in the depth of our being, we belong to each other) and the political principle of justice as solidarity (as we belong to each other, so, while celebrating our differences, we are to work together for the sake of us all).

Part 1
Human Rights

Ask, and it will be given you;
seek and you will find;
knock, and it will be opened to you.
—*Matthew 7:7*

"We have it in our power to begin the world over again."[1] Thomas Paine, pamphleteer of the American Revolution and defender of the French Revolution, captures in this phrase a central impulse conveyed through the idea of human rights: We have it in our power to begin the world again. That sentiment is cast in simple declarative form. As such it may seem naive. We are, after all, constrained—are we not?—by the inheritance of a world already accomplished, a world whose structures bind us in untold ways.

But the intention of Paine's statement is more than aspirational. It affirms a vision of what is possible—and what is desirable—given the deepest character of who we are and what we might become. If we comprehend the full dialectic between self and world, then we have it in our power to begin the world again even as the world is our matrix, the source and the condition, of our power. That's a central insight conveyed in the idea of human rights that has stirred up such controversy, philosophical and political, since it emerged in the beginnings of the modern era.

I would dare to suggest that the idea of human rights is expressive of the creative power of the universe that moves us, again and again, toward the consideration of new possibilities in our common existence. We are endowed by our Creator, Thomas Jefferson affirmed, with rights to life, liberty, and the pursuit of happiness. Whatever else that proposition signifies, I take it to assume that, in response to the lure of a new future, we have it in our power repeatedly to shape the world afresh.

The idea of human rights entails the responsibility, even the obligation, to respect that power by bending our energies and shaping the patterns of our common life towards its release and enhancement. The idea of human rights, so comprehended, stands in contrast to the clas-

17

sical liberal understanding of rights as a defense of the individual over against government, a protection against the arbitrary impositions of tyranny, a wall of separation between public and private spheres of life. There is some merit to that conception. However, I would insist that human rights are of greatest importance as a form of empowerment, enabling people, as individuals and in their associations, to participate effectively in and through the political community. But, in that respect, they are important. On that point, I diverge from those perspectives that tend to dismiss the idea of human rights on behalf of some sort of cost/benefit analysis (as in classical utilitarianism) or in deference to traditional ways and customary moral restraints (as in classical conservatism). The idea of human rights, I would contend, is of eminent significance politically and morally, but its meaning, its ground, its scope, its import are in need of reconstruction.

In the chapters that follow in Part I, I shall, first, propose a recasting of the basic idea of human rights within the framework of a relational, or communitarian, framework and to consider it, so revised, as the fundamental raison d'être of government. Second, I shall explore the concept, now formulated in a United Nations Convention, of the rights of children, arguing, inter alia, that human rights do not apply only to persons of mature age. Finally, in a brief essay—an interlude—I suggest that the idea of affirmative action is an extension of the same basic approach to political responsibility and participation.

2
The Idea of Human Rights:
A Communitarian Perspective

The Lord has anointed me
to bring good tidings to the poor;
he has sent me to bind up the brokenhearted,
to proclaim liberty to the captives,
and the opening of the prisons to those who are bound.
—*Isaiah 61:1*

We exist, at this historical moment, in the midst of a global political crisis, a crisis whose proportions extend throughout all dimensions of our common life. The crisis is centered on the question of whether, on balance, prevailing forms of life are more conducive to our mutual flourishing than to our mutual destruction.

Lest this formulation seem too extreme, consider the calculation that one-fifth of the world's human population is said to be barely surviving under conditions of absolute poverty. Consider that, given our intrusions into the living patterns of nonhuman creatures, whole species are confronting extinction at an accelerating rate. Consider the antagonistic divisions of ethnicity and race, gender and class that continue to break out in a frenzy of war in diverse human communities and that create well-nigh intolerable living circumstances for millions of peoples.

I intend, as a modest contribution to our reflections about this political crisis, to propose that the idea of human rights—or, more inclusively, the idea of natural rights—as that idea might be cast within a communitarian perspective, provides a fruitful framework within which to comprehend a central dimension of that crisis and to direct our minds toward future possibilities.

To be sure, the idea of human rights in its emergence in the modern period, at least as that idea has often been interpreted for some decades, has been tied to a political ontology—sometimes called classical Western liberalism—that has rightly been subjected to severe critique. However, although that critique has merit, the idea of human rights articulates a normative insight about the meaning of life that, in my judgment, must be preserved, albeit set within an alternative mode of thought. Where the political ontology of classical Western liberalism, reacting against hierarchical and organic forms of an aristocratic feudalism as well as against a rigidified scholasticism, was anthropocentric (even androcentric) and individualistic, the communitarian political ontology that I would propose—a political ontology that has a long heritage, although subordinated in the modern West—is more relational and ecological, even organic, in character (see appendix for table of contrasts).

Classical Western liberalism, at its best, properly draws our attention to the subjectivity of life and insists on that subjectivity as a locus of value. That is an insight that must be preserved. However, communitarianism, as I am construing that understanding, locates subjectivity not in one's isolation from others, but in a special moment within the context of the dynamic give and take of our historical and cultural life. Moreover, I would insist, subjectivity is found in all forms of life, not merely in human life. On this basis, I mean to suggest that, while affirming the idea of human rights, we need to encase it within a more encompassing idea of natural rights.

In pursuing this idea, I am using the term *political* in a special sense. Given the deep cultural influence of one strain of classical Western liberalism, the political tends nowadays to be associated with a continuous struggle for power, employing all available means in that struggle, however devious and however vicious. And so it is, at one level of political action. But the struggle for power is not necessarily devoid of a morality of means; it is not, in every instance, tied to deviousness and viciousness. Indeed, power, in one of its simplest renditions, is the ability to accomplish purposes or to realize desires. As such, power is an essential dimension of all life. And politics, as a process through which diverse agents, individual and collective, encounter each other in the constant flow of common life, is inseparable from the exercise of and the struggle for power.

But, more profoundly understood, the struggle for power is driven by an aim which influences, or should, for consistency's sake, influence the character of the struggle. Ends, that is, should infuse the character of the means employed to attain them. In the political process, the aim of the struggle for power is to inaugurate a more acceptable—ultimately a more just—manner of living together than prevails at any given time. If that be the case, then considerations of justice should color the strategies appropriated in moving in that direction. In that sense, but in that sense only, the ends justify the means. That is, the ends of political action constitute a criterion in assessing and justifying the means of political action. There is little glory in the pursuit of power for its own sake, however much that drive may seem to motivate political agents. Even in the political theories of Niccolo Machiavelli and of Thomas Hobbes, in which the drive for power is not improperly interpreted as central in the dynamics of social and political interaction, the aim of the drive for power is to institute a kind of peace, or at least a kind of social equilibrium, within which individuals find some security and encouragement to pursue their several desires.

But, in contrast to the political ontologies that inform the hermeneutics of Machiavelli and Hobbes (which, despite their popular reputation, are substantively different in character), I would propose that, in keeping with a theme that is critical in the tradition of a communitarian political ontology, the central question of politics is this: How might we so construct our lives together that all life flourishes? That question is inspired by the principle of relationality, although it derives, historically, from Aristotle's designation of the political community as the most encompassing of all associations, defined specifically by the inner need to provide all the conditions necessary and desirable for human fulfillment. Aristotle's deliberations over the political question are colored by his (substance) ontology and shaped by his (Greek city-state) circumstances.

However, the question, set within the circumstances of the end of the twentieth century and informed by the principle of relationality, retains its urgency and pertinence. Certainly, over against the deep strains of political alienation and political cynicism that are rampant in many circles nowadays in both West and East, the question as phrased is a reminder that, however distasteful political determinations and compromises may seem, the political task is intrinsic to our vitality. Given the dynamics of life, we are engaged in a constant definition and redefinition of the shape of those interrelationships that constitute the ever changing matrix of our thinking and our acting. We do live together. That is an inescapable feature of our identity. Our living together is a constitutive dimension of our individual lives. But how effectively the forms of our living together enhance the quality of our lives, severally and collectively, is a matter that we need, repeatedly, to ask. And that, I mean to suggest, is the central political question to which, in the modern (or, if you will, the postmodern) world, the idea of human rights, albeit in diverse permutations, has been proposed as a response.

In the Declaration of Independence (1776), for instance, Thomas Jefferson and his co-signatories affirm as the central premises of their revolutionary action that "certain unalienable Rights" constitute the purpose of government and therefore, presumably, the most fitting form of our political association with one another:

> We hold these truths to be self-evident, that all men are created equal, that they are endowed by their Creator with certain unalienable Rights, that among these are Life, Liberty, and the pursuit of Happiness.—That to secure these rights, Governments are instituted among Men, deriving their just powers from the consent of the governed.—That whenever any Form of Government becomes destructive of these ends, it is the Right of the People to alter or to abolish it, and to institute new Government.[1]

That we must take seriously the critique of the Declaration of Independence (and of similar seventeenth- and eighteenth-century declarations) from various perspectives, feminist and racial, goes without saying. The Declaration, which, on its surface, seems inclusive in its embrace, was, in practice, narrowly exclusive, pertaining particularly, it has often been noted, to white males of an affluent economic class.

However, my paramount concern at this point is to note that the idea of human rights is presented in the Declaration of Independence as the fundamental raison d'être of government and therefore as the proper quality of relationships pervading the political association. Over the decades, women (e.g., Mary Wollstonecraft and Elizabeth Cady Stanton) and African Americans (e.g., Frederick Douglass and Martin Luther King, Jr.) have used the premises of the Declaration as a foundation to expose and to undercut the sexist and racist practices that are deeply ingrained throughout the American polis. In their judgments on the perversities of the American political community, they were, in effect, affirming the central principle of Jefferson's text, namely, that the idea of human rights is a fitting, if not the most appropriate, response to the political question.

Jefferson, of course, did not create the idea of human rights *de novo*; he appropriated the idea from a strain of English thought expressed preeminently by, among others, John Locke in his famed seventeenth-century *Second Treatise of Government*. The *Second Treatise*, in which the idea of human rights occupies pride of place, has been subjected over recent decades to radically divergent interpretations, making Locke out to be, variously, a liberal democrat, a possessive individualist, and a devout Puritan. In part, these divergent interpretations derive from seeming ambiguities in the text itself that suggest, depending on an interpreter's perspective, either a more individualist or a more communitarian premise, a difference manifested in characterizations of the "state of nature."

When Locke affirms that in the "state of nature," we are—each of us—in a condition of perfect freedom to order our actions and to dispose of our possessions and persons as we see fit without asking permission or depending on the authorization of anyone else[2] and when he announces that the paramount end of governments is the preservation of our property,[3] he appears to assume that the idea of human rights is a means of sustaining our separateness from each other, an assumption that is central to classical Western liberalism. However, when Locke, invoking the doctrine of the "judicious Hooker," insists on the obligation of mutual love whereby we are to do what we can to preserve the life, liberty, health, and goods of each other[4] and when he declares that God put us under the obligations of the necessity and convenience of social interaction, and invested us with an inclination to engage in social intercourse,[5] he seems to suggest that the idea of human rights is a means of assuring our equal participation in the community whose purpose is to sustain and to enhance our lives together. At such points, Locke's presentation of the idea of human rights manifests the stamp of Hugo Grotius's "principle of sociability,"[6] according to which, in keeping with a communitarian perspective, our human rights are derived from and are intended to contribute to the enrichment of our interactions.

Whichever interpretation of John Locke's doctrine of the state of nature and its correlative idea of human rights—the individualist or the communitarian—is considered the more adequate as an interpretation of the *Second Treatise* as a whole, it is nonetheless the case that in Locke's understanding, as in Jefferson's, human rights are presented as a response to the political question. That is, the idea of human rights is centrally germane to the basic purposes of our living together.

On a very general, but not unimportant, level, the individualist and the communitarian interpretations of the idea of human rights converge. Both, at least in principle, turn our moral gaze toward the subject—each subject—as something to be cherished. By subject, I mean a center of feeling and sensibility, thought and creativity. To cherish each subject is to hold the subject up as of eminent value and therefore as possessing a justifiable claim to be respected. More particularly, to cherish each subject is to acknowledge that the subject is, in its own unique way, reflective of history past and, at the same time, within its own domain, responsible for history future. The subject, so understood, is the focal point of the idea of rights.

Moreover, the process of cherishing each subject composes the basis of an extensive moral judgment about the forms of our living together, social and familial, economic and cultural. These forms are not totally determinative of a subject's character and orientation, but they are among the constitutive and most intimate conditions of a subject's range of possibilities. In ways that reach far beyond economic calculation, they may enrich a subject's life or they may impoverish it; they may enliven it through the depth of insight and sensibility they bring to bear in everyday interactions or they may narrow its vision and motivation severely whether through coercive threats or, more subtly, through diverse means of cultural hegemony. To affirm that each person has a right to life, liberty, and the pursuit of happiness is to pose serious moral objections to any association in which and through which an individual or any class of individuals is subordinated to or subjugated by others in a manner that depreciates their inner life and thwarts their participation in the more encompassing community.

We should perhaps pause at this moment to distinguish between functional differentiation (where different persons assume different roles in performing a community task with authority distributed throughout the association) and hierarchical subordination (where some persons, whether a small elite or a large majority, hold authority of command over others without an effective possibility of recourse or appeal). The idea of human rights in its respect for subjectivity is compatible with the former, but not with the latter. On that point, classical Western liberalism and communitarianism seem to be in agreement. Both, in principle, are antithetical to all forms of association that deny or diminish the subjectivity of those whose lives are affected by an association. In more traditional language, they stand over against tyranny and despotism; in more recent language, they stand opposed to patriarchal associations and hegemonic structures.

However, despite that seeming agreement it is remarkable that the former tradition—classical Western liberalism—has, over the course of the past two centuries, been allied, in rhetoric and in practice, with forms of social and political interaction that have violated the principle of respect for subjectivity. American domestic policy and American foreign policy have repeatedly, in the (presumed) name of democracy and human rights, promoted and sustained systems of domination of various kinds—imperialism, racism, sexism, corporativism, ecocide—that belie what, on the face of it, constitutes the inner principle of the liberal tradition.

The contradiction is the result in part, I suspect, of the kind of ontology that underlies classical Western liberalism, an ontology which, on the surface, seems benign, but which, in its full measure, depicts life as a constant struggle of all against all. That each and every person—each one unique and separate from all others—has those rights needed to pursue life as she sees fit (e.g., rights to life, liberty, and the pursuit of happiness) seems most attractive. But when those pursuits clash, the results are not so attractive, particularly under conditions in which clusters of persons, joined in some fashion, are able to exercise control—directly or indirectly—over others, whether through political, economic, or cultural means, justifying that control in the name of human rights. Within this framework, the appeal to human rights fulfills an oppositional function instead of a unifying function. It pits person against person, group against group, class against class. Even as forces may collaborate, out of a concern for racial or sexual identity or for national or class interest, the appeal to human rights is separatist in its intent and dominative in its effect. We should recall, in this connection, Alfred North Whitehead's commentary on developments in nineteenth-century capitalism: "The mere doctrines of freedom, individualism, and competition, had produced a resurgence of something very like industrial slavery at the base of society."[7]

Thus, curiously, the presumed universalism of human rights doctrine (all persons are created equal, endowed by their Creator with certain inalienable rights) gives sway to structures of opposition and domination. Yet, even in such circumstances, the idea of human rights retains its power of moral insight, giving vision and courage to the dominated in their state of discontent. And so the struggles continue—whether between female and male, black and white, workers and managers, poor peoples and wealthy elites—with each party appealing to the idea of human rights to justify its struggle against the other.

The communitarian version of the idea of human rights, as I would propose it, rests on a different ontology, an ontology in which, to borrow a phrase from Bernard Eugene Meland, "events are primary."[8] An event, as intended in this context, is a moment in time. In a sense, each moment of time is discrete and has its own unique quality. But what must be understood is that at any given moment of time the whole creative passage is present in its inexhaustible complexity. On the human level, an event is a moment of experience, rich in its inheritance and laden with novel possibility. But I am referring here not to special moments, set apart from other, more routine times. I am referring to every moment of our lives, each one of which has its own special character and significance. I am referring to the experience of the everyday which bears in its depth more than we, with our conscious minds, can comprehend, ranging from the immediate to the ultimate and from the proximate to the ancient. As such, an event is a moment of transmission from a past to a future, but also a moment of eminent importance in itself in all that it bears and brings together in creative fusion—even if, given the peculiar circumstances of its inheritance, it is a moment of intense suffering.

The self, in this understanding, is not, in any simple way, a distinct and separate being, but a being both encumbered and, at least in some small degree, enlivened by its connectedness to places and times nearby and far away. As Whitehead remarks, "The self-sufficing independent man [sic], with his peculiar property which concerns no one else, is a concept without any validity for modern civilization."[9] We are not self-sufficing independent monads, but inimitable expressions of a host of far-reaching connections, which connections—biological and cultural, political and economic—are constitutive of the self. The full meaning of the self cannot be adequately understood apart from them. And yet the self is a creative agent, possessed with the power in some measure to shape those connections in a manner responsive to the moment at hand. At this point of creative formation, the genius of the self is put to the test, in the depth of its sensitivity to the past and in the reach of its vision of the future. In part, how well it meets that test is contingent on its political context.

The point of the idea of human rights is to designate the kind of context most conducive to the self's agency within the ongoing passage of events. The self as subject is to be cherished, but cherished not as a distinct monad, separate from all other subjects, rather as a sensitive and creative participant in an adventure in which all creatures are engaged and are dependent on each other for sustenance and fulfillment. Each self as subject bears a manifold responsibility for the character and quality of its participation: to itself, to others, to the world as a whole, and to that ultimate power of sensitivity that seeks the intensification of value in experience.

In this sense, the idea of human rights, within the framework of a communitarian ontology, is a function of human responsibility. The idea of human rights consists at any given time of that range and configuration of claims on the community and its members to provide, to whatever degree is at all possible, conditions of life optimal to the intensification of value not just for the self alone, but, through the self, for the community, the world, and the creative ground of all life. While, to be sure, in the immediate dynamics of social living, the claim to have rights may well set an individual person or a group of persons over against others, the full justification for the claim includes, as its import and intent, a contribution to the community's well being. The claims that bear the label of human rights are never, in principle at least, simply self-serving however much they are, in their momentary aim, of benefit to the self. Rights and responsibilities are bundled together, even though they may appear, at any given time, in tension with each other. A child's rights to adequate health care and appropriate educational facilities may seem, during its youthful years, to be a burdensome cost without commensurate benefit to the community, but where those rights are not effectively acknowledged, the quality of a child's participation in the community as a child and, later, as an adult is most likely to be diminished. The child suffers; the community suffers; the entire world suffers. That is the eventual fate of a failure to acknowledge human rights.

Hannah Arendt's felicitous phrase, "the right to have rights," intended by her to mark a general and enduring principle undergirding particular declarations of human rights, is instructive at this point, although I would extend the meaning of the phrase from her concern with the condition and significance of stateless persons in a world of massive organization to our concern with a communitarian political ontology.[10]

> The fundamental deprivation of human rights is manifested first and above all in the deprivation of a place in the world which makes opinions significant and actions effective.... We became aware of the existence of a right to have rights... and a right to belong to some kind of organized community, only when millions of people emerged who had lost and could not regain these rights because of the new global situation.... Not the loss of specific rights, then, but

the loss of a community willing and able to guarantee any rights whatsoever, has been the calamity which has befallen ever-increasing numbers of people....Only the loss of a polity itself expels [them] from humanity.[11]

The right to have rights, Arendt affirms, is tied intimately to participation in political community. To be politically excommunicated is to lose not only a cluster of particular rights; it is to lose the basic right to share in the give-and-take of our life together. However, from the perspective of a communitarian political ontology, there are objective limits to the force of explicit political excommunication. We may be, as many peoples have been over the centuries, ostracized, exiled, marginalized, excommunicated from social organizations, economic enterprises, nation states. We become, at such points, rightless; that is, before the courts of prevailing powers, even if we are granted standing at all, our claims are rejected as having no merit. We are an alien class, strangers, outcastes, a pariah people.

Nonetheless, in the more profound scheme of things, we can never be excommunicated from the community of life. In that sense, at least, our dignity—the fundamental ground of our claim to the right to have rights—can never be lost. However treated in organized political communities, we are denizens of the creative passage with all the rights and responsibilities that are appropriate to that condition. That is the insight of the idea of human rights. We can never, at least while living, be totally and unconditionally deprived "from a place in the world which makes opinions significant and actions effective." In the flow of events, each moment plays some role, each subject is an active participant in some degree, the experience of each individual is of some significance—however minimally. To be sure, the lives of many peoples throughout the centuries have been narrowly circumscribed by social forces that have virtually overwhelmed them. Yet, as historical events testify, despite outright oppression—or even the more silent treatment of dismissal and indifference—they have often been able, against the odds, to sustain a sense of their dignity and to make a difference in the world. This is why victims should never be considered as simply victims. The right to have rights, which is part and parcel of one's status as participant in the creative passage—as a member of the community of life—may be attacked, disregarded, or repudiated, but can never be alienated. Victims are never to be merely pitied as victims; however miserable their condition, they are to be treated respectfully as persons of dignity.

But, we might inquire, what is the range of human rights embraced in the "right to have rights"? Taking Arendt's phrase, "to make opinions significant and actions effective" as an initial clue to that inquiry, the question is, What sorts of rights are requisite "to make opinions significant and actions effective"? At this juncture, we encounter a long-standing controversy in debates over human rights. Is the idea of human rights properly limited to matters of civil liberties and political participation, assuring effective membership in the public forum? Or must the idea of human rights, given its full meaning and inner logic, be extended to embrace matters of social expectation, cultural enrichment, and economic security as well? The division indicated by those two questions is the traditional form of a controversy that finds some focus in continuing debates over the legitimacy of the United Nations' Universal Declaration of Human Rights (1948).

The United Nations' Declaration assumes the more encompassing understanding of human rights. Besides affirming the right to freedom of expression and peaceable assembly (a matter of civil liberties) and the right to take part in the government of one's country and to engage in periodic elections (a matter of political participation), the Declaration includes the following articles (composed, it should be noted, prior to the days of insisting on gender-inclusive language) as, respectively, matters of economic security (Article 25), social expectation (Article 26) and cultural enrichment (Article 27):

Article 25: Everyone has the right to a standard of living adequate for the health and well-being of himself and his family, including food, clothing, housing and medical care and necessary social services, and the right to security in the event of unemployment, sickness, disability, widowhood, old age or other lack of livelihood in circumstances beyond his control.

Article 26: Everyone has the right to education.... Education shall be directed to the full development of human personality and...shall promote understanding, tolerance and friendship among all nations, racial or religious groups.

Article 27: Everyone has the right freely to participate in the cultural life of the community, to enjoy the arts and to share in scientific advancement and its benefits.

Maurice Cranston is among those who, expressing a strong tendency in Anglo-American political culture, are critical of the United

Nations' Universal Declaration. Cranston objects strenuously to the intermixing of political/civil and economic/social rights as human rights on two grounds—philosophical and pragmatic.[12]

Philosophically, Cranston claims that the two sets of declared rights are logically distinct. His test of the difference is threefold: practicability, universality, and paramountcy. The former—civil/political rights—are immediately practicable since they merely require the removal of obstacles (to speech, association, participation, etc.). They are universal since they are applicable to all kinds and sorts of political circumstance, however primitive. And they are of paramount importance since they are reactive to the most elemental ways of stifling life and liberty (e.g., genocide, racial and sexual discrimination). But the latter—economic/social rights—are not immediately practicable; they are more like ideals and aspirations whose fulfillment is not everywhere possible. They are therefore not universal since they are realizable only under advanced economic and cultural circumstances. And, while they may be attractive, they are not of grave importance in the relief of the most heinous kinds of restrictions on human life. In their moral quality, they are more like desired virtues than strict moral duties.

Given this radical difference between the two sets of principles, Cranston would reserve the idea of human rights for the former (civil/political principles). The latter (principles of an economic and social character) might more appropriately be considered as moral goals, less pressing and less immediate in their claims on our energies than moral obligations, however attractive they may be to our moral imagination. That is Cranston's philosophical conclusion. Pragmatically, Cranston's fear is that the confusion of the two kinds of principles might "push all talk of human rights out of the clear realm of the morally compelling into the twilight of utopian aspiration,"[13] and, as a result, declarations of human rights will not be taken with the seriousness they deserve in directing our common life. If declarations of human rights are to have any effective punch in determining the shape of our interactions, they are best limited to political and civil obligations and claims.

Cranston's effort to draw a line of clear differentiation between the two kinds of rights clearly serves an ideological function by focusing exclusively on rights of participation in the political realm, and degrading any claims peoples might have in the economic and social system. Such a maneuver, in keeping with the tradition of modern Western capitalism, assumes a radical bifurcation between public and private life, identifies economic activity as essentially private, and resists moves directed toward the redistribution of wealth and income as improper for any but the most compelling of reasons.

However, Cranston's argument loses its force when one attends to the actual dynamics of human life, particularly if the communitarian principle has any merit. Consider, in this connection, Whitehead's affirmation that "The essence of freedom is the practicability of purpose."[14] I have suggested that central to the idea of human rights is the principle of respect for subjectivity. By subjectivity, I am referring to the moment of creative agency in the context of events, the moment in which one— each individual—confronts an opportunity to make what one can and what one will out of the give-and-take of historical and cultural life. The possibilities at hand may be rich and varied or, under conditions of natural catastrophe or political oppression, may be limited and cramped. Nonetheless, at such moments, each subject, pursuing some aim, makes a unique impress on the course of history. Each subject, drawing together the prospects and resources that life offers, finds its place and, thereby makes a difference in the world's future. Subjectivity, so understood, is more than a matter of internal feeling. It is a movement from imagination to realization. It pertains to the efficacy of feeling in the interaction between self and world. To respect the inner feelings of an individual or of a set of individuals is to provide resources for their expression in action. This is the reason Whitehead criticizes the confinement of freedom "to freedom of thought, freedom of the press, freedom of religious opinion," affirming, in contrast, that "freedom of *action* is a primary human need."[15] The prospects for genuine freedom are located as much in economic policy as in literary form—if not more so. The creative urge of the human spirit is contingent on the provision of both a rich cultural life to inform its imaginative explorations and an ample economic opportunity to allow for its effective realization.

If, in Arendt's phrasing, the "right to have rights" signifies the need for a "place in the world which makes opinions significant and actions effective," or if, as I have suggested, human rights constitute a function of human responsibility, then the range of rights embraced in the United Nations' Universal Declaration may not be as far off the mark as Cranston insists. For one thing, civil and political liberties are, by themselves, devoid of effectiveness without cultural and economic support. To declare, for instance, that all adult citizens have the liberty to participate in a system of electoral politics whose basic alternatives tend to be dictated, directly or indirectly, by massive industries and business corporations is to delimit the prospects of significant political freedom. That is the reason Carol Gould, in her highly cogent proposal that democratic principles be extended to economic organizations, affirms that the exercise of civil and political rights depends both on freedom from social domination and economic exploitation and on certain positive conditions, such as "a minimal level of well-being, some education or training and access to information."[16] But, more profoundly, Gould, whose central principle—that "positive freedom or self-development is a value grounded in the nature of human activity itself"—is congruent with what I have characterized as the principle of subjectivity, professes that such positive freedom "requires concrete social and material conditions for its realization." With that profession, she concludes that specifically human rights, whose "basic justification is that they are required by the nature of human activity itself, and therefore they belong to every human being simply by virtue of being human," must incorporate economic and social claims together with political and civil claims.[17] In short, the kinds of rights indicated in Articles 25, 26, and 27 of the Universal Declaration are not only supportive of political and civil liberties; more significantly, they delineate conditions requisite to the fulfillment of our place in life.

Beyond the issue of the range of rights embraced in the idea of human rights, we might also inquire, given a communitarian perspective, into the question of the status of rights as moral principles. Are they indicative of strict obligations, such that rights must always and everywhere be respected whatever the cost? Or are they long-range goals to be realized only when and where possible?

At one extreme, rights are conceived as stringent moral claims of a defensive character. That is, to invoke the classic rights to life, liberty, and the pursuit of happiness is to call for a strenuous form of protection of the individual against any possible infringement upon those rights by all other parties, whatever the interests of those parties in directing, circumscribing, or appropriating the energies and goods of that individual. In a word, in the game of life, rights are trump. That's a phrasing drawn from Ronald Dworkin: "Individual rights are political trumps held by individuals. Individuals have rights when, for some reason, a collective goal is not a sufficient justification for denying them what they wish, as individuals, to have or to do, or not a sufficient justification for imposing some loss or injury on them."[18]

Similarly, in Robert Nozick's lexicon, rights are side constraints, that is, "the rights of others determine the constraints upon your actions."[19] The presupposition of the idea of rights as side constraints, according to Nozick, is the principle that persons are always to be treated as ends. "Side constraints upon action," Nozick affirms, "reflect the underlying Kantian principle that individuals are ends and not merely means; they may not be sacrificed or used for the achieving of other ends without their consent. Individuals are inviolable."[20] We might add that Nozick is more consistently individualistic in his rights theory than Dworkin in arguing that rights as side constraints may never properly be sacrificed for some "overall social good," for the simple reason that "there is no social entity with a [lesser] good that undergoes some sacrifice for its own [overall] good. There are only individual people, different individual people, with their own individual lives."[21] To be sure, Nozick acknowledges that individual lives often conflict and, at times, in one party's pursuit of eminently valuable goals, the rights of other parties are, not without some degree of justification, violated. In such instances, Nozick insists on the need for some kind of appropriate remedial compensation. Nonetheless, rights in themselves are, in principle, inviolable. That inviolability, indeed, is the reason for compensatory action.

At another extreme, however, Gould suggests that human rights constitute not a kind of trump in the interplay of moral interests and claims, but rather a "regulative ideal" directing our actions and institutions toward a far-reaching goal. They depict an end state to be attained in and through the struggles of history. In the process, compromises are likely. Not all rights can possibly be honored at all times, although some elementary rights may be necessary if only for the sake of sheer survival. That is, in a full theory of human rights, we must "include not only the minimal conditions for survival and civility that make human activity possible at all, but also the fuller conditions that are required for the free and self-developing activity that marks human beings as distinctively human."[22] In Gould's comprehension, a complete theory of rights, encompassing all rights needed for the personal self-development of everyone, functions more as an historical ideal than as a side constraint. It acts more as a strategic aim than as trump. A "regulative ideal" lifts our moral imagination beyond what is immediately practicable, but then forces us to attend to the kind of political and economic changes needed to move effectively toward its realization. In this context, we should acknowledge that, in contrast to Nozick's individualism, Gould's social ontology is more communitarian. In her theory, the self is not an isolated monad. Rather, in a conception that is expressive of the principle of relationality, the self is always an individual-in-relation.

In the spectrum between understanding rights as trump and rights as a regulative ideal we might locate a third possibility, namely, the idea that rights constitute strong prima facie moral claims susceptible to modification depending on surrounding circumstances but that, in the full range of rights conducive to qualitative attainment in the passage of history, some are more basic, and therefore more compelling and less open to compromise than others. Given a communitarian perspective, to affirm that rights are strong prima facie moral claims is to introduce at least two kinds of consideration in the deliberation over such claims. First, whenever it is felt that the rights of a person or group should be delimited or compromised, the burden of proof falls not on the rights holder, but on those who feel or insist that the rights in question cannot (or should not) be fully honored. Second, the overarching criterion (as the measure of proof) in any proposed delimitation of rights should derive from the idea of human rights itself. That is, the argument must be that, under given conditions, such a modification or qualification is the best that can be accomplished to enhance the effectiveness of the self's interactions with the world promoting the intensification and deepening of value in experience.

Supplementary to the idea of rights as strong prima facie moral claims, we should add the distinction Henry Shue has instructively delineated between basic and nonbasic rights. Basic rights are those rights whose realization is essential to all others. As Shue develops the concept, without the provision of such things as economic subsistence, physical security, and political liberty, other rights (e.g., to education, to found a family, to share in scientific achievements) would be utterly ineffectual. Basic rights are not necessarily the most important rights in the scheme of historical life, but they are, as the term indicates, the most indispensable. All rights are, to some degree, prima facie rights, but some rights are properly to be considered more urgent than others. Those that occupy such a status in human life are closer in character to rights as trump than others, which might function more as a regulative ideal as we, in diverse forms of collaboration and conjunction with each other, engage in continuing political struggles. So understood, rights as trump and rights as regulative ideals are end points on a spectrum of rights, all of which constitute strong moral claims in the conduct of our political communities and in the fulfillment of our responsibilities.

So far, as a constructive response to the global political crisis of our times, we have focused solely on the idea of human rights. But that crisis reaches beyond the human community given the massive impact of modern life on the entire biosphere. It is time, I have suggested, to consider the incorporation of the idea of human rights as a special case in a more encompassing idea of natural rights, the rights of all life forms to whatever conditions might contribute to their flourishing.

I have declared that the focal point of the idea of rights is respect for each subject as a center of feeling and sensibility, of life and creativity. But human beings are not the only creatures marked with subjectivity. Within the context of a communitarianism informed by Whitehead's process ontology, each actual entity constitutes a subject. As a result, for consistency's sake, we must affirm the justifiability of each life form to be respected for its own integrity and fulfillment as well as for its place in the give-and-take of the overall dynamics of life. Such respect must attend to the subject in its distinctive individuality (this particular dog, this particular tree, this particular fish). But it must also attend to the conditions that led to its emergence and to the consequences of its presence and interaction with others. In this sense, the idea of natural rights properly provokes concern for whole species and for interdependent ecosystems as well as for individual organisms.

Recall that, from a communitarian perspective, the central political question is, How might we so construct our lives together that all life flourishes? The scope of that question, perhaps more so nowadays that at other moments of human history, must be enlarged to embrace all peoples and all creatures whose lives are caught up with each other in an intricate web of interconnectedness. The boundaries of our "lives together" are not so fixed and narrow as we sometimes tend to think. The modern nation-state system is a case in point. That system, to be sure, is well entrenched in our minds and in our institutions. But it has been qualified in untold numbers of ways, most evidently through the formation of political, economic, and cultural associations whose reticulations transcend our nationalist affirmations. Moreover, if we open our minds and spirits to the deeper conditions of our lives, we shall become aware of an even more extensive and embracing community that constitutes our identity, a community in which both human and nonhuman forms of life participate as companions and partners, each and every one of which possesses, in a manner in keeping with its own possibilities, the "right to have rights."

To affirm the idea of natural rights is not to insist that each and every form of life is deserving of exactly the same treatment, nor is it to adopt the utterly impossible position that under no circumstances may the life of any creature be sacrificed for the good of any other. But, in principled contrast to those for whom the environment is nothing but a reservoir of resources available for human use, it is to declare that each life form possesses its own intrinsic good, and to attenuate or to sacrifice that good is a matter of moral loss deserving of acknowledgment, or even, where such a sacrifice is necessitated for the sake of some other good, an expression of both grief and gratitude. Life, even that of a mite or a mosquito, should not be taken lightly. That, as I understand it, is a major point of Albert Schweitzer's doctrine of reverence for life:

> Whenever I injure any kind of life I must be quite certain that it is necessary. I must never go beyond the unavoidable, not even in apparently insignificant things. The farmer who has mowed down a thousand flowers in his meadows in order to feed his cows must be careful on his way home not to strike the head off a single flower by the side of the road in idle amusement, for he thereby infringes the law of life without being under the pressure of necessity.[23]

As the idea of human rights by itself has far-reaching implications for the character of our common life, massively violated as it is by prevailing political and economic structures, so the more encompassing idea of natural rights would entail a radical transformation of the styles of life—ranging from eating habits and agricultural techniques to residential patterns and forms of transportation—that dominate our globe under the hegemony of corporate capitalist civilization. Yet if respect for subjectivity and the intensification of value reside at the heart of the ideas of human and natural rights, then such an extensive transformation of our lives is the kind of moral vision that should capture our imagination. At the very least, with that kind of moral vision we shall be able to depict the global political crisis for what it is, in its depth and in its extent, a profound violation of principles of both social justice and ecojustice.

Perhaps even more importantly, with that kind of moral vision we shall be able to demonstrate in our own spirits and through our immediate spheres of influence the inner meaning of a life of sensitivity. In its deepest reach, justice is as much a principle of our dispositional character as it is a principle intended to permeate our institutional forms. As Aristotle acknowledged, justice is as much a virtue as it is a principle of governance. Even if the appeal to the idea of natural rights does not succeed in shaping the policies formulated through the public forum (for whatever reasons), it can be effected in the lives of those who participate in the deliberations of that forum. And at least to that extent the idea of natural rights is not an unrealistic projection of the moral imagination, but, rather, it is a sign embodied in the lives of those enthralled by its promise of a deeper realism yearning throughout the course of our common history for full expression.

APPENDIX
SUMMARY OF ISSUES IN HUMAN/NATURAL RIGHTS THEORY
(Acknowledging Rights = Cherishing Subjectivity)

	CLASSICAL LIBERAL ONTOLOGY	RELATIONAL ONTOLOGY
GROUNDS	Individualistic	Communitarian
INTENT	Protection	Empowerment
PURPOSE	Minimize Interference (individual life plans)	Intensify Value (self, others, world)
FOCUS	Personal Life (private sphere)	Common Good (public sphere)
GOVERNMENTAL ROLE	Negative	Affirmative
POLITICAL COMMUNITY	Instrumental Good	Instrumental Good and Intrinsic Good
SCOPE	Civil/Political	Civil/Political and Social/Economic
STATUS	Immediate Obligation	Immediate Obligation and Ideal Aspiration
STRINGENCY	Absolute	Prima Facie
LEVELS	Basic	Basic and Nonbasic
APPLICATION	Human Communities	Natural Communities

3

On the Suffering and Rights of Children: Toward a Theology of Childhood Liberation

> Whoever receives one such child in my name
> receives me; but whoever causes one of these
> little ones who believe in me to stumble, it would
> be better for him to have a great millstone
> fastened around his neck and to be drowned
> in the depths of the sea.
> —*Matthew 18:5–6*

I intend to speak a word on behalf of the children of this world. I do so from the perspective of a tradition of philosophical thought within which the ultimate aims for our world derive from the persistent intention of divine reality, namely, love. So writes Marjorie Hewitt Suchocki: "The togetherness of all things in the infinite satisfaction of God is the ultimacy of love, pervading and transforming each participant through the power of God's own subjectivity. The aims for the world that spring from this divine love are themselves aims toward a richness of community, which is as much named by love in the finite world as in the divine reality."[1] Against that measure—the richness of community—the lot of children is miserably deficient.[2] Given their condition throughout the world, children are deserving of their own form of a theology of liberation as a means of giving voice to their suffering and, in turn, articulating the character of their rights.

Children are among the most vulnerable and the most victimized of peoples. In part, children are victimized by their own immediate caretakers. As David Bakan remarks, "It has now become an open secret that people torture and kill their own children or children in their charge."

> Children have been whipped, beaten, starved, drowned, smashed against walls and floors, held in ice water baths, exposed to extremes of outdoor temperature, burned with hot irons and steam pipes. Children have been tied and kept in upright positions for long peri-

ods. They have been systematically exposed to electric shock; forced to swallow pepper, soil, feces, urine, vinegar, alcohol, and other odious materials; buried alive; had scalding water poured over their genitals; had their limbs held in open fire; placed in roadways where automobiles would run over them; placed on roofs and fire escapes in such a manner as to fall off; bitten, knifed and shot; had their eyes gouged out.[3]

Yet, however morally repulsive the widespread practice of direct child abuse by caretakers, a theology of liberation forces us to attend as well to those systemic conditions of our common life—economic, social, political—whose effects on the lives of children are at least equally violative of the meaning of childhood as direct physical abuse, if not more so. The lives of children are sharply delimited and irreparably damaged and degraded by structural forces susceptible to transformation but sustained by those in positions of power.[4]

How are we to respond to the suffering and death of children? There are times, as Stanley Hauerwas reminds us in a sensitive essay on "a child's dying," that the appropriate response is anguish and care.[5] But there are also times in our common life when anguish must give way to anger[6] and care must give rise to a cry for justice.[7] That is, we cannot, out of love, merely respond to a child's suffering with compassionate acceptance when the conditions effecting that suffering are the result of human agency. Death and disease are often as much political events as they are biological happenings. As political events, they should provoke rebellion. They should give rise to a drive for the emancipation of children from conditions that force them into such agony, that violate—intentionally or not—their childhood. They call for political transformation. That is the point of a theology of liberation. The anguish of suffering must not blind us to the mandate for emancipation.

THE INTENTION OF LOVE

Throughout the course of history, the suffering of children has been, in large part, a function of social systems. To this degree, the suffering of children is not "natural." That is, it is not the result of strictly inevitable forces in whose consequences we are advised to acquiesce as the better part of realism. In such cases, righteous indignation giving rise to moral reflection and action is the productive response.

Righteous indignation—the "sense of injustice"[8]—by itself seems negative in character. It is born of an experience of opposition and resistance. But, on its reverse side, righteous indignation emerges from a sense of love. Love, in this connection, is not merely a feeling of attraction nor is it merely a quality of personal relationships. It is a drive to act in a certain way, a motivation to expend one's energies toward the enhancement of relations, an effort, in its social manifestation, to shape institutional forms to enrich our common life. But then we must ask, what does love intend in the construction of forms of human interaction?

As an initial response to this question, Schubert Ogden provides a simple but significant answer: freedom. "[T]he one test of whether love is really present is always freedom—both in the sense that the test of whether one loves another is always whether one intends to speak and act in such a way as always somehow to optimize the limits of the other's freedom, and in the sense that the test of whether one is loved by another is always whether the limits of one's own freedom are in some respect thus optimized by what the other says or does."[9] To optimize the limits of one another's freedom is, in this understanding, a social principle entailed by love. The names of its antithesis are legion. Traditionally, it is called tyranny, patriarchy, oligarchy. Nowadays, it is labeled elitism, colonialism, hegemony, bureaucracy, alienation. But, whatever its name, its basic character is the same. It is manifest whenever and wherever, through means direct or indirect, the creative freedom of those affected is unduly circumscribed if not wholly denied. That is the charge brought by African Americans against white America, by women against patriarchal institutions, and by the Third World against the United States, and, I suggest, should be brought by advocates of children against the prevailing social system.

But freedom is a slogan for radically divergent social visions ranging from libertarianism to socialism. Its meaning is contingent on its context of interpretation. I shall here distinguish two significantly different meanings of freedom—negative and affirmative—and propose that the social principle of optimizing the limits of one another's freedom intends freedom in the latter sense.[10]

Freedom in the negative sense—"freedom from"—signifies the absence of external obstacles in the pursuit of one's desires. Liberation is the process of removing obstacles, smashing barriers, destroying constraints. In political and economic life, the constraints take the form of social domination—elite rule, oligarchic control, patriarchal authority.

With liberation from such constraints, those previously subordinated are presumably free to do as they will, to act as they please, to follow their own whim and fancy. That certainly is a significant dimension of freedom, and liberation so understood contributes to the optimization of the limits of freedom. Historically, negative freedom stands at the heart of apologies for a free enterprise economy and liberal democracy, although, in the twists and turns of history, those social forms have given rise to new patterns of domination, blatant and subtle.

The limitations of negative freedom are strikingly illustrated by the end of the Civil War in the United States. The legal institution of slavery was declared null and void. The tyranny of the plantation system was apparently destroyed. Former slaves were emancipated, only to be, as W. E. B. Dubois and others have noted, introduced to new forms of enslavement through their utter dependency on prevailing economic and political structures. Lacking in land and education, they were without the means to embark effectively on a new life of self-determination. The smashing of the legal wall of slavery removed an external impediment, but the former slaves remained encased in structures of power that persisted in degrading them.

Affirmative freedom, by contrast, means empowerment. Carol C. Gould construes affirmative freedom as self-development—"as freedom to develop oneself through one's actions, or as a process of realizing one's projects through activity in the course of which one forms one's character and develops capacities." As Gould insists, such a process is impossible apart from enabling conditions, material and social.

> Thus this conception stresses the importance of the availability of the objective conditions—both material and social—without which... purposes could not be achieved. Among the material conditions are the means of subsistence as well as the means for labor and leisure activity. The social conditions include cooperative forms of social interaction, reciprocal recognition of each one's agency, and access to training, education, and various social institutions.[11]

Where negative freedom, by itself, is not incompatible with the severe delimitation of human possibility, affirmative freedom, given its attention to the thick context of human agency, seeks out all forms of empowerment to assure as full a realization of self-development as is, in any given moment, possible.

Affirmative freedom is therefore not merely the opening of opportunity for the individual. It is, as well, a quality of interaction. It specifies a form of association. In this connection, I would distinguish three forms of association—organic, aggregative, and relational—and suggest that, of the three, the relational form is the most direct expression of the principle of affirmative freedom.

In an organic association, each participant fulfills a function within the system. That function is part of a larger whole and finds its significance in its contribution to that whole. One acts not on behalf of oneself, but for the benefit of the system. Corporations and bureaucracies tend to assume this character. Particular persons within a corporation or bureaucracy may come and go, but the association persists. What is deemed critical is that persons within the association do justice to the roles assigned to them.

An aggregative form of association is the reverse image of the organic. In this case, an individual enters into associative activity only if it will serve the individual's interests. The association is instrumental in character. When it no longer benefits the values of the individual, a break in the relationship, initiated by the individual, is likely. Clubs and interest groups are usually understood as cases of this form. In their narrowest construction, social contract theories of political association are of the same character.

In contrast to both organic and aggregative forms, a relational type of association is marked by reciprocity between and among its participants. The immediate agent in this form of association is the individual. Yet its participants are not isolated. They are engaged in a system of dynamic interaction through which what each accomplishes is both dependent on what others have done and contributory, in turn, to the agency of all others. A relational association thus is a structure of interdependency. Each life consists in a dynamic interplay between self and other. In a sense all associations—even the most oppressive—have this character, for each of us is caught up in a network of interrelationships all of which leave their impress, however destructive or constructive, on our life, its present condition and future possibilities.

But at its best, a relational form of association is empowering and enhancing. In its fullest expression, it is a structure of mutuality. Friendship, in its paradigmatic sense, bears this quality. In the traditions of Judaism and Christianity, a covenantal community bears the same character. Within a covenantal community, each member is acknowledged with deepest respect by all others and is nurtured and advanced by the relationship. In and through all other purposes served by this form of association, the common purpose pursued by all is to maintain and to enrich the association itself, but precisely because the association is integral to their own self-development as social beings.

The link between affirmative freedom and a relational form of association marked by the quality of mutuality, should at this point be clear. What Suchocki designates as the intention of love—the richness of community—is indicated by mutuality as the overriding quality of relationships. Love as the drive to press back the limits of freedom of the other therefore entails far more than the removal of external obstacles to action. It entails emancipation in the fullest sense of promoting the mutual self-development of all participants in the human community.[12] In its aim toward richness of community, love is, by intention, inclusive in its principle of participation. But precisely because of that aim, love cherishes the individuality and diversity of persons and groups within that community. If all this be true, we are pressed to consider the case of children: how we understand what children are (the meaning of childhood), what impact our institutions have on what children might become (the suffering of children), and how we should reconstruct the principles of our social life to provide optimal conditions for the flourishing of children's lives (the rights of children).

THE MEANING OF CHILDHOOD

Often in our common life, we draw a clear line of distinction between adults and children. Adults possess rights and privileges (e.g., to vote in elections, to drive on the public highways, to imbibe alcoholic beverages) prohibited to children. Children, on the other hand, are indulged in ways held inappropriate to adults, assuming that children have not yet attained the age of reason and that childhood is a time for playfulness and harmless experimentation. Childhood is an extended developmental moment, lacking in the attributes of full humanity. In traditional societies, the movement from childhood to adulthood is marked by rites of passage through which the young boy or girl is initiated into the ways of mature life.

But the distinction drawn between childhood and adulthood is more than a simple distinction between two stages. It constitutes a normative boundary, specifying what possibilities are appropriate to the class of persons assigned to either side of that boundary. More importantly, it constitutes a structure of domination: adults have the authority to control children, to direct their lives, to set the parameters of their behavior, to fix the structure of possibilities open to them. At its best, this structure of domination assumes the form of a benevolent paternalism; at its worst, it assumes the form of absolute property in which the owner (the adult) may use and dispose of what is owned (the child) at will.

The parallel of the structure of domination between adult and child to other dominative relationships is striking: white master and black slave in the old American plantation system, male and female in patriarchal institutions, industrialized North and colonized South under conditions of global capitalism. In each case, the dominating class pretends to a benevolent paternalism, assuming the subordinate class needs protection and direction. In each case, the control of the subordinate class is thought justifiable and beneficial—hence the force of doctrines ranging from "white man's burden" and noblesse oblige to technocracy and economic development.

African Americans, women, Third World peoples have properly denounced such doctrines as morally perverse. What, then, about the case of children? If the impetus of liberation theology derives from the struggle to emancipate dominated peoples, then should it not turn its energies toward the emancipation of children? Or is the control and care of children a special case? If love, as indicated above, intends to optimize the freedom of all others, what are the implications of this principle for children? If children, like adults, are creative participants in our common life, should they not be granted, in some sense, equal status in the distribution of rights and privileges? Or is childhood a stage of life so radically different from adulthood that it properly requires control and direction by adults?

Granting the complexities of childhood experience and the diversity of cultural settings within which children undergo their development to maturity, I suggest that, given the perspective outlined above, we should resist drawing a hard and fast line between childhood and adulthood. Instead we should entertain a twofold concept: first, that children, especially during their early years, are possessed of a much higher degree of dependency and vulnerability—physically and psychologically—than adults, but, second, that, from their earliest days, children are interactive agents possessed of a keener apprehension of their surroundings and a greater potential for creative intercommunication than is oftentimes understood. Hence, the nurturance and care that adults are expected to provide for children should be set in a context characterized not by domination but by mutual participation in a process of interaction.

At this point, we should attend to a long-standing controversy over the idea of childhood. Over thirty years ago, Philippe Aries argued that the "idea of childhood" is a "discovery" of the seventeenth century.[13] In the medieval world, childhood is not considered a separate and distinct stage of life. Medieval art, for instance, depicts children as miniature adults. Once weaned, the child is perceived as a diminutive member of the household's normal activity of work and play.

Childhood, as a time set apart, is a function of the modern era in which, gradually, children are subjected to a rigorous time-consuming discipline in preparation for entrance into the prevailing social system. In M. D. A. Freeman's version of Aries's thesis, the social cause of the invention of childhood is the emergence of capitalism. Given the ever-increasing complexities of bourgeois life, "it required its initiates to undergo more lengthy educational and training processes. It also produced wealth and this required an orderly transmission to a next generation which, having been controlled, could be trusted to use it purposefully."[14] Together with Freeman, Valerie Polokow Suransky criticizes the presumed development of the modern idea of childhood on the grounds that it constricts the creative powers of children: "In short, in the modern era of childhood . . . we have 'progressed' from the *forgetfulness* of childhood to the *containment* of childhood. Children as young as a year old now enter childhood institutions to be formally schooled in the ways of the social system and emerge eighteen years later to enter the world of adulthood having been deprived of their history-making power, their ability to act upon the world in significant and meaningful ways."[15]

Nearly twenty-five years ago, Lloyd deMause in a schematic psychohistory of the evolution of childhood argued directly against Aries that the social conditions of childhood have progressed, haltingly but steadily, over the centuries. They have evolved through several stages— from an era when infanticide, as means of resolving adult anxieties, was common practice; through an era of ambivalence when adults, though emotionally attached to their children, nonetheless coerced them, physically and psychologically, to fit an expected social mold; to the modern era, when, at their best, adults are fully sensitive to the particular needs of children. Of this current era, whose merits he admits have not been extensively realized, deMause remarks: "The helping mode involves the proposition that the child knows better than the parent what it needs at each stage of its life, and fully involves both parents in the child's life as they work to empathize with and fulfill its expanding and particular needs."[16]

More recently, Linda A. Pollack has criticized both Aries and deMause on the basis of historical evidence. In a close reading of Western sources from 1500 to 1900, she rejects any effort at a schematized periodization in the unfolding of the meaning of childhood. Whatever perceptible variations do occur from time to time in the understanding of childhood and in styles of adult-child relationships, they always confront two constraints: "the dependency of the child and the acceptance of responsibility for the protection and socialization of that child by the parents." Her dominant assertion, however, is that, throughout all cultural and historical variations, "Children . . . are far from passive creatures; they make demands on their parents" and that, in every century, "parents . . . accommodated to the needs of their offspring."[17]

Throughout this controversy, overriding the differences, we should take note of a remarkable consistency in understanding a central feature of childhood. In Pollack's phrasing, "children are far from passive creatures." That is, a child is conceived as an agent, a creative participant in the matrix of interactions that constitute the child's world of possibilities. In Suransky's phrasing, "understanding the child from the perspective of his [or her] world is to hold the view that despite biographical and developmental determinants, the growing child *is* an intentional actor constructing a life project with consciousness, that becoming in the world involves a dynamic self-representation, that the child, too, is a historical being, a maker of history, a meaning-maker involved in a praxis upon the world."[18] In her imagery, "the child lives in open communion with the world, and the world, in turn, invites exploration from the child."[19] Through constant interaction between the world as a reservoir of possibility and the child as a center of initiative and creativity, both world and child are formed and reformed. Even neonates, according to T. Berry Brazelton, regardless of vast cultural differences, display an astounding understanding of immediate surroundings and ability to respond in a self-determinative way to communications from those surroundings.[20]

In sum, children, like adults, are creative participants in the world. They are centers of understanding and action. Even in the earliest stages of infancy, they are citizens of a world community to be respected as such. They manifest a keen ability to interpret and to respond to the signals and disclosures that constitute their setting and present, more or less generously, possibilities for their lives. In this sense, lines that compartmentalize childhood, separating it in an absolute manner from adulthood, are deceptive, even destructive. To be sure, children, especially in their earliest years, live in a state of deep dependency and vulnerability. They are relatively unsophisticated in the ways of the wider world. They confront a sequence of stages of development that challenge them mightily as they proceed. These are features of childhood that must be recognized and that call forth the constant care of adults. The adult-child relationship is not wholly symmetrical.

But I would insist that children, whatever their historical time or cultural setting, are most accurately discerned as creative agents engaged in creative interaction with the world and, given that character, deserving of a loving context for their lives. Adults and children belong together and contribute to each others' lives. A child, from the very beginnings of its presence in the midst of the community, is a center of feeling, thought, and action. Children are not merely a neutral stuff to be shaped and molded through socialization, but are themselves sources of novel possibility and surprise.

Given the peculiar needs of child development, whatever lines are drawn between childhood and adulthood must be held to the test of love, namely, the drive to optimize the limits of freedom, to expand the possibilities for creative life. As such, love is the impetus to emancipate children from conditions of suffering through the effectuation of their rights.

THE SUFFERING OF CHILDREN

Rebecca Chopp declares that what sets liberation theology apart from other forms of modern theology is its persistent focus on suffering. Suffering, she asserts,

> confronts and disrupts human existence with the hunger of innocent children, the hopelessness of the poor, the marginalization of the oppressed, the extermination of the "other," and the agony of the dispossessed and despised of the earth. Suffering . . . is the representative experience of being human for the masses of nonpersons on the fringes or outside of modern history. Such suffering ruptures our ideologies about progress and security, revealing to us that for the

majority of our fellow human beings "progress" and "history" consist of a long, dark night of tragic terror.[21]

Suffering, in its most elementary meaning, is deprivation. It is the loss (or threatened loss) of something of vital importance in one's life, including life itself. Given this basic definition, two distinctions are pertinent. First, we should distinguish between objective and subjective dimensions of suffering. The latter is the feeling of pain or distress. The former is the actual deprivation. One may or may not be conscious of an actual condition of suffering. Second, we should distinguish between suffering resulting from causes beyond human control and suffering resulting from human injustice.[22] My concern here is particularly with the objective suffering of children (to whatever degree it is apprehended as such) so far as it results from injustice, or, alternatively, from the absence of love. Where love drives toward optimizing the limits of freedom, deprivation narrows those limits. Where love enhances the dignity of life through its promotion of creative possibility, deprivation is degrading. Where love celebrates difference and originality, deprivation is linked with domination and conformity. Where love enriches community, deprivation impoverishes our common life.

In the case of children, deprivation nowadays is often called "child abuse."[23] But understandings of the meaning and causes of child abuse vary widely. In its narrowest sense, child abuse refers strictly to interpersonal relations resulting in physical violence and is explained by a disease model. In its broadest sense, child abuse refers to a wide range of causes—interpersonal and structural—resulting in an array of assaults on a child's life that are best explained contextually. According to Jo Boyden and Andy Hudson, "The broadest definition of child abuse and neglect emphasizes 'any adverse social and environmental condition which interferes with the normal health and development of the child.'"[24] Similarly, Freeman proposes that the causes of child abuse are multiple, ranging from psychopathology (an individualist explanation) and sheer poverty (a social explanation) to attitudes and understandings (a cultural explanation).[25] The advantage of the broadest definition of child abuse is twofold. First, it focuses on what is ultimately at stake in the condition of children, namely, their self-development. Second, it allows for historical concreteness in uncovering the many manifestations and causes of childhood suffering.[26]

Physical violence. The effects of direct physical violence against children by their immediate caretakers goes beyond the immediate bodily injuries inflicted upon them. Such violence has a deleterious impact on their self-development and the quality of their interaction with others. Many children react by submission to parental desires, seeking to avoid attack, as a result of which "all the optimal conditions for learning are missing: sensitivity to and encouragement of innate potential, stimulating opportunities for exploration."[27] Others react to physical violence aggressively. Children who are physically abused have difficulty verbalizing their own feelings; they lack self-esteem; they may find it nearly impossible to trust others; they become depressed, even to the point of suicide.

Poverty. During recent years, major reports on the condition of children have tended to stress structural causes of their suffering, particularly poverty. In 1977, for instance, Kenneth Keniston for the Carnegie Council on Children notes that

> Poor children live in a particularly dangerous world—an urban world of broken stair railings, of busy streets serving as playgrounds, of lead paint, rats and rat poisons, or a rural world where families do not enjoy the minimal levels of public health accepted as standard for nearly a century. Whether in city or country, this is a world where cavities go unfilled and ear infections threatening permanent deafness go untreated. It is a world where even a small child learns to be ashamed of the way he or she lives. And it is frequently a world of intense social dangers, where many adults, driven by poverty and desperation, seem untrustworthy and unpredictable. Children who learn the skills for survival in that world, suppressing curiosity and cultivating a defensive guardedness toward novelty or a constant readiness to attack, may not be able to acquire the basic skills and values that are needed, for better or worse, to thrive in mainstream society. In some ways we might even say that such children are systematically trained to fail.[28]

The effects of the global economy on children throughout the world have been a consistent theme in the annual surveys of UNICEF. In its 1989 report, for instance, focusing on the Third World debt crisis, UNICEF's executive director notes that

> Three years ago, former Tanzanian President Julius Nyerere asked the question "Must we starve our children to pay our debts?" That question has now been answered in practice. And the answer has been "Yes." In those three years, hundreds of thousands of the developing world's children have given their lives to pay their countries' debts,

and many millions more are still paying the interest with their malnourished minds and bodies. In Brazil's impoverished north-east
alone, infant death rates increased by almost 25 percent in the course
of 1983 and 1984 as a result of the world's recession.[29]

Given current trends, UNICEF estimates that, during the decade of the
nineties, over 100 million children will die under the age of five and
many times that number will suffer from malnourishment. UNICEF
claims such suffering will be the result, not of natural forces, but of
political and economic policies. Among other things, they propose that
each nation adopt a "principle of first call": "That principle is that the
lives and the normal development of children should have first call on
society's concerns and capacities and that children should be able to
depend upon that commitment in good times and in bad, in normal
times and in emergencies, in times of peace and in times of war, in
times of prosperity and in times of recession."[30]

Within the United States, the same concern with the effects of
poverty on children is assigned a place of first priority in the 1991
report of the National Commission on Children, chaired by Senator
John D. Rockefeller IV:

> Today, children are the poorest Americans. One in five lives in a fam-
> ily with an income below the federal poverty level. One in four
> infants and toddlers under the age of three is poor. Nearly 13 million
> children live in poverty, 2 million more than a decade ago. Many of
> these children are desperately poor; nearly 5 million live in families
> with incomes less than half of the federal poverty level.[31]

The Commission's depiction of the effects of poverty on children are
grim and graphic:

> Many children go undernourished, are inadequately clothed, and live
> in substandard housing. For them, the world is often a dangerous and
> threatening place to grow up. It is crime-ridden streets where schools
> and playgrounds are the domain of gangs and drug dealers, or it is
> desolate rural areas without adequate roads or running water. It is
> dilapidated homes with broken windows, poor heating, lead paint,
> rats, and garbage. It is a world in which children grow up afraid and
> ashamed of the way they live, where they learn basic survival skills
> before they learn to read. Some poor youngsters succeed and prosper
> despite adversity. Many face limited futures outside the economic,
> social, and political mainstream.[32]

Child exploitation. By exploitation I mean the malappropriation of the labor of a subordinate group (in this case children) by a dominating group (in this case adults) to the detriment of the former. Child exploitation, which is closely related to their poverty, assumes diverse forms: child labor, child prostitution, the trafficking of children in international adoption rings, the use of children in pornography.

Estimates of the number of children under the age of fifteen who work vary from 52 million to 145 million.[33] Child labor is not itself exploitative or degrading. Exploitation begins with "the involvement of children in activities which are beyond their physical and mental capacity. . . . In many cases, children are forced into situations in which they are unable to give their informed consent and which may be morally and physically damaging."[34] On the effects of such labor, Caroline Moorehead asserts, "For children the major hazards of illegal and unregulated work lie in retarded growth, malnutrition, accidents, environmental pollution, separation from their families, and restricted education. What concerns people is not the fact that children work, but that, being defenseless, they are exploited when they so do, by being paid little or nothing, and by being made to work long hours in unsafe and unhealthy conditions."[35]

The remarkable increase of street children throughout the world—currently estimated at about one hundred million—is a result of several factors: urban migration, poverty, family disintegration, unemployment, urban blight. Some children choose to live in streets given the alternatives, but in any case, street children confront the same risks. In Moorehead's depiction:

> Street children, who are invariably small and undernourished, have to contend with stabbings, beatings, car accidents and the constant fear of prison. The consumption of drugs by street children is universal—from sniffing glue and cleaning fluid to injecting heroin. In Latin America children have become prime targets for drug dealers, who use them as couriers and for pimps—prostitution is now as common among boys as among girls.[36]

Boyden and Hudson report a study estimating about 300,000 boy prostitutes in the United States alone.[37] It is common knowledge that the prevalence of child prostitution in South East Asia is the result of the military presence of the United States in that region over many years and is openly sustained by the tourist industry.

Modern technology. Some forms and causes of childhood suffering are more subtle, but no less systemic, than poverty and child labor. Keniston, for instance, acknowledging the benefits of modern technology, nonetheless expresses reservations about the impact on children of technological developments in several industries—television, food processing, nuclear energy. Amidst the promises of technological advance, clear risks emerge:

> If the worst fears of the critics of television should be realized, our children would become mindless seekers of sensation, violence-prone illiterates. If the darkest worries about diet should prove true, our children would grow up laden with harmful chemicals and vulnerable to serious diseases. If the predictions of those who oppose nuclear power should be accurate, our children would, as adults, absorb radiation from the atmosphere, risk disaster from reactor breakdown, and live under conditions of restrictive security needed to protect nuclear materials from theft.[38]

Cultural ethos. The National Commission on Children singled out the "moral climate" of industrialized society as among the profound causes of childhood suffering: "As a commission on children, we could not avoid questioning the moral character of a nation that allows so many children to grow up poor, to live in unsafe dwellings and violent neighborhoods, to lack access to basic health care and a decent education."[39] Moreover, in the commission's judgment, the moral contradictions that pervade American society, expressed, for example, in racist practices, rampant materialism, and corporate greed, despite proclaimed values to the contrary, contribute to moral confusion among children and blunt the development of a society conducive to respect for human dignity and for cultural difference.

In sum, the suffering of children may take many forms. Its concrete manifestation may be culturally specific.[40] However, its generic meaning, given the framework I have developed above, is deprivation. From another angle, its deepest meaning is alienation, for, in effect, children are coerced by means direct and indirect to participate in a social system that runs counter to their own good. The suffering of children is more than a matter of pain and distress. It is to be deprived of the conditions and possibilities of positive freedom, of self-development, of a society characterized by friendship and mutuality. It is to endure constrictions on their creative participation as younger members of the world community. It is to incur an erosion of their rights, for the reverse side of the suffering of children—in the sense of deprivation induced by unjust practices—is the rights of children.

THE RIGHTS OF CHILDREN

Children, I have proposed, deserve their own theology of liberation given the extensiveness of their suffering throughout the world. In developing this point, I have presented three contentions. First, the underlying drive of love is toward richness of community entailing the optimization of the freedom of the other and a relational form of association epitomized by mutuality. The condition of children stands in stark contrast to this measure. Second, the distinction between adulthood and childhood is not absolute. Children, even while undergoing diverse stages of development, are, like adults, creative participants in the world community. Permeating cultural and historical differences in the social formation of childhood, each child, even as a neonate, is a creative agent and should be respected as such. Third, the suffering of children throughout the world is best understood as deprivation, whether caused by specific individuals or by systemic social factors. The forms of suffering are many, but in all cases the fundamental injury is to their self-development. Children, in short, are deprived of their rights.

Whether and in what sense children have rights, however, is a contentious issue that has been under intense discussion in the West for at least a century and a half.[41] Beginning in mid-nineteenth century, legislation was developed responding to the perceived needs of children in industrial society—regulating child labor, establishing compulsory education, developing a juvenile justice system. The effects of such legislation was, however, ambiguous, designed as much to control and to contain children as to enhance their creative freedom or even to serve their welfare.

Throughout the twentieth century, a sequence of international declarations of the rights of children displayed a dramatic shift in orientation from sole concern with child welfare to a more complex set of concerns, including the self-determination of children. The first such statement was promulgated by the League of Nations largely through the initiative of Eglantyne Jebb, founder of the Save the Children Fund. The brief five-point "Declaration of the Rights of the Child" (1924) invited the "members of the League to be guided by its principles in the work of child welfare."[42] Welfare is the sole theme of the principles. States, for instance, are to feed the hungry and help the sick and "backward"; they are to provide means requisite to normal development; they are to protect children from exploitation and prepare them for a livelihood.

Thirty-five years later, the United Nations Assembly adopted a "Declaration of the Rights of the Child"[43] composed of ten principles that amplify the League's statement, but sustain the same fundamental orientation—child welfare. Thus the preamble states, "the child by reason of his physical and mental immaturity, needs special safeguards and care, including legal protection." The principles range in style from crisp pronouncements of entitlement (Principle 3: "the child shall be entitled from his birth to a name and a nationality") to broad statements of aspiration (Principle 6: "the child, for the full and harmonious development of his personality, needs love and understanding"). The principles would create opportunities enabling children "to develop physically, mentally, morally, spiritually and socially in a healthy and normal manner"; they would provide mothers with prenatal and post-natal care; they would protect children from religiously and racially discriminatory practices. But the prominent concern is with the protection and welfare of the child. It does not acknowledge the child as a creative agent. That characteristic is, presumably, reserved for adulthood.

The acknowledgment of children as creative agents marks off the recently adopted United Nations "Convention on the Rights of the Child"[44] from its predecessors. Following the International Year of the Child (1979), the United Nations established a commission to prepare a convention which, by intention, was to be more specific and more binding on member states than prior declarations. After ten years of rigorous controversy, the commission submitted its results to the General Assembly which accepted the convention and distributed it to member states for ratification and implementation.[45]

The major part of the convention (the substantive part) consists of forty-one articles, many of which expand on the principles of the 1959 declaration, thereby perpetuating a long-standing concern for the protection and welfare of children. However, the convention diverges remarkably from earlier declarations by its inclusion of several articles whose import is to acknowledge a child's right to self-determination. Hence, for instance, the convention declares that the child shall "have the right to freedom of expression" (Articles 12 & 13), to "freedom of

thought, conscience and religion" (Article 14), to "freedom of association and to freedom of peaceful assembly" (Article 15), to protection
against "arbitrary or unlawful interference with his or her privacy, family, home or correspondence" (Article 17), and to freedom of "access to
information and material from a diversity of national and international
sources" (Article 17). In addition, the convention provides for a detailed
set of procedural rights when the child is, for whatever reason, caught
up in the judicial and penal system of a state (Articles 37 & 40).

The convention, in short, presupposes a more complex idea of
childhood than the declarations of 1924 and 1959. In this idea, childhood is not simply a passive, dependent stage of life in which the child
is subordinate to caretakers. While dependency is an important dimension of childhood, especially during the earliest years of life, self-development is another vital dimension of childhood to be supported and
celebrated. Through its forty-one articles, the 1989 UN convention
embraces two kinds of rights for children, welfare rights and self-determination rights, corresponding to the two dimensions of childhood.

In this respect, the convention properly consolidates diverse sides
of a long-standing controversy within the children's rights movement.
Three ways of understanding the rights of children are manifest in that
controversy. Each way contains some practical wisdom, but each by
itself neglects a crucial dimension of childhood. I propose a creative
synthesis of all three strands, modifying each through incorporation
within the framework I developed earlier. Of the three ways, the major
division in the children's rights movement is between protectionism
(stressing welfare rights) and liberationism (emphasizing self-determination rights).[46]

Protectionism. Protectionism is paternalistic. It supposes children
cannot care for themselves; parents must care for them. It supposes
children cannot even know what is good for themselves; parents, in
principle, are those who know. Children are subordinate to parents,
subject to their concern and their dictation.

Protectionism assumes that childhood is a time of utter helplessness or "total dependency."[47] Their dependency is physical and mental.
When threatened or attacked physically, they cannot defend themselves. Even when not threatened, they depend on others for sustenance. The adult community is a necessary source to protect them and
to supply everyday needs. Moreover, while children have their own likes
and dislikes, they lack the capacity to make wise decisions, prudentially
or morally. Adults must direct them. In sum, children are marked by

"imperfect rationality, need for guidance and protection, and material dependence."[48]

From this perspective, the rights of children are a function of their total dependency on adults for the fulfillment of their needs. A right, in this context, is a "moral power in virtue of which human beings may make just claims to certain things."[49] Children, in particular, have the right to claim that their specific needs be honored and fulfilled, else their life and development be jeopardized. The rights of children constitute claims, first of all on parents. But if parents are unable or unwilling to respond, then the claims run to the larger community of adults, in which case child welfare is the responsibility of government as the agent of the community. The rights of children, that is, must not be contingent on the condition of parents alone. No child, for instance, should be forced to suffer the consequences of poverty because of the poverty of parents. It is contrary to the rights of children to deprive them of health care or education by linking their fate with that of their mothers and fathers, their immediate neighborhood or surroundings.

Liberationism. Where the protectionist's version of children's rights supposes the "total dependence" of children on adults for sustenance and development, liberationists suppose the potential autonomy of children. Dependency is not the natural condition of children, but is imposed upon them: "We conspire as a society to keep children weak, innocent, helpless, and dependent."[50] The assumption of children's helplessness is an ideological means to suppress them, to keep them under control, to discipline them to conform to the expectations and interests of prevailing social institutions.

Within the movement for children's liberation, freedom as self-determination, an intrinsic value, is fundamental to all rights, but tends to be denied or violated by most institutions most directly concerned with children in modern society. Children are battered at home, indoctrinated at school, held incompetent by law, and denied representation in government. The purpose of children's liberation is not to do away with these institutions, but to transform them by bringing the child into direct participation in them given their own insights and expressed needs.

Adults, from this perspective, should concentrate less on what differences separate adulthood and children and more on the "common ground of humanity between ourselves and young children."[51] The currently prevailing double standard that treats adults and children differently—contrasting the vulnerability and dependency of children with the maturity and independence of adults—results in a denial of the rights of children.

As a liberationist, Richard Farson rejects that double standard and proposes a radical transformation of social institutions to conform to the central need of children: to exercise control over themselves and their environment. Toward that end, Farson outlines several rights of children. Children, for instance, have a "right to alternative home environments."[52] Granting that children have a need for love and care, for proper nutrition and adults with whom to identify, children should be assured options when parents cannot or will not meet those needs. Second, children have a right to information.[53] To keep them in ignorance by limiting their access to adult conversation, to school records, to books and various forms of art is to delimit their possibilities of self-understanding and self-development. Again, children have a right to economic resources and opportunities.[54] Farson is critical of child labor laws as perpetuating the myth of childhood dependency. Children should not, merely because of age, be prohibited from productive labor or from promotions or positions of leadership.[55]

Liberal paternalism. At first glance, the protectionist and liberationist understandings of children's rights seem antithetical. They presuppose radically different views of the meaning of childhood. Where the protectionist sees childhood as a time of total dependency, the liberationist argues that childhood is a time for autonomy. Where the protectionist stresses the care of children by adults, the liberationist focuses on the common humanity of children and adults. Where the protectionist assumes an organic connection between child and family, the liberationist proposes that each child is a unique person with the capacity for and the right of self-determination.

Despite that seeming antithesis, a third way of understanding children's rights draws them together in an understanding of childhood as a progressive unfolding of the child from an infantile stage of deep dependency to a mature stage of independence and autonomy. The task of the caretaker is to assist the child's becoming increasingly capable of independent thought and action. M. D. A. Freeman calls this position "liberal paternalism,"[56] but is cautious to distinguish it from the kind of paternalism that presumes a sharp and persistent division between classes of persons. The latter kind of paternalism is a form of domination. It is evident wherever employers adopt an attitude of superiority over the employed, the powerful assume the stupidity or laziness of the powerless, the rich dole out charity to the poor, or bureaucratic experts dictate conditions or regulations to the needy. As such, paternalism tends to perpetuate a structure of dependency and subordination. By contrast, where paternalism—as caring for those unable to care for themselves—is directed toward the maximization of self-determination, it may not only avoid that risk, but, especially in the case of the child, be a useful step on the way toward increasing autonomy.

From this perspective, paternalism in the case of children is justifiable only so far as it promotes the growth of the child toward self-determination. A child thus possesses two kinds of rights—welfare rights and self-determination rights—but the latter holds regulative priority over the former. Hence, rights to health care, to a standard of living sufficient for the child's physical and mental development, to education, to be protected from sexual abuse and economic exploitation are supportive of, but subordinate to rights of freedom of expression, freedom of religion, freedom of peaceful assembly, freedom of information, and freedom of privacy. The authority of parents and other caretakers of children is defined by its paramount aim and should progressively diminish as its work is accomplished. The pragmatic test of liberal paternalism is the eventual consent of those who have been subjected to it and whose lives have been conditioned by its influence.[57]

This construction of the rights of children—drawing together welfare rights and self-determination rights—is a compelling means of supporting the United Nations Convention on the Rights of the Child and of responding to many dimensions of the current suffering of children. Yet, whether the principle of autonomy (the aim of liberal paternalism) is an adequate statement of the ultimate meaning of the rights of children is susceptible to question. If the import of the principle of autonomy is negative freedom—the removal of obstacles to the pursuit of one's individual desires—then, I would suggest, it is severely limited as a moral principle.

Relationalism. As an alternative, I invoke, once again, the affirmation of Marjorie Hewitt Suchocki, "The aims for the world that spring from . . . divine love are themselves aims toward a richness of community, which is as much named by love in the finite world as in the divine reality."[58] Love drives toward optimizing the limits of freedom of the other. But freedom, in this context, is affirmative freedom. As such it denotes a quality of interaction through which the self-development of each member of the community contributes to the life of each other member. In this sense, individual freedom and social solidarity are not in conflict. The rights of children, I mean to assert, find their ultimate meaning and sense as an articulation of love so understood, for children even as children are, like adults, participants in the world community. Therefore, the rights of children are not all that different from the rights of all other members of that community.[59] The rights of children—their welfare rights and their rights to self-determination—consist in a justifiable claim to engage in that interactive process in which and through which the aims of love are realized.

From this perspective, rights are held by individuals to be respected for what are and might become. But they are not, in any simple way, claims over against the community. They are more adequately understood as a form of relationship among members of the community, a form of relationship supportive of diversity and difference. Where rights are jeopardized, the character of the community is threatened. That is, rights—including welfare rights and rights to self-determination as interdependent principles constitutive of social interaction—enhance the creative freedom of each person not only for that person's sake, but for the entire community.

The rights of children—to health care and education, to information and national identity, to love and security, to economic and political power—are supportive of the life and growth of each individual child (within that child's particular cultural setting) and create a context through which the child's life contributes to the life of the community in multiple ways. In this connection, I share Maxine Greene's insistence that the practice of rights must demonstrate respect for radical diversity in the lives of children: "If we are to come to terms with the matter of rights for children, we have to acknowledge a pluralism in the world of children."[60] Traditionally, in Greene's judgment, Western culture has reserved its "inalienable rights" for white males alone. Excluded from the domain of rights were women, minorities, slaves, and children: "It was assumed that children were property and were to be kept in good order by those in charge.... Whatever values were affirmed with regard to them were linked to notions of imprinting, molding, and controlling."[61] But, as Greene notes in developing a program of rights for children, each child is born a member of a cluster of particular groups—familial, ethnic, religious, racial, national. That immediate setting of a child's life is intimately associated with the child's identity. It is a resource for the child's survival, but more importantly, for the child's language and culture, expectations and aspirations. To respect the child requires respect for that setting. The rights of the child, while of universal significance, must be understood and realized contextually.

From a relationalist perspective, then, each child should, given that child's immediate setting and respecting its particularities, be granted a full spectrum of the rights of membership in the world community. That, I would claim, is the intention of the United Nations Convention on the Rights of the Child. That, I would insist, is the measure against which the suffering of children is so agonizing. That, I would declare, is a centerpiece in the kind of justice appropriate to the meaning of childhood. That, I would understand, is an implication of the "richness of community" that is the aim of love. That, I would suggest, is a key moral principle for any acceptable theology of childhood liberation.

To be sure, given the depth and intransigence of the historical forces that run counter to the needs of children, we cannot and should not be overly assured about prospects for the conquest of children's suffering or for the realization of their rights. But at least we can understand what each and every child brought into this world deserves. We can comprehend why the sufferings they experience are intolerable, even though they may seem, at any given moment, inexorable. We can be brought to realize that the deprivation of any child is, in the final analysis, a cosmic loss. And we can be driven by the persistent aims of divine reality to engage in the struggle for childhood liberation.

4

Interlude:
Affirmative Action
and the Deprivations of Racism

> They said to him, "We have only five loaves here
> and two fish." And he said, "Bring them here
> to me.".... And they all ate and were satisfied....
> And those who ate were about five thousand
> men, besides women and children.
> —*Matthew 14:17–18, 20–21*

Race matters![1] Whatever exactly the idea of race has been understood to signify from time to time, it seems to have occupied a place of eminent importance in the confrontation and conflicts among peoples throughout much of human history.

To be sure, racial differentiation and racial identity are not God-given realities, writ in the fundamental nature of things. Rather, "race" as a category employed to distinguish kinds of peoples is a construct of the human mind. It is a relational category, or, more strictly, a comparative category, used to classify peoples, to set them apart from each other, to assess their respective qualities and characteristics, and to determine their proper location in relationship to each other. But as such, race has become a harsh historical reality permeating all arenas of human interaction.

The idea of race—linked with its shadow companion, the practice of racism—has been a central feature in the cultural and political life of the United States of America since the days of its colonial beginnings in the sixteenth and seventeenth centuries. W. E. B. DuBois's oft-quoted declaration—that "the problem of the Twentieth Century is the problem of the color line"[2]—might just as well have been applied to earlier centuries in the history of this land and, given current trends in our common life, will apply as well to the twenty-first century, although assuming, as social context changes, new forms.

The controversy now percolating vigorously over the public policy of affirmative action is a clear indication that forces of racism (sometimes cloaked by a seemingly benign, if not righteous, appeal to equal protection of the laws) remain deeply embedded in the minds and hearts of an appreciable proportion of the population of the country. Racism, variously defined, although always entailing some sort of contrast concentrated on skin pigmentation as a prescriptive index, between Self ("us") and Other ("them"), tends to conjoin three factors: a cultural belief (we are different from them), a moral judgment (we are better than they are), and a political practice (we may, appropriately, circumscribe and delimit their rights and their power).

While racism may be, and all too often is, deliberately intentional, it need not be. The ultimate criterion of racism lies in its effects on the quality of relationship between Self and Other. In cases of aversive racism (where the Self, given feelings of discomfort, takes care to avoid the Other) and symbolic racism (where the Self declares high principles of racial equality, but resists correlative policies), malicious intent may be absent, but the results are nonetheless racist. That is, the effect is to reinforce the subjection of the (presumably) subordinate racial community—the Other.

Curiously, however, given the reflexive character of racism, the deprivations of racist attitudes and actions have a delimiting impact on *both* parties. "If racism brutalises and dehumanises its object, it also brutalises and dehumanises those who articulate it."[3] The agents of racism are themselves among the victims of racism. Unfortunately, this double effect of racism—on both Other and Self—is seldom acknowledged. More on the dynamics of this double effect later.

Over the course of the twentieth century in the United States, the practice of racism has assumed different forms, some more blatant, others more subtle. The practice of lynching African Americans, prevalent during the earlier decades of this century, constituted a particularly ugly case of *conspicuous racism*. Although lynching as such is now past history, conspicuous racism remains with us, for example, in incidents of "hate crimes" and in the spread of organized "hate groups" throughout the land. Beginning especially in the sixties, the idea of *structural racism* came into play to designate those practices and institutional patterns that, whatever their intent, tend to protect the advantages of a dominant racial community while sustaining or exacerbating the disadvantages of a subordinate racial group. Segregated residential patterns, for instance, not necessarily intended deliberately as racist, nonetheless have had an effect on the distribution of employment and educational opportunities among racial groups. More recently, the idea of the "*new racism*" has been conceived to point to instances where appeals to moral principle (e.g., fairness, equal rights, freedom of choice) have been used to justify moves to dismantle programs of affirmative action as themselves discriminatory or to defend persisting patterns of segregation in employment or residence as the result of voluntary decision. The "new racism" is also evident in instances where complaints about welfare, crime, and immigration are code words expressive of an underlying antipathy to people of color.

Affirmative action as a public policy in the United States was initiated, it has been suggested,[4] when President John F. Kennedy issued Executive Order 10925 in 1961 creating a committee on Equal Employment Opportunity and mandating federal agencies with contractual authority to take "affirmative steps" to end racial discrimination in hiring and subcontracts. President Lyndon B. Johnson introduced the words *affirmative action* in his 1965 expansion of that Executive Order, requiring from employers the submission of numerical goals and timetables (but not, it should be noted, quotas and target dates) to demonstrate their good intentions.

The idea of affirmative action was subsequently refined, expanded, modified, and particularized through legislation and executive orders at various levels of government to introduce a range of procedures dictated by a twofold purpose: to overcome the effects of racism (and sexism) in our common life and to facilitate the full participation of persons irrespective of racial (or sexual) identity in our economic, cultural, and political institutions.

Properly comprehended, affirmative action should be construed as part of an all-encompassing, highly visionary effort at social transformation, an aggressive attempt to bring the social reality of the United States into conformity with its alleged democratic principles. A major supposition underlying the idea of affirmative action is that racism (and sexism) in any and all of its forms is inconsistent with an authentic democratic community. Democracy, in this context, means something more profound than merely a narrowly construed bundle of civil rights—for example, to vote, to organize political parties, to hold periodic elections—however important these rights may be. Democracy, in a more abundant sense, means effective participation by each and every citizen and cluster of citizens in all those institutions—political, economic, cultural—that have a governing influence on the character of our common life, for the sake of creating as qualitatively profuse a common life as possible under given circumstances. Democracy, so understood, is part and parcel of the full intentionality of human rights.

As of this writing, however, affirmative action in its diverse programs, even as a general idea, is under severe attack. But those who have launched the countermovement against affirmative action are not, at least ostensibly, seeking a return to the legalized segregation of the pre-sixties era. Their approach, in their minds at least, is more progressive than that. That is, at its best, the countermovement derives from a plausible, albeit questionable, understanding of what the world is like and how we ought to live our lives, even though, at its worst, the counter-movement attracts support from a significant segment of those whose white supremacist persuasion, if not publicly expressed, is nonetheless evident in their moods and motivations.

On the surface, the controversy over affirmative action has to do with the effectiveness, if not the fairness, of the programs that have been instituted by federal, state, and local governments over the past thirty years to implement the idea. But the charges levelled against the programs—that three decades of affirmative action have, despite all the effort and expense they have entailed, accomplished little and that white men, despite their qualifications and competence, have suffered unduly because of the opportunities, educational and economic, reserved specifically for designated minority racial communities and for females—do not get at the deeper sensibilities at stake in the controversy.

At that deeper level, the controversy over affirmative action is a struggle between two (or three) alternative social ontologies, that is, understandings of social reality.[5] In the context of each of these understandings, the idea of affirmative action takes on a quite different meaning and its evaluation varies accordingly. Each of these social ontologies has roots in American cultural history—a beloved community, a meritocratic society, and a society of white privilege. But, of the three, the first is most in keeping with the allied principles of relationality and social pluralism.[6]

The "beloved community," with all its connotations, religious and political, was the name by which Martin Luther King, Jr., designated his social vision, a vision of possibility that he contrasted sharply with prevailing conditions of life in the United States. In the beloved community, all peoples, whatever their racial or ethnic or sexual identity would live together and work together, collaboratively and peacefully, for the welfare of all. King was aware that racial and class divisions were complexly intertangled in modern industrial society, and he thus promoted, for purposes of advancing his social vision, not only the civil rights of African Americans, but, more extensively, the economic rights of all citizens to employment, to a living wage, to decent housing, to adequate education. Those who, to some degree at least, shared in this social vision pressed for affirmative action as an institutional means— one among many—to accelerate the transformation of the social system of the United States, overcoming its long-standing and seemingly intransigent tradition of white male privilege to create a system in which brotherhood and sisterhood would constitute a genuine reality. That social vision—with its communal character—constitutes the deepest significance of affirmative action among those who continue to support the idea, however much they might be willing to refine its details as a public policy. Affirmative action is conceived not so much as compensation for injustices of the past as a stage in the unfolding of a morally persuasive and historically viable vision for the future.

A radically different social vision, I would suggest, informs those (or at least some of those) who are critics of the idea of affirmative action—a vision of a meritocratic society in which individuals should be set free to work as hard as they will and to advance as far as they can given their natural talents, their motivation, their industry, and their productivity. In a meritocratic society (which, it must be noted, is no less imaginary than the beloved community), traditions of special privilege and inherited status, whatever their origin, are considered dysfunctional. Individuals should rise and fall, progress and flounder depending strictly on the merits of their personal contributions to and success in the corporate marketplace. Such a social vision is individualistic and competitive in character, largely ahistorical in orientation, not given to forgiveness or mercy save insofar as a second chance might prove productive. In the vision of a meritocratic society, racial and sexual identity are in themselves irrelevant; but they are not irrelevant when and where they might make a difference in advancing (or in detracting from) the work of the market. Where programs of affirmative action might function to uncover previously hidden talents, thereby expanding the range of human resources, it might be appropriate. But, from the perspective of those who nowadays claim to be committed to a meritocratic society, the thirty-year experiment with affirmative action programs should be ended because of strong evidences of its inefficiency (its costs outweigh its benefits) and its unfairness (assessment according to merit precludes preferential treatment according to race or gender).

The contention between these two social understandings—the beloved community (with its democratic and communal sensibilities) and the meritocratic society (with its more individualistic marketplace orientation)—is compounded with the persistence of a third social vision—sometimes declared explicitly, but more often concealed by appeals to principles of fairness or efficiency, namely, the vision of a society of white privilege (or, more narrowly, white male privilege). At the deepest level of this social vision, racial differentiation seems to take on both an ontological (different races constitute different subspecies) and moral (some subspecies are more sophisticated and therefore more deserving than others) character, even where, on the surface, that assumption is denied. Where opposition to programs of affirmative action is most passionate, one may, not improperly, wonder if this kind of social vision—which once flourished in the grand plantation system of the deep South—is not lurking in the background. To be sure, as many commentators have observed, the strength of the opposition to affirmative action is roughly proportionate to the intensity of competition over scarce economic opportunities, but, it could argued, it is precisely that competition in a time of increasing scarcity that brings to the fore our most basic cultural sensibilities and beliefs.

Indeed, conditions of scarcity provide a revealing test case of the difference among the three social ontologies. In an envisioned meritocratic society, individuals confronting scarcity will scramble to outdo their fellows in competence and industriousness to get ahead. In a society of white privilege, people of color, whatever their talents and qualifications, will, given their racial identity, be the first and the longest to suffer. However, in a beloved community, under conditions of scarcity, all peoples seek to develop ways of enabling each other to survive. That is, in order to sustain the community, we are pledged to work together, to play together, to suffer together, to seek out means to aid and to assist each other—all because of the intrinsic good and intense joy of the communal adventure—to which our historical and cultural differences, racial or otherwise, properly serve as contributions. This vision of a beloved community, I would declare, is the ultimate rationale underlying affirmative action programs.

To return to an earlier theme, from that same perspective—the perspective of a beloved community—racism in its many manifestations has a deleterious impact on the entire social process. It has therefore a double effect, depriving everyone, including both the agents (the Self) and the objects (the Other) of racism, of the vibrancy and liveliness of creative interaction. More concretely, on a personal level, racism, in its reflexive effect on the Self, distorts understanding, promotes ignorance and insecurity, delimits our imaginary powers, narrows the future, results in lack of resiliency and openness. On a more institutional level, racism, in its effects on racists, precludes the prospects of authentic democracy, is neglectful of potential human resources and energies, tends toward cultural rigidity and conformism, inhibits the prospects for diversity of insight, is provocative of intense social resentment if not eventual social explosion.

In short, ironically, from the perspective of a beloved community, racism, however intentional or unintentional, runs contrary to the deepest interests of the racists, including those who, in the tops of their minds, do not think of themselves as racists. Even the seemingly innocent process of aversive racism—whether practiced in forms of personal behavior (e.g., avoiding the gaze or the proximity of the Other) or of institutional action (e.g., moving into self-contained, carefully secured residential clusters)—results in a loss of enriching possibility to the Self. For those versed in the lore of process theology, consider, in this connection, the political and moral implications of Henry Nelson Wieman's concept of "creative intercommunication."[7] Racism is, bluntly put, an obstruction to that kind of creative interaction through which both Self and Other might find their greater good.

James Baldwin, in his "Letter to My Nephew on the One-Hundredth Anniversary of Emancipation," captured this sentiment when he insisted that his nephew, despite his reluctance, must accept white people, "and accept them with love." Without the insistent presence of their black brothers and sisters, the white community cannot be released from the bonds of misperception and misunderstanding. They have been blinded for centuries by the myth of white supremacy, by the distorted belief that black people are inferior to white people. Given that long history of self-deception, they, too, stand in need of emancipation.[8]

More generally, if one assumes that the beloved community is the most morally compelling of social visions, then the entire cultural and economic system of the United States is in desperate need of radical transformation for the sake of us all, whatever our racial (or sexual) identity. That is why appeals merely to the principle of racial equality

Part II
Economic Relations

> You shall open wide your hand
> to your brother, to the needy and
> to the poor, in the land.
> —*Deut. 15:11*

We cannot live—in any meaningful and abundant sense—by bread alone. Yet we cannot live without bread. In the eloquent proclamation of the Declaration of Independence (1776), each of us is vested with rights to life, liberty, and the pursuit of happiness. To some degree, these rights have been vouchsafed us in the United States—or at least those among the more privileged classes of us—by the protective institutions of our common life. But protective institutions are insufficient to do what is needful for the full effectuation of these rights. We cannot live without bread.

Many decades later, the Universal Declaration of Human Rights (1948), acknowledging the breadth of meaning implied in that seemingly simple proclamation of the eighteenth century, announced that everyone has a right to bread, that is, to those economic resources and conditions requisite to the realization of life, liberty, and the pursuit of happiness—for example, food, clothing, shelter, medical care, education, cultural participation.

There are, however, multitudes of people—women, men, children—lacking in those conditions and resources. To be so lacking is the human meaning of poverty. The incidence of poverty throughout the world, even in industrialized lands, is astounding. Well over one-fifth of the world's population is making an effort to eke out an existence devoid of the most basic necessities of life. Such poverty stands in vivid contrast with the kind of luxurious life enjoyed by the wealthy.

From the perspective of the principle of justice as solidarity with its particular angle on the doctrine of human rights, we must admit that something must be radically awry in the structure of our common life given the contrast between the poor and the wealthy that presents itself

71

to anyone sensitive to the full state of our common life throughout the nations of the world.

But poverty—whether understood in absolute or in relative terms—is not an ineluctable necessity. It is a function of inherited forms of our life together. If, as I would like to suggest, economics consists of those forms of interaction—in spheres of production, distribution, and consumption—through which those goods and services are provided that are intended to contribute to the enhancement of our common life, then, given the pervasiveness of poverty, we are in need of reconsidering the basic character of our economic relationships with each other.

In the initial chapter that follows, I develop an extended reconception of the meaning of property from a relational perspective. In the second chapter, I affirm the desirability of extending the basic conception of democratic governance to economic institutions. In the brief interlude that follows, I propose the continuing relevance of the socialist vision. All three chapters are intended to direct our energies toward a new future in our economic relations beyond the forms of domination and exploitation that are currently rampant throughout the world toward a community of life through which we might be empowered to work together toward the benefit of all.

5

The Meaning and Use of Property

The land shall not be sold in perpetuity,
for the land is mine; for
you are strangers and sojourners with me.
—*Leviticus 25:23*

The great and chief end...of men's uniting
into commonwealths, and putting themselves under
government, is the preservation
of their property.
—*John Locke[1]*

The transformation of scattered private property,
arising from individual labour, into capitalist private
property is, naturally, a process incomparably more protracted,
violent, and difficult, than the transformation of capitalist
private property, already practically resting on socialized
production, into socialized property. In the former case, we had
the expropriation of the mass of the people by a few usurpers;
in the latter, we have the expropriation of a few usurpers
by the mass of the people.
—*Karl Marx[2]*

Conditions of the common life of peoples have undergone a radical transformation from the seventeenth century to the present. The character of daily work, the form of family life, the structure of nations and empires in our times are fundamentally unlike those of three centuries ago. In the economic sector, property is among the categories of thought and practice whose features have been transfigured during the period.

In the seventeenth century, John Locke, siding with the Whigs against the Tories, cast his renowned argument supporting individualized property at the center of his concept of civil government. The chief purpose of civil government, he insisted, is the preservation of property. Locke's argument, despite its ambiguities, is still invoked, particularly in disputes over social legislation, progressive taxation, and, more recently, government regulation.

However, in the nineteenth century, Karl Marx averred that the character of property has changed over the course of history and is in the process of changing once again. Individualized private property has given way to capitalist private property, but the latter, in time, will give way to socialized property. As C. B. Macpherson has noted:

> The meaning of property is not constant. The actual institution, and the way people see it, and hence the meaning they give to the word, all change over time. We shall see that they are changing now. *The changes are related to changes in the purposes which society or the dominant classes in society expect the institution of property to serve.*[3]

The term *property* has several specialized senses: to designate the essential features of a thing (e.g., each species has its own defining "properties") or to refer to parcels of land or buildings (e.g., a superintendent manages "properties"). But in economic relations, property is the claim or title someone has to something tangible or intangible. Locke and Marx use the term in this last sense, which is the sense with which I am concerned.

I intend to explore the meaning of property from a relational perspective. I shall focus not so much on the law of property as on its fundamental meaning, although the law of property cannot finally be divorced from some construction about its fundamental meaning. Legal forms of property enforced through, say, ancient Roman law, feudal law, or nineteenth-century American courts presuppose variant understandings about property in its most basic meaning. Moreover, such basic meanings assume, however dimly, some doctrine about the identity of self, nature, and society. In that sense, property is a symbol of cosmology.

What I shall propose is that a relational perspective synthesizes—within its own setting—dimensions of the meaning of property present in the thought of Thomas Aquinas (the principle of common use), John Locke (the principle of labor), and R. H. Tawney (the principle of social function). As such, a relational perspective requires a radical revisioning of the classical liberal or individualistic understanding of property.[4]

In the next section, I describe current controversies over the classical liberal understanding of property, distinguish several aspects of the basic definition of property over which there is contention, and amplify my proposal. In subsequent sections, I attend to understandings of property in Thomas, Locke, and Tawney. Finally, I show how central principles of these three understandings may be integrated through a relational perspective.

THE MEANING OF PROPERTY: CURRENT CONTROVERSIES

Property, in the classical liberal tradition, is a bulwark, protecting the individual against the arbitrary force of government. It specifies an arena in which no one may trespass without invitation or consent. As in the medieval distinction between dominium (ownership) and imperium (government), ownership constitutes a private sphere into which officials may not intrude. Together with civil liberties (speech, religious exercise, association), property is among the institutional principles promoted to affirm the superiority of the individual over political authority. But property also isolates individuals from each other. Within its boundaries, each controls one's own destiny and pursues one's own life plans. Property is an exemplary institution of individualism.

Within this tradition, property and contract are key features of economic activity, which is construed as a strictly private sphere, a business in which persons and groups interact independently of governmental authority. Governmental interference is perceived as a perversion of the proper order of institutional forms, a usurpation of the inviolable dignity of the individual. Private life (including economic life) is not only distinct from public life; it is superior to public life. Thereby a dominant tradition of social thought—from Aristotle to Aquinas—is turned on its head introducing an antagonistic standoff between politics (the domain of government) and economics (the domain of the individual).

John Locke is often interpreted as a seminal figure in the beginnings of classical liberalism. Though that interpretation may be overdrawn, Locke does affirm that protection of property is the chief end of civil authority and he allies the right to property with the life and integrity of the individual.

Near the end of the eighteenth century, William Blackstone formulated a definition of property epitomizing this tradition. Whether

Blackstone is merely stating a popular and naive view of property or forwarding his own constructive doctrine is a matter of debate.[5] In either case, the definition was widely influential in nineteenth-century American legal culture: "There is nothing which so generally strikes the imagination and engages the affections of mankind, as the right to property; or that sole and despotic dominion which one man claims and exercises over the external things of the world, in total exclusion of the right of any other individual in the universe."[6] Similarly, in the French Declaration of the Rights of Man and Citizen (1789), property is defined as "the rights to enjoy and dispose at will of one's goods, one's income, and fruit of one's labor and industry." Property, in brief, is the exclusive right of a person to possess, to use, to abuse, to dispose of a thing in any way one wishes. So conceived, property ("absolute property") is a bundle of rights against all other persons and groups, official or private.

This doctrine was vigorously supported in influential circles in nineteenth-century American jurisprudence. Hence Justice Joseph Story's dictum in the case of *Wilkinson v. Leland* (1829):

> The government can scarcely be deemed free where the rights of property are left solely dependent upon the will of a legislative body without any restraint. The fundamental maxims of a free government seem to require that the rights of personal liberty and private property should be held sacred. At least no court of justice in this country would be warranted in assuming that the power to violate and disregard them—a power so repugnant to the common principles of justice and civil liberty—lurked under any general grant of legislative authority, or ought to be implied from any general expression of the people. The people ought not be presumed to part with rights so vital to their security and well-being, without very strong and direct expressions of such an intention.[7]

On grounds such as these, efforts by American legislatures, state and federal, to act "in the public interest" but against the economic claims of private parties were forcefully opposed in courts throughout the nineteenth and well into the twentieth century. Even with changes effected under the New Deal, support for the doctrine of absolute property has persisted.

In recent years, Gottfried Dietze composed an apology "in defense of property" out of the conviction that twentieth-century social and political trends betoken a regressive move, contrary to the impulse of civilization—"a state in which men [sic] are emancipated and able to enjoy freedom."[8] Freedom, as the absence of coercive restraint, depends on the institution of private property. In Dietze's judgment, the evolution of Western civilization reached its climax "in the latter half of the eighteenth century when the idea of the natural rights of man—including those of property—came to be universally accepted."[9]

During the nineteenth century, the natural rights of property were largely respected. But the twentieth century marks the "fall of property" and thereby the decay of civilization. Dietze is frightened by the implications of this move, which he attributes to the emergence of egalitarian democracy. Classical democracy, governed by an elite, was respectful of the natural right of property. But egalitarian democracy acts without restraint; despite its rhetoric it is, in effect, authoritarian. In a revealing litany, Dietze illustrates his fear of the welfare state which, in its extremity, eventuates in socialism:

> This development implied the negation of the progress of civilization, a progress which had achieved its height in the nineteenth century. Private property, which has been one of the major incentives to human action throughout history, was deprived of that quality. The sick have conquered the healthy: social security, with benefits that are often out of proportion to needs, makes it less and less likely that the sick are eager to get healthy again and that they want to stay healthy for work. The lazy have conquered the diligent: unemployment compensation, having become more and more generous, makes it less and less likely that the unemployed are eager to get back to work, and that they do their best to stay in their jobs. The debtors have conquered the creditors: legislation having come to favor the debtor out of proportion to what is justifiable on humanitarian grounds, the debtor can take it easy in repaying his debt. To top it all, even work is being punished today: due to progressive taxation, the hard working individual will have a tax cut that is out of proportion to the amount he would pay if he did not work so hard. These examples are only a few demonstrations of the fall of property in the twentieth century.[10]

The classic liberal principle of property is thus set over against trends of the past century toward social legislation. In short, property and social justice are diametrically opposed.

Friedrich A. Hayek argues the same point in his tendentious treatise on "the mirage of social justice."[11] Since, he avers, society is nothing but an aggregation of individuals, it cannot act on its own and therefore cannot be just or unjust. In that sense, "social justice" is a mirage and concepts of distributive and economic justice are verbal nonsense. Unfortunately, however, such concepts are employed to excuse governmental interference into the lives of individuals thereby jeopardizing the central institution of free civilization—the market—which depends, in turn, on principles of property and contract.

Curiously, neither Dietze nor Hayek even mention the emergence of the modern corporation as a determinative reality in modern economic life, altering radically the meaning and forms of property.[12] If nothing else, the separation of ownership (stockholder), administration (manager), and production (worker) has split into many segments the bundle of rights gathered together in the single principle of absolute property. Such a development has "made it impossible to defend modern property rights in traditional Lockean terms."[13]

Undeniably, the institution of property as understood by the classical liberal tradition has been, at times, an important means of securing the liberties of the individual. However, as with most institutions, even those well intentioned, it has a reverse side as well. Karl Marx and Friedrich Engels, for instance, point to the irony of a capitalist civilization which, constructed on a principle of private property is, in its actual import, destructive of that principle for the bulk of people under its sway. The presumed intent of property is the protection of the individual; its effect, under conditions of capitalism, is the subjugation of the individual:

> We Communists have been reproached with the desire of abolishing the right of personally acquiring property as the fruit of man's [sic] own labor, which property is alleged to be the ground work of all personal freedom, activity and independence.... But does wage-labor create any property for the laborer? Not a bit. It creates capital, i.e., the kind of property which exploits wage-labor, and which cannot increase except upon condition of getting a new supply of wage-labor for fresh exploitation.... You are horrified at our intending to do away with private property. But in your existing society, private property is already done away with for nine-tenths of the population.... Communism deprives no man [sic] of the power to appropriate the products of society; all it does is to deprive him of the power to subjugate the labor of others by means of such appropriation.[14]

Later, in a contentious Supreme Court case, *Munn v. Illinois* (1877), Chief Justice Morrison B. Waite argued for the majority that private property is not absolute, that when private property is "affected with a public interest," the public, through its government, may properly control its use. Property, "affected with a public interest," is no longer merely private; it has a public aspect and is susceptible to principles of public life; the right to control passes into public agency: "property does become clothed with a public interest when used in a manner to make it of public consequence, and affect the community at large. When, therefore, one devotes this property to a use in which the public has an interest, he, in effect, grants the public an interest in that use, and must submit to be controlled by the public for the common good, to the extent of the interest he has thus created."[15] The full burden of Waite's doctrine, which entails a radical revision of the principle of absolute property, was rejected by mainstream nineteenth-century American jurisprudence and had minimal effect on the actual workings of the American economic system.

Following World War II, Walter Lippman, in his desperate call for a "public philosophy," launched a hard-headed critique of the principle of absolute property as it has worked out in practice in industrial society: "Absolute private property inevitably produced intolerable evils. Absolute owners did grave damage to their neighbors and to their descendents: they ruined the fertility of the land, they exploited destructively the minerals under the surface, they burned and cut forests, they destroyed wild life, they polluted streams, they cornered supplies and formed monopolies, they held land and resources out of use, they exploited the feeble bargaining power of wage earners."[16]

Then, twenty years ago, George Cabot Lodge announced the need for a radical ideological transformation given the impact of the "giant corporations." The old ideology was individualistic; the new ideology is communitarian. In the old ideology, property rights (in the Blackstonian sense) constituted an institutional means of assuring individual liberty. That made sense when centers of power were diffuse and social organization was localized. But it is no longer functional given circumstances of advanced capitalism in which the "central economic institution" is the "great corporation."[17] To support the lives of individuals in a corporative culture, Lodge proposed a principle of membership rights: "Today a new right has clearly superseded property rights in political and social importance: the right to survive, to enjoy income, health, and other rights associated with membership in the American community or in some component of that community, including a corporation."[18] Lodge proposes as well a new method to control the use of property. Under the old individualistic ideology, the market is the appropriate mechanism. Under the new communitarian ideology, a "criterion of community need" administered by the state is the more appropriate method to regulate the utilization of natural and human resources.

Thus a controversy of broad theoretical and practical significance has been joined over the status and meaning of property. On one side, absolute property is an essential principle of civilization; on the other side, absolute property is destructive and divisive, the antithesis of what is needed for a humane society. On one side, without sole and exclusive dominion over external things, freedom is a sham; on the other side, prevailing structures of ownership and use must be radically transformed and brought under some form of public control if freedom is to become a genuine possibility for all persons.[19]

More profoundly, the controversy is over what J. H. Bogart calls "root ideas—ideas which constitute fundamental moral commitments."[20] Root ideas, I would add, constitute social ontologies, fundamental understandings about social reality. The root idea underlying the principle of absolute property is the separateness of persons, a doctrine of external relations. The root idea underlying the alternative is of the connectedness of persons, a doctrine of internal relations. The two sides are at variance over the meaning of property and its place within the economy of human relations.[21] A relational perspective on property is more akin to the latter side of the controversy, but it incorporates deep respect for the creativity of the individual affirmed by the former side.

Several aspects are distinguishable in doctrines of property, over all of which there are contentions: (1) *status* (what kind entity is property?); (2) *subject* (who may hold property?); (3) *object* (what sorts of things are held as property?; (4) *import and extent* (what are the limits of property?); (5) *origin* (how is property initiated?); (6) *purpose* (what is the function of property?). The first four aspects are evident in Blackstone's definition. Property is:

1. *status:* that sole and despotic dominion which
2. *subject:* one man claims and exercises
3. *object:* over the external things of the world,
4. *import:* in total exclusion of the right of any other individual in the universe.

Blackstone's definition omits any reference to (5) *origin* and (6) *purpose*, although those aspects may be the more critical ones when probing the fundamental meaning of property. Locke, for instance, is specifically concerned with *origin*, that is, "how men [sic] might come to have property in several parts of that which God gave to mankind [sic] in common, and that without any express compact of all the commoners."[22] T. H. Green, a nineteenth-century English philosopher, is primarily concerned with the question of *purpose*, the "rationale of property," namely, "that everyone should be secured by society in the power of getting and keeping the means of realising a will."[23]

1. *Status: what kind of entity is property?* In popular usage, property designates things—houses, land, slaves, or capital in a variety of forms. But property is not the things themselves. It is some kind of claim over things. Property is not the land. It is my claim to possess or to use or to dispose of the land. It is a form of relationship between me and the land and, as such, between me and other persons. If I have a claim, others should honor that claim. Their actions should not conflict with mine.

According to C. B. Macpherson, a shift in linguistic usage from property as a right or claim, to property as a thing, began in the late seventeenth century as the extent of the claim became increasingly unlimited. Where in previous centuries a property claim was limited (several persons might hold different claims to the same piece of land), the doctrine of absolute property ("sole and despotic dominion") tended increasingly to prevail. To say, "that is my property" meant one claimed exclusive rights over the object and, in effect, the object itself began to be considered the property.[24] If Macpherson is correct, popular usage, seemingly innocuous, is in fact controversial. It bears the marks of the classical liberal tradition of absolute property.

But even now not all property claims are to sole and despotic dominion. I may invite friends to "my home," even though I hold it on a one-year lease. I claim possession to a seat in a theater, though only for a night's performance. I may own a share of stock, but have no dominion over any of the company's facilities.

As a claim, property is analogous to a promise. It is both an indicative (describing an institutional structure) and an imperative (incorporating a set of rights and obligations). Property indicates a form of relationship between persons and things, but, as a claim, it is a "performative utterance." If legitimate, it permits me to act in certain ways and obligates others to act or to refrain from acting in certain ways. At least in that sense, property seems to be a moral reality.

Whether it is strictly a moral reality, however, is the basis of another controversy. To Thomas Hobbes, private property is a creation of the state; property is therefore strictly a legal claim, not a moral reality. To ascertain the privileges and duties of a property claim, one must look to law, more particularly, to law as an expression of a sovereign political authority. That position is disputed by John Locke, for whom property is a *natural* right. Property is a claim antedating positive law, a claim to which positive law must conform to be valid. To Hobbes, property is a legal reality; to Locke it is more basically a moral reality.

2. *Subject: who may hold property?* In Blackstone's definition, the subject of property is "one man"; only a single person (at that time, most always a male) may hold full claim over a particular object. In accordance with the "root idea" of the doctrine, persons and things are taken as distinct and separable. No two persons may own the same thing: the bicycle is either mine (*meum*) or yours (*tuum*).

But legal systems over the centuries have varied on this issue. A. M. Honoré distinguishes two classes of legal system: unititular and multititular. In the former, "only a single independent title is possible."[25] Others may have an interest in a thing; the owner may permit various uses by them; but the law acknowledges only a single title. This is the character of the ancient Roman law of property.

In contrast, a multititular system acknowledges the possibility of several owners of the same object. Several persons may hold legitimate claims over the same parcel of land or the same building. Property arrangements may be so complicated that no one person can be said to be the "ultimate owner." This is the character of the medieval English law of property.

A similar difference prevails between the Roman conception and that of Germanic tribes. As Ewart Lewis demonstrates, the Roman conception "was simple and individualistic....Ownership was regarded as indivisible and unique, absorbing the object owned. It was a maxim that there could not be two lords over the same object."[26] Among Germanic tribes, on the other hand, property belonged to family and clan. Individuals had claims to use and to enjoy the fruits of the property, but the basic right of disposal did not rest in the hands of the individual. Hence the concept of multiple ownership: "Ownership could not absorb the object; it was simply a right in regard to the object; and such rights might be numerous and widely distributed." European feudalism followed the Germanic principle.

More broadly, a distinction may be drawn among three types of property: common, private, and state. Private property is specified by the right of the individual to exclude others from the use or enjoyment of the object owned. Nowadays, this is the image of property usually envisaged particularly when defenders champion the right of property or, like Gottfried Dietze, bemoan the "fall of property." However, in a significant twist in nineteenth-century American jurisprudence, the idea of the individual person was extended to include corporations. In *Santa Clara County v. Southern Pacific Railroad* (1886), Justice Stephen Field argued that the Fourteenth Amendment's due process clause ("nor shall any State deprive any person of life, liberty, or property, without due process of law") was intended to include corporations as *personae fictae*. Thenceforward corporations were to enjoy all the "privileges and immunities" of individuals.[27] Thereby a constitutional amendment formulated to protect emancipated slaves became a legal defense enabling corporations to thwart efforts at public control. The principle of private property, for centuries an essential component of constitutionalism, became a central feature of corporate capitalism.

Common property, as distinguished from private property, is vested in a community and is specified by the right of all members of the community to access. Members have a right not to be excluded from the use or enjoyment of the object owned. Highways and city streets, public parks and recreational facilities are cases of common property. A similar right extends to facilities and conveniences deemed open to the public, though in some sense privately owned, such as inns and railroads. State property, on the other hand, is vested in the public agency which, although created to serve the public, maintains strict control over that which is owned, permitting only limited access. Instances include military bases, state laboratories, administrative buildings.

How this tripartite distinction—private, common, state property—is construed is part of the current controversy over the fundamental meaning of property and its significance in the economic system. James Gewartney focuses primarily on the tension between private and state property, arguing that "the intellectual case for private ownership is stronger than at any time in the past," that "private ownership minimizes social conflict and provides a shield against oppressive concentration of power," and that "where private property is most widely respected…personal freedom is most secure."[28] Gwartney's ultimate interest is to support free-market capitalism over against socialism.

On another side of the controversy, C. B. Macpherson focuses primarily on the contrast between private and common property, asserting that strong pressures are developing against the image of property as strictly private,

> as a fairly direct result of the unpleasant straits to which the operation of the market has brought the most advanced societies. The more striking of these pressures comes from the growing public consciousness of the menaces of air and water pollution. Air and water, which hitherto had scarcely been regarded as property at all, are now being thought of as common property—a right to clean air and water is coming to be regarded as a property from which nobody should be excluded.[29]

Moreover, Macpherson argues that, under current economic conditions, property as the right of all members of the society "not to be excluded from the use or benefit of the achievement of the whole society" should include "an equal right to access to the accumulated means of labour" if not also "a right to an income from the whole produce of the society, an income related not to work but to what is needed for a fully human life."[30]

3. *Object: what sorts of things are held in property?* Within a strict doctrine of absolute property, distinctions among kinds of things owned is unimportant. However, in recent times, distinctions have been drawn out of concern for fundamental social policy.

Charles Donahue, Jr., for instance, distinguishes property for production from property for consumption: "What Karl Polanyi called 'the great transformation' of the eighteenth and nineteenth centuries wrought a radical change in the object of property law. Family farms, of course, continued, reflecting the older pattern; but increasingly property for consumption and property for family became disassociated from property for production, which fell into the hands of the corporations."[31] Kenneth R. Minogue extends the distinction, but suggests that the same object may function in more than one way—for example, a toothbrush, an object of intimate hygiene to most persons, may be a tool of trade in a studio of commercial art.[32]

Nonetheless, from a socialist perspective, the distinction between personal and productive property is significant. As Hastings Rushdall remarks, "critics of Socialism seem to forget that Socialism does not aim at the extinction of private property but only at that of private capital."[33] Public control of productive property is an essential component of socialism, but that does not mean individuals and families will not hold property at all. The line between the personal and the productive must be settled from time to time by argument and experience. However, "We cannot justify the whole capitalistic system *en bloc* by the bare formula that property is necessary to the development of individual character. The most we can claim, as a general principle..., is that without some property or capacity for acquiring property there can be no individual liberty, and that without some liberty there can be no proper development of character."[34]

Earlier, John Stuart Mill insisted that certain realities should be excluded from the realm of property altogether, citing particularly persons and public positions. These are

> things which are or have been subjects of property, in which no proprietary rights ought to exist at all.... At the head of them, is property in human beings. It is almost superfluous to observe, that this institution can have no place in any society even pretending to be founded in justice, or on fellowship between human creatures.... Other examples of property which ought not to have been created, are properties in public trusts; such as judicial offices...a commission in the army, and...right to nomination to an ecclesiastical benefice.[35]

Over three decades ago, Charles Reich announced that a "new property" emerged in the United States subsequent to World War II, creating a complicated problem in public policy. The new property is an effect of the growth of multiple forms of government largess which, taken altogether, are "helping to create a new society."[36] Government largess includes income and benefits (e.g., social security, veterans' benefits); jobs (e.g., civil service); occupational licenses (e.g., physicians, longshoremen); franchises (e.g., television channels, park concessions); contracts (e.g., defense industries, highway construction); subsidies (e.g., shipping industry, scientific research); public resources (e.g., public lands, rivers and streams); services (e.g., technical information, postal service). Individuals and industries have become increasingly dependent on the effectiveness of their claims to governmental largess, that is, on the "new property." Therein lies the problem. As government gives, so government may take away. The new property is not secure. Claims may be dismissed or nullified in the name of "public interest." In response to that problem, advocates of a free-market economy press for the abolition of government largess altogether. Reich instead proposes that at least some of the new property be guaranteed as a matter of fundamental right: "Only by making such benefits into rights can the welfare state achieve its goal of providing a secure minimum basis for individual well-being and dignity in a society where each [individual] cannot be wholly master of [one's] own dignity."[37]

4. *Import and extent: what are the limits of property?* Property, whatever its definition, is never merely an arrangement of persons (the subject of property) and things (the object of property). It betrays an ontological ground of broad social significance, which ground bears on the issue of the extent and limitations of the practice of property.

In Blackstone's definition, property is the sole dominion a person exercises over external things to the total exclusion of other persons. That definition, straightforward on the surface, conceals its full import. The definition presupposes an understanding of self (as monadic), society (as aggregative), and nature (as instrumental). The principle of absolute property is a correlative of an individualistic understanding of the self, a contractualist doctrine of society, and a view of "external things" as a neutral stuff to be used and exploited at will.

Even within the dominant liberal tradition, however, property is subject to some kind of limitation. Individualism contains its own boundary, namely, the being of the other individual, honored by the no-harm principle. In a now classic essay on "the 'liberal' concept of 'full' individual ownership," A. M. Honoré argues that property is not merely a bundle of *rights*. The "incidents of ownership" include *responsibilities* as well. An owner's rights and interests are "subject to the condition that uses harmful to other members of society are forbidden."

> I may use my car freely but not in order to run my neighbor down, or to demolish his gate, or even to go on his land if he protests; nor may I drive uninsured. I may build on my land as I choose, but not in such a way that my building collapses on my neighbor's land. I may let off fireworks on Guy Fawkes night, but not in such a way as to set fire to my neighbor's house.[38]

Within this conception, the responsibilities and limitations of property bear the marks of a fundamentally individualistic "root idea."

With a change in root idea, the meaning of property is transformed, the dynamics of property are viewed differently, and the responsibilities of property are delineated in new ways. Early in this century, Bishop Charles Gore appropriated Leonard Hobhouse's dis-

tinction between "property for use" and "property for power" to indicate an alternative understanding of self as "in its fundamental being a
social thing—a relation of one individual to another." Gore, at a time
when corporate capitalism was coming into its own, "cannot get rid of
the feeling that individualism in property has overdone itself; that it is
working disastrous havoc."[39] Property for use is what people need for
"true freedom" but that constitutes "a very limited quantity on the
whole." As the accumulation of property by an individual or group
expands, it becomes property for power: "it becomes at last the almost
unmeasured control by the few rich, not of any amount of unconscious
material, but of other men [sic] whose opportunity to live and work
and eat becomes subject to their will."[40] Property, in short, is a political
reality and must be assessed according to its effects on the structure and
quality of the community.

Somewhat later, Morris Cohen proposed a similar understanding of
the dynamics of property. The Romans, Cohen notes, distinguished
dominium ("the rule over things by the individual") from *imperium*
("the rule over all individuals by the prince"). An analogous distinction—between private and public law—persists in modern jurisprudence. But, to Cohen, these dimensions are not so clearly distinguishable. Property confers on the owner a power over others, especially if they want or need those things over which the owner declares
dominium: "we must not overlook the actual fact that dominion over
things is also *imperium* over our fellow human beings." Property is a
form of sovereignty.

> The character of property as sovereign power compelling service and
> obedience may be obscured for us in a commercial economy by the
> fiction of the so-called labour contract as a free bargain and by the
> frequency with which service is rendered indirectly through a money
> payment. But not only is there actually little freedom to bargain on
> the part of the steelworker or miner who needs a job, but in some
> cases the medieval subject had as much power to bargain when he
> accepted the sovereignty of his Lord. Today I do not directly serve my
> landlord if I wish to live in the city with a roof over my head, but I
> must work for others to pay him rent with which he obtains the per-
> sonal services of others. The money needed for purchasing things
> must for the vast majority be acquired by hard labour and disagree-
> able service to those to whom the law has accorded dominion over
> the things necessary for subsistence.[41]

In Cohen's judgment, since large property owners are holders of sovereign power over the lives and fortunes of fellow citizens, then the law should develop a doctrine of "their positive duties in the public interest."[42] Property is a political reality and should be subject to political control, that is, control by the community whose principal end is neither profit nor efficiency, but "how to promote a better communal life." Cohen thus berates individualists and socialists who limit their debate primarily to questions of productivity and distribution. The "more profound question" is "what goods are ultimately worth producing from the point of view of the social effects on the producers and consumers." That question "requires the guidance of collective wisdom."[43]

Aldo Leopold extends the context for assessing doctrines of property beyond the human community to include the "land," taking "land" as a symbol for the world of nature. Land is not merely an exploitable resource: it is our habitat, our place of dwelling: "We abuse land because we regard it a commodity belonging to us. When we see land as a community to which we belong, we may begin to use it with love and respect.... That land is a community is the basic concept of ecology."[44] The community of land includes soil, waters, plants, animals. It also includes humans who should be identified not as owners and controllers of land (as intimated in Blackstone's definition), but as members and citizens of the living community of land. Land is not, in any simple sense, an "external thing." It is a commonwealth of which we are part and for which we hold responsibility.

John Cobb, appropriating Leopold's image of the biotic community, insists we are participants in nature, part of a complicated process of life and death, growth and decay, sickness and healing. Participants have responsibilities; they are not masters. Yet we have acted as masters and wreaked havoc on the biotic pyramid.

> Our interference in most places and at most times has reversed this process [of maximizing life] by impoverishing the soil and reducing the complexity of the biotic pyramid. To extend concern to all living things calls us to work with rather than against the evolutionary process. We must adapt our actions so that both the base and the complexity of the biotic pyramid may again grow, both for our own sake and for the sake of other species of which it is composed.[45]

Underlying the direction indicated by Gore, Cohen, Leopold, and Cobb is a "root idea" radically divergent from that of the doctrine of absolute property. Blackstone's definition supposed an understanding of self as monadic, society as aggregative, and nature as instrumental. The alternative doctrine assumes the self is relational, society is constitutive of the self, and nature is a community of which humans are a part and for whose life and health humans have responsibility. The ontology of the former doctrine is individualistic and anthropocentric; the ontology of the latter is relational and holistic.

5. *Origin: how is property initiated?* The Blackstonian definition of absolute property does not address questions of origin and purpose explicitly. Yet these questions are more basic than the other four questions in ascertaining the fundamental meaning of property. Moreover, these two questions belong together.

Origin may be construed chronologically as beginning (when and how did property as the claim to some object first occur?) or foundationally as principle (what is the basic ground of the claim to a particular object or to objects in general?) These constructions are not necessarily unrelated, for an interpretation of the beginning of property may be intended to express its foundation.

As already intimated, Thomas Hobbes and John Locke are at variance on the topic of the origin of property. To Hobbes, private property is, strictly, a creation of law, which is the dictate of the sovereign of the commonwealth:

> annexed to the sovereign [is] the whole power of prescribing the rules whereby every man may know what goods he may enjoy, and what actions he may do, without being molested by any of his fellow subjects: and this is it men call *propriety*. . . . This propriety, being necessary to peace, and depending on sovereign power, is the act of that power, in order to the public peace. These rules of propriety (or *meum* and *tuum*) and of good, evil, lawful, and unlawful in the actions of subjects are the civil laws.[46]

To John Locke, on the other hand, responding to Sir Robert Filmer's defense of royal sovereignty, property originates not in law but in the natural right all humans possess severally to their own person. The labor of their bodies and the work of their hands belong to them; therefore the results of their laboring are theirs as well. Property is an extension of the life activity of the individual. Civil law should protect property, but does not in itself create property.

I shall develop Locke's doctrine at greater length later. For the moment, I would note that, in Hobbes and Locke, questions of origin and purpose are intimately connected. To Hobbes, the origin of property is civil law; its purpose is social harmony. To Locke, the origin of property is labor; its purpose is the preservation of life and creativity.

6. *Purpose: what is the function of property?* In a study of doctrines of property in the West from Locke to Mill and Marx, Alan Ryan distinguishes two traditions about the purpose of property: instrumental and self-developmental.[47] The former is characteristic of Jeremy Bentham and utilitarianism. The latter is typical of Hegel and idealistic philosophy. In some cases, such as John Locke, the traditions are intermixed. In the instrumentalist tradition, property is a means to some further end: prosperity, security, independence. In the self-developmental tradition, property is a direct expression of one's person—an unfolding of the progress of the self, the objectification of one's inner spirit.

Ryan suggests that legal systems vary in their approach to this question. Where, for instance, the English common law system is primarily concerned with what constitutes clear title to a possession but is unconcerned with how a possession is used, the Roman law system focused on the query, What does it mean to be an owner of something?

More directly, the two traditions are linked with alternative views of work. From an instrumentalist tradition, work is a cost to get on with one's life. Working is "making a living." A job may be more or less pleasant, but in all cases it is a necessary burden to engage in activities more intrinsically satisfying. Productive work makes possible the joys of consumption. In the self-developmental tradition, work is one's mode of being in the world. It projects one's energies. It realizes one's inner being in concrete form. Some working conditions, however, distort the self: this is the point of Marx's thesis about work under conditions of capitalism entailing self-alienation.

Within the instrumentalist tradition, systems of property and work are justified when they contribute effectively to extrinsic purposes: economic progress, financial security, political independence, moral character. Within the self-developmental tradition, property and work are justified as expressive of the meaning of human existence. The difference is discernible in alternative arguments for economic democracy. Democracy in the workplace may be promoted as a means toward higher productivity. That's an instrumentalist argument. But it may also be supported as a way of showing due respect for the freedom of the human spirit.

Whether Ryan's classification scheme is adequate to do justice to modern theories of property, it serves to indicate that contentions over the purpose of property manifest a deeper stratum of understanding. The contrast between Bentham and Marx is not merely a difference in social policy. It is a difference in philosophical anthropology and social ontology. It is a difference that reaches into questions about the character of human life and social existence. Bentham's individualism and Marx's socialism manifest radically divergent comprehensions about our identity as human beings. At this level, theories about purpose and origin—final cause and efficient cause—of property are linked, as are debates about all other aspects of doctrines of property: status, subject, object, import (see summary in the appendix to this chapter). This, I suggest, is the level at which a relational perspective has a contribution to make to reflection about the fundamental meaning of property.

I have proposed that a relational perspective incorporates in its own setting dimensions of the meaning of property present in the thought of Thomas Aquinas, John Locke, and R. H. Tawney. This proposal is two-sided: historical and philosophical.

On the historical side, the thesis counters a suggestion of Charles Donahue, Jr., linking the concept of property in the West with individualism:

> The Western legal concept of property has always been associated with various forms of individualism.... Individualism has always had an opposite. There is a tension between individualism and communalism, the individual and society, self-protection and self-giving. The concept of property in the West, however, has normally been associated with one side of this basic dichotomy. Both sides, of course, embody fundamental values, and the legal system must resolve tensions between them. The issue ... is whether it continues to be useful to have a legal concept that expresses what lies on one side of the dichotomy. For those who believe that something may be said for the Western concept of individualism, I suspect the answer is yes.[48]

Against Donahue, I propose there is a tradition of thought about property in the West transcending the dichotomy between individuality and sociality because of an understanding about the relational character of the self. To be fair, we should note Donahue's focus on the *legal* concept of property: he is not directly concerned with debates over property on the philosophical level. However, "legal," in Donahue's usage, refers to systems of *positive* law. There is a tradition in Western thought in which a doctrine of higher law or natural law is invoked as superior to positive law as such. Thomas Aquinas, John Locke, and R. H. Tawney—each from his own perspective—present a relational understanding of self and society that constitutes a grounding for a higher law concept of property.

To be sure, Thomas (Dominican monk of the thirteenth century), Locke (English statesman and philosopher of the seventeenth century), and Tawney (economic historian of the twentieth century) lived in and were responding to fundamentally different social and cultural contexts—medieval feudalism infused with the ideals of Christendom, the beginnings of modern bourgeois capitalism influenced by the spirit of Puritanism, and advanced bourgeois capitalism driven by the force of utilitarianism. However, although these three theorists belong to fundamentally different times and their doctrines of property are at variance with each other on some levels, each formulates a kind of communitarian understanding of social relations that, I suspect, derives from the influence of a Christian (or, more broadly, an Abrahamic) vision of ultimate reality. Each, including Locke, casts his doctrine of property within an understanding of the connectedness of the world in which each individual is responsible for the welfare of all. From this perspective, property is not a principle simply of private life; wealth is not merely a matter for private enjoyment. Property is both a right and a responsibility of the individual. Property is to be held and used in trust as part of the common wealth of all peoples and nations.

On the philosophical side, I propose that the central principles in the doctrines of property of Thomas, Locke, and Tawney may be drawn together as three dimensions of a relational doctrine of property (particularly as that doctrine is represented by process thought). Central in Thomas's doctrine of property is the principle of common use; in Locke's, the principle of labor; and in Tawney's, the principle of social function. The correlative dimensions in process thought are the principles of objectification (analogue for the principle of common use), creativity (analogue for the principle of labor), and relativity (analogue for the principle of social function). These three principles, in this context, constitute a theory of human action. Creativity is a moment of freedom and innovation: it signifies that each action is sui generis, is unique, is something to be cherished for itself. Objectification is a moment of inheritance, of passing on to others: it signifies that each action is not just for itself, it is, as well, for all others, a datum for all future actions. Relativity means that each action has its own special place in the entire realm of things; it is not and cannot be all things: it has its own special contribution to make to the world. In the final section of this chapter, I shall develop this correlation and indicate how a doctrine of property derived from such a relational perspective stands in opposition to the Blackstonian principle of absolute property.

HISTORICAL INTERPRETATIONS: THOMAS, LOCKE, TAWNEY

1. Thomas Aquinas's understanding of the meaning of property has been interpreted in widely divergent ways. Some interpretations are oversimplified to the point of distortion.

Gottfried Dietze, for instance, locates Thomas in the Western tradition favoring the principle of private property: "St. Thomas proclaimed that property [i.e., private property] is natural and good."[49] There is a modicum of truth in this judgment, but Dietze uses it to support a position that is non-Thomistic if not anti-Thomistic. Dietze, in effect, transforms Thomas into a forerunner of modern bourgeois liberalism.

From a different angle, E. K. Hunt identifies Thomas with a conservative version of the "Christian corporate ethic," a version reflecting the ethos of feudalism. In Hunt's rendition, Thomas argues

> that private property could be justified morally only because it was a necessary condition for almsgiving. The rich, he asserted, must always be "ready to distribute...[and] willing to communicate." Aquinas believed...that "the rich man, if he does not give alms, is a thief." The rich man held wealth and power for God and for all society....Aquinas'...profoundly conservative addition to the Christian corporate ethic was [his] insistence that the economic and social relationships of the medieval system reflected a natural and eternal ordering of these relationships....[He] stressed the importance of a division of labor and effort, with different tasks assigned to different classes, and insisted that the social and economic distinctions between the classes were necessary to accommodate this specialization.[50]

In sum, to Dietze, Thomas's doctrine of property is a precursor of modern natural rights theory, whereas to Hunt, Thomas's doctrine of property is irretrievably feudalistic. Both interpretations are misleading.

Thomas's understanding of property should be cast within the larger context of his thought. As Anthony Parel notes, "Aquinas' doctrine of property forms part of his wider teaching on the nature and destiny of man, of his humanism."[51] Thomas's doctrine of property is located in his theory of human action. To Thomas, the primary question of property is the role external things are meant to play in the economy of human life. The primary principle is common use. The predominant problem is the temptation to transmute instrumental goods into ultimate ends. According to Thomas, we live in a purposeful world. We are directed, throughout our lives, toward our own perfection. We are born weak and deficient. But we are driven toward the realization of our given potentialities, ultimately toward the fulfillment of the summum bonum, toward perfect happiness.

Material things, the stuff of property, are in some sense good, but they are not the highest good. They are ephemeral and transitory. They cannot, despite any pretense to the contrary, finally satisfy the inner yearnings of the human spirit. The summum bonum cannot be found in "riches, honours, glory, power, bodily well-being, sensory pleasures, even self-preservation."[52] Yet external things are of instrumental value. As Thomas writes, for that happiness "such as can be had in this life, external goods are necessary, not as belonging to the essence of happiness, but by serving as instruments to happiness, 'which consists in an operation of virtue.'"[53]

The locus classicus of Thomas's doctrine of property is found in his *Summa Theologica*, II–II Question 66, on the topic of theft and robbery understood as "sins opposed to justice." In the first article, Thomas argue that people have a natural dominion over external things, but not in an absolute or unlimited manner. Their dominion extends to the use of things to sustain and enrich human life. As such, external things are a *bonum utile*.

In the second article, Thomas asks whether it is legitimate for individuals to possess things as their own. At this point, Thomas devises a critical distinction. On the one hand, humans severally have the capability *to care for and to administer* external things. Moreover, there are cogent reasons why individuals should exercise that capability. First, responsibility: each person takes more trouble to care for what is his or hers than what is held in common by many. Second, efficiency: human affairs are more productive if each person is charged with caring for particular things, whereas confusion results when everyone is to look after everything. Third, harmony: people live together in greater peace if everyone is satisfied with his or her own. Thus there are compelling reasons for a system of private property.

However, on the other hand, humans have the capability *to use* external things. Indeed they need external things for sheer survival and, beyond that, for the development of their potentialities as humans. Given that need, Thomas propounds a principle that sets him in total opposition to the doctrine of absolute property: individuals ought to possess external things not as their own, but as common so that they may more readily communicate them to those in need. Thomas's understanding of property is, in a way, synthetic, combining private or individual possession with common use. But the two sides of this understanding are not equivalent. Individual possession is secondary. Common use is primary. Individual possession is not so much a right or privilege to do with things as one wishes as it is a burden or obligation to care for and to manage things in a responsible and orderly way. The purpose of care is use, but use is common. This is why Anthony Parel insists that, according to Thomas, "the ontological essence of property is common use."[54]

Furthermore, systems of private property are not, to Thomas, ordained directly by natural law. They are "devised by human reason for the benefit of human life."[55] But what is devised by human reason may be defeasible. The justification of private property depends on circumstances. In Parel's explication:

> It is to be sought...in historical conditions which vary from time and place and culture. Assuming that men [sic] are better motivated to care for material things if owned privately, assuming further that there will be less social conflict on the basis of private ownership, and assuming still further that each owner will be content with the satisfaction of his [sic] own legitimate need and will not invade others', private ownership may be necessary and beneficial. But this is something for the times, for the cultures and the good legislators to determine. Natural law itself is silent on how private property should be arrived at. That is left to human law.... Private property, in other words, is a historical institution.[56]

More vital in systems of property than ownership is use: "the benefit of human life."

The priority of common use over private possession is explicit in Thomas's discussion of economic surplus and economic necessity. In

both cases, the principle of need supercedes the principle of private
ownership.

> Things established by human law cannot derogate from natural right
> or divine right. Now, according to the natural order established by
> divine providence, inferior things are ordained to the purpose of suc-
> couring human needs. And therefore the division and appropriation
> of things, based on human law, cannot overrule the principle that
> human needs are to be succoured by such things. Thus whatever one
> has in superabundance is due, by natural law, to the sustenance of the
> poor.[57]

Thomas even wonders if it is proper to accumulate a superabundance
in the first place. Avarice includes going "too far" in getting or keeping
material things: "In this way avarice is a sin directly against the neighbor, because with material possessions it is impossible for one person to
enjoy extreme wealth without someone else suffering extreme want."[58]
This is Thomas's indignant reaction to the judgment that "keeping
what belongs to oneself is no injury to others." An editor of the Blackwell edition of the *Summa Theologica* adds the following gloss to the
passage: "Implicit here is the point...that avarice so taken is a sin
directly against justice. One cannot but be impressed by the unqualified
principle of social and economic justice, so flatly stated in the 13th century, that still remains an unfulfilled, even revolutionary ideal."[59]

Thomas's response to the question of whether it is legitimate to
steal under conditions of economic necessity is even more striking.
Under ordinary circumstances, each person is entrusted with the
administration of his or her property to assist the needy, although in
neglecting that duty, "it is the hungry one's bread you withhold, the
naked one's cloak you store away."[60] The goods belong not so much to
the one who possesses and administers as to the one who needs—the
hungry and the naked. Under extraordinary circumstances, that judgment may be enacted in extraordinary ways to the extremity of taking
from another whatever is needed without consent.

> If the need is so manifest and so urgent that it is evident that the
> immediate need must be remedied by whatever means are available,
> as when a person is in imminent danger and no other remedy is pos-
> sible, then it is lawful for one to succour one's need by means of
> another's property, by taking it either openly or secretly. And this is
> not, properly speaking, theft or robbery.... It is not theft, properly

speaking, to take secretly and use another's property in case of extreme need; because that which one takes for the support of one's life becomes one's own property by reason of that need.[61]

Avarice, defined by Thomas as the "immoderate desire of temporal things which serve the use of human life and which can be estimated in value by money,"[62] is the vice that contravenes the proper use of material things. On its psychological side, avarice is an undue desire for wealth or for any kind of temporal good. On its social side, avarice is unjust action, directed toward the getting and keeping of wealth. On both sides, avarice is a form of dehumanization. It is a perversion of human life.[63] Thomas is aware of the systemic effects of avarice. Its progeny—the "daughters of avarice"—include "treachery, fraud, falsehood, perjury, restlessness, violence and callousness to mercy."[64] Thomas would, most likely, appreciate Marx's charge against capitalism as given to a "fetishism of commodities."[65] Avarice is a disposition of the psyche, a flaw of character, but, as Thomas is aware, its effects extend to institutional forms and organizational designs.

Remedies for avarice are of two kinds: psychological and institutional. The psychological remedy is to transform the vice of avarice with moral virtues, particularly the virtues of liberality and justice.[66] Liberality as the right use of material things is both an attitude and an action. In attitude, liberality means detachment from wealth. Wealth is valued for what it is, but only for what it is, a stuff useful in a limited way to meet human need and to enhance human life. In action, liberality is manifest in a generosity of spirit in spending and in giving, again, for the enhancement of the human life of the entire community of humankind. The purpose of justice, according to Thomas, is to hold people together "in companionable living in common."[67] Justice, as the stable and continuous will to give each one's due, is manifest in forms of interaction through which the needs of all, individually and communally, are met. With respect to material things, justice is the application of the principle of need to the distribution of property.

The full impact of avarice cannot, however, be overcome by virtue alone. Thomas is, in this sense, a social realist. While voluntary action derived from a character imbued with liberality and justice is a vital dimension of social life, it must be supplemented with institutional remedies to assure justice in the distribution of property throughout the society. That is the purpose of political governance and human law. In the distribution of property, rulers, even where they may employ force, are not necessarily engaged in taking property from some to give it to another, but are instead serving the fundamental purpose of property as a system, namely, common use.[68] The foundation of a legitimate claim to material things is not possession but need; possession is more a responsibility than a right. Among the obligations of government is to direct the interactions of the economy toward the realization of need and therefore to see to it that possessors of material things fulfill their responsibility.

Richard Schlatter remarks that "The Thomist theory of property has been repeated in one form or another from the fifteenth century to the present day by the theologians of the Church. When they use it to demand that the state shall intervene to provide the necessities of life for everyone it seems to be a radical theory; when they use it to defend the rights of property against proposed reform it appears as a conservative doctrine."[69] In either case, the inner sense of Thomas's understanding of property is that the common good must be served by material things, that ownership by individuals is never absolute, that property is subordinate to the higher purpose of enhancing human life.

Underlying Thomas's understanding of property are all the elements of his grand scholastic synthesis which, taken altogether, is a far cry from the relational perspective I am proposing. Yet, historically, it demonstrates against Donahue that the Western concept of property, at least in its philosophical renditions, has not always been individualistic in any simple sense. And, constructively, it is suggestive of the notion that the world, under the principle of common use, is a repository of possibilities properly available for the general enrichment of life. It is not a set of things to be distributed according to the doctrine of absolute property.

2. John Locke is often interpreted as making a radical break in his psychology and in his political theory with medieval modes of thought and practice. He is presented as a herald of classical modern liberal individualistic possibilities. In Henry Kariel's judgment: "Determined to define a new regime in opposition to repressive feudal institutions, Thomas Hobbes, John Locke, Adam Smith, and James Madison... frankly proclaimed that a society was wanted in which everyone would be committed to the rational pursuit of self-interest. They elaborately announced their faith in salvation through private endeavor."[70] Similarly Richard Schlatter identifies Locke as a champion of an emerging bourgeois class and its concern to establish a doctrine of absolute property:

John Locke's theory of property became the standard bourgeois theory, the classical liberal theory. Wherever middle-class revolutionaries rebelled against feudal privilege and royal absolutism, they ascribed on their banners the slogan of "life, liberty, and property."... The theory that property was a natural right triumphed with the Glorious, the American, and the French Revolutions.[71]

Yet, as with intellectual history generally, interpretations of John Locke diverge radically. Since the early nineteenth century, they have ranged from a reading of Locke as a progenitor of modern socialism to a rendition of his work as supportive of modern libertarian philosophy.[72] Among the more influential interpretations is C. B. Macpherson's through which, in John Dunn's words, Locke is characterized as writing "a moral charter for capitalism every bit as brutal as any that Marx alleged": "Macpherson's analysis of Locke's discussion of property sees its key function as the removal of the sufficiency limitation on private accumulation and the consequent sanctioning of unlimited appropriation. At the individual level the effect of this is to make property a pure private right, excised from the context of social responsibility implied by the medieval understanding of the duty of charity."[73]

In Macpherson's own formulation, "Locke's astonishing achievement was to base the property right on natural right and natural law, and then to remove all the natural law limits from the property right."[74] Locke thus undermines the traditional view that property is a social function and ownership entails social obligations: "He has erased the moral disability with which unlimited capitalist appropriation had hitherto been handicapped.... But he does even more. He also justifies, as natural, a class differential in rights and in rationality, and by doing so provides a positive moral basis for capitalist society."[75] "Possessive individualism" is the social ontology of Locke's understanding of property.

Persuasive though it seems, Macpherson's rendition of Locke has been convincingly charged with neglecting the full cultural context of Locke's reflections. Given that context, Locke should be interpreted not as representative of modern bourgeois interests, but as formulating a political and economic doctrine out of a Calvinist theological interest.[76]

The immediate occasion for Locke's *Two Treatises of Government*—in the second of which appears his central statement on the meaning of property—seems to have been the Exclusion Crisis in England. The

Tories favored the accession of James, Duke of York, to the throne following the reign of Charles II. The Whigs, fearing arbitrary government and a return to Catholicism under James, sought to exclude him from that office. Sir Robert Filmer published a series of tracts and a treatise, *Patriarcha*, arguing the Tory position on monarchy. Locke was provoked to respond, attacking Filmer's doctrine, but, more importantly, building a case for representative government and for popular resistance to arbitrary rule.

Yet Locke's argument is not a simple repetition of Whig conventions. He instead employs the language of natural law and natural right within a specifically theological frame of reference. Locke's doctrine of property should be viewed as part of a Puritan understanding of the dynamics and purposes of human life.

The preeminent concern of Locke's theory of property is how individuals lay claim to a world that is given by the Divine Creator to humankind in common. The fundamental principle is that of labor which, in John Dunn's interpretation, is a version of the Puritan doctrine of calling. The chief function of government is to assure that the purpose and therefore the limitations of property are sustained.

The setting for Locke's theory of property is formulated early in the second treatise, in a chapter on the "state of nature." The state of nature is a condition of liberty, but not to do as one will, rather to do as one ought given the intentions of God: "For Men being all the Workmanship of one, Omnipotent, and infinitely wise Maker; all the Servants of one Sovereign Master, sent into the World by his order and about his business, they are his Property, whose Workmanship they are, made to last during his, not one anothers Pleasure."[77] Filmer and Locke agree on one premise: "The entire cosmos is the work of God."[78] But in keeping with his doctrine of absolute monarchy, Filmer construes this to mean that Adam and all subsequent authority, acting in the place of Adam, possessed full authority to distribute the things of the created world to its human denizens. Property is a privilege bestowed by the king.

Locke, on the other hand, construes the premise of God's creation to mean that every individual is assigned an assemblage of responsibilities and correlative rights. The assemblage is the Law of Nature: "The *State of Nature* has a Law of Nature to govern it, which obliges everyone."[79] Law, to Locke, is a directive force: "For *Law*, in its true Notion, is not so much the Limitation as *the direction of a free and intelligent Agent to his proper Interest*, and prescribes no farther than is for the general Good of those under that Law."[80]

Out of the premise that the world, especially the world of humankind, is the "workmanship" of God, Locke announces that "the *fundamental Law of Nature* is *the preservation of Mankind.*"[81] Three basic rights are derived from this law.[82] First, all persons have a "right to their preservation."[83] That is, once having entered the world, they have the *right to life.* Second, all persons have a right to do what they must and should to assure the preservation of themselves and others. This is the *right to liberty,* but the right to liberty, it should be noted, is derived from an obligation: "Every one as he is *bound to preserve himself...* so by the like reason... ought he, as much as he can, *to preserve the rest of Mankind.*"[84] Third, all persons have a right to things needed for their preservation: "Men, being once born, have a right to their Preservation, and consequently to Meat and Drink, and such other things, as Nature affords for the subsistence."[85] This is the *right to possession.*

These three rights—to life, liberty, and possessions (taken altogether, Locke calls them "by the general name, *Property*")[86]—are, it must be stressed, functions of an overall obligation: to assure the preservation of all humankind. In this sense, Locke is not an individualist if that means, in Kariel's phrase quoted above, commitment to "the rational pursuit of self-interest."

Yet it is the individual who lives, acts, and enjoys possessions. Locke is therefore challenged to show "how Men might come to have a *property* in several parts of that which God gave to Mankind in common."[87] At base, the world is a commons; everyone has a right not to be excluded from the use of that commons; how, then, is that which is held in common to be distributed? How does each individual gain control and possession of that which is needed to fulfill the natural law?

Locke answers these questions in a single word: *labor.*

> Though the Earth and all inferior Creatures be common to all Men, yet every Man has a *Property* in his own *Person.* This no body has any Right to but himself. The *Labour* of His Body, and the Work of his Hands, we may say, are properly his. Whatsoever then he removes out of the State that Nature hath provided, and left it in, he hath mixed his Labour with, and joyned to it something that is his own, and thereby makes it his *Property.*[88]

Locke's labor theory of property has been appropriated by both socialists and libertarians to support their causes. Certainly the theory begs many questions.[89] But, assuming the fundamental theological context of the theory, it cannot be taken to sanction a Blackstonian version of the meaning of property. According to Alan Ryan, "The natural thrust of Locke's initial claim is ... towards a doctrine of stewardship, not one of absolute individual rights—men possessing such rights over things as enable them to fulfill God's intention in creating those things. The ultimate source of property rights is God."[90] Locke's labor theory of property is, however, individualistic in one sense: the individual is the locus of rights of possession which, in turn, rest upon the right of the individual to his or her own person and therefore to his or her own action. One's life, one's labor, and one's possessions belong to one's self as a unique individual. These rights are primordial. They obtain to the individual prior to the construction of any social organization or governmental form and constitute the raison d'être of such institutions.

Yet these natural rights are inextricably conjoined with natural duties. As John Dunn remarks, "It is apt enough to note that Locke makes property a pure private right, but that in no way impairs the social responsibilities which emanate from it. The individualization of the right is matched symmetrically by an individualization of the duty."[91]More generally, Locke's theory of property must be understood within the context of the Protestant ethic of vocation. God calls each individual to a creative task, an activity of shaping and molding the world for the conduct of His business—the preservation and enhancement of human life.

Given this context, Locke's concept of labor must be defined broadly. It embraces all creative endeavor in response to and in imitation of the Divine Creator. It is definitive of the inner nature of being human. This is James Tully's interpretation of Locke's position: "Labour ... is a moral form of activity in two senses. Not only does it take place within a context of, and is the means of, performing moral duties, it is a moral form of activity itself. It is the form of activity characteristic of man [sic] ... and so his duty."[92]

As natural law sanctions private property, though within the context of an ethic of divine calling, so also natural law set bounds on the accumulation and use of property. In his chapter on property in the second treatise, Locke seemingly proposes three principles of limitation, at least prior to the invention of money. First, whatever one's possessions as created by one's labor, there must be an adequate supply of materials remaining for others (the sufficiency principle): "no Man [sic] but he can have a right to what that [Labour] is joyned to, at least where there is enough and as good left in common for others."[93] Second, one must never own so much that any goes to waste (the spoilage principle): "As much as any one can make use of to any advantage of life before it spoils; so much he may by his labour fix a Property in."[94] Third, in the case of land, one may never own more than one can work (the labor principle): "*As much Land* as a Man Tills, Plants, Improves, Cultivates, and can use the Product of, so much is his *Property*."[95]These limitations are not artificial additions to the theory of property. They are logical extensions of the basic theological understanding of which the theory is a part.

However, the invention of money by the common consent of humankind effected a radical change in the conditions of human life. The hoarding of money does not necessarily violate the sufficiency principle. Money can accumulate without spoiling. And money makes it possible to till and cultivate much more land than otherwise. Hence money "introduced...larger Possessions, and a Right to use them."[96] Moreover, through the invention of money, humankind in effect "agreed to disproportionate and unequal Possession of the Earth, they having...found out a way, how a man [sic] may fairly possess more land than he himself can use the product of, by receiving in exchange for the overplus, Gold and Silver, which may be hoarded up without injury to any one, these metalls not spoileing or decaying in the hands of the possessor."[97]

At this point, interpretations of Locke's intentions diverge irreconcilably. Macpherson reads Locke as approving of this revolution, thereby creating a justification for market capitalism and the unlimited accumulation of wealth. "Locke has justified the specifically capitalist appropriation of land and money."[98] Tully, on the other hand, reads Locke as disapproving of at least the results of this revolution for it stimulated "a state of contention, covetousness and acquisitive desire": "The acceptance of money brings with it the fall of man. Prior to its appearance men were motivated by need and convenience; now they are driven by the most corrupt of human motives: the desire for more than one needs."[99] Given Macpherson's reading, civil government is introduced as a means of securing the unlimited accumulation of wealth; the state is an agent of capital. But given Tully's reading, civil government is required as a means of restoring and assuring the obligations and rights of natural law; the state is an agency "obligated to distribute to each member the civil rights to life, to the liberty of preserving himself and others, and to the requisite goods or 'means of it.' This is a governmental duty from natural law and the public good, and it is now backed up with the threat of legitimate revolution if not discharged."[100]

The cogency of Tully's version of Locke is derived from his placement of Locke's theory of property within the broad theological-cultural context of his thought. Assuming Tully's position, Locke must not be seen as a champion of private property in any one-dimensional manner. Rather what Locke depicts is "a system in which private and common ownership are not mutually exclusive but mutually related: private ownership is the means of individuating the community's common property and is limited by the claim of all members. What particular legal form this might take in a given commonwealth is not a problem of theory but of prudence."[101]

Yet labor is the critical point, for without labor, human life is impossible. Labor is the creative formation and reformation of the conditions of human life, if not the substance of human life. Labor is the direct expression of one's self, the materialization of one's visions, the realization of one's being. Property within the framework of Locke's understanding should be viewed dynamically, not statically. It is not a stuff that one possesses and hoards. It is an activity necessary on the most basic level for survival, but needed on the highest level for fulfillment. Labor is the investment of one's energies in the conduct of history. In its origins, it depends on a common world, a world that is given—God's creation. In its intended consequences, it forms a heritage supportive of the life of all. But in its moment of immediacy, it is an individual's own special calling which is simultaneously an obligation and a right which subsist independent of and prior to all political forms.

3. R. H. Tawney is best known as an economic historian. But economic history to Tawney is not a specialty set apart. It is a branch of moral philosophy.[102] Its impetus derives from interests of the present.

> History, as I understand it, is concerned with the study, not of a series of past events, but of the life of society, and with the records of the past as a means to that end...there is truth in the paradox that all history is the history of the present; and for this reason each generation must write its history for itself. That of its predecessors may be true, but its truth may not be relevant. Different answers are required because different questions are asked. Standing at a new point on the road, it finds that new ranges in the landscape come into view. It discovers that phenomena, which formerly appeared irrelevant, are a vital part of itself. It realises, in short, and sometimes realises too late, that what is supposed to be the past is in reality the present.[103]

Tawney's famed works on the *Agrarian Problem of the Sixteenth Century* (1912) and *Religion and the Rise of Capitalism* (1926) are studies "of the resistance of groups and individuals to the imposition on them of capitalist modes of thought and behavior."[104] They deal respectively with two of the "main pillars of capitalism": the "doctrine of the sanctity of private property rights" and the "elaborate ethical support given to the creed of economic individualism by religious opinion."[105] They are studies of the historical origins and persistent character of modern capitalism as, in Tawney's judgment, the critical social problem of our age. Thus, in the closing passages of *Religion and the Rise of Capitalism*, he gives voice to his own commitment that "Compromise is as impossible between the Church of Christ and the idolatry of wealth, which is the practical religion of capitalist societies, as it was between the Church and the State idolatry of the Roman Empire."[106]

Tawney, during his college years, "became infected with socialist principles, principles which in Tawney's case were strongly infused with Christian ideals."[107] Within a few decades, he became with others such as William Temple and Charles Gore, "one of the most influential spokesmen of Anglican socialism."[108] While the adequacy of his approach to socialism has been questioned,[109] the force of his arguments, historical and constructive, were directed toward the need for radical social transformation, including the transformation of the meaning of property as a central institution in economic relations.

> According to Tawney, social transformation requires most basically a change in attitude. The attitudes of governments to social questions is wrong, profoundly wrong. But it is wrong because the attitudes of individuals to each other is wrong, because we in our present society are living on certain false and universal assumptions.... What we have got to do *first* of all is to change those assumptions or principles.[110]

Economic relationships, in Tawney's judgment, are not autonomous; they are reflective of the deep moral sensibilities of a people who, given the character of modern industrialism, must be brought to a new vision.

> Too much time is spent today upon outworks, by writers who pile up statistics and facts, but never get to the heart of the problem. That heart is not economic. It is a question of moral *relationships*. This is the citadel which must be attacked—the immoral philosophy which under lies much of modern industry.[111]

At the heart of that "immoral philosophy" is a principle of absolute property. Tawney asserts this at the beginning of his essay, "The Sickness of Acquisitive Society" (1919), which was later expanded to book length:

> The right to the free disposal of property and to the exploitation of economic opportunities is conceived by a large part of the modern world, and in particular by the most socially influential part of it, to be absolute, and this volume of interest and opinion rallies instinctively against any attempt to qualify or limit the exercise of these rights by attaching further conditions to them.... To-day that doctrine, if intellectually discredited, is still the practical foundation of social organization.[112]

The dominant concern of Tawney's theory of property is to construct an alternative to modern industrialism, an alternative inspired by a conception of equality. The central principle of his theory of property is social function, which requires a transformation of "rights which are absolute into rights which are contingent and derivative, because it is to affirm that they are relative to functions and that they may be justly revoked when the functions are not performed."[113] The focus of Tawney's critique is on the perverse character and conditions of modern industrial capitalism.

In his critique, Tawney contrasts two kinds of social order: acquisitive and functional. The former is the predominant character of Western societies since the eighteenth century. The latter, nowhere realized in fact, has long been a moral ideal and is, in Tawney's judgment, derived from the purpose—the *real* purpose—of economic relationships. Tawney is, at this point, a classical teleologist in moral analysis.

Modern societies typify an acquisitive society because their primary aim is to protect economic rights "while leaving economic functions, except in moments of abnormal emergency, to fulfill themselves." Their governing motivation is "to increase the opportunities open to individuals of attaining the objects which they conceive to be advantageous to themselves," and not "to secure the fulfillment of tasks imposed for the public service." Such a conception, Tawney avers, "has laid the whole modern world under its spell."[114] In an acquisitive society, "the enjoyment of property and the direction of industry are considered ... to require no social justification, because they are regarded as rights which stand by their own virtue, not functions to be judged by the success which they contribute to a social purpose."[115]

A functional society, on the other hand, aims "at making the acquisition of wealth contingent on the discharge of social obligations," seeks "to proportion remuneration to service," and esteems not what people possess, "but what they can make, or create, or achieve."[116] The main subject of social emphasis in such a society "would be the performance of function." In its economic dimensions, a functional society consists of four features. First, *purpose*: "the purpose of industry is obvious...to supply man with things which are necessary, useful or beautiful, and thus to bring life to body or spirit."[117] Second, *efficiency*: "pay for service and for service only, and when capital is hired to make sure that it is hired at the cheapest possible price." Third, *control*: "place the responsibility for organizing industry on the shoulders of those who work and use, not of those who own, because production is the business of the producer and the proper person to see that he discharges his business is the consumer for whom, and not the owner of the property, it ought to be carried on." Fourth, *accountability*: "insist that all industries shall be conducted in complete publicity as to costs and profits, because publicity ought to be the antiseptic both of economic and political abuses, and no man can have confidence in his neighbor unless both work in that light."[118]

These two kinds of social order—acquisitive and functional—are essentially incompatible. Their primary point of contention is at the level of purpose: "The essence of industrialism...is not any particular method of industry, but a particular estimate of the importance of industry.... [I]t is elevated from the subordinate place which it should occupy among human interests and activities into being the standard by which all other interests and activities are judged."[119] Industrialism confuses means with ends. It turns business into a fetish. It is a form of idolatry.

> The chief enemy of the life of the spirit, whether in art, culture, or religion, or in the simple human associations which are the common vehicle of its revelation to ordinary men, is itself a religion. It is, as every one knows, the idolatry of wealth, with its worship of pecuniary success, and its reverence for the arts...by which success is achieved, and its strong sense of the sanctity of possessions and weak sense of the dignity of human beings, and its consequent emphasis, not on the common interests which unite men, but on the accidents of property, and circumstance, and economic conditions, which separate and divide them.[120]

Because of its individualistic, self-centered character, an acquisitive society is intrinsically divisive. But a functional society is communal; it engages its members in mutually supportive endeavor. These two types of social order represent radically different understandings of the meaning of property.

While acknowledging that property is an ambiguous category, embracing a multitude of rights which "vary indefinitely in economic character, in social effect, and in moral justification,"[121] Tawney tends to distinguish two basic meanings of property: "property which is used by the owner for the conduct of his profession or the upkeep of his household, and property which yields an income irrespective of any personal service"[122] or, alternatively phrased, "property for use and property for power or exploitation."[123] The correlation between these two meanings of property and the two kinds of social order is obvious.

Since the seventeenth and eighteenth centuries in England and France, the principle of private property, initiated through revolutionary struggle to honor the idea of property for use, has been transformed, given changing historical conditions, to represent the idea of property for power. Originally the principle of the inviolability of private property seemed justified because of the social circumstances under which the principle became a fundamental social policy. First, property in land and in capital—a condition of effective work—was widely distributed. Second, major forces threatening property for use were the persistence of feudal authority and the fiscal policies of government. Third, private property was, in principle at least, a resource and citadel for the laborer; it protected "the yeoman or the master craftsman or the merchant from seeing the fruits of his toil squandered by the hangers-on at St. James or the courtly parasites of Versailles."[124] Under these conditions, private property was an aid to creative work. It promoted public purposes. It supported those who worked and their dependents. Moreover, given these cultural and political conditions, "the idea that the institution of private property involves the right of the owner to use it, or refrain from using it, in such a way as he may please, and that its principal significance is to supply him with an income, irrespective of any duties he may discharge, would not have been understood by most public men of that age, and, if understood, would have been repudiated with indignation by the most reputable of them."[125]

Yet the principle of private property was transmuted into such an idea as the conditions of modern industrial capitalism emerged. The whole structure of the social order changed during the late nineteenth and twentieth centuries. At the present time, first, ownership of the national wealth is highly concentrated in and controlled by a small class of people. Second, what threatens the original intent of private property is the "insatiable expansion and aggregation of property itself, which menaces with absorption all property less than the greatest"— the small business, the family farmer, the country bank—and which "has turned the mass of mankind into a proletarian working under the agents and for the profit of those who own." Third, the modern property system does not protect the laborer. Instead, "ownership is not active, but passive, ... to most of those who own property to-day it is not a means of work but an instrument for the acquisition of gain or the exercise of power and ... there is no guarantee that gain bears any relation to service, or power to responsibility."[126] Tawney concludes that passive property distorts the meaning, the essential purpose, of the institution. Such property, he claims, is functionless.

Tawney draws a spectrum of kinds of proprietary rights protected by societies—ranging from more active property (e.g., property as payments for personal service, personal possessions needed for health and comfort, land and tools used by owners) to more passive property (e.g., property in monopoly profits, urban ground rents, royalties such as mining rights). Societies vary in the ratios of kinds of proprietary rights protected by them. In modern society the preponderance of property is passive. Given the inner meaning of property, the consequences of this shift toward passive property are morally unacceptable. The consequences are special privilege, institutionalized inequality, the erection of a whole apparatus of class associations, "which make not only the income, but the housing, education, health and manners, indeed the very physical appearance of different classes ... almost as different from each other as though the minority were alien settlers established amid the rude civilization of a race of impoverished aborigines."[127]

As an alternative to modern industrialism, Tawney constructs the moral vision of a society based on the principle of function. Within the envisioned society, rights—including the right to property—are not absolute, but contingent.

> The individual has no absolute rights; they are relative to the function which he [sic] performs in the community of which he is a member, because, unless they are so limited, the consequences must be some-

thing in the nature of a private war. All rights, in short, are conditional and derivative, because all power should be conditional and derivative. They are derived from the end or purpose of the society in which they exist. They are conditional on being used to contribute to the attainment of that end, not to thwart it.[128]

A central imperative of the envisioned society is equality—a "practical equality" given to the elimination of all forms of social inequality obstructive of the creative energies and works individuals have to contribute—given their differences in talents and abilities—to social well-being: "it is the mark of a civilized society to aim at eliminating such inequalities as have their source, not in individual differences, but in its own organization, and that individual differences, which are the source of social energy, are more likely to ripen and find expression if social inequalities are, as far as practicable, diminished."[129] So understood, practical equality is a means of moving beyond the intrinsic divisiveness of industrial capitalism toward the communal spirit of a humane society.

> If a high degree of practical equality is necessary to social well-being, because without it ability cannot find its way to its true vocation, it is necessary also for another and more fundamental reason. It is necessary because a community requires unity as well as diversity, and because, important as it is to discriminate between different powers, it is even more important to provide for common needs.... Social well-being does not only depend upon intelligent leadership; it also depends upon cohesion and solidarity. It implies the existence ... of a conviction that civilization is not the business of the elite alone, but a common enterprise which is the concern of all.[130]

Thus equality of opportunity is a vital precept in a functional society. However, Tawney distinguishes two meanings of that precept. In one sense, the opportunities sought are "to rise, to get on, to exchange one position for a succession of others, to climb, in the conventional metaphor, the educational or economic ladder." This meaning of the precept is characteristic of the acquisitive society. In its second meaning, typical of a functional society, the opportunities sought are "to lead a good life in all senses of the term, whether one 'rises' or not." The aim of this kind of equality of opportunity is not individual self-advancement, but solidarity, participation in and contribution to the whole community.[131]

While Tawney insists that "the application to property and industry of the principle of function is compatible with several different types of social organization,"[132] he nonetheless urges a range of fundamental social policies whose implication is that industry—its wealth and power—should be transmuted into a form of public or common property.

With respect to industrial wealth, Tawney promotes the progressive taxation of corporate enterprise to create a communal provision for social income. He interprets this policy as "the pooling of its [industry's] surplus resources by means of taxation, and the use of the funds thus obtained to make accessible to all, irrespective of their income, occupation, or social position, the condition of civilization which, in the absence of such measures, would be enjoyed by only the rich."[133] As social income, Tawney would include programs "to raise the general standard of health," "to equalize educational opportunities," "to provide for the contingencies of life" (sickness, old age, unemployment), to secure housing, and to protect the beauty of the environment.

In addition to the redistribution of industrial wealth, Tawney promotes a radical reconstruction of the corporate organization to mitigate the heavy concentration of economic power typical of modern industrial capitalism. He admits that, at times when liberty and equality are incompatible, liberty is to be preferred: "The spiritual energy of human beings, in all the wealth of their infinite arrangements, is the end to which external arrangements, whether political or economic, are merely means. Hence institutions which guarantee to men the opportunity of becoming the best of which they are capable are the supreme political good, and liberty is rightly preferred to equality, when the two are in conflict."[134] However, given the prevailing form of modern industry, the dominant threat to liberty is corporate autocracy. Under such conditions, an equalization of economic power is a requisite of economic liberty. Thus, while acknowledging the need for authority in economic organization, Tawney proposes more direct participation of the worker in the governance of industry—from the workplace to the board room—and more extensive subjection of major industries to public policy. Such moves, declares Tawney, will both have the effect of increasing the efficiency of industry[135] and, more importantly, give expression to the true meaning of industry "as a social function."

Industry, as the most prominent form of property in the modern world, should not be conceived as owned by its shareholders in the Blackstonian sense of absolute property. Rather, in Tawney's doctrine, it should conceived as a public service, as a contribution to the enhancement of the whole community, as a kind of common property.

A CONSTRUCTIVE PROPOSAL:
A COMMUNITARIAN UNDERSTANDING OF PROPERTY

The works of Thomas Aquinas, John Locke, and R. H. Tawney were accomplished at different periods of social history. Thomas wrote during the maturity of the Western feudal and manorial system. Locke was responding to tensions and struggles of an emergent bourgeois capitalism. Tawney was engaged in interpreting and reacting to a time of advanced corporate industrialism. These differences of social and historical setting are reflected in their respective doctrines of property. Nonetheless, their doctrines of property display a remarkable continuity.

On the negative side, none is supportive of the principle of absolute property formulated by William Blackstone. To be sure, Locke's doctrine has often been invoked as a case of "possessive individualism." But, if John Dunn and James Tully are correct, such an invocation distorts the actual character of Locke's argument. On the positive side, all three of these doctrines conjoin two dimensions in their understandings of property—communal and individual. Property as a claim on the use of resources is neither exclusively an individual right nor simply a matter for political and social determination. Charles Donahue's dichotomy between individualism and communalism is overdrawn and his identification of the concept of property in the West with individualism is dubitable. At least in some of its philosophical forms, the concept of property manifests a more complicated, perhaps more justifiable approach to social and economic arrangements.

The historical side of this study, however, is subordinate to its philosophical concern, namely, to explore the meaning of property from a relational perspective. That perspective, I would propose, embraces, in its own way, dimensions of the meaning of property found in the thought of Thomas (the principle of common use), Locke (the principle of labor), and Tawney (the principle of social function). In keeping with the continuity among these three otherwise disparate theorists, a relational doctrine of property requires a radical revisioning of the classical liberal or absolute principle of property with its strictly individualistic import.

The question of property is intimately related to a broad issue of political and economic philosophy—the relation between public and private. The doctrine of absolute property is correlative with an insistence on the priority of private life. Public life is of secondary, perhaps only instrumental, importance. In extreme form, such an insistence poses doubts about the possibility of any genuinely public life at all. What appears public is reducible to the private.

As Lois Livezey argues in her interpretation of Alfred North Whitehead's "conception of the public world," a privatistic understanding of action is incompatible with the principle of relationality.[136] Furthermore, a privatistic understanding of action constitutes a major problem in the modern world. Commenting on the diffusion of a Cartesian form of thought throughout modern life, Whitehead remarks:

> The doctrine of minds, as independent substances, leads directly not merely to private worlds of experience, but also to private worlds of morals. The moral intuitions can be held to apply only to the strictly private world of psychological experience. Accordingly, self-respect, and the making the most of your own individual opportunities together constituted the efficient morality of the leaders among the industrialists of that period. The Western world is now suffering from the limited moral outlook of the three previous generations.[137]

What has been ignored over these generations and even yet under conditions of corporate capitalism is "the true relation of each organism to its environment."

In contrast, to Whitehead, each entity—each decision, each action—consists of two sides, public and private. In a concise statement of his doctrine of prehensions (the way in which entities relate to each other in the ongoingness of the world), he formulates this point explicitly:

> The theory of prehensions is founded on the doctrine that there are no concrete facts which are merely public, or merely private. The distinction between publicity and privacy is a distinction of reason, and is not a distinction between mutually exclusive concrete facts. The sole concrete facts, in terms of which actualities can be analysed, are prehensions; and every prehension has its public side and its private side. Its public side is constituted by the complex datum prehended; and its private side is constituted by the subjective form through which a private quality is imposed on the public datum.[138]

More precisely, to take account of "the creative advance" of the world, one must understand actualities dynamically, as in process from public moment to private moment, then again to public moment:

> An actual entity considered in reference to the publicity of things is a "superject"; namely, it arises from the publicity which it finds, and it adds itself to the publicity which it transmits. It is a moment of passage from *decided public facts* to a *novel public fact.* Public facts are, in their nature, coordinate. An actual entity considered in reference to the privacy of things is a "subject"; namely, it is a moment of the genesis of *self-enjoyment*. It consists of a purposed *self-creation* out of materials which are at hand in virtue of their publicity.[139]

Of these three moments, I suggest that Thomas's *principle of common use* pertains primarily to that of "decided public facts"; that Locke's *principle of labor* is focused on the moment of self-creation and self-enjoyment; and that Tawney's *principle of social function* is predominately a statement about the moment of "novel public fact." Thomas's primary concern is that the world be understood as a common resource belonging to the entire community. Locke's interest is with the manner and sense of individuation, with the particular rights of each person, with how each person is enabled to make something of that common resource. Tawney's point is to direct self-creation toward the enhancement of the community's future. With this construction, these three principles are conjoined in a single understanding of property that stands in stark opposition to Dietze's defense of a doctrine of private property as a central institution of human civilization.

Profound reservations about the doctrine of absolute property are evidenced in Whitehead's *historical thesis* about the genius and deficiencies of the prevailing philosophy of the past three centuries. In *Science and the Modern World*, for instance, Whitehead links scientific materialism with an individualistic social philosophy, expressing, among other things, his critique of the tradition of economic thought inaugurated by Adam Smith.

> It is very arguable that the science of political economy, as studied in its first period after the death of Adam Smith (1790), did more harm than good. It destroyed many economic fallacies, and taught how to think about the economic revolution then in progress. But it riveted on men [sic] a certain set of abstractions which were disastrous in their influence on modern mentality. It de-humanised industry.[140]

Along with its individualism, this philosophy assumed a principle of the value neutrality of matter, thereby inculcating "the habit of ignoring the intrinsic worth of the environment," including both the social and the physical environment.[141]

> Thus all thought concerned with social organization expressed itself in terms of material things and capital. Ultimate values were excluded.... A creed of competitive business morality was evolved, in some respects curiously high; but entirely devoid of consideration for the value of human life. The workmen [sic] were conceived as mere hands, drawn from the pool of labour. To God's question, men gave the answer of Cain—"Am I my brother's keeper?"; and they incurred Cain's guilt. This was the atmosphere in which the industrial revolution was accomplished in England, and to a large extent elsewhere.[142]

In *Adventures of Ideas*, Whitehead's historical thesis is both more complex and more explicit in its judgment about the modern doctrine of property. From ancient to modern times, a massive shift in social organization and social thought transpired, redounding to the benefit of all humankind: "Slavery was the presupposition of political theorists then; Freedom is the presupposition of political theorists now."[143] This gradual development, halting and limited, has meant a growth in "the conception of the dignity of human nature" and therefore in "the idea of the essential rights of human beings, arising from their sheer humanity."[144] However, the notions of human freedom and human rights, embodied in institutional and ideational form in the nineteenth century, took an ironical turn. The amalgamation of classical liberalism with corporate industrialism produced a new kind of enslavement. "The mere doctrines of freedom, individualism, and competition had produced a resurgence of something very like industrial slavery at the base of society."[145]

As a result, in Whitehead's judgment, "economic organization constitutes the most massive problem in human relationships."[146] In particular, doctrines of contract and property have been eviscerated of their earlier significance by the emergence of the modern corporation as a presumed or fictitious person with all the essential rights and liberties that, gradually over the course of centuries, had attached to natural persons.

> The necessity for large capital, with the aid of legal ingenuity produced the commercial corporation with limited liability.... The

introduction into the arena of this new type of "person" has considerably modified the effective meaning of the characteristic liberal
doctrine of contractual freedom. It is one thing to claim such freedom as a natural right for human persons, and quite another to
claim it for corporate persons. And again the notion of private property had a simple obviousness at the foot of Mount Sinai and even
in the eighteenth century. When there were primitive roads, negligible drains, private wells, no elaborate system of credit, when payment
meant the direct production of gold-pieces, when each industry was
reasonably self-contained—in fact when the world was not as it is
now—then it was fairly obvious what was meant by private property,
apart from any current legal fictions. Today private property is
mainly a legal fiction.[147]

At this point, Whitehead directs his critique beyond the problem of
corporate industrialism to the central idea of individualism on which
the modern doctrine of classical liberalism is grounded. The alternative
to individualism is an understanding of the intrinsic relatedness of
human life and of the need for a new social arrangement in which freedom and coordination, individuality and participation are correlative.

The whole concept of absolute individuals with absolute rights, and
with a contractual power of forming fully defined external relations,
has broken down. The human being is inseparable from its environment in each occasion of its existence. The environment which the
occasion inherits is immanent in it, and conversely it is immanent in
the environment which it helps to transmit.... There is no escape
from customary status.... On the other hand, the inherited status is
never a full determination. There is always the freedom for the determination of individual emphasis.[148]

Underlying Whitehead's historical thesis about the ironic character
of the modern world is his *cosmology*. Whitehead's cosmology concentrates on actual entities as "the final real things of which the world is
made up."[149] An actual entity is a creative synthesis of a complex inheritance; it has, for a time, a life of its own; it then becomes part of the
heritage for all future entities. That, in stark form, is the fundamental
character of the world in all its many forms.

Three moments are distinguishable in that process: an inheritance from the past, the enjoyment of the present, a possibility for
the future. Simplifying Whitehead's language, I suggest the terms of

objectification, creativity, and relativity may be employed to designate, respectively, these three moments. *Objectification*, Whitehead writes, "refers to the particular mode in which the potentiality of one actual entity is realized in another actual entity."[150] Objectification is the moment an individual receives the common world, positively or negatively, into itself. *Creativity*, to Whitehead, is an ultimate category:

> It is that ultimate principle by which the many, which are the universe disjunctively, become the one actual occasion, which is the universe conjunctively. It lies in the nature of things that the many enter into complex unity. "Creativity" is the principle of *novelty*. An actual occasion is a novel entity diverse from any entity in the "many" which it unifies. Thus "creativity" introduces novelty into the content of the many, which are the universe disjunctively. The "creative advance" is the application of this ultimate principle of creativity to each novel situation which it originates.[151]

Finally, according to the principle of *relativity*, "it belongs to the nature of a 'being' that it has a potential for every 'becoming.'"[152] Although each actual entity has its day and then, in a sense, it perishes, it still persists as a datum, whatever its character, to be reckoned with by all subsequent entities. As evident, *objectification* and *relativity* are correlative ideas which, nonetheless, I distinguish to focus on aspects of past and future as both public dimensions in the passage of life. Life moves from a common world to the solitariness of private experience, but then it moves again into the realm of the common. That is the ineluctable character of all reality.

Whitehead's cosmology is the framework for his philosophy of civilization, which is his contribution to *social and political theory*. Where, on the cosmological level, life has a certain fixed character about it, in human association, wide variation is possible. Civilization in Whitehead's thought is a normative concept. As such it functions on several levels: it is a groundwork for a doctrine of human rights; it is a version of common good; it incorporates an understanding of human virtue.[153] According to Lois Livezey, of the features that make up civilization, "Adventure and peace represent Whitehead's novel contribution to ... [its] defining character."[154]

Adventure is the feature of creativity in civilization. It is the character of experimentation and novelty. It is a function of the capacity for self-transcendence. Freedom is the requisite of adventure. Flexibility of association, provision for new opportunity, respect for difference, appreciation of robust debate, affirmation of the unusual are among the expressions of the sense of adventure. Adventure is thus a ground for individual rights and rights of association. Peace, on the other hand, in its social dimension, is a feature of our relatedness. It elicits actions of mutual support and reciprocal enhancement. Loyalty and trust, concern and care, harmony and order are among its political aspects. Peace is a basis for the obligations and responsibilities of citizenship. Where adventure favors the sensibilities and actions of individuals and groups, peace affirms the solidarity of the total community. Together, adventure and peace are responsive to a central problem of social life: the commingling of freedom and coordination:[155] "One of the most general philosophic notions to be used in the analysis of civilized activities is to consider the effect on social life due to variations of emphasis between Individual Absoluteness and Individual Relativity. Here 'absoluteness' means the notion of release from essential dependence on other members of the community in respect to modes of activity, while relativity means the converse fact of essential relatedness."[156]

Whitehead did not systematically set out the implications of his cosmology and social theory on the *question of property*. But, in connotation, I suggest that he would stand in the tradition I have traced through Thomas Aquinas, John Locke, and R. H. Tawney. Given his concept of civilization as the norm for social arrangements, he would conjoin two dimensions in his understanding of property—communal and individual. There are two (interrelated) sides to the appropriation and manipulation of environmental resources, the possession and use of external things. Such resources and things are intended for the support and extension, expression and self-formation of the individual's life (the principle of labor), but not exclusively so. They are meant also for enhancing the quality and character of the lives of others and for the life of the community as a totality (the principles of common use and social function). Property is a bundle of individual rights and social responsibilities. Respect for individual determination and public concern are linked. Precisely how they should be linked at any given time may depend on historical considerations. But under no circumstances is property exclusively an individual and absolute right. Likewise, under no circumstance is property exclusively a matter for autocratic concession and dictate. The meaning of property must be cast within the framework of the concept of civilization with its qualities of adventure and peace.

Within that framework, a relational perspective on the several aspects of the meaning of property would take the following form. I have altered the order to begin with the paramount concerns of Whitehead's cosmology and social theory.

1. *Origin: How is property initiated?* Property originates in the dynamics of human life. Property in the sense of claims to environmental resources is a natural part of the interactive process of living. It is the appropriation of "decided public facts" for purposes of self-creation.

2. *Purpose: What is the function of property?* The ultimate purpose of property is captured in the concept of civilization. Property is a means and an expression of the creativity of the individual and the quality of a society. A relational perspective synthesizes the instrumentalist and the self-developmental traditions.

3. *Status: What kind of entity is property?* Property is most fundamentally a moral claim to the appropriation and use of things of all kinds for the purposes stated above. The legal claim to property should provide whatever institutional support is necessary or desirable to advance the more basic moral claim.

4. *Subject: Who may hold property?* Given the complexly interactive character of human life, property must be understood as multititular. No one possesses absolute or exclusive title over anything, even one's own life. Particularly in the instance of material things, a right not to be excluded from access to what is necessary or might be helpful for the conduct of one's life is as critical as, if not more critical than, the right to exclude others is conceived to be in the classical liberal tradition.

5. *Object: What sorts of things may be held as property?* In a sense, given the actual dynamics of human life, everything constitutes property to an extent. We even appropriate each other in the simple actions of our everyday existence. What is at stake is not so much what we appropriate, as how we appropriate. More important than the question of what we command as resources is the issue of whether in the process of appropriation and in the forms assumed by appropriation, the lives of individuals affected in the process are enhanced and the quality of social life, as well as the life of nature, is sustained or improved. This is sufficient reason to reject slavery and forced labor as inappropriate and to support

a distinction in principle between property for consumption and property for production.

6. *Import and extent: What are the limits of property?* The limits of property are dictated by its purpose. The limiting question is, What advances the cause of civilization? Given the breadth of the relational perspective, however, the cause of civilization must be undertood to embrace care and concern for the entire ecosphere.

In sum, from this perspective, property should be conceived of simultaneously as (1) a public resource (principle of common use); (2) an individual province (principle of labor); and (3) a public responsibility (principle of social function). Within the spectrum of economic philosophies currently under contention, this conception is closer to the democratic socialism of an R. H. Tawney than to the libertarianism of a Friedrich Hayek. The relational perspective, in its approach to "the most massive problem of human relationships"[157] of the present time, points toward a communitarian form of the meaning of property.

APPENDIX
SUMMARY CHART:
CONTROVERSIES OVER THE MEANING OF PROPERTY

1. *Status:* What kind of entity is property?	property as things	property as claims a. moral claims b. legal claims
2. *Subject:* Who may hold property?	unititular system	multititular system a. private property b. common property c. state property
3. *Object:* What sorts of things may be held as property?	i. property for production ii. property in persons and public offices iii. (old property)	property for consumption (property in things) "new property" (gov't. largess)
4. *Import and Extent:* What are the limits of property?	self as monadic society as aggregative nature as instrumental	self as relational society as constititive of self nature as community
5. *Origin:* How is property initiated?	creation of law	natural right: labor
6. *Purpose:* What is the function of property?	instrumentalist tradition	self-developmental tradition

Corporate Governance and Democracy

> He has put down the mighty
> from their thrones, and
> exalted those of low degree;
> he has filled the hungry with good things;
> and the rich he has sent empty away.
> —*Luke 1:52–53*

THE FUTURE SHAPE OF CORPORATE GOVERNANCE

Is democracy, in any sense of that ambiguous concept, an appropriate ethical principle for the governance of the modern corporation? The question may seem both innocent and innocuous on its surface. But, within the context of Western capitalist civilization, the question is, in fact, highly contentious. Consider the judgment of G. A. Borgese: "The capital error of capitalist democracy, still unabjured in some tory quarters, is the identification ... of political freedom with a freedom of economic enterprise inclusive of the freedom to subjugate the other fellow."[1] From this perspective, "capitalist democracy" is, in short, an oxymoron. Borgese's judgment, I shall suggest, is not without merit. But, I mean to suggest, the democratic vision, if pressed toward its full ramifications, must be extended to what nowadays is called "economic democracy" and should drive us toward the transformation of corporate structures.

Democracy has long been cherished as the most appropriate form for governing human relations. To be sure, those who exalt the ideal of democracy have often been at odds with each other over its precise meaning. The famed symposium sponsored by UNESCO shortly after World War II is evidence of that contention.[2] More recent debates over the character and scope of the democratic vision, to which we shall turn later, constitute additional evidence of the ambiguity of the concept. But, within the modern period, the virtually unanimous coalescence of sentiment over the desirability of the democratic principle has been remarkable. Democracy in its many forms is favored as the social

expression of specifically human qualities—freedom, equality, rationality, cooperation. At the very least, democratic institutions, it is
claimed, unless they are abused, are protective of those qualities. In its
more perfect envisionment, democracy embodies them directly.

Within the course of Western history, modern democracy and capitalism emerged simultaneously and seemed, in the view of many defenders, to be basically compatible with each other (although even in
seventeenth-century England, there were detractors from that position,
Gerrard Winstanley and the Diggers among them).[3] To many, the new
politics of parliamentary democracy and the new economics of capitalism were both part and parcel of a general movement of liberation and
enlightenment, throwing over the restrictions and impositions of
medieval tradition and enabling the people (or at least some classes of the
people) to order their own lives as they saw fit and for their own benefit.

However, since the industrial revolution and the rise of the modern
business corporation, social critics from a wide range of perspectives
have voiced serious concern over the increasing development of a tension, if not outright contradiction, between forms of governance in the
political and economic sectors. In the former, democracy (rule by the
many) is the claim and promise, although, sadly, too often honored in
the breach. In the latter, in its dominant corporative form, hierarchy
rules. Principles of private property and freedom of contract may be
invoked to justify the practice, but its central institutional principle is
oligarchy (rule by the few).

The tension, if not contradiction, between political democracy and
economic oligarchy, has been stated in stark terms:

> There is incompatibility between socio-cultural values and norms
> concerning human equality, self-reliance, and freedom, and the hier-
> archical and constraining nature of social control in capitalist systems
> of production. Indeed, the work place is the most authoritarian milieu
> in democratic societies (with the obvious exception of the military
> and total institutions such as prisons and mental hospitals). Employ-
> ees are compelled to lead a double existence: outside their work they
> may enjoy considerable liberties...; in their places of work they are
> subject to strict authority and control, particularly those at the lower
> end of the hierarchy, and to forces of technological and social organi-
> zational change over which they have little or no control.... Capitalist
> production, as a distinct nondemocratic social order, has difficulties
> in legitimizing itself in democratic societies.[4]

This thesis, as formulated, may seem tendentious. But it presents, in bald terms, an ethical issue of critical historical importance, particularly if one views developments in our common life in the West over the past several decades from a radically democratic perspective and is concerned about the fate of democratic principles in the twenty-first century.

Over fifty years ago, James Burnham published his controversial "theory of the managerial revolution," which he later modified, but did not repudiate.[5] The emerging social and political world, Burnham insisted, is neither capitalist nor socialist, but managerial, a world in which a new class of persons has assumed the reins of social control, those whose function consists in the technical direction and coordination of processes of production. Under such conditions, Burnham argued, the prospects for democracy are limited and dim.

Slightly over a decade later, Kenneth Boulding asserted that, since the final third of the nineteenth century, especially in the economic sphere, our common life has been utterly transformed by a phenomenal increase in the size, complexity, and impact of large organizations: "So striking is this movement that it deserves the name of the organizational revolution."[6] In a moment of uncanny premonition, Boulding mused that the forces of militarism conjoined with the organizational revolution might drive us toward a militarized garrison state. But, apart from that prospect, he discerned no inherent tension in principle between a society of large organizations and democratic governance.

Twenty years following the publication of Boulding's argument, Peter Drucker, in his classic work on management, suggested that the organizational revolution formed the necessary beginnings of a subsequent "management boom" to which his work is addressed. In an age of large organization, the managerial role is an inevitability. Some set of people—the "management group"—must assume responsibility primarily for the results of the enterprise and secondarily for directing the work of others. Drucker's intent was to instill in that role a rigorous discipline, a sense of professional duty, measured by economic performance. Only a responsible managerial class, Drucker insisted, might preserve us from the threat of tyranny.[7] Given the historical emergence of a professionalized managerial class, together with a "mixed economy" and the multinational corporation, Drucker called for a new model of government-business relations—but nowhere in this text did he address the question of the democratic principle and its relation to managerialism.

However, where Boulding and Drucker seemed sanguine about the rise of the modern business corporation and the emergence of a professional managerial class, others have been far less confident. Twenty years ago, Robert Heilbroner, in a series of essays forecasting long-range prospects for the shape of our common life, painted a somber portrait of the eventual decline and fall of "business civilization."[8] Its very success in promoting economic growth will lead to its demise. Problems of population expansion, resource depletion, scarcity of energy, and environmental decay will gradually but ineluctably drive us toward a complexly organized, highly centralized, and tightly controlled form of social order. Somewhat plaintively, he allows that democracy may continue to be effective in the transition, but unlikely so. Heilbroner has explored variations on this same theme in a series of publications up to the present time.[9]

From a different perspective, Roberto Mangabeira Unger, after a compelling analysis of the tensions inherent in liberal society and the resultant move toward the formation of the welfare-corporate state— an expression, in effect, of the organizational and managerial revolutions, presents us with two possibilities for the future. We confront, at the moment, a massive decision about the shape of our social life. The first possibility is captured in "the idea of a hierarchical or closed community"—"the ideal of conservative corporativism." The second possibility is "an egalitarian or open community in which the exercise of power is subordinated to the condition of internal democracy."[10] These possibilities constitute alternative conceptions of community, alternative directions for the historical future. There is no certainty that either will necessarily prevail. Which alternative eventuates will be a matter of moral decision.

If Unger is correct—I am inclined to think that he is—then the historical future is not predetermined. But then also, the question posed above—Is democracy, in any sense of that ambiguous concept, an appropriate ethical principle for the governance of the modern corporation?—is indeed an ethical issue of critical historical importance. We do exist, as Boulding has argued, on the far side of an organizational revolution of immense and far-reaching proportions. The multinational business corporation and the corporate-welfare state constitute a dominant force in our lives. Managerialism, as Burnham predicted, is prominent in the governance of all our institutions, directly or indirectly. And, despite our rhetoric and valiant efforts to sustain traditional forms, democracy, certainly in the sense of the town meeting, seems increasingly ineffective if not anachronistic. But whether it is anachronistic depends on the fundamental legitimacy of the idea and the decisiveness with which those convinced of its rightness develop its meaning and implications. That is the force of the question before us.

Assuming the importance of the question, how might we begin to address it? As a point of entry, I propose, first, to sketch a theory of democracy as an ethical aspiration, if not ethical obligation; second, to characterize some of the significant lines in recent debates over the meaning of democracy; and third, to survey diverse experiments and proposals for democracy within the corporate economic sector.

THE MORAL IMPORT OF DEMOCRACY

Ethical principles and judgments are intimately connected with fundamental beliefs about the character of the world and the nature of being human. More succinctly, ethos and cosmos are correlative. This is the position of ethical holism. How we think about what we ought to do reflects, more or less directly, how we think about what we are. Ideas about what is right and good and virtuous find their basic validation through their conformity with background beliefs of a philosophical or religious character. Even if they are not articulated, such background beliefs are presupposed in the formation of ethical judgments.

The basic view of the world that I have found compelling entails a doctrine of the social character of reality. That doctrine applies to all levels of reality, not just the human. For purposes of this reflection on democracy and corporate governance, however, I shall focus primarily on its implications for human relationships. According to that doctrine, we are not, initially, individual beings separate from all others. We are born in and depend for our very life on a vast context of multiple lines of relationship, biological and cultural, present and past. As Bernard Meland has put it, we are re-presentations of the world as much as we are individuals: the sea water flows through our veins; the chemicals and ores of the earth give structure to our bodies; the atmosphere provides us with breath and life; whole civilizations vibrate through our language.[11] At the same time, we bring to each moment the stamp of our own individuality. We are, in however negligible a fashion, a fount of creativity, a reality of unique import. Each person, each event is marked with some kind of special genius. Yet as such, each of us is dependent on resources and powers bequeathed us by the whole community of being and we, in turn, contribute what we have wrought to all others, however enhancing or degrading that contribution might be. In short, the fundamental theme of life is individuality-in-community.

Daniel Day Williams frames this theme as the "logic of sociality."[12] The logic of sociality is, on an encompassing level, a statement about the character of human life—what it is and what it ought to be. It constitutes, I suggest, the beginnings of a doctrine of democracy as the most appropriate principle for the governance of human relations. Requirements of the logic of sociality include the following:

1. *Individuality and participation:* "*A first requirement would be that all existential relations would involve both the freedom and individuality of each member of the society as well as the participation of each member in the life of others, drawing upon them and contributing to them.*"[13] Each self is both individual and social. Privacy and publicness are both constitutive of our being. Yet private life and public action are not wholly separate spheres, for each influences and shapes the other. Any effort to draw an absolute distinction between private sector and public sector as if they had no bearing on each other is called into question.

2. *Action and interaction:* "*[A]ll action involves being acted upon.... [A]ll action is self-transformation through relationship to the other.*"[14] How employers act in relation to their employees has a reflexive action on the employers themselves. It gives shape to their disposition. What revolutionaries do to established power has a formative impact on their own mind and being. In economic relations, in military action, in political policy, there is a solidarity of effect on all parties, active and passive, that alters the character and conditions of the life of each.

3. *Present and future:* "*Every present good must be appraised in relation to what is now given, but also in relation to the continuum of means and ends, conditions and consequences, which stretches into the future.*"[15] This requirement is a version of the principle of seasonal relevance as applied to social life. A policy, an institution, a form of action appropriate in one time and place may (or may not) be appropriate in a different circumstance: "What is relevant, releasing and effective for the increase of social communion in one situation may become obstructive habit in another context."[16] All cultural and institutional constructions, however valuable they might have been and might still be must be subjected eventually to the emergence of new times, new demands, new expectations. Among other things, this requirement gives warrant to

the practice of dissent and the claims of conscientious objection. It extends the idea of loyalty and fidelity to include principled negation.

4. *Continuity and novelty:* "*[T]he logic of a genuinely social relationship must include the logic of an ever-enlarging experience.... A society requires new being, freedom, spontaneity of the members bringing new value into the increasing life of the whole.*"[17] Given the dynamic character of reality, perfection should be conceived not as a static condition, but as a condition of openness. An open society means, at the very least, a deep respect for difference and opposition, creativity and experimentation, novelty and adventure as contributions to the life and health of the whole community.

The logic of sociality as construed in these four requirements is both descriptive (ontological) and prescriptive (ethical). On the one hand, the features of sociality are always present in some configuration in the interactions among persons. But the configuration may be unbalanced and skewed in the forms, for instance, of an extreme libertarianism, a rigid conservativism, an oppressive collectivism, or a revolutionary frenzy. Even such distortions have some element of truth about them which lends them some degree of credence and legitimacy. On the other hand, the logic of sociality suggests a social ideal, a possibility of social interaction that sustains the features of sociality in a balance productive of the greatest intensity of experience. That social ideal as it pertains to the governance of human relations I would call democracy.

Democracy in this sense is more than the range of institutions customarily associated with a democratic government—civil liberties, popular assemblies, independent judiciary, parliamentary legislatures, direct elections, party politics. Certainly without some kind of institutional embodiment, democracy is but a largely ineffective sensibility. Yet the institutions by themselves are vacuous and insubstantial—or worse, they may become instruments of manipulation and control— unless quickened by the democratic principle.

What, then, is the democratic principle? In one of its classical formulations, democracy means government grounded on the consent of the governed.[18] The adequacy of that formulation depends on how "consent of the governed" is understood. Such a phrase can too easily be called upon to justify demagoguery in the political sector or indentured servitude (including its more modern version, wage labor) in the economic sector. A more satisfactory formulation, I suggest, is derivable from Lincoln's felicitous phrasing: democracy is "government of the people, by the people, for the people."[19] As I understand this formulation, it addresses four interrelated questions about the character and conduct of our common life.

A Question of Authority. The initial phrase *of the people* means that government belongs to the people. The people, as a community, authorizes the government. The authority of government (and therefore all governmental officials) is derivative. Government is subordinate to the people. It is the agent adopted to act on behalf of the people. And what the people have authorized, they may, in their good judgment, modify, supplement, or totally transform.

A Question of Procedure. The middle phrase *by the people* signifies the engagement of the people in the conduct of public affairs. Government is their business. How precisely they go about that business may vary, including methods direct and indirect, through their own voice or the advocacy of representatives. But it is their prerogative, if not their responsibility, to be present in the conduct of governance, in the formation and in the implementation of policy. Participation is critical in democracy.

A Question of Purpose. The final phrase *for the people* indicates the beneficiary of governmental action. The needs and interests of the people, severally and collectively, compose the purpose of governmental processes. In traditional terms, government is conducted for the public interest, the common good, the general welfare. The good of the people is the reason for government, the most genuine sense of *raison d'état.* The final justification of governmental action is not merely that the people have so willed, but as importantly that it redounds to their benefit.

A Question of Constituency. Finally, the term *people* is intended inclusively: rich and poor, old and young, lame and whole, male and female, straight and gay, black and white. The people is neither an organic collectivity nor an aggregate of individuals, but a composition of persons and groups, each possessing a singular uniqueness yet altogether forming a community. Separately and together, the people live through time, experience variable historical fortunes, threats, and challenges, and, in moments of lucidity, are aware that, even at times of solitariness, their lives are inextricably caught up with each other in diverse webs of connectedness.

Democracy, so understood, is not without inner tensions and discords. For example, the people may decide ("government by the people") on a course of action that is *not*, in every respect, in their own best interest ("government for the people"). But those are the inner tensions and discords of life itself. Accepting such dissension as integral to the interplay of life, I would suggest that democracy as government of, by, and for the people is an optimal exemplification of the logic of sociality in the organization of relationships between and among diverse persons and groups. As such, democracy is the most appropriate ethical principle for the governance of human relationships.

FOUR PERSPECTIVES ON DEMOCRACY

From the perspective outlined above on the ethical import of the democratic principle, I turn to an extensive debate that has transpired since World War II among American social critics over the meaning of democracy. The debate is more than semantic. It is, in its deepest significance, both ontological (it presents claims about the basic character of our lives) and normative (it articulates a vision of how we should construct our relationships with each other).

I shall isolate four prominent voices in that debate. I shall contend that, while there are vital if not irreconcilable differences among these voices, each is expressive of an important insight of ethical importance and that, as the debate has proceeded, it has properly moved toward the inclusion of large corporate enterprise within the conception of the public realm, thereby subjecting the economic sector to the requirements and strictures of the democratic principle. The four voices to which I shall attend are liberal democracy (principle of individuality), elite democracy (principle of accountability), strong democracy (principle of solidarity), and economic democracy (principle of welfare).

Liberal Democracy (Principle of Individuality). In a compact summary, Carl Cohen has properly accentuated individuality as the core feature of liberal democracy:

> Individualist democracy is rooted in the primacy of the individual human being. Democracy protects the right of each citizen to participate in making the laws that govern all and maintain social order. The larger purpose of these laws is to enhance the lives of the private citizens they serve. The freedom of individuals to live as they think best is the highest democratic idea.[20]

John Locke, Jean-Jacques Rousseau, Jeremy Bentham, James Mill, and John Stuart Mill are among the diverse political theorists whose ideas are invoked in the tradition of liberal democracy. They differ considerably. Yet each stresses some variation of the principle of individuality.

An exemplary case in point is John Stuart Mill's assertion of the "one very simple principle," which he insists must govern all compulsory dealings of social and political organization with the individual: "That principle is that the sole end for which mankind [sic] are warranted, individually or collectively, in interfering with the liberty of action of any of their number is self-protection. That the only purpose for which power can be rightfully exercised over any member of a civilized community, against his will, is to prevent harm to others."[21] Government's role is secondary and protective: to secure a realm of privacy within which individuals may live and do as they please.

Yet Mill also insists on an educative role for government. In deliberating about "the criterion of a good form of government," he avers that "the most important point of excellence which any form of government can possess is to promote the virtue and intelligence of the people themselves."[22] That is the genius of true democracy through which the active participation of all classes of people has the effect of advancing each person's mental powers, moral sentiments, and practical effectiveness, thereby improving the quality of government, but also and more importantly, enhancing the life of each individual.[23]

Shortly following World War II, two versions of liberal democracy, both reacting to the terrifying if not nihilistic political tendencies manifest in that convulsive event through which the forces of fascism threatened to engulf the world, were proposed. The traditionalist version invoked a doctrine of human dignity rooted, by claim, in the Hebraic-Greek-Christian tradition.[24] Democracy, it was (and is still) argued, is that form of governance grounded on faith in each person as a rational, moral, spiritual creature with a destiny that surpasses the temporal order and a right to all those conditions of life requisite to the realization of that destiny. The freedom that is secured through democracy with its attendant protection of human rights is the optimal political condition for all individuals to direct their respective lives toward the perfection of their human powers.

The interest group version of liberal democracy was more closely allied to the utilitarianism of Bentham than to the human rights doctrine of the traditionalist school.[25] Moreover, it was ostensibly more explanatory in its intent than normative, although implicitly it celebrated the presumed pluralism of American democracy as far superior to any more monolithic, centralized alternative. The political process in the United States, it was argued, consists of two crucial features: multiple interest groups with overlapping memberships and potential interest groups, especially those with concerns about sustaining the "rules of the game." These features "serve as a balance wheel" in a pluralistic society such as the United States.[26] In their actual operation they assure multiple points of access by individual and groups to governmental decision. They thus serve to effectuate a kind of representative democracy protective of individual interests.

More recently, a renewed defense of liberal democracy has been launched in light of challenges that have emerged in the last few decades: the enormous growth of public bureaucracy; the increased control of the military over public policy; the expanded impact of multinational corporations on our common life; and the gradual disruption of the biosphere through the depletion of natural resources and the effects of environmental pollution.[27] Given these threats, it has been argued, a genuinely "viable democracy" must establish effective ways for the people to control large organizations and to secure ample opportunities for alternative styles and diverse modes of self-development. Once again, the central concern of liberal democracy is the preservation of individuality, however dim that prospect might prove in an era of large organization and centralized control over the disposition of resources.

Elite Democracy (Principle of Accountability). The concept of elite democracy was initially formed out of an admission that, given the social transformations of recent history, humankind has entered upon an era of massive organization and that individualism, at least in the economic sector, is no longer a pertinent ideology. The classical apology for the concept is located in Joseph Schumpeter's famed study of capitalism, socialism, and democracy, initially published in 1942, although the term *the elitist theory of democracy* was coined only much later.[28]

With grave reluctance, Schumpeter was driven to the conclusion that socialism, defined as "an institutional pattern in which control over means of production and over production itself is vested with a central authority" is an historical inevitability.[29] The very success of capitalism presses toward that end. But, then, does such a move entail the demise of democracy? It does, if democracy is understood in a "classical" sense as the people, out of their wisdom, determining the common good through the selection of persons assembled to carry out their will.[30] Granting that many hold to such an ideal with religious zeal, Schumpeter is skeptical about that construction on several grounds. First, concepts of common good and the general will of the people are chimerical in light of the rifts and variances that run throughout large populations. Moreover, the hypothesis of human rationality and wise judgment has been shattered by strong evidences that a primitive irrationality and susceptibility to influence run rampant throughout the masses. Again, that concept of democracy ignores the inevitable surfacing and powerful role of leadership in all organized life—which is Schumpeter's modest version of Michels's "iron law of oligarchy."

Yet, Schumpeter argues, socialism and democracy are not necessarily incompatible if, given the actual configurations of modern life (following the social and managerial revolutions), a more realistic theory of democracy is espoused, toward which Schumpeter turns. First, Schumpeter insists that democracy is merely a method of political decision. It is not an end in itself; indeed, it may eventuate in results that are highly unacceptable.[31] More precisely, democracy means "competition for political leadership": "the democratic method is that institutional arrangement for arriving at political decisions in which individuals acquire the power to decide by means of a competitive struggle for the people's vote."[32] More tersely, "Democracy means only that the people have the opportunity of accepting or refusing the men [sic] who are to rule them."[33]

Thus, within the framework of modern society, while it is not true that the people rule, or can expect to rule, in any direct manner, it is possible that an electorate (or its majority) can hold political leaders accountable through regular elections. The electorate determines whom it will accept and whom it will evict as leaders, although the leaders themselves constitute a special class with the power to settle basic policy and to conduct the business of the social order.

In Seymour Lipset's version of the elitist perspective, "democracy in modern society may be viewed as involving the conflict of organized groups competing for support."[34] Lipset, whose delineation of elitist democracy is very close in character to Robert Dahl's concept of "polyarchy,"[35] suggests that some semblance of the democratic vision may be sustained by the active contention of diverse organized groups throughout the social system. However oligarchic the groups may be arranged internally, through their interminable conflicts with each other, the "egoistic misuse of power" is limited: "Democracy in large measure rests on the fact that no one group is able to secure a basis of power and command over the majority so that it can effectively suppress or deny the claims of the groups it opposes."[36]

Elite theory stands in marked contrast with features of liberal democracy. It demonstrates greater concern for the stability of the social system than for the education and self-development of individual citizens.[37] It focuses more directly on competition among elites for positions of leadership than on the protection or, more importantly, the empowerment of marginalized classes and fringe groups.[38] Its intent is more to explain (if not to justify) the actual workings of current political arrangements than to articulate a moral vision of how our common life ought to be lived and how distant we are from that ideal.[39] Yet elite democracy as conceived at least promotes the need for an effective method of accountability of rulers to ruled in an age of concentrated power and large organization.

Strong Democracy (Principle of Solidarity). "Strong democracy," a term devised by Benjamin Barber, designates a mode of political thought and practice intended to move us beyond the crisis of liberal democracy and toward "participatory politics for a new age."[40] It incorporates a transformation of the underlying cosmology of the democratic tradition and it extends the democratic principle beyond its customary limits to embrace the organization of economic relations. In contrast to elite democracy, it concentrates not on competition for positions of leadership, but on the development of a full-fledged sense of citizenship and on citizen participation in public affairs. In contrast to liberal democracy, it argues that without an extensive and effective program of social equality and political equality, democratic forms are but a fraud and a pretense. The result is "pseudodemocracy."[41]

In Barber's judgment, the deepest flaw of liberal democracy is its unalloyed individualism. This feature he traces back to a Newtonian view of the world: each of us is, at base, an isolated being, driven in a singular direction, oblivious, except at points of collision, of the interests and projections of others. Such a view infuses the epistemology and psychology of classical liberalism, culminating in a doctrine of rationalized self-judgment and aggressive acquisitiveness. We are, by nature, ultimately lonely and alone. But, declares, Barber, such a view is

neglectful of a vital dimension of human experience: our connectedness and our transformative influence on one another—"liberal theory
cannot be expected to give an adequate account of human interdependency, mutualism, cooperation, fellowship, fraternity, community, and
citizenship. To take but a few examples, we contravene the corollary of
mutual exclusivity daily, in every human interaction that engages us in
friendship, partnership, community, or love."[42]

The alternative to liberal democracy rests on an understanding of
the necessity for public action on issues of broad consequence, of the
presence of conflicting judgments about what should be done, of the
absence of any certain way of determining policy, but of the possibility for reasonable public choice. Given such conditions, strong
democracy proposes the formation of an ongoing political community in which we may talk together, decide together, and work together
in the formation and transformation of our common life, thereby
adopting the genuine character of citizenship. Strong democracy, in
short, "posits the social nature of human beings in the world,"[43] that
is, our solidarity even under conditions of difference and opposition.
Through various means—neighborhood assemblies, electronic ballot-
ing, workplace democracy—Barber would have us create an "unmedi-
ated self-government by an engaged citizenry."[44]

In an analogous move, Jane Mansbridge concludes a lengthy study
of decision processes in a small town and in a crisis center with the
admonition that a legitimate mode of governance must, on all levels,
national and local, integrate features of two kinds of democracy—
adversarial (with its equitable distribution of power to protect variable
and conflicting interests) and unitary (with its grounding in the principle of friendship and its drive toward consensus).[45]

In Philip Green's version of strong democracy (although he does not
use the term), the question of economic relations is critical because, he
asserts, "political equality, the real spirit of democracy...cannot be
achieved without fundamental changes in the social and economic base;
without a new commitment to social equality."[46] Social equality consists
of three components, all of which are needed for equal citizenship, but all
of which would require a massive transformation of the capitalist system.
First, "constrained inequality": Green would assure everyone of sufficient
economic resources to lead a productive life and to prepare for active participation in public affairs. Second, a "democratic division of labor":
work, education, and family should complement each other; hence, for
instance, socially valued work, education, child care, and shared parent-

ing should be available for all. Third, "equal access to the means of production": economic processes should be made susceptible to detailed surveillance and control by all whose lives are affected by them through whatever diversity of arrangements might be made possible.

To Green, only with social equality can we attack seriously problems of political equality: how to assure opportunity for all to participate in determining the contours of our common life; how to keep elected or appointed representatives from forming an elite class in pursuit of their own special privilege; how to safeguard against the persistent subjection of any class or group of persons.

The aim of social equality is a kind of solidarity, that is, to create "a relatively classless (and casteless) society" and hence "a genuine collectivity with a genuinely collective interest in peaceful conflict resolution."[47] The solidarity of strong democracy does not mean the cessation of opposition and difference, but it does intend a communal context within which democratic citizenship is possible. But, as Green and others[48] acknowledge, such an intent requires a fundamental transformation of both political and economic institutions. These sectors have become so intertwined and interconnected, they cannot be neatly segregated into public and private; both direct and fix the shape of our lives; if the democratic principle is to be effective, it must inform the entire structure.

Economic Democracy (Principle of Welfare). The essence of economic democracy is defined as "the transfer of economic decision making from the few to the many." Its primary features in current circumstances are construed to be "(1) the shift of investment control from corporate domination to the public; and (2) the reconstruction of economic decision making through democratic, worker- and worker/consumer-controlled production."[49]

Underlying the concept of economic democracy—a close ally to strong democracy—is the argument that, pretenses to the contrary, the large modern business corporation is not a strictly private institution. It is, because of its character and impact, public and should therefore be subjected to the procedural and substantive principles of public institutions. Assuming the cogency of democratic theory, the corporation should therefore be directed to serve the public welfare in both its procedures and its results. But welfare in this context means not some grudging handout to the poor and powerless, it signifies instead whatever will conduce to the well-being of the human community.

Peter Bachrach is among those who have persistently insisted that the modern corporation must be identified as fundamentally political: "There is no serious challenge among scholars today to the view that gargantuan multinational corporations are political institutions in the strictest sense of the term; that oligarchical self-perpetuating heads of these leviathans 'authoritatively allocate values' that affect millions of people, both within and without the corporate constituency; and that not infrequently the vast power resources of the oligarchies are drawn upon to compel compliance of potential recalcitrants."[50]

Bachrach's argument is simple and direct: if politics is defined in functional, not structural, terms; if, for instance, politics means the "authoritative allocation of values in society"; if corporations do in fact with some degree of authoritative force shape our social and cultural lives by their determinations; then corporations are engaged in political action.[51]

Robert Dahl charges a possible counterposition—that corporations are instruments of private property and therefore immune, in principle, from public control—as historically illusory. It neglects the vast social transformations of the past century. It transforms the ideology of private enterprise of farmer and small merchant to the modern corporation, the "corporate leviathan." But, "nothing could be less appropriate than to consider the giant firm a *private* enterprise."[52] On the contrary, the modern corporation, particularly those of multinational scope, is "for all practical purposes a new, shadowy, unregulated polity with resources greater than those of most nation-states."[53]

Dahl dismisses the customary view that corporations are properly controlled by stockholders on two grounds. First, he reiterates the long-acknowledged argument of Berle and Means that the meaning of ownership has been irrevocably modified in the modern era as evidenced in the emergence of a managerial class separate from stockholders in corporate enterprise. Managers more than stockholders control the resources and operations of the enterprise. Second, Dahl invokes the "Principle of Affected Interests": "Everyone who is affected by the decisions of a government should have the right to participate in that government."[54] Granting all the puzzles and difficulties provoked by that precept, Dahl promotes it as having prima facie authority. In the case of corporate governance, this means that employees, customers, even the general public have a compelling basis to claim corporate citizenship, however that might be worked out in detail.[55] In a work in which Dahl has set out, with some stringency, the argument for economic democracy, he presents the claims in strong moral terms:

> Members of any association for whom the assumptions of the democratic process are valid have a *right* to govern themselves by means of the democratic process. If, as we believe, those assumptions hold among us, not only for the government of the state but also for the internal government of economic enterprises, then we have a *right* to govern ourselves democratically within our economic enterprises.[56]

From another perspective, given the democratic principle, the measure of modes of governance is twofold: (i) results and (ii) procedures. That is, human need includes not only goods and resources that sustain and enhance life; it includes as well—perhaps even more importantly—the satisfaction and growth attained from active engagement with others in deliberating about the means and ends of life, in deciding what might conduce most clearly to the public good, and in cooperating in the realization of whatever plans emerge from that process.[57] Welfare, in the sense of human well-being, is not merely a matter of commodities and material wealth; it is, more significantly, a process of creative intercommunication through which all parties gain more intense insight into themselves and one another than is otherwise possible and through which, therefore, the quality of the entire community is enriched.[58]

The argument for economic democracy—for extending strong democracy into corporate governance—is thus two-sided. First, as some economists have reasoned persuasively, economic democracy, in comparison with the present American system, would result in a more productive utilization of resources and decreased wastefulness in the kinds of goods and services produced.[59] Second, economic democracy would establish conditions within which the humane values of the logic of sociality—including liberty, equality, and community—might more effectively be actualized.

FORMS OF ECONOMIC DEMOCRACY

The strong affirmation of the need to subject economic organization to the democratic principle has been repeated constantly over the past century, often under the rubric of "industrial democracy." Sidney and Beatrice Webb used that term as the title of their classic study of trade unionism originally published in 1897.[60] Two years later, Henry D. Lloyd praised the labor movement as an effort "to add to political democracy industrial democracy."[61] Woodrow Wilson, during the second term of his presidency, called for "the genuine democratization of industry, based upon a full recognition of the right of those who work, in whatever rank, to participate in some organic way in every decision which directly affects their welfare in the part they are to play in industry."[62] In 1942, Henry Wallace, then vice president, asserted that "the new democracy, the democracy of the common man, includes not only the Bill of Rights, but also economic democracy."[63] In the early 1960s, the founding manifesto of the Students for a Democratic Society insisted that "the economy...is of such social importance that its major resources and means of production should be open to democratic participation and subject to democratic social regulation."[64]

However, such terms as *industrial democracy* and *economic democracy* have been used to designate a broad range of diverse proposals.[65] Here I shall explore four kinds, each of which expresses some aspect of the democratic principle, although only the last two seem to press that principle toward the basic question of ultimate authority. The four kinds are collective bargaining (limited empowerment); human relations (circumscribed respect); economic rights (variable autonomy); and social ownership (solidary participation).

Collective Bargaining (Limited Empowerment). In an extensive survey covering a century (1865–1965), Milton Derber has argued that the "American idea of industrial democracy" is best represented by the model of collective bargaining. By the beginning of the twentieth century, "the single most widely accepted idea of industrial democracy was bilateral collective bargaining between a trade union and an individual employer or group of employers, with the working rules expressed in a written trade agreement, disinterested outsiders playing a very limited role as conciliators or arbitrators when requested by the parties, and government serving primarily as a source of factual information, as the guardian of women and children in certain limited respects, and on occasion as the protector of the public peace and safety."[66] With modification, the model has endured over the decades, but it now confronts significant challenges from the implications of high technology, multinational corporate organization and conservative forces in circles of federal and state governments in the United States. Labor unions are struggling nowadays for their survival and include only a small minority of workers throughout the country.

Yet it is precisely under circumstances of the centralization of power in government and corporate industry that the principle of collective bargaining may be salutary in sustaining the intent of the democratic principle. That was the argument of H. A. Clegg, whose "new approach to industrial democracy" was constructed in the sixties under the aegis of the Congress for Cultural Freedom in response to threats of collectivism. His thesis was that, in general, the active presence of pressure groups is the preservative of democracy in modern society and that, in particular, trade unions constitute a critical kind of pressure group:

> In all the stable democracies there is a system of industrial relations which can fairly be called the industrial parallel of political democracy. It promotes the interests and protects the rights of workers in industry by means of collective bargaining between employers and managers on the one hand, and on the other, trade unions independent of government and management. This could be called a system of *industrial democracy by consent,* or *pressure group industrial democracy,* or *democracy through collective bargaining.*[67]

Clegg's view of democracy has been criticized, not improperly, as more protective than participatory in character.[68] Yet Clegg's emphasis on the importance of power in effecting workers' rights ought not be ignored, especially in a social system where to work means to be subjected to the control and authority of others and where unions are widely understood as an unwarranted threat to the rights and responsibilities of management.[69] The principle of collective bargaining, where effective, at least empowers employees to engage, to some degree, in the settlement of matters that bear on their working life. But the range of decisions is largely limited to "workers' issues." "Management issues"—for example, choice of products, markets, and pricing; investments in new buildings and machinery; divestitures, mergers, and plant relocations; distribution of profits—are considered totally outside the range of matters appropriate to the bargaining table.[70]

Human Relations (Circumscribed Respect). The famed Hawthorne studies initiated in the late 1920s by Elton Mayo generated an influential movement of managerial thought and practice, the Human Relations school, proposing diverse forms of direct participation by employees in the conduct of corporate enterprise. In that sense, the Human Relations school promotes a delimited kind of economic democracy, which, in contrast to collective bargaining, has been adopted by some corporate managers because of its presumed effect on efficiency and productivity.[71]

In Douglas MacGregor's version of the human relations doctrine, all forms of management rest on some understanding of human nature. The conventional view (Theory X) supposes that people dislike work; that they must therefore be coerced to bend their energies toward the achievement of the corporation's objectives; and that most people shun responsibility and need to be directed and controlled. An alternative (Theory Y) assumes, on the contrary, that work is as natural as play; that people will exercise self-control toward objectives to which they are committed; that most people seek responsibility; and that, under current industrial conditions, the full potentialities of the average person have not been tapped.[72]

To draw people into the counsels and conduct of an enterprise is to motivate them by appealing to the deepest human needs, needs not just for survival and security, but, more importantly, for belonging, for self-esteem, and for continued self-development. Thus MacGregor, Rensis Likert, and others suggest the formation in the corporation of teams or small groups of employees to design, organize, conduct, and evaluate their own way of accomplishing their tasks.[73]

A variety of programs have been attributed to the human relations doctrine: job enlargement, job enrichment, quality circles, works councils, joint production committees. In addition, although many profit-sharing plans have been and still are efforts motivated by anti-union sentiment to solicit loyalty to the corporation,[74] the Scanlon Plan, it has been argued, was formed out of the sensibilities of the Human Relations school.[75] The primary purpose of the Scanlon Plan is to draw all workers into collaborative interaction to improve procedures of production and thereby to increase the economic gain of the enterprise which is, subsequently, distributed regularly to the entire work force.

Programs derived from the perspective of the human relations school have a democratic complexion to the degree that they support active worker participation in the conduct of the corporation. Moreover, given its theory of motivation allied with its emphasis on interactive engagement in the productive process,[76] the human relations school demonstrates deeper respect for the full character of human reality and the logic of sociality than the traditional form of hierarchical governance directed by a narrow principle of economic rationality.

But that respect is scrupulously circumscribed and controlled. Peter Drucker charges the approach as manipulative, as promoting an "enlightened psychological despotism," for ultimately in such programs the inner needs of employees are subject to exploitation by and on behalf of a higher command.[77] The human relations approach, in short, neglects the fundamental democratic question of power and authority.[78]

Economic Rights (Variable Autonomy). The concept of "economic rationality," at least since the eighteenth century, has a distinctively utilitarian cast. That is, the predominant morality of business enterprise has consisted in (a monetary form of) cost/benefit analysis. Profitability—the "bottom line"—has been accepted as a basic test, if not the basic test, of corporate strategies and procedures, and a measure for assessing the performance of employees. But utilitarianism has been severely criticized for its failure to respect human rights and thus to honor one of the vital components of democratic theory.

During the bicentennial celebration of the Declaration of Independence, David Ewing argued that American society is riven with an organizational paradox.[79] Principles of constitutionalism, as represented in the Bill of Rights, secure an extensive range of civil liberties in the political realm. But such liberties do not extend into economic relations. In the corporation itself, there are no rights to free speech or dissent, little protection for conscientious objection to unethical orders, no rights securing desks and papers from search and seizure, seldom any assurance of formal procedures for appeals or due process—unless a particular corporation establishes its own policy on such matters. As a remedy, Ewing proposes a special bill of rights for the workplace, enacted, if need be, by constitutional amendment to extend the principle of civil liberties—free speech, privacy, association, due process—to employees of all private and public organizations.

Nearly a decade later, in a statement of far greater philosophical sophistication, Patricia Werhane presented the case that corporations are moral agents, not just producers of wealth, and, as such, are under the obligation to conform to the strictures and directions of moral rights.[80] Moral rights are claims one may make on the actions of others justified directly or by implication by one's humanity. Basic moral rights include claims to equal consideration, security and subsistence, life, freedom, and privacy. On this basis, Werhane argues decisively, for instance, against the traditional capitalist doctrine of "employment at will" and for a prima facie right not to be fired. The bill of rights for employees (and, correlatively, for employers) with which she concludes is more extensive than Ewing's, including, for example, rights to a safe workplace, to information about the corporation, its condition and future, and to participate in decisions pertaining to one's job and to the corporation as a whole.

Ewing's and (to a large extent) Werhane's understandings of human rights manifest the individualism of liberal democracy. While in both cases, the principle of rights places significant moral and constitutional constraints on corporate practice, neither poses a radical democratic challenge to corporate authority. That, however, is the import of the economic bill of rights proposed by Samuel Bowles, David Gordon, and Thomas Weisskopf. The "democratic economics" of Bowles, Gordon, and Weisskopf features, among other things, the "right to shape our economic futures," which includes national democratic planning based on a social needs inventory; community-based control over investments; subjecting the Federal Reserve Board to election by the House of Representatives; community initiative in determining plant location and infrastructural development; and the development of extensive procedures to engage communities in protecting their natural environment.[81] In brief, their intent is to shift, as a matter of basic right, the authority of corporate decision to the people affected by such policies and practices. Their underlying philosophy is more akin to strong democracy than to liberal democracy.

Social Ownership (Solidary Participation). Social ownership as a form of industrial democracy exacts an explicit turn from the liberal principle of individualism to the logic of sociality. In this context, moreover, ownership signifies not merely title, but effective control. Again, control, as a matter of social ownership, is vested in the community for the benefit of the community. This is the import of Tom Schuller's conclusion that "democracy at work, whatever shape it takes, must entail at least one element: a degree of collective identity and collective definition of interests. The ability of individuals, under whatever regime, to control their own work cannot justify the label of democracy unless they also participate in some form of collective decision making." Thus Schuller insists that "atomistic, wholly individualized systems are not compatible with industrial democracy." [82]

The idea of worker directors (e.g., the principle of codetermination in Germany and the Bullock Committee proposal in Great Britain) is a severely delimited but nonetheless controversial version of social ownership.[83] The supposition of the idea is that workers gain a position of significant control when represented on the corporate board which is, presumably, a locus of strategic power in determining fundamental policies of the enterprise. Even where introduced, however, the program has been resisted strongly by both management and unions. Management views worker directors as an encroachment on ownership rights and managerial authority. Unions are fearful lest worker directors jeopardize their bargaining strength. Moreover because of structural constraints on the worker directors' role, critics are doubtful that the presence of workers on boards has had much appreciable effect on the direction or character of corporate practice.

The Meidner plan in Sweden, a version of which has been proposed for the United States,[84] offers a more extensive form of social ownership than worker directors. According to the plan, a percentage of corporate profits—as much as 20 percent—is transferred annually to one of several employee investment funds. Among the objectives of the system is "to give workers direct responsibility for the use of risk capital, a share of future profits, and a greater measure of influence in the enterprise."[85] Over the years, the boards of the employee funds are expected to control a significant proportion of corporate capital. Dividends may be distributed various ways, but, in Sweden, strong preference has been expressed to use them for long-term, collective benefits: education and training, research and safety projects, reinvestment, and support for weaker firms.

Producers' cooperatives constitute still another form of social ownership, in this case, on the level of the firm. With wide variations in size and character,[86] cooperatives generally share the following characteristics: "(i) the establishment is autonomous, (ii) employees are able to become members of the enterprise by nominal holdings of share capital, (iii) the principle of 'one-member-one-vote' prevails, (iv) formal provision exists for direct employee participation at all levels, (v) employees share in profits."[87] Producers' cooperatives—ranging from the complex Mondragon system in Spain to the several plywood cooperatives in the American Pacific Northwest—confront several critical problems: dependency on external (sometimes hostile) sources for operating capital; combining democratic procedures internally with the apparent need for professional management and job specialization;

sustaining commitment to the cooperative principle given divergent expectations among the workers.[88] However, as Schuller muses, "Perhaps the most significant feature of co-operatives is that they claim the formal right and the formal responsibility to confront those issues explicitly."[89]

In contrast to collective bargaining, human relations programs, and workplace rights (in their more limited versions), social ownership is directed ultimately toward the transformation of prevailing structures of corporate authority into a more democratic form. Recently, both Peter Abell and Joyce Rothschild-Whitt have developed, independently of each other, an "ideal type" of democratic organization in direct contrast to Max Weber's well-known construction of the hierarchical-bureaucratic model which, it has been argued, is typical of corporate enterprise. To Abell and Rothschild-Whitt, the question of authority is critical.[90] In Rothschild-Whitt's formulation:

> Decisions become authoritative in collectivist organizations to the extent that they derive from a process in which all members have the right to full and equal participation. . . . All major policy issues, such as hiring, firing, salaries, the division of labor, the distribution of surplus, and the shape of the final product or service, are decided by the collective as a whole. . . . Only these decisions, changing as they might with the ebb and flow of sentiments in the group, are taken as binding and legitimate. These organizations are collectively controlled by their members or workers; hence the name *collectivist* or *collectivist-democratic* organization.

DEMOCRACY AS ASPIRATION AND OBLIGATION

The question we have been exploring is whether democracy is an appropriate ethical principle for the governance of the modern corporation. On its surface, the question may seem somewhat strange. The current global corporation, in intent and in operation, is anything but democratic. Yet, since the emergence of the modern corporation, that question has been asked persistently. Properly so. The question is particularly urgent at the present time when massive corporations have command of resources across the world and can, through their policies, determine the life circumstances of masses of individuals and communities.

From the standpoint of the politics of relationality, democracy—as government of, by, and for the people—is the optimal form for the arrangement of human relations. In that sense, the question, however strange it may seem given the concentrations of oligarchic control that dominate the global economy, must be answered affirmatively. Such an affirmative response would mandate a profound transformation of the structure and procedures of corporate enterprise, particularly since, in my assessment, strong democracy and social ownership seems most akin to the logic of sociality as sketched above.

To be sure, the central principle of each position in the debates I have characterized bears some cogency. Within the logic of sociality, principles of individuality, accountability, solidarity, and welfare all assume a proper place. Considerations of the empowerment of marginalized groups, respect for the full range of human needs, protection of the autonomy—including the rights and responsibilities—of individual agents, and solidary participation in the decisions and conduct of the corporation are all critical. But it is, I would insist, only in the framework of a strong and vibrant form of democratic control and ownership of corporate enterprise that all these principles and considerations are brought together in an integrated and mutually enforcing way.

Democracy, within this framework, is an ethical aspiration, yet not without grounding in reality, ontological and historical. Given the fundamental character of human life, it is the most fitting pattern of organizational interaction. As such, democracy has the force of an ultimate obligation. It possesses the quality of a compelling moral vision. In the terms of political theory, democracy is expressive of the common good. In religious language, it is the social counterpart of the divine intent for peace and justice. To the extent that our institutions and associations fall short of the vision, our humanity is diminished. That may be the tragedy of our condition, but then there is some measure of grace to be drawn from the honest acknowledgment of our limitations and our failures.

7
Interlude:
The Socialist Vision Revisited

And all who believed were together
and had all things in common; and
they sold their possessions and goods and
contributed them to all, as any had need.
—*Acts 2:44–45*

"Socialism is finished.... The socialist experiment is over and the capitalist experiment roars to its own conclusion." So declares Norman Rush.[1] Although unhappy with that conclusion, Rush nonetheless thinks it indubitable given the surprising dissolution of state socialism in Eastern Europe not long after the dismantling of the Berlin Wall.

To be sure, as Rush notes, we are indebted to those long devoted to the socialist cause. In and through their political struggles over the decades, they have been influential in promoting and shaping much of the "moral infrastructure of modern capitalist society": labor unions, the eight-hour working day, diverse forms of social insurance, improved working conditions, child-labor legislation, credit unions, and so on. But, at the present moment it is uncertain what forces will press for the expansion, or even merely the retention, of such humane modifications of the seemingly relentless drive of corporate capitalism to increase the "wealth of nations"—or, more accurately, to increase the wealth of the upper socioeconomic class—whatever the cost to other dimensions of our common life.

Socialism—centered, Rush asserts, in the demand for material equality through mandated public ownership—received its coup de grace during that unanticipated and amazing turn of events that transpired from 1989 to 1991, during which the USSR utterly disintegrated into multiple fragments, many at odds with each other; the Baltic states were liberated; the Berlin Wall was obliterated; and Eastern European nations broke away from their enthrallment by the Soviet Communist system. Throughout these nations and others once considered, by their own definition, socialist, massive movements have subsequently been undertaken toward the development of a market economy with its (presumably) commensurate political and social system under the political slogan of freedom.

Hence, Rush concludes, even if prevailing forms of capitalism stand in need of persistent and hard-headed moral critique—which they do—that critique must now derive from some alternative, more pragmatic, source: "Forget socialism, now."

However, I am not so sure we should "forget socialism, now." Despite Rush's pronouncement of the death of socialism and notwithstanding Robert Bellah's speculations of two decades ago about socialism as an American taboo,[2] I suggest the need to revisit the socialist vision as, in its most alluring versions, a social expression of the principle of relationality and, as such, a social possibility worthy of our commitment.

Since the emergence of the concept of socialism in the early decades of the nineteenth century, it has taken on diverse forms and given rise to various movements—some of which, such as Stalinism, have transformed its original impulse into its virtual antithesis. But that should not be surprising. Such reversals are not without precedence in human experience. Consider, in religious history, the kinds of viciousness perpetrated in the name of Christianity or on behalf of the Hindu tradition or to preserve Judaism. Consider, moreover, in political history, the forms of authoritarian control and racist practice conducted under the pretense of democracy and freedom. Reversals of this kind are worthy of close historical study: how they happened, why they happened, whether they had to happen. But that they happened need not detract us from a reexamination and reappropriation of the original impulse of these movements. Stalinism may, in some sense, be finished, but that does not necessarily mean that the socialist vision is without merit.

In its inner core, I would contend, socialism captures a sensitivity about our common life that retains its power and pertinence at the present time despite those kinds of repressive regimes that have over the past century been proclaimed as socialist. Indeed, socialism may have a special currency nowadays over against the forms and tendencies of corporate capitalism. Corporate capitalism, despite its presumed genius as a force for economic growth, is simply neglectful (as socialism at its best is not) of issues of the public good. Moreover, through its attention to issues of the public good, socialism may be more heedful of the welfare of the individual than corporate capitalism with its proclaimed concern to preserve individual freedom.

Socialism is not, at least by intention, a political and economic ideology in the Marxist sense of that term. That is, it is not merely a rationalization of narrow class interests. Rather, in its original context, it was an affirmation about the meaning of human life constructed in opposition to unfolding political and economic forms that were discerned as delimiting human possibility and unresponsive to human need. The concept of socialism emerged during the first third of the nineteenth century as a social principle constructed almost simultaneously in France by followers of Saint-Simon and in England by devotees of Robert Owen in direct reaction against what Saint-Simonians called "individualism," that is, the social doctrine underlying developments of early capitalism.

The term *individualism* was coined by Saint-Simonians to designate the kind of social consciousness stimulated by the Enlightenment that defined associations as strictly instrumental—as meant to serve the private interests of the individual. So understood, individualism opposed efforts by public institutions to regulate or control economic relations, which were conceived to be solely of private concern. And it was supportive of an idea of natural rights as protecting the individual against undue intrusion by governmental forces. On the surface, individualism seemed, in the context of early modernism given its reaction to inherited traditions, to be an attractive social ideal.

However, as the Saint-Simonians and others argued, through its neglect of the more organic and communal dimensions of human experience and by virtue of its egotistic implications, individualism became a force promoting competitive and exploitative practices in political and economic life. Through its elevation of self-interest, individualism, as it took form in the dynamics of social interaction through the development of early forms of industrialism and urbanization, uprooted people from their communities of origin and resulted in a kind of social anarchy. Ironically, individualism, in stark contrast to its moral rhetoric, eventuated in the manipulation and subjugation of the individual or, more precisely, in the utilization of the energies of working people to serve the interests of the owners of property. In short, individualism tended, in social practice, to support the individual interests of some (the few) at the expense of the individual life of others (the many). In the course of events, the rhetoric of individualism served to conceal the reality of class hierarchy and class oppression.

The term *socialism* was coined to designate an alternative social philosophy, acknowledging the communal dimension of human life and promoting the welfare of all through collaborative action. *Associationism* was the original term employed by the Saint-Simonians to contrast their social vision with individualism. More generally, socialism, as it emerged in common usage among Saint-Simonians, Owenites, and others in the 1830s conveyed, according to Bernard Crick, the image of "an invented system of society that stressed the social as against the selfish, the cooperative as against the competitive, sociability as against individual self-sufficiency and self-interest; strict social controls on the accumulation and use of private property; and either economic equality or at least rewards according to merits (merits judged socially), or (a middle position) rewards judged according to need."[3]

Underlying this image of socialism, I would contend, is a fundamental understanding about life, a cosmology—a theology—according to which our lives are intricately intertwined, the destiny of each caught up with the destiny of all. The principle of relationality is a way of designating this understanding. Whereas in the individualist vision, we are monads, each pursuing a separate path, each concerned to avoid obstructions to our chosen adventure in life, in the socialist vision, we are companions, each having a more or less direct influence on all others for better or for worse as we appropriate the resources of this world while shaping and directing the future. The moral intent of socialism is so to construct the forms of our common life that the experience of all individuals is enlivened and enriched through their interactions with each other.

Against this backdrop, I would revise Norman Rush's formulation of the central predicate of socialism. The central predicate is not so much the demand for material equality through mandated common ownership as it is the yearning to shape a form of social interaction through which the life of each might enhance the lives of all, thereby contributing to the creative advance of value in the world. That, in theological language, is what it means to love God with all one's heart and soul and mind and strength. Of the triadic set of normative social principles that emerged in the French Revolution—liberty, equality, community—socialism's primary focus is on the formation of community, with the insistence that thereby the liberty of each should be strengthened and the equality of all promoted.

In the formation of community, from a socialist perspective, the question of property is pivotal. Property is a normative term, signifying a bundle of rights over things: rights of possession and control, use and disposal. In ordinary usage in the modern Western tradition, particularly with its individualist propensities, the question of property tends to be construed as a question of mine versus thine. Principles of property draw definitive lines between what distinct peoples may control and use to the exclusion of all others. Such an exclusivist understanding of property underlies the development of modern capitalism throughout its diverse stages, from its earliest (small market) phase to its more recent (transnational corporative) phase.

However, from a broader, more theological perspective, the question of property takes on an appreciably different tone. In the final analysis, whose world is it anyway? Who properly controls the direction and disposition of the world? Who should benefit from the world's resources and how they are employed? Who should bear the burdens when all cannot benefit? Should not all those whose destiny is at stake in the shaping of the future be enabled to participate in that shaping?

Within the Western theological tradition, the world belongs, ultimately, to God. The human community—or, more inclusively, it must nowadays be argued, the entire biotic community—has ownership of the world and its resources, but only on condition, namely, that they use the resources of the world to contribute to its qualitative advancement. The socialist vision can be construed as a means of instantiating this theological understanding in its social dimension.

That is, ownership of the means of production is contingent on whether those means are employed to contribute to the flourishing of the human community (if not the entire biosphere) and each of its members. Given this criterion, Karl Marx, witnessing the exploitative effects of modern capitalism, asserted that the distinguishing characteristic of socialism is, negatively, the abolition of private property. But, it should be noted, this negative characteristic—the abolition of private property—bears not so much on personal things (toothbrushes, books, bicycles, shoes, coffee cups) as it does on those means—technological and organizational—through which a community generates the goods and services that are foundational to the lives of its members.

The alternative to private property is common ownership. Common ownership of the means of production does not (necessarily) mean state possession, but it does mean public accountability (a question of control) and it entails concern for the public good (a question of use). In my judgment, the most effective and appropriate form of public accountability of the modern corporation that has been proposed in recent times is economic democracy: "an extension of the democratic process to economic enterprise."[4] That is, some form needs to be devised to empower all those who have a stake in a productive process (workers, consumers, neighborhoods, and others, including, if only through surrogates, nonhuman creatures) to participate in the formulation of policies governing that process—what is produced, how it is produced, where it is produced, by whom it is produced. That kind of empowerment or control constitutes one of the traditional dimensions of "ownership." In this sense, the participation of stakeholders in the process of economic policy formation should be understood not as an imposition but as a right, a property right.

Such a form of public accountability need not preclude some version of a market economy, especially given the virtues of a marketplace in bending production to the express needs and wants of people (in their limited role as consumers), in developing innovative and diverse products and services for use throughout the community, and in encouraging efficiencies and technical advances in the creation of the stuff of life. But, I would insist, the marketplace must be located within the embracing context of a democratic sensibility. Means must be devised to guard against concentrations of economic power, to assure widespread access to capital, to block forms of production and exchange that run contrary to principles of social justice, and to encourage those that might contribute to the enhancement of the community of life. The process of market exchange, by itself, is lacking in the possibility of that kind of deliberative intercommunication about the public good (or common good) that is, in principle at least, the governing concern of a public forum. What I am reaching for is a "third way" beyond a strictly command economy (as in state socialism) and a strictly market economy (whatever its mode, laissez faire or corporate). Call it, if you will, a relational economy.

Public accountability is, from a democratic socialist standpoint, directed by a criterion of the public good. Contrary to current practice, the productive process is properly measured not so much by how much is produced (a principle of the Gross National Product [GNP]) as by the impact of the productive process—what is produced and how its results are distributed—on the quality of life throughout the human community and the biosphere (a principle of the General Welfare). For this purpose, we need to develop at least a rough measure of General Welfare, more sophisticated and nuanced than the GNP, to ascertain the genuine health of an economic system.

That the socialist vision I have adumbrated in this sketch is "utopian," I would not deny. Yet, I would claim, it is not therefore unrealistic. On the contrary, its realism is grounded in its understanding of the prevailing conditions of life throughout the world, where corporate capitalism seems to run roughshod over human and ecological communities in the press for economic growth measured in the narrowest of terms. Moreover, its realism is located in its intended function, that is, to serve as a counterhegemonic force to the cultural mythologies that tend to suppress the kind of philosophical and social reflection that might enable us to change our forms of social consciousness and social practice in a manner more responsive to the needs of the twenty-first century. Socialism is not finished; although it is but a small voice in the public forum at the moment, it is yet a force to reckon with in the political struggle over our destiny.

Part III

Religious Commitment

I hate, I despise your feasts,
and I take no delight in your solemn assemblies....
But let justice roll down like waters,
and righteousness like an ever-flowing stream.
—*Amos 5:21, 24*

Like it or not, religion and politics are inextricably caught up with each other. We may, for good reason, support the conventional American slogan promoting the separation of church and state. But whatever principles and policies that slogan may represent—for example, that religious nonaffiliation (or affiliation) shall be no bar to public office—it is impossible to remove all traces of religious attitude from political interaction or, for that matter, all traces of political implication from religious practice.

If religious faith, as some would argue, betokens the most ultimate of our concerns, giving color to all that we feel and do, then if we would clarify the full character of our political interactions, we must uncover the religious qualities expressed in and through those interactions. Conversely, if politics constitute the manner in which and through which we give shape to our common life, then if we would understand all dimensions of our religious life, we must take cognizance of its political forms and the kind of political orientation it sustains.

However, while acknowledging that the religious and the political dimensions of our common life are intimately associated, we cannot assume that religious influences are always to be celebrated. We must, instead, admit to the profound moral ambiguity of religious community.

At their best, religious traditions give presentation to the deepest yearnings of the human spirit: peace (Islam), compassion (Buddhism), justice (Judaism), love (Christianity). From this angle, religious community sets before our ordinary life an aspiration in contrast to which our everyday associations are too often found wanting. At their worst, however, religious traditions have sparked a kind of crude passion and fervent fanaticism that have been destructive of those delicate lines of relationship that enable the community of life to flourish.

In the chapters that follow, I suggest that even as religious traditions provide resources for an understanding of and response to critical issues in our common life, so they themselves are susceptible to critique from the perspective of those principles of compassion and justice which must be honored in the ordinary routines of our life together if we take the politics of relationality seriously. Chapter 8 is addressed to the "history of suffering" in modern times, what it means and how religious traditions participate in that history. Chapter 9 unfolds the political presuppositions of a "thick" understanding of the theology of interreligious dialogue within the context of radical religious plurality. Chapter 10, delivered in its original version as a baccalaureate homily, seeks to demonstrate the moral implications of the kind of understanding (presumably) promoted by institutions of higher learning.

8

Religion as Critique and the Critique of Religion: The Problem of the Self in the Modern World

> What does the Lord require of you
> but to do justice and to love kindness,
> and to walk humbly with your God?
> —*Micah 6:8*

Circumstances of life at the present epoch in our history—with its globalized economy, world wars, new forms of colonialism and imperialism, subtle and not so subtle expressions of racism and sexism, advanced technology, widespread poverty—have given rise to a range of questions all of which, taken together, constitute the problem of the Self in the modern world: What is the fundamental condition and ultimate meaning of the Self under such circumstances? What is and what should be the shape of the Self's relationship to the Other? What is the destiny of the Self over the course of the future—short range and long range? This topic is of immense concern to religious traditions within which questions of the human condition and human destiny have always been, in some form or another, paramount.

Diverse procedures are possible as an entrée to that topic—of the problem of the Self and the response of religious traditions to the problem of the Self. I shall take as a clue to my approach a quotation from Aloysius Pieris, a Jesuit priest and director of the Tulana Research Center in Sri Lanka:

> I submit that the religious instinct be defined as a revolutionary urge, a psycho-social impulse, to generate a new humanity. It is none other than the piercing thrust of evolution in its self-conscious state, the human version of nature's thirst for higher forms of life.... This revolutionary upsurge can be sidetracked to regressive states of inertia. Revolution could turn reactionary, religion irreligious. But...it is

159

this revolutionary impulse that constitutes, and therefore defines, the
essence of *homo religiosus.*[1]

Pieris's main theme—that the religious instinct is a revolutionary
impulse to generate a new humanity—is daring and tendentious. I
would have us ponder that theme for a while and consider what its
implications might be.

In pondering that theme, I would have us begin with where we are,
denizens of the modern world—a world, it is claimed, in the throes of
radical transition, confronted with the question of the Self and society
as an issue of practical thought, or *phronesis,* in Aristotle's language. I
would have us begin with the question of the anguish of the Self and
the fate of the Self as an issue in social practice, but also as a proper
claim upon—and therefore an accusation against—religious communities. I shall begin, that is, with the matter of justice which is, as John
Rawls would have it, the first virtue of social institutions, for justice, in
its various permutations, addresses the problem of the Self, its circumstance and destiny. Moreover, justice is a force intrinsic to the religious
spirit in its multiple expressions and might, as a matter of internal critique, be turned back upon religious traditions as a mode of engaging
the entire discipline of *Religionsgeschichte.*

In this reflection, I set before you five propositions. First, the problem of the Self, revealed dramatically in moments of suffering, is a
problem of relationship. Self and Other, that is, are correlative terms.
Second, religious traditions are both resource and obstacle in responding to the problem of the Self. Third, justice names that quality of relationship through which the Self might flourish. Justice, in this
connection, is both a receiving and a giving. Fourth, justice is a perspective from which the vast religious plurality of the human world
might be susceptible to interpretation and evaluation. Fifth, in its
depths, justice, as I am rendering the term, is expressive of a communal
cosmology, which as such generates visions of a new social world in
which and through which the prospects of human flourishing might be
greatly enhanced.

*The problem of the Self, revealed dramatically in moments of suffering, is a
problem of relationship. Self and Other, that is, are correlative terms.* Suffering, construed as event of deprivation, presents the problem of the
Self with emblematic intensity. Lest we become too lost in abstraction, I
would present, at the start, an instance of suffering—an instance taken
from Albert Camus's *The Plague.* In that masterful novel, the bubonic

plague had overcome the town of Oran, a French port on the Algerian coast during the 1940s. Several persons were deeply engaged in struggling against the plague, including Rieux, an agnostic but compassionate physician, and Paneloux, an honest and deeply devout priest. At a key moment in the story, these two, with others, witness the long, excruciating death of an innocent child, despite the use of a newly developed serum to combat the disease.

> They had already seen children die... but... they had never had to witness over so long a period the death-throes of an innocent child. And just then the boy had a sudden spasm... and uttered a long, shrill wail.... From between the inflamed eyelids big tears welled up and trickled down the sunken, leaden-hued cheeks. When the spasm had passed, utterly exhausted... the child lay flat, racked on the tumbled bed, in a grotesque parody of crucifixion.... All were waiting. The child... seemed to grow calmer. His clawlike fingers were feebly plucking at the blanket over his knees, and suddenly he doubled up his limbs, bringing his thighs above his stomach.... For the first time he opened his eyes.... In the small face, rigid as a mask of grayish clay, slowly the lips parted and from them rose a long, incessant scream... filling the ward with a fierce, indignant protest, so little childish that it seemed like a collective voice issuing from all the sufferers there.... Paneloux gazed down at the small mouth... pouring out the angry death-cry that has sounded through the ages of mankind. He sank on his knees, and all present found it natural to hear him say in a voice hoarse but clearly audible across that nameless, never-ending wail: "My God, spare this child!"... And now the doctor grew aware that the child's wail... had fluttered into silence.... The fight... was over.... The end had come.... His mouth still gaping, but silent now, the child was lying among the tumbled blankets, a small, shrunken form, with the tears still wet on his cheeks.[2]

In the presence of the agonizing death of a child, who can fail to be moved? But what, in Camus's rendition, does it signify? What did Camus intend to convey through this story, particularly, through this scene? To some critics, Camus has captured the perennial character of the human condition. Death and suffering constitute our lot, whether or not deserved, and that is a reality causing us to pose difficult, if not impossible, questions, including, in Western religious traditions, the question of theodicy. To other critics, Camus's story is an allegory of the vicious spread of Nazi fascism throughout Europe and into North Africa, a social pathology whose degenerative consequences threatened the utter decimation of whole populations.

I have appropriated the story to symbolize what Johann Baptist Metz calls the "history of suffering"—especially in its exquisitely modern (perhaps I should say its postmodern) form, that is, in a time during which we have presumed to take historical destiny into our own hands. The irony of the modern age is located precisely in that presumption. We took hold of history through our technology and our associations in order to reduce suffering and to enhance human life, but, instead, in Metz's formulation, "Unhappiness and depravation, misery and evil, oppression and suffering have remained and intensified and increased to planetary proportions."[3]

The history of suffering is not the result merely of so-called natural evil, although that is a factor not to be ignored. The history of suffering is perhaps now more than in prior epochs attributable to the quality of relations between Self and Other, even where it may seem to be the result of natural causes.

That is a thesis that underlies Richard Rubenstein's grim study of the modern age as an "age of triage." Triage, in medical usage, means the allocation of treatment in times of disaster to optimize the number of survivors. As such, its purpose seems most laudable. But its reverse side means the consignment of some persons to sure and certain death. Triage, in its socio-political application, means the implementation of policies whose impact, more or less deliberately intended, is to assure the elimination of whole populations, albeit ostensibly for good reason. To some, triage may seem to be a necessity for survival. But to others, triage is another word for genocide.

The prime case of genocide in the twentieth century is the Nazi holocaust, the results of a deliberate policy to exterminate the Jewish people (as well as, we might add, Gypsies and homosexuals). The sheer horror of the event has brought us to treat it as an aberration. But, Rubenstein argues, it is not unique; it does not stand alone; it is not sui generis. It is part of a pattern initiated long before and continued since. In a sense, it epitomizes a central theme of modern history.

In the instance of Great Britain, often considered among the most civilized of nations, Rubenstein demonstrates how the enclosure movement of the sixteenth and seventeenth centuries, the poor laws of the eighteenth and nineteenth centuries, the emigration policies and the Irish famine of the nineteenth century can be compellingly interpreted as moves, designed and enforced by governmental policy, to dispose of unwanted populations. In the twentieth century, similar cases are evident: the Armenian massacre by the Turkish government, Stalin's treatment of peasants and diverse ethnic and religious groups, and, subsequently, practices of the Cambodian and Vietnamese governments. But Rubenstein does not spare the United States government from his critique: if one pursues the social consequences of recent policies respecting matters of welfare, employment, taxation, and education—all promoted as if necessitated by economic constraints—one is driven to conclude that they constitute at least a modified form of triage. Taken altogether, they are productive of a massive underclass within the social system, an underclass of marginalized peoples entrapped in a condition of psychic hopelessness and physical suffering.

The age of triage, Rubenstein asserts, was made possible by the triumph of instrumental rationality in the modern world. Instrumental rationality enhanced humankind's powers of knowing and doing. It infused all disciplines of investigation and it promoted new methods and means of production and organization. It introduced a utilitarian calculus of means and ends and it advanced efficiency as a paramount norm in social practice. But it also enabled policymakers to consider the human Self as simply another resource or liability to be weighed in the balance.

Conjoined with social Darwinism and possessive individualism, instrumental rationality forms, for classes in positions of power and privilege, all the delineaments of a "viable religion," the kind of deep-seated faith that undergirds and sustains the lived experience of the everyday world of the elite:

> it provides an overarching structure of meaning in terms of which a group's experiences and values can be comprehended. It enables its adherents to believe that their social location, way of life, and fundamental values are cosmically grounded.... In a time of acute socioeconomic crisis, ... [it] could provide decision-makers with the legitimating ideology for political decisions that would spell disaster to millions of their fellow citizens.[4]

In Rubenstein's judgment, to counter the policies and practices of the age of triage, supported as they are by the deep religiousness of modernity, we stand in the need, ultimately, of a religious transformation. We are in need of an inclusive structure of meaning in which no person can be considered surplus, in which the fate of our neighbors is more than a prudential calculus, in which relations between Self and Other are governed by considerations of decency and concern. Under current world conditions, such a religious transformation must be informed by a new, encompassing vision:

> it must be an inclusive vision appropriate to a global civilization in which Moses and Mohammed, Christ, Buddha, and Confucius all play a role. We can no longer rest content with a humanity divided into the working and the workless, the saved and the damned, the Occident and the Orient. Our fates are too deeply intertwined.... In truth, we must be born again as men and women blessed with the capacity to care for each other here and now.[5]

The capacity to care for each other: that single phrase encapsulates the quality of the Self-Other relation, which Rubenstein sets over against the age of triage and which constitutes the centerpiece of a postmodern social vision and the foundations of a social policy in which the alleviation of human suffering would be the first order of business.

Yet that phrase—the capacity to care for each other—may be too simple. Tzvetan Todorov, in his powerful study of the "conquest of America"—which he constructs as a paradigm for the modern era—asserts that the relation of Self to the Other consists of several dimensions. He distinguishes three. First, an axiological level: one may love or hate the other; one may find the other good or evil; that's an evaluative question in Todorov's lexicon. Second, a praxeological level: one may treat the Other as identical with the Self, as inferior or superior to the Self, or one may be indifferent to the Other; that's an actional question. Third, an epistemic level: one may know and understand the Other in varying degrees of detail or intimacy; that's a cognitive question.[6]

As Todorov presents the case, distinguishing the varying attributes of the *conquistadores* in their relations to native Americans, these levels are not necessarily correlative. One may, in some sense, love but lack detailed knowledge about the Other. Conversely, one may possess an intricate and intimate understanding of the Other, but not love. What, then, might we envision as an appropriate relation between Self and Other? Perhaps this: One loves the Other. One knows and understands the Other. But one also accepts and supports the Otherness of the Other and engages in that kind of interaction in which both Self and Other find themselves enhanced by the relationship. If that is what caring means, then the capacity to care for each other is the most crucial component of a social policy that takes the history of suffering seriously and of a religiousness that is worthy of our commitment.

Religious traditions are both a resource and an obstacle in responding to the problem of the Self. Throughout history, religious traditions have been subjected to critique—as an inhibition to creativity, a falsification of reality, an agent of injustice. The critique ought not to be ignored, for it contains, in its various forms, significant insight into the peculiar risks of religious commitment. Whether religious commitment and the practices it engenders do in fact represent, in Pieris's terms, "a revolutionary urge to generate a new humanity" is a question that needs pondering.

Friedrich Nietzsche, for instance, in his brief treatise on *The Anti-Christ*, subjects Christianity to an intensive and insightful critique as diametrically opposed to the conditions of vitality and genuine happiness: "Christianity has taken the side of everything weak, base, ill-constituted, it has made an ideal out of *opposition* to the preservative instincts of strong life." In contrast, he avers, "I consider life itself instinct for growth, for continuance, for accumulation of forces, for *power*: where the will to power is lacking there is decline. My assertion is that this will is *lacking* in all the supreme values of mankind—that values of decline, *nihilistic* values hold sway under the holiest of names."[7] This contrast is connected with Nietzsche's famed doctrine of the *Ubermensch*—the genius who stands out above the mass and whose life gives witness to the will to power.

Whatever our judgment about the *Ubermensch*—it has often been linked with the National Socialists' doctrine of the Superrace—we should not forget Paul Tillich's transmutation of the will to power into the power of being. Without the power of being, the power, that is, of creative self-expression, the Self is nothing. Can we deny that religious traditions have, in many times and places, stifled creative self-expression, crushing the human spirit in the name of the divine?

Consider, secondly, Sigmund Freud's critique of religion, concentrated on its illusory foundations. Religious understandings, he argues, are "fulfillments of the oldest, strongest, and most urgent wishes of mankind." Such wish-fulfillment explains the strength and durability of religious faith. In Freud's construction, the subjection of the Self to divine powers is a repetition of the child's deep dependency on the father:

> As we already know, the terrifying impression of helplessness in childhood aroused the need for protection—for protection through

love—which was provided by the father; and the recognition that this helplessness lasts throughout life made it necessary to cling to the existence of a father, but this time a more powerful one. Thus the benevolent rule of a divine Providence allays our fear of the dangers of life; the establishment of a moral world-order ensures the fulfillment of the demands of justice, which have so often remained unfulfilled in human civilization; and the prolongation of earthly existence in a future life provides the local and temporal framework in which these wish-fulfillments shall take place.[8]

These are, Freud admits, honorable concerns. But, given these concerns, better to respect the reality principle, to confront the tragic limitations of life for what they are, and to take on the tasks of civilized life courageously and deliberatively than to assume through faith that some heavenly agent controls all details of the universe to our ultimate benefit. Can we deny that the psychodynamics underlying religious motivation ofttimes detract the faithful from direct confrontation with the problem of the Self?

Consider, thirdly, Karl Marx's critique of religion as a construct of consciousness, emerging out of the concrete realities of historical existence. To understand the meaning of religious doctrine and practice, we must uncover the social struggles and class antagonisms out of which they arise. Religion, in this sense, is ideological in its most basic character. In each of its particular institutional manifestations, it serves to reinforce some position or other in those struggles and antagonisms.

As such, religion may be an expression of false consciousness, constructing an imaginary world, thereby concealing the actual dynamics and contradictions of historical life. Yet it may also be a force productive of change. Religion may function therefore in diverse ways: legitimating the intention of the powerful to perpetuate their position of privilege, responding to the prayers of the sorrowful to find solace in their pain, but also, in some cases, such as primitive Christianity and the Left Wing of the Reformation, motivating the yearning of the dispossessed to press for revolutionary action. But in any case, religious sentiments, while products of the imagination, are never wholly out of touch with the actual conditions of life, however much they may cloak them in supernatural terms. Thus Marx writes:

> *Religious* suffering is at the same time an *expression* of real suffering and a *protest* against real suffering. Religion is the sigh of the oppressed creature, the sentiment of a heartless world, and the soul of

soulless conditions. It is the *opium* of the people. The abolition of religion as the *illusory* happiness of men, is a demand for their *real* happiness.[9]

Can we deny that the mythologies and rituals of religious traditions are susceptible to the hermeneutics of suspicion, that, if we would penetrate their full meaning and significance, we must uncover their interaction with the social tensions that constitute their historical context, that they may, despite their elegance and grand promise, function to sustain structures of oppression?

In short, Nietzsche, Freud, and Marx—each out of his own framework of interpretation—presents a compelling critique of religion from the standpoint of the problem of the Self. But there is another side to the equation.

A few years ago, Robert Ackerman proposed that the discipline of philosophy of religion turn away from its traditional textual and analytic approach to religious thought in order to investigate instead "religion as critique." "Religions," he noted, "have arisen as legitimate protests against societies and ways of life, providing in the process the overpowering foundations for laying down one's life to improve the lot of humanity."[10] By juxtaposing an ideal world to an actual society, a religion breaks the bonds of cultural hegemony. It is a resource for distancing oneself from inherited routines. It enables one to look afresh at the institutional and historical context of one's life and to hold it up to critical scrutiny. It is a source of dissonance and, through its vision, it furnishes the makings of social reconstruction.

Ackerman does not claim that religion is nothing but social critique, but he does insist that religion is a constant source of critique. Moreover, he asserts that a religion without critical edge "is already dead."[11] A living and vibrant religion gives rise again and again to the "power of disruption."[12] As such, religion, in Ackerman's rendition, "is a source of pictures of how the world ought to be, pictures that can be repeatedly reinterpreted to evaluate new and even unexpected social patterns. The longevity of religion is related to its continuing ability to adapt its highest level pictures to new situations and to new forms of critique."[13] The Judaic concept of the covenant is an instance of this dynamic. The covenantal relationship is, in Ackerman's judgment, "sheer religious genius": the constant personal relationship between God and the people signified by the covenant is a source of continuing critique not only of other societies, but of Judaic social practice as well.

Now, we might ask, is there any point of convergence between the critique of religion and, on the other hand, religion serving in its function as social critique? Are these two modalities of religious understanding at any juncture isomorphic? I believe they are. The point at which these movements converge is where each addresses the problem of the Self, the history of suffering, the question of that quality of association in which and through which Self and Other in their linkage with each other both flourish because of their interaction. In this respect, the point of convergence acknowledges the ambivalence of the religious enterprise, but directs our attention and our energies in a common direction toward an envisioned future, a future, I would suggest, in which justice prevails throughout the human community—if not the entire community of life.

This point of convergence is keenly illuminated in the reflexive dialectics of the feminist movement. Carol Christ and Judith Plaskow, for instance, affirm at one and the same time that "religion is deeply meaningful in human life" and that "the traditional religions of the West have betrayed women."[14] Thus from the perspective of women's experience, an extensive internal critique and reconstruction of religious tradition has been initiated to purge the tradition of its sexism and all the suffering sexism entails in its violation of the selfhood of women. But it pursues this reconstructive work in a manner that sustains the deepest insights and resources of the tradition itself.

Riffat Hassan, for instance, is unremitting in her critique of Islamic societies in which Muslim women, presumably on grounds of Islamic authority, "have been kept for centuries in physical, mental, and emotional bondage and deprived of opportunities to see themselves as fully human."[15] Hassan, a Muslim originally from Pakistan, declares that the women's revolution is, in Muslim countries, "a terrifying reality that threatens to shake the world of Islam from within."[16] But the foundation of Hassan's critique is the most sacred text of Islam, the *Quran*. Through close textual and linguist analysis, she demonstrates how verse after verse of the *Quran* has been mistranslated and misinterpreted to favor the oppression of women. Where traditionalists find male hierarchy, she demonstrates a principle of reciprocity. Where traditionalists affirm inequality, she discovers equality. Where conservatives find authority for opposing family planning, Hassan asserts that "in this day and age there can be no doubt that a woman who has no control over her own body or who is compelled by social and religious pressures to play the part of a reproductive machine becomes less than a fully autonomous human being."[17] Over against the long-standing practices of Muslim societies, she affirms "the basic intent of the *Quranic* statements of women's status as autonomous human being capable of being righteous as an act of choice."[18] Aware of a long history of oppression, Muslim women are asking for their rights—"rights given to them not by an Islamic government but by Allah."[19]

Justice names that quality of relationship through which the Self might flourish. Justice, in this connection, is both a receiving and a giving. I have adopted as a theme Pieris's proposition that the religious instinct is a revolutionary impulse to generate a new humanity. I have suggested that we begin by acknowledging our complicity in a modern world confronted with the problem of the Self as an issue in practical thought, with the question of the anguish of the Self and the fate of the Self as an issue in social practice. I have incorporated Rubenstein's thesis that the modern age is an age of triage in which whole classes of persons, considered redundant and superfluous, are either exterminated summarily or condemned by political and economic policy to live in conditions of crushing deprivation if not premature death. But I have also quoted, with approval, Rubenstein's challenge: "In truth, we must be born again as men and women blessed with the capacity to care for each other here and now."[20]

The problem of the Self on the plane of social practice consists of two dimensions: the struggle against suffering and the possibility of human flourishing, or, in other words, the struggle against ill-being and the formation of structures of well-being. In this connection, Marjorie Hewitt Suchocki points to a paradox present in social practice and religious traditions, namely, ill-being is ofttimes ordained and sanctioned as well-being. Poverty and misery, for example, are deemed acceptable, perhaps not as good in themselves, but good instrumentally as a means to some higher end—for instance, the long-range welfare of the social order as a whole or the ultimate salvation of the human soul. But the convoluted argument entailed in such a paradoxical identification she finds repugnant, at least as it pertains to marginalized and deprived peoples:

> The ill-being of women, blacks, and others outside the dominant cultural value system has been called well-being within a posited system of order. Irony rather paradox might be a more appropriate name for such twists, and I, a feminist, cannot in any way consider these views as functions for dealing salvifically with social situations not easily

changed. Rather, using justice as an internal basis for criticism, I name such practices evil, and call for their reform.[21]

I share Marjorie Suchocki's sentiment. The critique of justice names such practices evil and calls for their reform. But we must be cautious at this point. The meaning of justice is a highly contestable issue. In traditional phrasing, justice is rendered: to give to each one's due. That tells us something, albeit of a formal character. Justice, as such, embraces both a giving and a receiving. It is a correlation between a duty and a right, an obligation and an expectation. In its full meaning, justice specifies a structure of reciprocity. It is therefore a relational term. In its multiple forms and levels, justice designates the proper structure of relations between persons and groups. It represents a quality that should permeate our several social practices through which we are linked with each other and our interactions are canalized. It is both distributive and aggregative. It intends a certain distribution of the powers and privileges, goods and services that flow through a social system. And it intends the coalescence of the lives and energies of persons into structures of collaboration and cooperation.

As giving to each one's due, justice is properly understood as a dominant if not the paramount virtue of social institutions. But such an understanding of justice is highly generalized. It states what justice is about, but it does not specify what justice is. It portrays what counts for justice, but it does not define what substantive conception of justice might suffice to give body and soul to notions of ill-being and well-being. The controversies—philosophical and political—that rage over plausible meanings of justice are focused at that precise point. They are contests over substantive conceptions of that social virtue.

Contestants within these controversies are many and diverse. At the risk of oversimplification, I shall cite three types. As representing conceptions of justice, each comprehends both a negation and an affirmation. That is, these types differ in both what they are against (some idea of ill-being) and what they aspire to (some idea of well-being).

To libertarians, for instance, the central quality of justice is the freedom of the individual. The coercive hegemony of social practices frustrating the wishes and desires of the individual constitutes the evil to be conquered. Individuals should be free to think as they will, to act at they desire, to use their property as they determine. The fewer the constraints on self-determination and free choice, the better.

To egalitarians, in contrast, the primary trait of justice is equality in the distribution of the benefits of social life, including political power and economic goods. The unequal allocation of fundamental social resources among classes and groups within a social system is the primary cause of suffering and misery. Individuals should not be deprived of equality of opportunity because of social policies and cultural expectations. If political and legal constraints are required to assure the equal distribution of opportunity, then such constraints are legitimate and acceptable.

To communitarians, the driving purpose of justice is the construction of forms of mutuality. The dominant social problem is the prevalence of structures of alienation, that is, institutions within which persons are entrapped in patterns of activity that contradict their own good. The practice of slavery is a classic example; patterns of sexist and ethnic degradation are no less illustrative. Justice, as the antithesis of alienation, is located where all persons are fully fledged participants in the creative give-and-take of systems of intercommunication. In this case, a fundamental goodness is present in the process of creative interchange itself, for it is in that process that the lives of all are enriched.

Are these understandings of the substantive meaning of justice irreconcilable? Perhaps. Certainly proponents of these understandings are at loggerheads over a wide range of fundamental social policies—from taxation to welfare, from corporate governance to affirmative action.

Yet, at one level at least, there is something that seems compelling about all three perspectives. Each of the three, I would urge, gives voice to a significant dimension of the experience of the Self and thus bears some relevance to the problem of the Self.

Individuality is one dominant feature of the experience of the Self. The Self is unique, *sui generis*, has a character and a history different from all others. There is an inevitable solitariness that attends our experience, a solitariness that sometimes takes the form of loneliness. But our solitariness is also an opportunity, even a challenge, to shape our life's energies within whatever context is bequeathed us in a manner that contributes to the common adventure of history. Each of us is, to some degree, a creative agent even in those moments when we are subjected to unyielding constraints.

Comparability is a second feature of the experience of the Self. That is, as we evaluate ourselves in comparison with others, while acknowledging certain kinds of relative superiority and inferiority in talent and ability or in function and task, we have a deep sense of equal dignity. At some profound level, we experience ourselves as, in principle, no worse though no better, than others. This aspect of our experience is invoked in our demand for equality of respect and universal human rights.

Solidarity is a third feature of the experience of the Self. Our lives are caught up in webs of interrelatedness. We live out of a common history and we live in association. We are engaged in forms of shared existence from which we cannot in any full and complete way extricate ourselves. We are social beings whose lives and identities are caught up with each other.

Individuality, comparability, and solidarity are all essential features of our experience of ourselves as Selves. If justice is to give to each one's due, then justice requires that all these features be honored and respected in our several associations and social practices. The history of suffering is the history of injustice. It is the denial of our individuality, the rejection of our comparability, the distortion of our solidarity. It is, in short, the violation of the Self.

But we must be cautious at this point. Among others, those schooled in *Religionsgeschichte* would remind us of the radical differences in the identity of the Self expressed in the various cultures of humankind. Even within a single cultural history, variations abound. The Jain doctrine of jiva, the Vedantist theory of Brahman-Atman, the Buddhist principle of anatta—although all are strains within the cultural history of South Asia—seem at odds with each other in their interpretations of the condition and destiny of the human Self. Pluralism in religious and philosophical understanding and pluralism in cultural ethos and social practice are indisputable features of our common life however much we may lament the fact. Yet, I would contend, pluralism does not necessarily undercut the principle of justice I have adumbrated. On the contrary, that principle of justice, acknowledging such pluralism, would honor it, encourage it, and support it, as expressive of the very features of the Self that give justice its substance.

Justice is a perspective from which the vast religious plurality of the human world might be susceptible to interpretation and evaluation. Twenty-five years ago, Alan Race developed a useful, albeit controversial, typology of approaches by Christian theologians to the presence of divergent religious traditions within the community of humankind.[22] From its beginnings, the Christian community has encountered alternative forms of faith, but the question of how properly to take account of religious diversity has become an increasingly critical issue in modern times. Each faith lays claim, in some fashion or other, to the truth and wisdom of its professed way of life and manner of thought. But, as our knowledge of divergent religious traditions has become more sophisticated, we—whether Christian, Jewish, or whatever—become more keenly aware of the radicality of the differences and the seeming impossibility of rendering these traditions wholly compatible with each other. We are therefore forced to confront the question of relationship: What is the proper way to understand and to interpret how these divergent traditions stand in comparison with each other?

Race constructs three alternative ways Christian theologians have responded to that question: exclusivism, inclusivism, and pluralism. *Exclusivism,* in its most rigorous Christian form, declares that Christianity is the sole repository of truth. From that perspective, other forms of faith, however attractive, are grounded in error. There is but one valid faith and one way to human fulfillment, and that is located in the apostolic tradition. *Inclusivism* at least appears on the surface more appreciative of alternative religious communities. It declares that each tradition has merit, each tradition bears some truth and conveys some wisdom through its rituals and doctrines. But each is, in the final analysis, deficient. The fullness of truth is borne only in the Christian witness. There may be "anonymous" or "hidden" Christians among other traditions, even among professed atheists, but, while lacking the explicit name, they are measured by the meaning of Christian dogma.

Pluralism, the third approach Race distinguishes, is more nearly relativistic in its embrace of difference. But it often assumes that underlying all forms of faith is a common ultimate reality, although the apprehension each faith has of that reality is limited and partial. The pluralist, acknowledging the historicity of religious cultures, the deeply conditioned character of the language and practice of religious tradition, is characteristically tolerant in the face of incompatibilities and patient in the presence of religious argument and conflict.

The debate among these three parties, at least as Race has constructed it, is concentrated on a single basic question: the question of truth in religious belief and religious practice. At that point, of course, we encounter all the confusions and contentions that occupy much of contemporary philosophical and theological discourse over the meaning of language and the status of religious doctrine, all of which bear on the sense in which we can (or cannot) affirm any declaration or expostulation "true." The question of truth, we must admit, is of eminent importance, however it is cast, especially if the truth (or claims to truth) pertain to our destiny.

But in that connection—to take a turn that is congenial at least to some strains in that discourse—might it not be instructive to shift our focus of attention for a time from long-standing questions of dogmatic divergency to immediate questions of pragmatic urgency (granting that these sets of questions are, in important ways, tangled up with each other)? Might it not be wise to turn, for the moment, from the seeming abstractions of pure doctrine to those pressing issues of practical reason so vividly present in our lived experience? Should we not take up, as our first order of business in encountering religious plurality, the question of the anguish of the Self and the fate of the Self in the modern world? Should we not consider the history of suffering as our preeminent priority as we proceed in our interpretations and evaluations of all forms of faith, including our own?

Once again, I would invoke an insight from Marjorie Suchocki. Liberation theologians, she notes, are keenly aware of "the invidious effects that follow when one mode of humanity is made normative for others." That dynamic applies to relations between men and women, whites and blacks, First World and Third World. It applies as well to relations among the religions. She is led thereby to promote a radical form of religious pluralism (that is, the respectful acknowledgment and acceptance of deep-seated religious diversity) but, significantly, permeated and governed by the principle of justice:

> universalizing one religion such that it is taken as the norm whereby all other religions are judged and valued leads to oppression, and hence falls short of the norm that liberationists consider ultimate— the normative justice that creates well-being in the world community. A feminist perspective, therefore, suggests that one must radically affirm religious pluralism, but not without bringing a critical consciousness of well-being in human community to interreligious and intrareligious discussion. Justice is thus to be the fundamental criterion of value and the focus of dialogue and action among religions.[23]

Suchocki is not unaware of the seeming inconsistency of her proposal. She resists the old imperialism of religious claims—that imperialism "leads to oppression." But she then, it seems, promotes a new imperialism. She calls it justice, the mandate to create "well-being in the world community." But whose conception of well-being, whose vision of social order, whose justice is the "fundamental criterion of value" by which religious traditions are to be assessed?

Suchocki's response is complex. First, she insists that, in the investigation of the religions of humankind, one might find some degree of unanimity on "the value of freedom from suffering."[24] But, in any case, "there is a certain intransigence to the norm" of justice "when it comes to fundamental aspects of human existence, such as peaceful access to food, water, health, shelter, work, and community."[25] Second, she proposes that, as an implication of the meaning of justice, "the primary visions within each religion of what societal life should be in a 'perfect' world is [sic] a source of judgment that can be used internally within each religion to judge its present societal forms of justice."[26] Third, she suggests that proponents of the world's religions have an obligation to engage in common discourse about their several understandings of ill-being and well-being with the intention of concerted action, where feasible, toward the transformation of oppressive social structures. In that very process, she notes, the several understandings of religious traditions might be modified and transformed. Fourth, she asserts that justice in its attentiveness to the historicity of the human condition, is itself supportive and protective of cultural and therefore religious diversity.

Paul Knitter, as well, has proposed that the question of justice take precedence in the interpretation of religious plurality and the conduct of interreligious discourse. Taking his cue from theologies of liberation, he adopts three concepts for this purpose: a hermeneutics of suspicion, a preferential option for the poor, and a soteriocentric criterion of judgment.

First, a hermeneutics of suspicion. Proponents of religious traditions, especially those in privileged positions, must be constantly reminded that religious practice has often been employed to cloak and to promote class interests. "All too often the truth that we propose as 'God's will' or as divinely revealed is really our own disguised, subconscious will to maintain the status quo or to protect our own control of the situation or our own cultural-economic superiority."[27] Under the broad mandate of justice, a hermeneutics of suspicion requires a rigorous and meticulous form of self-critique within every given religious community.

Second, a preferential option for the poor. Knitter asserts that a preferential option for the poor—"that is, the option to work with and for the victims of this world"—is or should be the driving purpose of interreligious discourse.[28] Knitter is aware of potential resistance to, as well as the potential fruitfulness of, such a starting point.

> *If* (a big if!) followers of various traditions could agree to a shared commitment to confronting the cross-cultural and cross-religious crises of our age, if they could share a "preferential option" for suffering humanity and suffering earth, they would have a common starting point or context on the basis of which they could, possibly, construct together some always shaky common ground of mutual understanding and cooperation. In such a soteriocentric (rather than theocentric) model for discourse, norms for discerning truth and value are derived from the shared but always relatively grasped ideal of humanity's and the earth's *well-being*. What that well-being requires can be known only in the dialogue.[29]

Third, a soteriocentric criterion of mutual judgment. In contrast to the methodological principle of strict neutrality, Knitter proposes that proponents of diverse religious traditions not shy from evaluative judgments of each other. Yet, to avoid the pitfalls of utter arbitrariness and ideological abuse, such judgments must be directed to specific doctrines and practices (not to the tradition as a whole). They must be governed by the intention to do justice in the world (not to advance the hegemony of one's own faith over the other). And they must be receptive to countercritique (not presented as unassailable dogma). The driving aim of such judgments is collaboration in addressing the history of suffering, particularly as that history is bodied forth in the crises of the modern world. Their common concern must be the advancement—ultimately the fulfillment—of the community of life.

In its depths, justice, as I am rendering the term, is expressive of a communal or relational cosmology which as such generates visions of a new social order in which and through which the prospects of human flourishing might be greatly enhanced. I have suggested that liberty, equality, and community are three of the defining touchstones of justice. Justice, as the disposition to give to each one's due, mandates the incorporation of the qualities of individuality, comparability, and solidarity in our common life. The violation of justice is the human cause of suffering. The sustenance of justice is the human cause of life's flourishing. Justice is therefore a cardinal virtue of social institutions and a requisite in the advancement of life. Justice, I have declared, is the proper response to the anguish of the Self in the modern world. Understood as such, justice finds historical rootage in religious tradition, but may also, in a reflexive turn, be employed as a fulcrum of judgment upon religious practice. While justice construed in this manner does not and cannot provide sure and certain solutions to all the detailed issues of our social existence, it does, at least, give warrant to our profound sense of malaise about conditions of modern life and it does give inspiration and direction to our constructive energies. It sets out an agenda whose extent and urgency betrays the perversities of contemporary civilization: sexism and racism, neocolonialism and poverty, militarism and the threat of nuclear annihilation, the extinction of innumerable species and the prospects of massive degradation of the biosphere. All these items bear witness to the problem of the Self—the fate of the Self—in the modern age.

Yet, let us admit that these pronouncements about justice, however much they may appeal to the deliberations of our practical reason, are, in some other portion of our minds, troubling. We may yearn for some foundation on which to respond to the history of suffering. We may crave some assured ground on which to understand the meaning and from which to advance the growth of the Self. But is there such a ground? Or must we, in our maturity and our sophistication, acknowledge the absence of any firm standing place? Have we not become so imbued with historical consciousness and, as a consequence, so aware of the relativity of our several perspectives on life that we are properly wary of any effort to secure a benchmark for judgment, theoretical or practical? In one way or another, this issue, dubbed the issue of foundationalism, pervades virtually all contemporary disciplines of the mind—philosophy of science and ethics, *Religionsgeschichte* and literary analysis.

In response to this issue, I would invoke the effort of Richard Bernstein to discover a way "beyond objectivism and relativism," that is, to determine whether there is an alternative method in the formation of judgments beyond the dogmatisms and certainties of the objectivist tradition and the buzzing, blooming confusions of relativism. Bernstein construes objectivism as "the basic conviction that there is or must be some permanent, ahistorical matrix or framework to which we can ultimately appeal in determining the nature of rationality, knowledge, truth, reality, goodness, or rightness." The job of the theorist is to uncover that foundation without which we would be at a loss in our thinking and in our doing. Relativism, on the other hand, Bernstein

defines as "the basic conviction that when we turn to...those concepts...taken to be the most fundamental—whether...rationality,
truth, reality, right, the good, or norms—we are forced to recognize...all such concepts...as relative to a specific conceptual scheme,
theoretical framework, paradigm, form of life, society, or culture." To
the relativist, there is a nonreducible plurality of such references. There
are no overarching standards of judgment among the possibilities. Fundamental forms of life are radically incommensurable.[30]

We confront, Bernstein declares, a dilemma. Given the acknowledged idiosyncrasies of relations between Self and world, objectivism
is passé. However, given the urgencies of the crises at hand, relativism
seems unacceptable. Is there a third way? Bernstein argues that there
is. He discovers its emergence among a range of contemporary social
critics. In a word, it is a dialogic alternative. The language of dialogue, communication, solidarity, community is indicative of a move
beyond the classical principle of objectivity and the modern turn
toward a principle of subjectivity to a new possibility: a principle of
intersubjectivity.

Within the dialectic of intersubjectivity—when and where it is
unobstructed and undistorted (an all too rare moment under modern
conditions)—divergence of perspective is deeply respected, but only so
long as it sustains and enriches the dialectic. In principle at least, relativity is there conjoined with continuity. Such an understanding of
rationality as dialogic is not without its import in social practice. The
social counterpart of dialogic rationality is that kind of energetic
democracy depicted by Hanna Pitkin and Sara Shumer:

> Democratic politics is an encounter among people with differing
> interests, perspectives, and opinions—an encounter in which they
> reconsider and mutually revise opinions and interests, both individ-
> ual and common. It happens always in a context of conflict, imperfect
> knowledge, and uncertainty, but where community action is neces-
> sary. The resolutions achieved are always more or less temporary,
> subject to reconsideration, and rarely unanimous. What matters is
> not unanimity but discourse. The substantive common interest is
> only discovered or created in democratic political struggle, and it
> remains contested as much as shared. Far from being inimical to
> democracy, conflict—handled in democratic ways, with openness
> and persuasion—is what makes democracy work, what makes for the
> mutual revision of opinions and interest.[31]

The dialectic of intersubjectivity together with its political corollary, energetic democracy, is contingent, I suspect, on an often unspoken premise, a premise we must lift to the surface and ponder, namely, that with all our differences and through all our conflicts, we belong together. We can speak with each other, even engage in deathly struggles with each other, because we are connected with each other. The Self, even in its solitariness, is always, as Caroline Whitbeck puts it in her feminist ontology, "a relational and historical being": "the realization of the self can be achieved only in and through relationships and practices."[32] The premise, however, must be extended to surmount its anthropocentric limitations. We are members not only of a sociosphere, but of a vast biosphere in whose intricate lines of interdependency we are thoroughly engaged, however little we comprehend of that engagement.

I am claiming, in short, that the dialectic of intersubjectivity, extended to include its connotations about the meaning of the Self as relational and the cosmos as communal, provides a grounding for the principle of justice. The dialectic of intersubjectivity and the principle of justice are congruent in their concern for the quality of relationships and therefore the forms of our associations with each other.

Justice betokens a style of life whose theme is Self-in-Community and whose driving purpose is two-sided. Its purpose, negatively, is to shatter structures of oppression and domination, to reform patterns of indifference and insensitivity. But its purpose, in the long haul, is to construct the conditions whereby the genius of each individual and each culture (including each religious community) might enrich the lives of all others; it is to encourage new forms of creative intercommunication. Under the circumstances of modern history, that is no mean task. But, I would declare, that is the mandate of practical reason.

And, if I would be faithful to my opening quotation from Aloysius Pieris, that is the implication of the religious instinct. Recall Pieris's primary proposition: "I submit that the religious instinct be defined as a revolutionary urge, a psycho-social impulse, to generate a new humanity."[33] I am reminded of Alfred North Whitehead's maxim: "Religion is world loyalty." In its context, that maxim affirms at one and the same time the value of the individual for itself and the value of the objective world in its dynamic interconnections with the individual: "The moment of religious consciousness starts from self-valuation, but it broadens into the concept of the world as a realm of adjusted values, mutually intensifying or mutually destructive."[34]

9

Crossing the Boundaries: Interreligious Dialogue and the Political Question

> The stranger who sojourns with you
> shall be as the native among you,
> and you shall love him as yourself.
> —*Leviticus 19:34*

During recent decades, the topic of a theology of religions has occupied an increasingly significant place on the agenda of Christian theologians. Discussions about the topic have concentrated, by and large, on the question of truth. Exclusivists declare, for instance, that, among all the world's religions, Christianity alone is true. Inclusivists argue that other religions are bearers of some degree of truth, but in Christianity they find their culmination. Pluralists insist that all religious communities, each in its own way, bear witness to the same ultimate truth. And, as one can imagine, there are many variations on these themes, even efforts to develop new alternatives.[1]

But the question of truth may be approached at various levels and from various angles, including that of the political question. Indeed, the political question is of crucial importance at this particular historical moment. The political question—which cannot, in the final analysis, be divorced from the question of truth—provides a potentially fruitful angle on the issue of relations among the religious communities of the world—Christian and Native American, Islamic and Jewish, Hindu and Sikh. The political question, most simply put, is, How shall we live our lives together?

The political question is crucial at the moment because we live in a world riven with deep antagonisms—ethnic and racial, sexual and religious, cultural and class. Perhaps such antagonisms will be with us always. But perhaps not. The shape of the future depends on how we think and what we do in the present. However, in the commitment to overcome these antagonisms, we are properly reminded not to seek

sheer uniformity in our respective ways of life and religious understandings, but instead to be respectful of the otherness of the Other. In
short, the celebration and encouragement of the otherness of the Other
should be among our paramount aims in the struggle to overcome the
antagonisms that set us over against each other and that threaten to
devastate us all.[2]

In this connection, the idea of interreligious dialogue—one of the
dominant ideas in current discussions of the theology of religions—is
intriguing. It provides, I believe, a significant response to the political
question, but a response laden with far-reaching implications, theoretical and practical. Current movements inspired by the idea of interreligious dialogue—for example, among Christians and Buddhists,
Muslims and Jews—can be viewed as a kind of struggle against divisive antagonisms which incorporates at one and the same time a deep
concern for the otherness of the Other and yet a conviction that religious communities—however much at odds they appear to be in their
respective understandings of the world—have an interest in creating
lines of communication with each other about their respective patterns
of thought and forms of practice.

The idea of interreligious dialogue, I would stress, is much more
than merely a device to bring members of various religious communities into discussion with each other. That is a thin version of the
idea. In its thick version, the idea of interreligious dialogue bears its
own philosophical understanding and displays its own implications
for the broader political life of humankind.[3] Taken seriously, it forces
us to broaden the circle of theological discourse in dramatic ways and
to become open to new possibilities and new mandates in our thinking about and living in the world. Moreover, it constitutes, at least in
principle, a model for a more extensive dialogue we must initiate
among all kinds of communities across the globe. As such it is a
prospective historical ideal, yet deeply rooted in the historical realities of the present time.

At its center, the thick version of the idea of interreligious dialogue
is, in a sense, deeply ironical. It begins with an affirmation of radical religious pluralism and incorporates, as it governing principle, respect for
the otherness of the Other. It celebrates difference. Yet it also begins with
an affirmation of connectedness (otherwise dialogue would be an utter
impossibility) and it proceeds with an expectation that, through the dialogic process, each participant will be, to some degree, transformed.
That is, it acknowledges that each religious community—Christian and

Muslim, Jewish and Confucian—is significantly different from all others. Each religious community has its own history, displays its own unique character, has its own perspective on the shape of the world. But it also assumes that religious communities, in some sense, belong together and, for the sake of the common good, should enter into collaborative discourse with each other. Moreover it assumes that religious communities are permeable and susceptible to creative transformation through their encounters with each other. In short, while they live in different worlds, they nonetheless live in the same world. Or, alternatively, while they live in different histories, they live in the same history—and the future remains yet to be determined. The political question is, How, given that irony of identity, shall they live together?

The irony that inheres in the idea of interreligious dialogue is no different, perhaps, from the irony that constantly attends our personal and social lives. On a personal level, though each of us exists as a unique and solitary individual, yet our lives are inextricably linked together and the character of that linkage has a massive effect on the quality of our individual lives, even as the individual's identity has an effect on that linkage. On a social level, though each community—racial, ethnic, cultural—has its own mythos and praxis, yet all communities are participants in a more inclusive community, ultimately, the entire ecosphere. The idea of interreligious dialogue betokens an understanding of our human condition that moves beyond any simple universalism (according to which we are all, essentially, the same) and any simple historicism (according to which we are all, culturally, different).

In what follows, I intend to pursue this line of thought, outlining the political meaning of the idea of interreligious dialogue in its thick sense as a means of reflecting about the theology of religions it signifies and about its broader implications for our living together.

THE DIALOGIC IMPERATIVE

> If to be human is to live in community...
> then to alienate ourselves from community,
> in monologue, is to cut ourselves off
> from our own humanity.[4]

A dialogue, summarily defined, is a form of relationship in which each participant enters into the life of the other through a process of interaction, as a result of which, even when that process entails hard-headed confrontation and opposition, the lives of all are enriched.[5] Not all conversations or collaborations are dialogues in this sense, but a dialogic relationship is always a possibility whenever any person or group, religious or otherwise, encounters another. In the sheer absence of that kind of relationship, our lives would be radically impoverished. On this point, feminist theology has reminded us repeatedly of the web of connectedness that constitutes the necessary matrix of our subjectivity.[6] From the time of birth to the time of death, the richness of our lives is contingent on the depth and extent of the dialogic interactions in which we have been engaged.

I suspect this is why David Lochhead, from a Christian perspective, declares that interreligious dialogue is an imperative. It is an implication of the command to love one's neighbor, but it is also a law of our most basic character as humans. Hence his affirmation: "If to be human is to live in community... then to alienate ourselves from community, in 'monologue,' is to cut ourselves off from our own humanity."[7] Interreligious dialogue to Lochhead is but a special instance of the more inclusive mandate of love, namely, to engage in dialogue with all the world, in short, to engage in a "cosmic dialogue."

Leonard Swidler presents more immediately historical reasons—institutional and cultural—for promoting the idea of interreligious dialogue. As a result of a host of modern institutional developments, technological and economic, we now live in an intricately interdependent world in which hostility and violence have become rampant. If for no other reason, then at least, "for the sake of survival, meeting in dialogue and cooperation is the only alternative to global disaster." As a counterpoint to these institutional developments, Swidler notes a gradual but dramatic shift in our prevailing form of consciousness in the West from the individualism and separatism of classical liberalism to a worldview in which mutuality and relationality are constitutive features of the cosmos and of ourselves, who we are and how we ought to act.[8] The idea of interreligious dialogue, in its contemporary form, emerges from these historical conditions—as a pragmatic response to threats to the human future and as an expression of the growing consciousness of mutuality as central to the character of reality. Given this context, Swidler calls religious communities to move across the boundaries that separate them from each other and to enter into a dialogic process lest they become historically irrelevant in their isolation and parochialism.

In John Cobb's judgment, the idea of interreligious dialogue, in a sense, points beyond itself. That is, its purpose is not merely to exchange views. Rather its aim is mutual transformation, or, as he elsewhere terms it, "creative transformation."[9] The sensibilities and feelings, thoughts, and understandings of those engaged in the dialogic process are inevitably qualified at least in some measure through the interaction. On a general level, the range of what they can know and appreciate is expanded; their ability to empathize with peoples across barriers of estrangement, even hostility, is increased; their capacity to integrate into their own individuality a vast diversity of experiences and alternative visions is enhanced; their power to absorb the effects of sundry conditions of life is deepened.[10] On a particular level, Christians and Buddhists, Muslims and Hindus—should they proceed to unfold their respective histories and practices to each other—may find illuminating points of contrast and complementarity, drawing each to deeper respect for and understanding of the other and thereby moving toward a more adequate comprehension of the complexities of human possibility and a more profound sense of responsibility for the future of the world.

Such a procedure entails, as Cobb renders it, drawing on the work of John Dunne, a "passing over" and a "coming back." In John Dunne's phrasing, "Passing over is a shifting of standpoint, a going over to the standpoint of another culture, another way of life, another religion. It is followed by an equal and opposite process we might call 'coming back,' coming back with new insight to one's own culture, one's own way of life, one's own religion."[11] In this two-way process of passing over and coming back, interreligious dialogue does not assume that all religious communities are directed to the same ultimate reality. Nor does it assume the desirability of full and complete consensus. But it does assume that that process constitutes a mutually enriching way of living together and, at least as Raimundo Panikkar renders it, a way of responding in concert to forces threatening the future of the world.

Panikkar repeatedly insists that the peoples of the world are divided from each other by a radical pluralism. Religiously and culturally, we encounter fundamentally incommensurable systems of thought and forms of action. Our languages and our practices, our perceptions and our expectations are qualitatively different. That difference is a function of our historical embeddedness. Nonetheless Panikkar stands in agreement with Lochhead and Cobb that a mutually enriching dialogic intercommunication is not impossible provided each community attains a mature apprehension of its own tradition and is genuinely open "to be fecundated by the insights of the other."[12] Panikkar then adds another proviso, that all religious communities must be infused, at this moment in the world's history, with a certain attitude of trust—a "trust that sustains a common struggle for an ever better shaping of reality."[13] Religious communities "can no longer live in isolation, let alone in animosity and war."[14] The contemporary political and ecological situation of the world requires a radical reconsideration of the place of humanity in the cosmos which will only be possible if the diverse traditions of the world collaborate, each bringing to that collaboration its own unique and peculiar insights. The purpose of the collaboration is concord—which Panikkar defines as "neither oneness nor plurality. It is the dynamism of the Many toward the One without ceasing to be different and without becoming one, and without reaching a higher synthesis."[15]

Cobb agrees with Panikkar on the need for various communities—religious and otherwise—to collaborate in response to the most urgent problems confronting our common life. That, at this moment in our history, is a vital dimension of interreligious dialogue. But if that collaboration is to be thoroughly honest and tough-minded, then a strategy of critical deconstruction must accompany efforts at political reconstruction. The value of deconstruction is its effectiveness in exposing the oppressive mystifications of our doctrines and languages and the distortions of our practices and institutions both inside and outside religious communities:

> Feminists especially have used deconstructive techniques to show how pervasive are patriarchal motifs in our languages, and how language both furthers and masks the universal oppression of women. To a lesser extent deep ecologists have shown how pervasive in our language is anthropocentrism and how this has obscured the degradation of the biosphere.... The deconstruction of inherited assumptions may help also to expose and overcome the deep-seated homophobia that engenders so much suffering in a large segment of humanity. The urgency of such deconstruction can hardly be exaggerated.[16]

The strategy of deconstruction means that, even as communities engaged in interreligious dialogue must be open to learn from each other, they must, precisely because of that, be open to critical question by each other. The idea of interreligious dialogue at this point incorporates an ethics of discourse that stands in judgment against all forms of distortion and hegemony in communication.

The reverse side of critical deconstruction is political reconstruction, that is, the transformation of our common life governed by the minimal, but not inconsiderable, concern that "we leave to our descendents a habitable planet in which society can so structure itself as to make life at least tolerable for most of its members."[17] On a more maximal level, I shall suggest later on, the reconstructive effort entailed in the idea of interreligious dialogue should be aimed at a common life infused with practices of nonviolence and social justice. In moving toward the consensus required for reconstructive work, the participants to the dialogue across religious communities must "acknowledge that their own positions do not exhaust truth and reality, that they can be corrected and enriched by hearing what others have learned . . . [and that] each enters the encounter with the other ready in principle to revise what one brings."[18] Underlying the deconstructive and reconstructive moves in interreligious dialogue is the supposition that, at some level of sensibilities, we are aware of a "shared destiny" that "is important for all of us."[19]

At this point, the ironical character of the idea of interreligious dialogue is clearly evident. We enter the dialogic process out of respect for the otherness of the Other. But that very respect for the otherness of the Other forces us to acknowledge our shared destiny. We belong together. Moreover, if we would honor the uniqueness of each religious community, we must engage in a critical judgment on all religious communities, including our own, as a stage in the reconstruction of our life together. That, perhaps, is the same irony that attends Iris Marion Young's "politics of difference." The first stage of a politics of difference, Young notes, is the liberation of oppressed groups—in the case of the United States, "women, Blacks, Chicanos, Puerto Ricans and other Spanish-speaking Americans, American Indians, Jews, lesbians, gay men, Arabs, Asians, old people, working class people, and the physically and mentally disabled," each group with its own history, experiences, and perceptions.[20] But the driving purpose of a politics of difference is the empowerment of each group in its distinctiveness to participate in the public forum in which all groups belong together as coparticipants in our common life. That is the meaning of social justice in a politics of difference. The idea of interreligious dialogue, I propose, has a similar import in its response to the political question.

THE NECESSITY OF NONVIOLENCE

> A pragmatics of nonviolence
> opens a horizon of encounter... thereby
> transforming the violence of exclusion
> into a solidarity from which speech may arise.[21]

A dialogue, I have asserted, is a form of relationship in which participants enter each other's lives through a process of interaction, as a result of which, even where that process entails confrontation and conflict, the lives of all are enhanced. Recently, David Krieger, posing the question of whether and how interreligious dialogue across the globe is possible, has argued that nonviolence is among its pragmatic conditions.[22] Violence may occasion the arising of dialogue, but, in itself, it contradicts the impulse and intent of dialogue. Where violence is exclusionary, nonviolence is inclusive. Where violence is destructive of the Other, nonviolence displays respect for the Other. Where violence silences, nonviolence opens the possibility for listening and speaking. Nonviolence, as Krieger presents the case, is an integral part of the political meaning of the idea of interreligious dialogue.

The concept of nonviolence is often used merely to designate devices of conflict resolution or techniques of social change that eschew resort to physical violence—for example, negotiations, demonstrations, peaceful forms of civil disobedience. That use of the concept of nonviolence may derive from a superficial reading of some of the more notable cases of its practice in this century—Mohandas K. Gandhi's struggle for national independence in India and Martin Luther King, Jr.'s campaign against legalized racial segregation in the United States. That narrow understanding of nonviolence, however, does not do justice to its full meaning even in those cases. More broadly understood, nonviolence is a substantive response to the political question. It is a form of living together. In particular, it is a way of encountering the otherness of the Other by which, even in moments of aggression and opposition, an effort is made to sustain the fundamental integrity of all parties, yet through which, at least in intention, each party is drawn to an appreciative awareness of the Other, opening up the prospect of a new mode of symbiotic relationship. This more inclusive meaning of nonviolence is what is implied by the idea of interreligious dialogue.

Nonviolence, in Krieger's judgment, creates the possibility of honoring radical pluralism, but moving toward a "new universalism." In that dynamic, nonviolence replicates the ironical character of the idea of interreligious dialogue. Krieger agrees with Panikkar, Cobb, Young, and others that radical pluralism is a central feature of contemporary life—a feature that constitutes both a threat and a promise as we confront the political question. Radical pluralism, he writes, is "a matter of different worldviews, that is, different ways of thinking and ways of life which are constituted by their own criteria of meaning, truth, and reality, and which, therefore claim absolute validity."[23] Each cultural complex, each religious community, each body politic, each social class, each racial grouping tends to create its own world and to interpret and assess all others from that perspective. We are fragmented into multiple circles of meaning, not all of which are compatible, but, at the same time, we are aware of that fragmentation and of its threats to our common life. The threats are all too evident: indifference to the suffering of others, the construction of protective walls of separation between communities, the denigration and exploitation of outsiders, outbreaks of aggressive violence against others to the point of annihilation.

In response to the threats engendered by conditions of radical pluralism, Krieger promotes a "new universalism," but a universalism that incorporates respect for the otherness of the Other. For that purpose, he argues that we need to develop a new kind of discourse, a "discourse of disclosure," which forces us to break through the boundaries of ordinary discourse. In our ordinary communities, religious and otherwise, we have been, by and large, trained in how to speak and how to act. We know what the rules and expectations are. We know how to cope in cases of emergency and how to adjudicate differences in cases of conflict. The Christian community is not different in this respect from any other. The faithful participate in the holy sacraments without a second thought or, if some issue should arise, procedures are generally available to settle them. On occasion, controversies may erupt over the encompassing rules and expectations of a community. That is, the "boundaries" of the community are called into question and the community, through some means, must deliberately determine its basic character and distinctiveness anew. In the Christian community, for instance, discourse about the boundaries may involve the reinterpretation of basic dogmas or the reformulation of its sacraments and rituals.

As long as religious and cultural communities remain relatively isolated from each other, everyday discourse and boundary discourse may suffice for the common life of those communities. But these two kinds of discourse are deficient in circumstances where radically different communities encounter each other. At those moments, according to Krieger, a new kind of discourse, a discourse of disclosure, must be formulated, enabling us to speak across and beyond the boundaries. "Dis-closure," in Krieger's usage, means to open the boundaries. It is the antithesis of closure. It requires revealing oneself to the Other and receptivity to influence from the Other. It entails, at least for the time of the encounter, moving beyond the rules and expectations of the everyday, even stepping outside the procedures through which boundaries may be reinforced or redefined. But, at the same time, the discourse of disclosure does not mean that communities must bracket or suppress their identity. On the contrary, they bring to the dialogue their respective histories and narratives, their basic understandings and practices.

Violence is antithetical to the discourse of disclosure because where the intention of the latter is to create a forum for difference, the intention of former is to subdue difference. The primary form of violence is "the exclusion and suppression of the 'other,' who threatens our lifeworld with total transformation."[24] Where the discourse of disclosure welcomes alternative forms of logic and reasoning, violence stands opposed to "other rationality." Violence, as Robert McAfee Brown reminds us, assumes many guises.[25] Some are more overt, as in cases of assault and war, police brutality and government-sponsored terrorism. Others are more covert, as in cases of institutionalized racism and traditional patterns of sexism as well as in patterns of economic deprivation and religious imperialism. But in all its manifestations, violence, perhaps never wholly absent in our relationships with each other, is the denial of the otherness of the Other. In contrast, the drive of nonviolence is toward the transformation of all practices of violence, overt or covert, out of respect for the Other.

Young's politics of difference, especially her depiction of the ideal city, is indicative of the political significance of the discourse of disclosure: "In public life [group] differences remain unassimilated, but each participating group acknowledges and is open to listening to the others. The public is heterogeneous, plural, and playful, a place where people witness and appreciate diverse cultural expressions that they do not share and do not fully understand."[26] Analogously, Krieger argues that, in circumstances of confrontation and conflict, nonviolent action presses, in its final intention, not so much merely to negotiate a compromise among opposing parties, as to create an open space—"a space of difference, of dis-continuity, of dis-closure"[27]—in which they may move toward an understanding of each other to the point of a mutual transformation of mind. As such, nonviolent action, as Joan Bondurant interprets Gandhi's doctrine, is both a method of inquiry and a means of enlarging rationality.[28] That is, nonviolent action entails the admission that each community is historically embedded and therefore limited in its perspective on reality, but that, through creative conflict with the Other, its understanding can be refined and its perspective expanded.

The irony of the idea of interreligious dialogue is nicely reflected in the pragmatics of nonviolence, for the pragmatics of nonviolence is premised on two seemingly countervailing insights: our radical pluralism and our ultimate connectedness.[29] Where communities clash, the techniques of nonviolence constitute means of conflict resolution which, by intention, honor both our differences and our unity. As such, the pragmatics of nonviolence, as a response to the political question, conjoins the means and ends of our common life. In Bondurant's phrasing, nonviolence "proceeds as a means which assumes the proportion of an end in itself."[30] That is, the principle of nonviolence is an implicate of the dialogical imperative. However visionary—some would say unrealistic—nonviolence as a form of life may appear under prevailing historical circumstances, it is no less necessary if the full meaning of the idea of interreligious dialogue is to be taken seriously both in itself and in its broader political meaning.

THE CRITERION OF JUSTICE

> Justice is . . . to be the fundamental
> criterion of value and the focus of
> dialogue and action among religions.[31]

Marjorie Hewitt Suchocki, approaching the idea of interreligious dialogue from a feminist-liberationist perspective, draws a compelling parallel between religious imperialism and sexism. Both practices entail the hegemony of one community over another, resulting in the degradation of the latter and a distorted understanding of both. In the case of sexism, "The consequence of the absolutized masculine norm is oppression of women in all areas of life: public and private, social and spiritual."[32] In the case of religious imperialism, the consequence is much the same as evidenced in the original impact of the Christian community on native Americans, to cite but one example. Both cases violate the otherness of the Other. Both cases are denials of difference. Both cases militate against "the mutuality necessary for full dialogue."[33]

In contrast to religious imperialism, Suchocki would have us "radically affirm religious pluralism," thereby honoring the uniqueness and, perhaps, in some sense, the validity of all religious communities. At the same time, she insists on "bringing a critical consciousness of well-being in human community to interreligious and intrareligious discussion"—a critical consciousness whose central principle is justice.[34] The ironical character of the idea of interreligious dialogue is clearly discernible at this juncture in Suchocki's position. To avoid imperialism, we must affirm pluralism; yet pluralism finds its limits in a principle of justice which "knows no boundaries":

> The ultimate test of justice is precisely the degree to which it knows no boundaries to well-being. A justice which establishes well-being within the context of its own community and ignores the well-being of those outside that community is to that degree unjust. Likewise, a community that establishes its own well-being through exploitation of the well-being of those outside the community is to that degree unjust. A supposition underlying this statement is that the world is a network of interrelationship and interdependence.[35]

Suchocki is cognizant of the uneasy tension that resides between her repudiation of religious imperialism and her promotion of a principle of justice that "knows no boundaries." Why, she asks, is not the latter mandate simply a new form of imperialism? She seeks to resolve this tension in various ways, for example, by diversifying the demands of justice, with the exception of its most elementary drive for sheer physical well-being. In this move, I suggest, she blunts the more incisive critique social justice levels against the prevailing conditions of our moment of history: its critique of oppression. In this context, I would distinguish between social justice as a distributive concept (whose most basic concern is to provide means of sustenance) and social justice as a structural concept (whose immediate concern is with the liberation of oppressed peoples).

On this point, Paul Knitter, invoking the dynamics of liberation theology, takes a somewhat bolder step than Suchocki by asserting that, given the current condition of the world, "both basic humanitarian concerns as well as the soteriologies of most religions would seem to dictate that a preferential option for the poor and the nonperson constitutes both the necessity and the primary purpose of interreligious dialogue." Preferential option for the nonperson—that is the central theme pervading liberation theology in all its forms. It is liberation theology's version of respect for the otherness of the Other, but pointed more precisely at those peoples who have been subordinated, cast aside, subjected to humiliation, if not annihilation. Whatever other interests sustain interreligious dialogue, its preeminent concern, to Knitter, is "to work for justice," that is, to participate in the struggle of "removing the oppression that contaminates our globe."[36] Social justice in this sense means more than a redistribution of resources to assure the physical well-being of all peoples; it embraces as well an empowerment of peoples, a reconstruction of our systems of living together to give as full effect to the principle of mutuality as is possible.

While social injustice includes a skewed distribution of economic goods and social power, it is more amply construed as a matter of oppression. Young distinguishes five "faces of oppression": exploitation, marginalization, powerlessness, cultural imperialism, violence. In all its forms, some classes or groups of persons suffer from deprivation because of systemic institutional conditions. They are deprived from learning and using cultural skills in conventional social settings. They are inhibited from communicating their understandings and perspectives in contexts where others might listen. They are lacking in the power and opportunity to participate effectively in working to shape the social circumstance of their lives. Oppression is not always intentional, but it is sustained wherever some communities are privileged and others deprived.[37]

By its very character, oppression is antithetical to dialogue. It is antithetical to those kinds of interactions contributory to human flourishing. It is antithetical to the meaning of love. Conversely, social justice is a requisite of dialogue and therefore integral to the idea of interreligious dialogue. Where injustice disables and denigrates, justice enables and empowers. Where injustice deprives and constrains, justice esteems and encourages. Where injustice nullifies and destroys, justice enlivens and regenerates. In the utter absence of justice, dialogic interaction is impossible.

Knitter, like Suchocki, Panniker, Cobb, and Krieger, is sensitive to the radical differences in mythos and praxis that exist among religious communities. But, at the same time, he affirms that all religious communities now reside in a common context—in a "global situation consisting of concerns and questions that transcend differences of culture and religion and so touch all persons."[38] Permeating the differences that distinguish us in our several forms of faith are dimensions of experience that call for a collaborative response, namely, the massive suffering of populations throughout the world and, correlatively, a deep yearning for liberation and social reconstruction on the part of the nonperson. That situation—our common context—creates both the historical possibility and the moral necessity of an interreligious dialogue in which social justice is the highest, though not the only, priority.

Knitter proposes three related considerations for the shaping of interreligious dialogue to assure its responsiveness to the oppressive realities of contemporary history.[39] First, *a hermeneutics of suspicion.* It is by now a truism that communities of all kinds, out of an impulse to justify themselves, are deceptive, even self-deceptive. However elegant their self-identities, they are blind to their blemishes. They sometimes simply overlook, but sometimes deliberately conceal, their perpetuation of oppressive practices. Aloysius Pieris has demonstrated, for instance, how, throughout modern history, Christianity—sometimes through its linkage with movements of colonialism and neocolonialism, at other times through its pietistic tendencies—has served in the creation and reinforcement of structures of poverty and dependency throughout the Third World.[40] A hermeneutics of suspicion is an exercise in critique—both of self and others. It is liberation theology's version of Cobb's strategy of deconstruction. It presses beyond explicit statement to structural reality in its drive for honesty.

Second is *the perspective of the victim.* If social justice is a fundamental criterion of value in interreligious dialogue, as Suchocki and Knitter declare, then the outsiders, the victims of this world must have voice in that dialogue. Without incorporating the perspective of the victim, interreligious dialogue is deficient in assuring "the full right to speak and the genuine ability to hear."[41] Moreover, as Knitter affirms, "Without a commitment to and with the oppressed, our knowledge is deficient—our knowledge of self, others, the Ultimate. This is not to imply that we can know the truth only in such a commitment but, rather, that without this option for the poor, the truth that we may know is, at best, incomplete, deficient, dangerous."[42]

Third is *a praxis of liberation*. As noted above, according to Cobb, the idea of interreligious dialogue, in a sense, points beyond itself. That is, it is more than an exchange of beliefs and ideas. It has a transformative intent. Knitter would extend that transformative intent to embrace the common context of the dialogue and to be directed toward the liberation of the oppressed. On this point, he would link the praxis of dialogue with the praxis of liberation:

> The criteria—what elements contribute to authentic, full liberation—can be known only in the actual praxis of struggling to overcome suffering and oppression, and only in the praxis of dialogue. What are the causes of suffering, of oppression? How best to eliminate them? What kind of socio-cultural analysis is needed? What kind of personal transformation or alteration of consciousness is required? The preferential option for the poor does not provide prefabricated answers to such questions. And yet the starting point for struggling, together, toward answers is given in the fundamental option for and commitment to the oppressed.[43]

Notwithstanding Knitter's commitment to social justice as a central feature of a liberationist theology of religions, he is not unaware of the ironical character of that commitment. Like Suchocki, he is wary of religious imperialism—in itself, a form of social injustice—which that commitment seems to entail. So while he asserts that "concern for liberation and for the promotion of human welfare in this world constitutes...a *soteriocentric core* within the history of religions," and that "all religious soteriologies begin by identifying a...broken state of human affairs which they then try to repair"[44] he is forced to admit that around this core, "there grows a stubborn, prolific plurality—a plurality that contains not only variety but contradiction." That plurality demands that we "embrace a Hindu and Buddhist perspective that is less concerned with disarmament than with nonappropriation, nonpossession...or that is less concerned with social transformation than with *karman* (selfless action) and *yajna* (sacrificial action) by which the cosmic order is constituted."[45] Given that irony, he is led to propose that the agenda of liberation theology at least constitute a starting point for interreligious dialogue: "we will be able to dialogue all the more fruitfully if all the partners can share—as share they *must*, it would seem—a common conversion to human and planetary welfare—to removing the sufferings of our fellows and of our Mother Earth. Such a conversion, and the depth of experience that it contains, will be our starting point."[46]

THE FEMINIST PARADIGM

> [T]he human oppressed, regardless of age, class,
> race, ethnicity, or creed, are peopled predominantly
> by women against whom violence is directed
> specifically because they are female human beings.[47]

To this point, I have presented mutuality, nonviolence, and social justice as qualities integral to the political meaning of the idea of interreligious dialogue in its thick sense. Mutuality is the most encompassing of the qualities, incorporating nonviolence and social justice as dimensions of its full meaning. Feminist theology, as I have suggested at various points, celebrates this same set of qualities. Indeed, I am led to assert that feminist theology, in some of its strains, constitutes a paradigmatic case of the idea of interreligious dialogue, particularly as feminist theology, cutting across the boundaries of traditional religious communities—Christian and Islamic, Buddhist and Native American, Hindu and Jewish—and drawing on the experience of women from diverse cultures, projects a postpatriarchal political model.

Feminist theologians are drawn together from diverse religious communities by a common experience and a common cause. The common experience of women embraces two dimensions in tension with each other. In its negative dimension, the common experience has been that of oppression. While feminist theologians differ in many respects, they are joined in their opposition to patriarchy as the general form of women's oppression. Patriarchy is hierarchical and androcentric.[48] As hierarchical, patriarchy means domination: a more powerful class controls a less powerful class (in this case male over female). As androcentric, patriarchy means that a woman's identity and power are secondary to and derivative from a male-dominated social system. She is confined to predetermined roles which are allocated strictly according to gender, and expected to conform to culturally transmitted models of what womanhood means.

Yet, the common experience giving rise to feminist theology has an affirmative dimension as well, a dimension that stands over against the distortions and constrictions of patriarchy and that is a source of strength and vision. As Beverly Harrison has asserted, there are qualities of women's experience that are to be cherished as more authentic and informative about the character of all our lives than the mystifications of a patriarchal ideology. The most important of these qualities is relationality:

> To speak of the primacy of relationship in feminist experience...is, above all, to insist on the deep, total sociality of all things. All things cohere in each other. Nothing living is self-contained.... The ecologists have reminded us of what nurturers always know—that we are part of a web of life so intricate as to be beyond our comprehension. Our life is part of a vast cosmic web.[49]

The moral implication of relationality, as Harrison and other feminist theologians develop it, is solidarity, reciprocity, mutuality, a form of interrelationship that enriches the lives of all its participants. This cluster of moral qualities—solidarity, reciprocity, mutuality—indicates the common cause of feminist theology and points toward a postpatriarchal age.

> A post-patriarchal age is one in which women and men find possibilities for the fullness of life, not through rule over one another, but rather through freedom and mutuality, trust and ecstasy. The mutuality at issue is not between people alone, but between people and other creatures, between people and the earth. It is the fullness of *all* life—not human life alone, much less male life alone—toward which so many rightly aspire.[50]

The vision of a postpatriarchal age characterized by mutuality is daring in its critical and reconstructive implications. These implications have been explored by feminist theologians from a wide variety of religious communities, Western and Eastern, oftentimes working in concert across the traditional boundaries that distinguish them.[51] That collaboration is an instructive case in the practice of interreligious dialogue both in itself and in its broader political significance.

Maura O'Neill, who draws on feminist thought specifically to refine the idea of interreligious dialogue, issues a warning, however, to be cautious in the struggle against oppression and in the adoption of mutuality as a common cause lest we, in effect, slip into a new form of Western imperialism, glossing over the historical particularity of women's experience in different cultural and religious communities. What may, for instance, appear oppressive from the perspective of Western feminists, may not be experienced as oppressive from the perspective of women in other cultures. O'Neill cites, as specific instances, practices of purdah and polygamy.[52]

At the same time, without ignoring wide variations in women's experiences of oppression throughout the world, O'Neill adduces evidence to support the claim that the feminist experience is, in some sense, universal. Feminism, she writes, "can be seen as emerging everywhere. Women all over the globe are demonstrating a growing determination to be actors who participate in shaping society rather than remaining victims. There *is* such a thing as global feminism."[53] The exact experience of oppression and the precise shape of the yearning for liberation may be culturally specific. Yet, to O'Neill, permeating all these differences, which are to be respected in their concreteness, women are becoming increasingly determined throughout cultures all over the world to speak for themselves, naming that which is experienced as oppressive to them in their particular communities, and to participate, as full agents, in "the struggle for justice and liberation in all those areas of life that encompass women's concern."[54] In that sense, feminism is a universal movement.

As she develops more fully the philosophical dimensions of her idea of interreligious dialogue from a feminist perspective, O'Neill proposes an interactional understanding of the self and a conversational view of epistemology which, in her judgment, are more fitting for the mutuality necessary for dialogue than the androcentrism she finds among several proponents of that process.[55] Given an interactional understanding of the self, our identities—as male or female, or, for that matter, as Christian or Buddhist—are not fixed. They are in a process of continuous formation and reformation, their quality contingent on the range and depth of our interactions with others. Given a conversational view of epistemology, which O'Neill presents as an alternative to naive forms of objectivism and relativism, we must be constantly open to the insights and perspectives of others—whatever their gender, race, or religious background—in our efforts at understanding. And, in matters pertaining to our social condition, as Knitter would remind us, we must be particularly mindful of the voice of the oppressed.

The concept of mutuality is a key point of convergence between feminist theology and the idea of interreligious dialogue in its thick sense. It is because of that convergence that I have suggested feminist theology as a paradigmatic case of the idea of interreligious dialogue. Mutuality, at least as intended in this context, embraces the irony of both feminism and the idea of interreligious dialogue by embodying both respect for the otherness of the Other and an affirmation of our connectedness with each other. In that conjunction resides the political meaning of the idea of interreligious dialogue.

In sum, the idea of interreligious dialogue is rich in its implications, both theoretical and practical. That the idea has emerged at this moment in our history is, I suspect, no accident. It is responsive to the agonies and antagonisms of our times. It is, perhaps, indicative of a yearning for a new axial age[56] in which our radical differences—religious and political—will no longer constitute an excuse for destructive conflict and genocidal fury, but become a creative resource for the enhancement of all our lives. There is no assurance, alas, that that yearning will be realized. Yet, I submit, that yearning bespeaks a manner of responding to the political question and a direction for constructive work in the theology of religions that is worthy of our commitment.

10

Interlude: Wisdom and Compassion— The Deeper Dimensions of Understanding

> Go down, Moses,
> Way down in Egypt land.
> Tell old Pharaoh,
> To let my people go.

This chorus from a powerful African American spiritual conjures up from our memories two images of history past.

Out of ancient times, these words signify a narrative of singular importance in the self-understanding of Judaism, a narrative of suffering and liberation, a narrative through which God is portrayed as an advocate of the oppressed. God calls Moses to return to Egypt to secure the release of an enslaved people and to direct them, out of deep concern for justice, to establish themselves as a new people in a new land with a new lease on life. This is a story retold again and again in the Jewish community, indicating who they have been, who they are now, and how they are to live toward the future.

Given the character of that story, we should not wonder that African Americans, during the centuries of their enslavement in this land of ours, found in it insight and inspiration. They, too, were a people oppressed; they, too, were a people full of sorrow; they, too, yearned for a time of release. Through their songs and poetry, through their heart's desire and most vivid dreams they called upon the divine power to act on their behalf, to serve as an agent of their liberation, to establish a kingdom of justice: "All o' God's children got shoes."

These images of history past, I suggest, are, in their ultimate reach and intention, more than just that. They constitute a statement about times present and a possibility for times future. They provide a means of reflecting about the shape of our self-identity and the form of our interaction with the world. They indicate a revealing perspective on the whole of human history, a perspective, if I may be so bold, that is

201

implied whenever we earnestly and sincerely seek understanding—which I like to think is the primary mission of all education—which, at least ostensibly, we honor so highly, but whose deeper dimensions we too often neglect.

To cast this perspective in brief compass: Wisdom is the culmination of understanding. Compassion is the direct expression of wisdom. Justice is the impulse of compassion. Or, in alternative phrasing, if we would understand the world, we must understand the world's suffering, and in understanding the world's suffering, we are driven to respond in compassion and justice.

The virtue of wisdom is an old-fashioned concept, expressed with some embarrassment nowadays, for what, after all, is wisdom? Even if we had some intimation of the meaning of wisdom, who, we wonder, would claim to be wise? Perhaps, if I may put the matter this way, there is some wisdom in our uncertainties and doubts about wisdom!

Yet, in a sense, we all claim to be wise at least implicitly. We all claim to be wise by virtue of our efforts, however halting and however limited, to embody our understanding in and through the course of life's activities—professional and personal. We all claim, at least implicitly, to be wise by the manner in which we shape and reshape the forms of our interactions with others. In this assertion about our implicit claim to wisdom, I am taking a hint from Alfred North Whitehead. In a well-known lecture on education, he observed:

> Though knowledge is one chief aim of intellectual education, there is another ingredient, vaguer but greater, and more dominating in its importance. The ancients called it "wisdom."... Now wisdom is the way in which knowledge is held. It concerns the handling of knowledge, its selection for the determination of relevant issues, its employment to add value to our immediate experience.[1]

That final phrase is instructive: wisdom concerns the employment of understanding "to add value to our immediate experience." To be sure, that phrase may be construed too narrowly, as dictating a criterion of instantaneous utility—even more stringently, of instantaneous economic utility—of all our courses of study and all our principles and theories: "Cash value"—that's what really counts!

But, in keeping with the spirit of Whitehead, that phrase—"to add value to our immediate experience"—should instead be construed in a more extensive manner. Understanding, if it be genuine understanding, is driven by the intention of qualitative attainment, by a deep concern for goodness and beauty, by a yearning for the enhancement of life, by the moral necessity to assess how every specific action bears on the world's future. Our immediate experience, you see, embraces a profundity, a depth of which we are ordinarily only dimly aware. Through all that flows in and through us—biologically and culturally, physically and socially—the world constitutes our matrix. But, in turn, what we say and what we do, how we feel and how we act makes a difference in the coming of every tomorrow.

The point of understanding is to become more keenly appreciative of the depth of immediate experience. We cannot understand ourselves unless we understand the world. And, I would suggest, we cannot understand the world unless we understand the world's suffering.

The world's suffering—that concept is, alas, too abstract. I mean the malnourished child, the war-ravaged village, the jobless worker, the political prisoner. I mean the raped woman, the disenfranchised refugee, the persecuted believer. I mean the mentally tormented, the ostracized, the ridiculed, the stereotyped. I mean those racked with unrelenting disease, threatened by political repression, confined by racial identity, mesmerized through cultural mythology, held in thrall by corporate bureaucracy. That's what I mean by the world's suffering.

Suffering is an index of something gone awry in the texture of our relationships. Suffering is a sign of needs unfulfilled or, worse, of an attack, direct or indirect, on creative possibility. The key to suffering is not always pain, nor is consciousness a requisite of suffering. Rather suffering is marked by deprivation, by the absence of those conditions that are conducive to the flourishing of life or, to borrow once again from Whitehead, by the absence of those conditions that might "add value to our immediate experience."

So defined, the world's suffering extends to the entire biosphere. It includes the extinction of species, the degeneration of ecosystems, the interruption of natural rhythms. It includes the poisoning of streams and oceans, the erosion of soils, the deterioration of atmosphere. It is present wherever and whenever any form of life or community of life is deprived—intentionally or unintentionally, with good reason or with no reason—of what might otherwise promote its creative extension, its flourishing, its goodness, its beauty: "His eye is on the sparrow, and he watches over me."

We cannot, I have suggested, understand the world unless we understand the world's suffering. And, given the depth of immediate experience, we cannot understand the world's suffering unless we understand it as, in some sense, our suffering. That, I would assert, is the ground of compassion. Recall, at this point, the perspective I am unfolding: wisdom, which is the employment of knowledge to "add value to immediate experience," is the culmination of understanding, and compassion is the expression of wisdom.

Compassion—as empathetic participation in the life's experience of another, especially in the life's suffering of another—is a dominant concern expressed through central symbols of the world's religions. Consider the following.

I have already referred to the Exodus story derived from the ancient Hebraic tradition. The God of Abraham, Isaac, and Jacob is portrayed as responsive to the suffering of his people. Even God's anger is a manifestation of his compassion, when directed as it is at perpetrators of injustice. Beverly Harrison has properly reminded us that anger, provoked by the distortions and degradations of patriarchal institutions, has its proper place in the service of love.[2] Moreover, as God is, in the Exodus story, presented as compassionate, so he expects compassion among his people: "You shall not oppress a stranger; you know the heart of a stranger, for you were strangers in the land of Egypt."[3]

Again, at the heart and center of Christianity is the solemn symbol of the crucified Christ. Whatever else that image is taken to mean, it epitomizes suffering love. It conveys the sensibility of one whose reach embraces the world in all of its agony and who absorbs that agony into his very being. Love, as presented in this story, is far more than warm feeling and kind sentiment. Love is participation in the life of the beloved—the ultimate sense of compassion. When a community is permeated with love, then "if one member suffers, all suffer together."[4] As John puts it: "By this we know love, that he laid down his life for us; and we ought to lay down our lives for one another."[5] Compassion is the name of that kind of sensitivity in which one feels as the other feels, through which one stands where the other stands, by which one grieves when the other weeps. Compassion, in its extremity, is the willingness to die that others might live.

In Buddhism, compassion is exquisitely manifest in the symbolism of the Bodhisattva, the one who, though strongly tempted to withdraw from the world, to detach oneself from the miseries of the everyday, is instead drawn deeply into the world to do what is necessary to enable all forms of life to find a path out of suffering: "I have taken upon myself, by my own will, the whole of the pain of all things living."[6]

Compassion, in this context, is the flip side of right mindfulness. One's identification with the other is, in effect, a function of understanding the other.

In Black Elk's "Great Vision" we find another symbol of the scope and import of compassion—the symbol of the Broken Hoop: "Behold the circle of the nation's hoop, for it is holy, being endless, and thus all powers shall be one power in the people without end."[7] But the nation's hoop is broken. Its brokenness is emblematic of the distortions and deformities of life's circumstance—of starvation and struggle, of exploitation and extinction. Trees, horses, birds, people—all are in a state of disease and disarray. Yet, take care, declares Black Elk, for beyond the brokenness of the hoop can be envisioned a restoration: "And I saw that the sacred hoop of my people was one of many hoops that made one circle, wide as daylight and as starlight, and in the center grew one mighty flowering tree to shelter all the children of one mother and one father. And I saw that it was holy."[8]

All these images and symbols—the Exodus, the crucified Christ, the Bodhisattva, the Broken Hoop—each in its own way informs us that understanding, in the most complete sense of that process, provokes compassion. Without the sensitivity of compassion, we cannot understand. Moreover, together with Bernard Meland, I would like to affirm that "Existence in most instances is sustained by a perilously slight margin of sensitivity."[9] It is precisely that sensitivity—which I have called compassion—that provides the possibility of creative advance in the world, that opens up the structures of our life to allow for the increase of value in immediate experience, that stimulates a constructive response to the pains and deprivations that wreak havoc in the world.

That is why these revelatory religious images point to the prospects of a new future, of a new time, of overcoming the conditions that are productive of suffering: a promised land, a sanctified people, an enlightened world, the Sacred Hoop restored. And that is why I have suggested that, as wisdom is the culmination of understanding and compassion is the expression of wisdom, so justice is the impulse of compassion.

Justice is the principle that requires us to attend with care to all the patterns of interaction in which we are engaged every day—friends and family, work and play, school and politics, earth and sky, nation and neighborhood. Justice poses a question of these patterns: Do they, in their character and in their effects, conduce to the enhancement of life?

Do they "add value to our immediate experience"? Are they worthy of celebration? Do they contribute to the deepening of fulfillment? Are they productive of the creative advance of the world in all its magnificent diversity?

Justice demonstrates its kinship with compassion when it mandates that, as we ponder this question, we stand in the shoes of the other, we see ourselves as others see us, we seek out the perspective of the marginalized and the exploited, we open our hearts and our minds to the voices of those whose welfare is most profoundly dependent on our forms of life. Justice, in this sense, mandates an enlargement of self. In its ultimate extension, it results in solidarity with all others, but manifests special concern for those whose lives are particularly jeopardized by the patterns we have created in our history.

In that concern, justice bends our energies toward transformative action—to do whatever we can do, within the grave limits of our finitude, to bring to fruition the vision of the Sacred Hoop, the Beloved Community, the covenant of peace: "The wolf shall dwell with the lamb, and the leopard shall lie down with the kid...and a little child shall lead them....They shall not hurt or destroy in all my holy mountain."[10] That's the far import of the cry for justice, even as its work attends to very particular matters very close at hand—ranging from sexual harassment and racial inequality to the cessation of military hostilities and the conservation of wetlands.

The work of justice is quite mundane, even though, in its visionary motivation, it is quite glorious: "'Lord, when did we see you hungry and feed you, or thirsty and give you drink? And when did we see you a stranger and welcome you, or naked and clothe you? And when did we see you sick and visit you?' And the Lord will answer them, 'Truly, I say to you, as you did it to one of the least of these my brothers and sisters, you did it to me.'"[11]

We should, in sum, recognize an intimate association—acknowledged in the imagery of many religious communities—between the drive for understanding and the mandate to do justice, an association whose name is compassion. That association comprises the deeper dimensions of understanding—dimensions in the absence of which, all our ordinary claims to understand are but dross. When those deeper dimensions—I am referring to the mind of wisdom, the heart of compassion, the will to justice—are quickened, then we cannot but be responsive to the world's suffering and seek to "add value to our immediate experience."

Part IV
Social Conflict

Love your enemies, do good to
those who hate you, bless those who curse
you, pray for those who abuse you.
—*Luke 6:27*

Harmonious intercommunication among tribes and nations, groups and associations has not, in any simple sense, been characteristic of life throughout the history of the human community. Thomas Hobbes (with his concept of a "war of all against all" in the state of nature) and Karl Marx (with his understanding of "class struggle")—each from his own perspective—had it right. If we would be wise in the ways of the world, we must be aware that peoples—as individuals and in their associations—conflict with each other. Some conflicts are relatively insignificant and are smoothed out easily through mutual agreement, compromise, or third-party mediation. Other conflicts, however, are intensive and life threatening, resulting in the employment of violent methods as each party seeks to dominate, if not annihilate, the other. Besides class struggle and the war of all against all, *Kulturkampf*, the battle of the sexes, "there shall be wars and rumors of wars," survival of the fittest—are among well-known phrases giving cognizance to the pervasiveness of massive social conflict in the course of our common life. Carl Schmitt once argued that, as the basic categories of moral analysis are good and evil, so the basic categories of political understanding are friend and enemy. And if that be true, Schmitt suggested, war is a central, indeed necessary, method of political action, for only through war and the threat of war might enemies be subdued and the political community be sustained.

Yet there is a deep-seated irony to social conflict, too often ignored, but acknowledged as a principle of dialectical logic—the unity of opposites. Those in conflict with each other, nonetheless, in some sense, belong to each other. As Hegel so shrewdly cast it, in the dynamic struggle between master and slave, they are mutually dependent. The identity of each is contingent on the identity of the other.

207

But the association is not static and fixed; it is laden with the possibility of moving to a new stage of interaction in which the lives of both parties might be enlarged and enriched. But the movement toward that new stage is contingent on an intentionality that confronts the conflict for what it is, yet moves into and through the conflict seeking a creative resolution of a transformative character.

The chapters that follow pursue this theme. In the first, I suggest that education, committed as it supposedly is to understanding (and therefore, I would argue, to social justice) is among the institutional means of countering the politics of annihilation that has so pervaded twentieth-century relations, domestically and internationally. In the second, I urge that the tradition of nonviolence is a repository of moral and political possibilities through which we can (and should) respond constructively to moments of serious social conflict. In the third, a brief interlude, I propose a "peacemaking perspective" on criminality, asserting that those whom we identify as criminals are, despite that, still our companions in the adventure of life and they deserve the respect of companionship.

11

The Politics of Annihilation
and the Mission of Higher Education

> It's not just hating war,
> despising war,
> sitting back and waiting for war to end.
> It's not just loving peace,
> wanting peace,
> sitting back and waiting for peace to come.
> Peace, like war, is waged.
> —*Walker Knight*[1]

We live in the present, but we live toward the future. In a sense, the present consists of pressing the conditions that surround us into the next stage of our living together. That is the importance of normative considerations in our understanding of the present and in our determinations of what the future shall be. That is, I would declare, the importance of the concept of social justice. The concept of social justice pertains, at the very least, to the shape of our relationships with each other, even with the entire biosphere. Social justice, I shall claim, bears special meaning at this point in our history, because, I fear, if its instruction is ignored, human life will become even more miserably impoverished than it now is; nay, it may well become impossible. There is an intimate link between social justice and the human survival into the future.

In explaining that link, I shall develop three propositions—broad in scope, perhaps excessive in claim. In summary form, the propositions are these:

- First, although the modern period has often been touted as an age of enlightenment, we have during this very period practiced a perverse politics, a politics of annihilation.
- Second, in response to the politics of annihilation, we confront the challenge of social justice, whose elementary maxim is this: So act

that the life of the entire community and each of its participants might flourish.

• Third, social justice as a critical principle is central to the mission of higher education in general and to religious studies in particular. From the standpoint of this principle, an adequate understanding of our historical condition cannot be divorced from moral judgment.

POLITICS OF ANNIHILATION

The idea of social justice is, in a sense, an ancient inheritance. Yet each age must reflect about it anew. Within recent history, John Rawls has brought us to consider afresh the force of justice as a central principle in our political life.[2] For too long in this land, we had thought that the only sort of moral calculus that made sense in our common life was utilitarianism—whether in the grand form of Jeremy Bentham ("so act to realize the greatest pleasure of the greatest number") or in the rather stingy form of the nineteenth-century Robber Barons ("so act to maximize the profits of me and my firm"). Both forms of utilitarianism are with us yet. But Rawls's stunning argument about equal rights and about the proper claims of the least advantaged on the resources and benefits of our social system has posed some hard questions to any simple form of utilitarianism in our public life.

I would propose a rather grand thesis about the pertinence of social justice for our times. Here I shall, with some modification, draw on a brief hint from Robert Neville—who suggests the need nowadays to expand a broad historical interpretation originally constructed by Paul Tillich.[3] Tillich once argued that Western history has developed through three dominant moments, in each of which humankind experienced a distinctive form of anxiety—of threat to their well-being.[4] During late ancient times, a perceived threat of death induced an ontic anxiety, and immortality became a dominant concern. During late medieval times, a perceived threat of guilt provoked a moral anxiety, and forgiveness was of paramount interest. During advanced modern times, a perceived threat of meaninglessness elicited a spiritual anxiety, and the search for meaning became a consuming question. We are never, it seems, without some despair, without some apprehensiveness about the limitations and uncertainties of finite existence. But in each moment, despair assumes a distinctive form, in response to which the "courage to be" is the power—the power of self-affirmation—that enables us to endure.

Tillich's historical interpretation is suggestive, but it needs an extension to account for the realities of our moment of history, a moment when a new threat and a new concern have become pervasive. The dominant threat of our time is not so much the threat of mortality or guilt or meaninglessness. It is the threat of social injustice. It is, put more starkly, the threat of a politics of annihilation. This threat confronts not only Western peoples. It confronts the entire community of human life, even more inclusively, the entire community of life—human and nonhuman—that constitutes the richness of this earth.

In the encounter of nation with nation, of group with group, the politics of annihilation has become dominant across the world. By politics in this context, I do not mean necessarily a jockeying for power and privilege, a manipulation of peoples to gain personal advancement—although that is the character that politics has tended to assume over the course of time. Rather, by the political I mean the basic structure and content of our interaction—which may or may not assume the character of a power struggle. The key political question is not so much, Who gets what, when, where, and how? as it is, How shall we live our lives together? Politics is the designed structure of our togetherness. *The politics of annihilation is present whenever and wherever, through social policies and political institutions, we create or sustain systems of interaction where classes of people—identified by race, ethnicity, gender, sexuality, nationality, religion, class—are isolated, exploited, subjugated, marginalized, exterminated.* We have, throughout the modern period, practiced a politics of annihilation in many ways, blatant and subtle—although, I would affirm, the politics of annihilation is not a necessity of history. It is a consequence of human determination. It need not be. Permit me to amplify this judgment.

Tzvetan Todorov's revealing study of *The Conquest of America*—subtitled significantly, *The Question of the Other*—may assist in the amplification of this judgment.[5] The "question of the Other" is a question of relationship, a question of the encounter between Self and Other. As such, it is a political question, focused on the character of our interactions; it is also a question of social justice.

For Todorov, a study of the "conquest of America" is of double significance. First, it is a paradigmatic case of "the discovery *self* makes of the *other*."[6] Second, it informs us not only about an event that occurred long ago, but, given the impress of past on present, it illuminates the realities and propensities of our times. In his words, "the conquest of America...heralds and establishes our present identity.... We are all direct descendents of Columbus, it is with him that our genealogy begins, insofar as the word *beginning* has a meaning."[7]

Remember that Todorov's overarching interest is the encounter between Self and Other—in this paradigmatic case, *conquistadores* and indigenous peoples. What are the dynamics at work in that encounter? In pursuing this inquiry, we must not forget the following statistic, admitting that it results from historical reconstruction and is susceptible to critique: Within a fifty-year period following Columbus's landing on these shores, out of eighty million indigenous peoples in what we now call the Americas, seventy million died—some by direct killing, some by maltreatment, most by diseases introduced by the Europeans. Some would call that genocide.

Todorov is concerned not only with the enormity of that happening, but with the processes of Self-Other encounter between intruding and indigenous peoples that gave rise to that happening. He focuses primarily on three figures: Christopher Columbus, Hernando Cortés, and Bartolomé de Las Casas—each of whom represents a special form of that encounter.

Columbus's motivations are so thoroughly imbued with traditional Christian sensibilities and lust for wealth, he is unable to discern the indigenous peoples for what they are to themselves in their own world. Despite initial words of admiration, his impulse is to convert and to exploit, to assimilate and to enslave. To Todorov, Columbus represents "egocentrism"—the imperialist projection of his values, of his self-identity, upon the universe and all its peoples—"in the conviction that the world is one."[8]

Cortés is more sophisticated, yet more vicious, than Columbus. His conquest of Montezuma displays a keen comprehension of the myths and rituals, the communicative practices and cultural boundaries of the Aztecs. Given that comprehension, he is much more able than Montezuma, his prey, to break into the mentality of the Other—the stranger—and to understand how the Other—in this case, the Aztecs—view the world and react to events in the world. But he employs his knowledge to confuse Montezuma, to manipulate the tribes, and ultimately to subjugate the kingdom. With Cortés, understanding the Other is separated from respect for the Other; knowledge is wholly divorced from love. In Cortés's relation with the Otherness of the Aztecs, his actions are shaped by two (not wholly compatible) motivations—both of which, Todorov contends, typify the mentality of modern times—wealth and massacre. In Todorov's striking assertion, the reduction of all values to money and riches is a new phenomenon; it "heralds the modern mentality."[9] More generally, the sheer "barbarity" of the Spanish in their slaughter of native Americans is a deliberate action that "heralds the advent of modern times."[10] That is, the singular drive for wealth and prosperity as well as the powerful drive to exterminate the alien and the different comprise an enduring legacy whose fruits remain most obvious in our era. They are forces of negation in the Self-Other relation; they are expressive of the politics of annihilation.

Las Casas, a Dominican, whose perceptions of native peoples matured over time, came to this complicated experience of alterity (Otherness) in the so-called "new world" infused with a sensibility radically different from both Columbus and Cortés. From a Christian postulate of the equality of all peoples and the universality of natural (moral) law, Las Casas defended the integrity and dignity of these newly "discovered" peoples over against the *conquistadores*. However, equality, in his comprehension, meant identity. These peoples were not really strange; they were, rather, very much like us. Hence while he loved them and defended them in the courts, his understanding of them in their own unique ways was constricted. His love was a function of prejudgment. Except near the end of his life, it was not linked with an empathetic apprehension of the communal identity of the indigenous peoples from their own perspective.

Todorov's narrative of the "conquest of America" is intended as a moral tale, informing us not just of what has happened, but of what is happening, telling us about the character of our times as a legacy of times past. The modern world, born, by claim, as an age of enlightenment, has, ironically, been a dark age, an age of massive destruction, an age in which to be an "Other" has meant to live in a constant state of threat of annihilation. The myth of progress through modern ways of thinking and doing barely conceals the perpetuation throughout the centuries up to the present moment of the mentality and the practice of the *conquistadores*. Our pride in modernity has been perversely misplaced.

Consider, in this connection, Richard L. Rubenstein's dramatic thesis that ours is an "age of triage." Triage, in original usage, refers to the selection of which injured persons are to be treated medically when (it is thought) resources are insufficient to treat all. On its reverse side,

triage determines that certain persons shall die. Evidence that triage—
in a form, however, that allows the rich and powerful to retain their
position and prestige—has been and remains a fundamental social policy is stark and compelling. Rubenstein sets out a litany of cases. The
peasant class in England was, in effect, designated for near extinction
through the enclosure movement beginning in the sixteenth century.
The Irish famines in the nineteenth century, which could have been
mitigated by British policies, were instead exacerbated by government
action. The outright massacre of Armenians by the Turks was in part
sheer opposition to an ethnic minority and in part the result of a mod-
ernization program. Under policies of the Stalinist government, eighty
million persons, it is estimated, met their death. The gas chambers of
Nazi Germany were intended to eliminate all European Jews and came
close to the realization of that goal. The fate of Vietnamese boat people,
refused refugee status in land after land, is another case of the politics
of annihilation. In more subtle, but no less effective, ways, social policies that sustain conditions of structural unemployment, systemic
poverty, homelessness, malnutrition in any society (including the
United States) are another expression of the age of triage—for, we must
not forget, such policies result, even if only indirectly, in the death,
albeit the quiet death, of thousands of people, particularly the young,
the old, the vulnerable, the marginalized.

Both Gil Elliot in his "twentieth-century book of the dead"[11] and
Edith Wyschogrod in her study of "man-made mass-death"[12] make the
case that, beginning with World War I, we have developed a military
technology and a political culture of devastation. In Eliot's calculation,
the "death machine," employing diverse agents—ranging from the
direct violence of bombs to the slow strangulation of blockades—has
resulted in the deliberate destruction of 110 million lives from 1914 to
1970. Wyschogrod argues that a new sort of reality has entered our
public life—the "death event," that is, the systemic and calculated creation of means of massive annihilation within a compressed period of
time. In the concept of the "death event" she embraces the creation and
deployment of weapons of extensive destruction; the establishment
and use of techniques such as embargoes and deportations whose effect
is the extermination of peoples; and the creation of "death worlds,"
such as concentration camps and relocation centers, wherein vast populations are subjected to forms of life "conferring upon their inhabi-
tants the status of the living dead."[13] I would extend Wyschogrod's idea
of death world to include refugee camps (consider the Palestinians

from the time of the Israeli war of independence in 1948 to the initiation of a "peace process" between the communities of the Israelis and the Palestinians) and inner-city ghettos (consider the circumstance of the Latino and African American poor in urban America).

Death machines and death events are blatant forms of the politics of annihilation. But we must not neglect more subtle forms of the same threat to the well-being of massive groups of peoples given political and economic policies that, with proper vision and concerted will, could be transformed. Ponder, for instance, the full import of the astounding datum, announced in the 1991 report of the National Commission on Children in the United States: "Poverty among children varies considerably by race.... About 44 percent of all black children and more than 36 percent of all Hispanic children are poor, compared to fewer than 15 percent of white children."[14]

In sum, in this presumed age of enlightenment, the politics of annihilation—the denial of the Otherness of the Other—occupies a dominant if not definitive role in our common life. But the politics of annihilation, the practice of constructing systems of interaction through which whole classes of persons are subjugated, marginalized, exterminated is, I have asserted, a form of perverse politics. It runs contrary to the inner meaning of politics understood as the process through which peoples may, in deliberation with each another, determine how, in their diversity, to live together and to support each other under given constraints and conditions of history. Living together is the premise of such an understanding of politics, and living as well as we can with each other and through each other is its aspiration. That is why social justice is a central component of politics so construed.

SOCIAL JUSTICE

In response to the politics of annihilation, we confront the challenge, nay, the obligation, of social justice whose elementary maxim is this: So act within the circumstances at hand that the life of the entire community and each of its participants might flourish.

We may distinguish two ways of understanding social justice—as a distributive concept and as a structural concept. The predominant way of rendering social justice nowadays is the former. That is, the subject of social justice is how the stuff of a given society is distributed among its members. Debates over social justice are contentions over what principles to employ in allocating the wealth produced by the economy or the offices and jobs, privileges and responsibilities available in the social system.

John Rawls, for instance, promotes a principle of modified equality, that is, each person has, virtually, the same claim as any other to the products of the social order, qualified only in a way to assure that those who are, at any given time, least advantaged be given special attention. In sharp contrast, Robert Nozick argues for an entitlement principle according to which people have a right to hold and to enjoy whatever they have already acquired or what has been transferred to them by established legal principles. From this libertarian perspective, efforts at a deliberate redistribution of income or position by governmental policy—given, say, the imposition of a Rawlsian principle of modified equality—are no less than a form of institutionalized theft, if not slave labor.

The question of distribution is of obvious importance in our lives. On the side of things to be allocated, it is a question of jobs, income, pensions, education, health care, housing, cultural expression, political voice. On the side of recipients (or nonrecipients) of things allocated, it is evident in controversies over sexism, homophobia, racism, ethnocentrism, neocolonialism, xenophobia. It provokes contentions between highly privileged and underprivileged, rich and poor, white and black, upper class and outcaste, capital and labor, ethnically dominant peoples and ethnically subordinate peoples.

However, focusing predominantly on the distributive concept of social justice is constrictive. It neglects a deeper dimension of social justice—the qualitative character of relationships between persons and groups within the human community. So, for instance, while self-respect is not unrelated to one's place within a distributive system, it is, more profoundly, a matter of the continuing regard with which one—including the relata of one's identity (racial, sexual, ethnic)—is held by others.

The classic formula for social justice is "to each one's own" (*suum cuique*). On the surface, that formula seems to require only some reasonable criterion for determining *what belongs to each* (that is, what is "one's own") for its implementation. However, on a deeper level, to provide that formula with sum and substance, a doctrine of *what it means to speak of "each"* is required (that is, who "we" are such that certain things belong to "each" of us.)

At this point, I would distinguish two forms of social ontology, that is, two ways of declaring who "each" of us is. The basic difference has to do with the character of the Self and the nature of the Self's relationship with the Other. In one form, an individualist understanding of Self is paramount; in another form, a relational understanding predominates. In the former, each of us is a separate and distinct being. Interactions with others must be constructed and are more or less useful as they accord with one's individual desires and projects. This individualist understanding of Self is of enduring significance, for solitariness is a vital dimension of our lives. We are, each of us, a unique center of feeling and thought, a source of creative action. Yet individualism is deficient in its neglect of the matrix of our lives. We are, from a relational standpoint, born in a nexus of interaction. We are as much the progeny of social relationship as we are sources of novel activity.

I propose that a relational ontology is indicated by the deepest dimension of our experience. We are, in a sense, always alone, yet never wholly alone. We exist in a constant state of dynamic interaction with others—sometimes, to be sure, primarily through the languages and images, memories and feelings we bear with us wherever we go and whatever we do. We are social selves even as we are individual selves. Individuality-in-community: that is our condition. This duality is constitutive of what "each" of us is.

The meaning of social justice as a structural concept is a reflection of this ontology, of this understanding of what "each" of us is. *To each one's own*: what belongs to each of us, most fundamentally, given what we are, is a form of interaction in which and through which the lives of all participants are enriched. I am daring to suggest that the meaning of social justice is rooted in the deepest dimension of our experience, that we have some apprehension, however dimly sensed and lacking in reflective rigor, that some forms of interaction are more productive of creative life than others. Social justice is a standard derivable from that apprehension, although, to be sure, any and all of its formulations are susceptible to reconsideration and restatement measured always in relation to its persistent intent.

Given this background, I have proposed that the elementary maxim of social justice is this: So act that the life of the entire community and each of its participants might flourish. According to this maxim, individuals and associations have an obligation to be supportive of and to contribute to our common life. So Robert O. Johann, after asserting that our lives are, most basically, "a shared undertaking in a shared world," insists, "What this means is that in forming my aims and purposes, I, the subject, am unqualifiedly obliged to do so in a way consistent with the requirements of our common life. These come down essentially to a certain respect for, and responsiveness to, the other as you, i.e., as an equal partner with me in the joint enterprise which is our common life."[15]

However, Johann's insistence on the objective worth of our common life must be refined lest it be taken to promote an oppressive subordination of creativity to conformity, of social critique to social expectation. For that purpose, I would distinguish two types of relational theory: consensual and conflictual. In general, relational theory—in its contrast to individualism—is defined by its celebration of our relations with each other and its assertion of the obligation we all bear to contribute to our common life. To that point, Johann is on the mark. Within that framework, however, the consensual type of relational theory favors harmony, where the conflictual type cherishes dissent. The consensual type stresses compliance with prescribed rules for sustaining institutional life, where the conflictual type encourages political argument and opposition. The consensual type presses for full agreement of all parties, where the conflictual type is respectful of plurality and difference while sustaining a commitment to civic friendship.

At times, partnership in our common life may mean we are yoked together in a task whose goals and procedures are definite and clear. At such moments, we must collaborate and cooperate. We must get on with the task at hand. But partnership may be just as vividly manifest in the presence of vast cultural difference and political division and in moments of struggle among contending groups. Then, in contrast to the well-known narrowly xenophobic slogan, "America, Love It or Leave It," an alternative may be more appropriate, "America, Love It through Resistance."

Creative freedom and radical difference, opposition and dissent are not alien to the flourishing of our common life. On the contrary, they contribute to its enhancement—excepting, perhaps, cases where they constitute a clear and present danger to the Other. Yet we must be exceedingly cautious about this exception. At least under present historical conditions, it is more likely that established institutions rather than oppositional groups constitute a clear and present danger to the Other—as in cases of institutionalized racism, entrenched patriarchalism, or fervent nationalism—in which cases radical social and cultural transformation may be requisite to the flourishing of our common life. At such moments, the maxim of social justice properly gives rise to a revolutionary impulse. Perhaps, indeed, we should, out of a relational theory in its conflictual version, sustain a permanent revolutionary impulse given the fallibilities and ambiguities that accompany us throughout our history.

In this connection, I am drawn to Iris Marion Young's rejection of a politics of assimilation on behalf of a "politics of difference." The assimilationist ideal, epitomized in the melting pot version of American history and in current social policies insisting that all persons be treated exactly alike, is, in its effect, neglectful of radical differences that distinguish us and separate us. Young affirms the resurgence of a politics of difference within recent decades in this nation, "not only among racial and ethnic groups, but also among women, gay men and lesbians, old people, and the disabled."[16] A politics of assimilation presses for homogeneity within the body politic (e.g., promoting the legal establishment of English as the official language of the country, or opposing "multiculturalism" in public education). A politics of difference is supportive of heterogeneity and promotes group solidarity. Within a politics of difference, social justice may well require a differential treatment of groups, depending on their particular history and needs. Conditions among Native American tribes, for instance, are appreciably different from circumstances among varying groups of Latinos, although both peoples have been effectively marginalized and denigrated in American society.

In its minimalist form, the maxim of social justice can be cast as the prima facie duty of nonmaleficence. That is, without compelling moral reasons to the contrary, we are obliged to avoid any action, personal or collective, that will harm or injure the Other. (Consider, e.g., the placement of a new superhighway directly through the center of an urban ethnic neighborhood.) Even in this minimalist form of the maxim, we are mandated to subject our personal lives and our social systems to critical scrutiny, for harm to the Other can be caused without deliberate intention—sometimes merely by acquiescing in long-standing patterns of action whose effects have been ignored. To cite one example, it is unconscionable, given the duty of nonmaleficence, that the quality of public schools in districts throughout this nation should depend on the relative wealth of those districts.

I would suggest several corollaries to the maxim of social justice in its more complete form. First, *a principle of effective participation.*

In whatever settings in which the conditions of our lives are most forcefully shaped (schools, families, workplaces, neighborhoods), persons and groups should be enabled to give voice to their judgments and to exercise power to influence governing policies. Consider, as an implication of this principle, its import for a massive redesign of multinational corporations—their internal governance and their investment practices.

Second, *a principle of common use.* The fundamental consideration governing the wealth of the human community should be, not entitlement, but need. The first claim on the resources of the social system should be determined by what is required to fulfill the basic needs of the community and all its members. At its most basic level, I would define need as embracing what Henry Shue terms "minimal economic security, or subsistence," that is,

> unpolluted air, unpolluted water, adequate food, adequate clothing, adequate shelter, and minimal preventive public health care. Many complications about exactly how to specify the boundaries of what is necessary for subsistence would be interesting to explore. But the basic idea is to have available for consumption what is needed for a decent chance at a reasonable healthy and active life of more or less normal length, barring tragic interventions.[17]

As a third corollary of the maxim of social justice, I suggest *a principle of creative expression.* Individuals and groups should be empowered to give free play to their sensibilities and inspirations in diverse forms, cultural and organizational. This principle stands opposed to "cultural imperialism," the sometimes but not always subtle subjugation of the Otherness of the Other through the "gaze" of normality and assumptions of respectability.[18] Consider, for example, the suppression of certain works of art as odd, indecent, obscene, blasphemous, or just plain too radical.

These principles—effective participation, common use, creative expression—do not stand alone; they are not autonomous. They are linked as corollaries of the elementary maxim of social justice: So act that the life of the entire community and each of its participants might flourish. By adherence to these principles in the formation and conduct of our common life, the lives of each of us might indeed be enriched. These principles, taken together, stand in opposition to and judgment upon the politics of annihilation in all its forms, blatant and subtle.

HIGHER EDUCATION AND RELIGIOUS PLURALISM

According to my first proposition, throughout the modern period a politics of annihilation—typified in the encounter between *conquistadores* and indigenous peoples in these lands—has been a prevailing practice. In the practice of a politics of annihilation, the intent, in instances of serious social conflict, is to isolate, to exploit, if not to obliterate, the Other. In response to the persisting, at times escalating, threat of a politics of annihilation (a threat directed, in its extremity, to the entire biosphere) I have proposed a maxim of social justice: So act that the life of the entire community and each of its participants might flourish. Under conditions of a dominant politics of annihilation, the "courage to be,"[19] given a relational understanding of the Self, finds its appropriate expression in the strength to act—to act in such a way that, so far as it in us lies, social justice is our overarching purpose. This maxim applies to the life plans of individuals as well as to the institutional designs of societies.

In that light, I would have us turn to my third proposition: social justice as a critical principle is integral to the mission of higher education in general and to religious studies in particular. Understanding, which is, I assume, the governing purpose of the educational process at all levels, cannot be wholly divorced from moral judgment. From another angle, the educational process, when it is effective in promoting its basic mission of understanding, is a constructive means of approaching questions of serious social conflict in a manner that affirms the life of all parties to the conflict. However, unfortunately, educational institutions, even institutions of higher learning, do not always serve their basic mission very well.

In a thoughtful study of *The Moral Collapse of the University*, Bruce Wilshire announces, "The sickness of the university is primarily ethical."[20] Wilshire is not here making a comment about the mores of fraternity houses, the need for courses in values clarification, or the corruption of intercollegiate athletics. His diagnosis—his accusation—is much more fundamental and far reaching. In his assessment, the contemporary university tends, despite its vast array of departments and programs, to be neglectful of the central meaning of education. Education, at its best, poses the most fundamental questions we can ask: Who are we? What have we been? What might we become? How shall we construct our lives, individually and collectively? What should be the shape of our tomorrow?

At first blush, these questions appear—in some sense, they are—highly personal. Unless and until they become questions of intense interest to teachers and to students, the act of education is sharply delimited. But they are not merely personal. They are not questions that pertain merely to the inner feelings and agonies of each student in the privacy of her heart and mind. They are, rather, questions whose sophisticated exploration requires educators and students to engage in joint ventures of learning through which our consciousness of ourselves is deepened and broadened and through which our patterns of interaction are increasingly informed with critical insight. They are questions whose character compels us to consider the whole world in all its diversity and our place in it. Consciousness of *World* is a necessary correlative to consciousness of *Self*. Self and World do not, in any simple way, stand apart. They are entangled intimately with each other. Precisely because of that entanglement, how we think and how we act are dialectically intertwined, for our action is always interaction, shaping and reshaping the contours of both World and Self. Our reflections and our practices are part and parcel of each other.

Of vital importance to the mission of higher education and its contribution to our common life is how, at the very outset, we construe the relationship between Self and World or, if you will, between Self and Other. It is precisely at this juncture Wilshire properly identifies the central problem—the central flaw—of contemporary higher education in modern industralized nations, namely, its separatist thesis of the relation between Self and World. From the perspective of this separatist thesis, the Self gazes on the World as an external reality, susceptible to dispassionate investigation and technological manipulation. Once the World's features and dynamics are known, the Self may use it, modify it, control it, bend it to the Self's use, or, for that matter, destroy it—as in the politics of annihilation. In the telling phrase of Francis Bacon, knowledge is power. The more intricate our knowledge of nature, the more extensive our ability to exploit it as a resource. The more precise our knowledge of human behavior, the more complete our capacity to shape and mold what people do—whether for purposes of political power, economic profit, or personal pleasure. Recall the case of Hernando Cortés who employed his knowledge of Aztec culture to crush Montezuma. Consider as well the case of modern marketing techniques, used alike in business enterprise and political electioneering.

Knowledge, in this framework, requires objective distancing, a purely disinterested approach to investigation. This way of construing the Self-World correlation assumes the Self is a detached ego, a solitary soul, a private individual whose inner desires, whatever they happen to be, dictate what is and is not valuable, what is and is not of ultimate importance. Things moral, as things beautiful, are, in the final analysis, in the eye of the beholder. The Self as ego, given its version of the good and the beautiful, mobilizes whatever power it possesses to force the World to conform to its image of what is desirable. Knowledge, by itself, is morally neutral. Its value is strictly instrumental—save, perhaps, for those few who, because of an archaic disposition, find intrinsic joy in its pursuit. The congruence between this construction of the Self-World correlation and a politics of annihilation is, I assume, evident.

I have already proposed an alternative to the separatist thesis, namely, a relational ontology according to which Individuality-in-Community is our condition. The Self is not separate from the World, but a creative participant in the World. Self and Other are inextricably engaged in an "all-inclusive field of interactivity."[21] In the process of broadening our understanding of the World, we have an effect both on the World and on ourselves. As any keen physicist or anthropologist knows, observer and observed stand not over against each other. They are not wholly separate from each other. Rather they are closely related to each other—each, by virtue of the relationship, having an influence on the Other. In our observations and investigations, we bear with us a deep background of feelings and sensibilities which colors our hunches and our findings, our knowledge of the World and of ourselves. On the reverse side, what we discover contributes in some way to those feelings and sensibilities. The very process of understanding is therefore not without direct moral consequence. Understanding is an expression of and has an impact upon the quality of our relationship with each other.

More pointedly and more controversially, I propose that understanding is in fact enhanced as we accept moral responsibility for the character of that relationship. I understand this as an implication of Wilshire's explication of the principle of reciprocity:

> To understand best what in fact I am doing to the other I must imagine what it would be like to have the act done to me, for this counteracts the ego's blinkered awareness, caught up as it is in the instant of action, not being acted upon. Take a mendacious and self-serving act of seduction. I will not begin to comprehend what I am doing unless I imagine the act done to me—or, differently put, unless I empathize

with any other to whom this act is done.... Ethical facts are facts of a particular sort of reciprocity: that deliberate mimetic response and empathy with others which is compassion. This is to be morally centered as a field being.[22]

Understanding in the absence of compassion is not only morally irresponsible; it results, as well, in a constricted, nay, a distorted form of understanding. The depth of our understanding of the World—of the Other—is contingent in no small measure on a moral assessment of the condition of the World and the quality of our interaction with it. In an exploitative relationship, the lives of both Self and Other are restrained and deformed. Only in a relationship of reciprocity—or, more profoundly, of mutuality, where Self and Other are enriched by the interaction, is the quality of life advanced.

From this perspective, if the dominant purpose of higher education is to advance our understanding of the world, then social justice as I have framed it in the maxim—so act that the life of the entire community and each of its participants might flourish—is integral to its mission. Higher education, as such, has a vital role to play in resisting the politics of annihilation and in promoting the enrichment of our common life. In the language of Jürgen Habermas, the predominant interest governing our pursuit of knowledge in the university should be neither technological control nor hermeneutical understanding, but political emancipation for the sake of Self and the World which constitutes the matrix of our existence.[23] If anyone is oppressed, none of us is free.

Religious studies occupies a special place in higher education. Here I adopt William James's generic depiction of religion as our "total reaction upon life":

> Total reactions are different from casual reactions, and total attitudes are different from usual or professional attitudes. To get at them you must go behind the foreground of existence and reach down to that curious sense of the whole residual cosmos as an everlasting presence, intimate or alien, terrible or amusing, lovable or odious, which in some degree everyone possesses. This sense of the world's presence... is the completest of all our answers to the question, "What is the character of this universe in which we dwell?"[24]

If we would comprehend the reality of any people (including ourselves), we should probe into their most basic memories and aspirations, into the mythic patterns and dominant institutions that govern their lives. We must, in James's terms, "reach down to that curious sense of the whole residual cosmos as an everlasting presence," which infuses their consciousness and their practice. That is the predominant focus of religious studies, whatever their more particular focus or subject—traditional or nontraditional.

We have, perhaps, become more aware in modern times than before of the vast plurality of the world's religions (and, I should add, the world's cultures). Each has its own integrity. Each bears its own worldview. Each practices its own rituals and promotes its own style of life. Each cherishes its own historical development and sustains its own traditional ways. Each, over the course of time, has experienced transformation, sometimes splitting into antagonistic divisions. To the devotees in each religious community, the form of faith expressed through its beliefs and rituals provides a total orientation to life, an understanding of Self and World, an affirmation of the meaning of existence that seems sufficiently persuasive to warrant their ultimate commitment, even as they split into multiple groupings and undergo historical change.

What, we must ask, are we to make of the vast plurality of these "total reactions upon life" presented to us? How are we to respond to them? Given the position I have been unfolding for our consideration, I have found a judgment of Marjorie Hewitt Suchocki instructive. From the perspective of a feminist form of liberation theology, she "suggests that one must radically affirm religious pluralism, but not without bringing a critical consciousness of well-being in human community to interreligious and intrareligious discussion. Justice is...to be the fundamental criterion of value and the focus of dialogue and action among religions."[25] Stimulated by that judgment, I offer the following suggestions.

First, assuming the kind of relationship between Self and Other I have already sketched, I suggest we consider religious plurality on a parallel with a politics of difference. Whatever our own inherited or adopted "total reaction to life"—Christian, Islamic, Buddhist—our initial obligation is to cherish the Otherness of the Other, to esteem the particularities in thought and practice of alternative forms of faith, to comprehend as thoroughly and empathetically as we can the inner dynamics of other kinds of religious community—traditional and nontraditional. We should acknowledge and be supportive of the integrity of each religious tradition, its holistic character and its varieties, the manner in which, through its myths and rituals, it captivates the lives of its members.

Second, I suggest that, given the principle of reciprocity, we take the occasion of our appreciative consciousness of the Otherness of the Other among the world's religions to engage in a process of self-criticism and self-correction. By listening to the Other, we may gain purchase on a fresh understanding of ourselves, our limitations, our conventionalities, our viciousness, our prejudices, our hidden assumptions. We may well be brought to a transformation of our previous ways as we are persuaded that the insights of the Other might enrich our own understanding of and actions in the world.

Third, I propose that the maxim of social justice—so act that the life of the entire community and each of its participants might flourish—together with its corollaries provides, at this point in our common history, grounds for a critical judgment of all the world's religious communities, our own and others. Recall my assertion that the maxim of social justice pertains to the life plans of individuals and to the institutional designs of our diverse associations and social systems—among which I would include our religious communities. To put this proposal in a negative form, religious communities have no more justification than any others to sustain oppressive social practices—practices whose systemic effect is—to appropriate Iris Marion Young's categories— exploitation, marginalization, powerlessness, cultural imperialism, violence.[26]

Fourth, acknowledging profound differences among religious communities, in history and orientation, and the integrity of each to its communicants as a "total reaction upon life," I nonetheless propose that we should understand them, each and all, as participants in a more encompassing community, ultimately the entire biosphere, and as therefore responsible for the present and future condition of that community. While respecting the particularity of each form of faith, we have good reason to call them into a collaborative forum to explore and to promote the meaning of social justice throughout the world. As an instance of this kind of collaborative forum, I cite the struggle of women of many forms of faith—Christian and Judaic, Hindu and Islamic, Buddhist and Native American—against patriarchalism with its hierarchical and androcentric structures on behalf of a radically different pattern of life, characterized by principles of mutuality and creative interaction.[27] This feminist vision is intended for the transformation of religious communities narrowly understood, but, more extensively, for the total transformation of our common life. The oppression of women, under any guise and in any setting, is, from this perspective, a matter of social injustice and must be acknowledged as such in any adequate comprehension of the character of the World.

In pursuing these lines, religious studies has a vital role in contributing to the emancipatory mission of higher education. The university (or, for that matter, any genuinely educational association), as I am interpreting it, is, at its heart, a moral community whose central task—that of expanding and deepening our understanding of both Self and World—is, by virtue of that task, properly directed by the principle of social justice. Only as the university deliberately takes up that task will it be, as it should be, an explicit force against the politics of annihilation, against, that is, those principalities and powers whose effect is the denial of the Otherness of the Other.

A brief final word. I am not sanguine about prospects for the human future. The dominance of the politics of annihilation is overwhelming. And institutions of learning seem more captivated by the separatist thesis and more driven to serve the powers—economic and political—that prevail than to advance the cause of a deeper understanding infused with compassion. At the very least, however, we can, each of us in our several groups and associations, adopt David Tracy's strategy of resistance and hope—resistance against the politics of annihilation and hope for a community of social justice.[28] In every act of resistance, there is displayed some measure of hope, for to resist on behalf of social justice is already to manifest a profound confidence in that reality which constitutes the ground of our courage to be and the source of our strength to act. In that light, I can think of no more fitting words to conclude this reflection than Micah's rhetorical question, "what does the Lord require of you but to do justice, and to love kindness, and to walk humbly with your God?"[29]

12

On Making Peace: Nonviolence and the Principle of Relationality

They shall beat their swords
into plowshares,
and their spears
into pruning hooks.
—*Micah 4:3*

We are at a moment in human history when, I would propose, we must take more seriously the tradition of nonviolence than we ever have heretofore. To be sure, we have, on occasion, praised the life and works of such diverse figures as Mohandas Gandhi, Dorothy Day, Thich Nhat Hanh, Martin Luther King, Jr. They have given us, in their respective struggles to bring about radical social transformation, some insight into the genius and relative effectiveness of nonviolence as a form of praxis through which seemingly indomitable structures of oppression have been, to some degree at least, undone and new possibilities of living together in a more humane manner have been realized. But too often we have tended to circumscribe their works, confining their significance to specific times and places, without exploring the prospect of nonviolence as an integral dimension of any kind of morally sensible concrete historical ideal for the future, more particularly, at the moment, for the twenty-first century.

The particular aim of such an exploration is to consider the principle of nonviolence as a basis for reconstructing the ways in which we understand and respond to serious conflicts between and among peoples both domestically and across the globe. In this connection, the principle of nonviolence may provide us with an alternative to war and an innovative approach to police work and penology as well as a method of pressing for needed social change—although in their detail these prospects lie beyond the scope of our immediate discussion.

For our immediate discussion, I propose four themes:

- First, in contrast to earlier epochs of human history, the principle of relationality, according to which we are, constitutively, members of each other, provides the grounding for a morally sensible concrete historical ideal for the future. Self and Other, while differentiated, belong to each other and, in their most mature forms of living together, contribute to the enrichment of each other's experience and of the world's ongoingness.

- Second, violence, whatever its motivation or form—aggressive or defensive, institutional or revolutionary—is, in the strict sense of the term, destructive of the Other and, reflexively, destructive of the Self. As such, violence runs counter to the moral import of the principle of relationality.

- Third, nonviolence, which is an approach to conflictual encounter through which the agent seeks to sustain the integrity of both Self and Other, even in their opposition to and struggle against each other, moving them through a process of interaction toward a new stage of creative synthesis, embodies in exemplary fashion the moral import of the principle of relationality.

- Fourth, peacemaking, as the unfolding of the full meaning of nonviolence in human relationships, is an endeavor that requires individual commitment and practice. But also, given its moral importance, it must assume a central role in the reconstruction of basic social policies and energies at least to the same degree as does warmaking at the present time.

THE PRINCIPLE OF RELATIONALITY

Each epoch, Jacques Maritain mused some decades ago, has its own "concrete historical ideal."[1] A concrete historical ideal in Maritain's usage is a "prospective image," a model of civilization responsive to the deepest yearnings and most serious deficiencies of the time. It is, by intent, not a product of sheer fantasy, an utterly impossible dream, a utopia out of touch with the character of our lives. It is rather an image of what might be and can be—"with more or less difficulty, more or less imperfection . . . realizable as something on the way to being made . . . a rough draft which may later be determinative of a future reality."

Maritain employed this notion of a concrete historical ideal as a means of prodding his community of faith, Roman Catholicism, to break its fixation with medieval times (with its commitment to the ideal of maximal organic unity) and to direct its energies, however grudgingly, toward a moral image more in keeping with the most attractive dimensions of modern culture (with its commitment to the ideal of autonomy). Maritain's focus was on the development of civilization in the West; his concern was to outline the makings of a New Christendom while sustaining, as compatible with that project, the sensibility that each individual has a right to freedom in all realms of social life.

We are now, I would suggest, at a new moment in our history (broadly understood as it must be these days as the history of the entire community of life across the globe), a moment defined by its own critical needs and deep yearnings. Those needs and yearnings are expressed through diverse liberation and ecological movements that have arisen in cultures throughout the world. All such movements, not always in concert with each other, are nonetheless conjoined in their effort to transform the systems—political, economic, cultural—that hold their communities in thrall. On their negative side, these movements are engaged in a struggle against oppression, against forces that would exploit them if not annihilate them. On their affirmative side, they are, at their best, engaged in a struggle for respect and recognition, for equity in the distribution of the stuff of life (its benefits and its burdens) and for effective participation in the continuing forum of life. On both sides, they may be interpreted as reaching out for a quality of relatedness throughout the community of life that is mutually respectful and mutually enriching.

Within such a historical moment as this, I would propose, neither the principle of maximal organic unity nor the principle of autonomy provides us with an appropriate concrete historical ideal. The former is neglectful of the drive for self-determination and the worthiness of honoring radical cultural diversity. The latter is neglectful of the need for responsibility and care even across the lines that distinguish and divide us. The principle of relationality within whose dynamics life is a continuous dialectic between participation and individuation provides us with an alternative that is more fitting given the urgent needs of our time.

That is, each of us, on the one hand, is an inheritance from times past both distant and immediate. Our physical characteristics and our cultural sensibilities are the result of the confluence of generations that have gone before us and of multiple factors, human and nonhuman, that constitute the context of our current living. Our identity is determined in no small part by the coming together of all these relationships. We are, in this sense, members of each other, located on a grid that is in constant motion, that extends far and wide, embracing an entire ecosphere. We are participants in the community of life as it is configured at this historical moment and cannot be adequately understood independently of that community.

Each of us, on the other hand, is, to some degree and within some circle of influence, a creative agent, making our own way through the concourse of these interrelationships. We do something with our inheritance. We place our own individual stamp on the flow of life. The ecological grid and the historical process are shaped by the paths we choose to walk and by the manner and mien of our feelings and emotions. We make a difference. We are, on this side of our being, self-determining and self-constructing (and, as such, makers of history and molders of the world). Even under conditions that are narrowly confining, we manage to sustain some measure of independence, whatever we may do with it, either in the privacy of our own thoughts or in our response to the world that surrounds us.

The dialectic between participation and individuation is, within this worldview, a constant of our life. But the quality of that dialectic is not a constant. It is a matter susceptible to manipulation and transformation. The quality of relations may be refined or impaired; it may be redirected or radically altered. Consider, in this connection, events ranging from the dynamics of parent-child relationships (which may be in a process of estrangement or reconciliation) to political revolutions (which end, sometimes in tyranny but sometimes in a move toward democracy). History, which is in continuous flux, is the development of changing configurations in the dialectic between participation and individuation.

At this point the moral question intrudes. What is to be done to advance the quality of that dialectic between participation and individuation such that all life—the life of both Self and Other—might flourish?

If this is the most appropriate form of the moral question in our time (as, it seems to me, is testified in both liberation and ecological movements), then perhaps we might move toward the development of a new type of ethical theory that I deign to designate "koinonology."

Teleological ethical theory is directed to purposes and objectives to be realized and engages in means/ends analysis. Deontological ethical theory concentrates on one's obligations and duties, dealing with the give and take of rights and responsibilities. But koinonology's predominant concern is with the tenor of relationships. Its drive is to promote the creation of forms of interaction characterized by genuine reciprocity through which the integrity and creativity of each party (Self and Other) are respected, yet each intends to contribute to the life of the Other as they move together into a new and not always predictable future. In the dynamics of life, koinonology is sensitive to the interplay and clash of structures of alienation and reconciliation at all levels of our association with each other, seeking constantly, in all kinds of circumstances, for the release of those energies productive of creative transformation.

Friendship, at least as we tend to envision it in moments of lucidity, is a model case of genuine reciprocity. However, I would hasten to add, we should not construe friendship as limited solely to immediate personal relationships. Friendship, in the sense of civic friendship, is of broad political relevance. I am here, inspired by the Aristotelian tradition, considering the political community as the most embracing of associations, although, under the influence of the ecological movement, I would propose that we should extend the lines of that association from polis to cosmopolis. I would dare to suggest that, from the perspective of the principle of relationality, civic friendship resides at the heart and center of politics properly understood.

Politics, in this rendition, is not fundamentally a struggle for power, although power is an important component of political association. The motif of struggle for power, which seems to cast politics as a zero-sum game consisting, as the game arrives at its key turning points, of winners and losers, is pervasive throughout contemporary political rhetoric and political practice. But the sensibility of that way of considering politics is contingent on the kind of worldview represented in Thomas Hobbes, according to which each of us is an isolated individual (or part of an aggregate in the form, for example, of an individualized sovereign nation-state), bent on maximizing the realization of our desires in whatever way we can, given a world of individuals with the same drive. From that standpoint, Karl von Clausewitz's famous maxim—that war is nothing other than the extension of politics with other means—is intelligible. But this Hobbesianlike worldview, however much it may have served in times past to release the individual from the hegemonic control of inherited social forms, is, I would propose, ultimately self-destructive in its import. Though seemingly realistic ("that's the way the world works"), it must now be seen and assessed as dysfunctional given the conditions of life as we now confront them. In short the world cannot much longer work that way and, in fact, when it works and works well, other kinds of forces sustain it, forces of mutual respect and civic friendship.

From the perspective of the principle of relationality, politics is understood as that process of interaction through which forms of community are created and recreated with the aim of assuring, so far as possible, that each participant, while contributing to all others, flourishes. Within this context, war (or, more generally, violence) is not the extension of politics with other means. Per contra, violence is the antithesis of politics.

THE MEANING OF VIOLENCE

Hannah Arendt, in a searching study of the glorification of violence in the twentieth century, is careful to distinguish power from violence.[2] In keeping with her understanding of politics in the human community, she reserves the term *power* to designate the ability to act in concert. Power emerges out of deliberation and association. It is the result of consensus attained in and through a public forum. Power is the expression of community. And Arendt is keenly aware (as, we shall note, was Gandhi) that "people of power" are, in the dynamics of their position, empowered by a supportive group, the group they "re-present." When that group withdraws its support, the power "re-presented" through those people dissipates. Power and consent are two sides of the same reality. Alternatively phrased, power entails a collaboration between Self and Other and, as the circle of Self and Other expands, so power intensifies.

Violence, in contrast, is the employment of "technique" (that is, technological means, instruments of force) to have one's way over the determinations of an opposition. In acts of violence, Self stand against the Other. Violence is a matter of imposition, not a matter of consensus.

Both power and violence are forms of human interaction. Both can effect dramatic historical change. Both can bring about something new. Moreover, in some instances, violence may seem to be an extension of power. However, given their basic meanings, power and violence are incompatible with each other. They move in opposite directions. In puzzling over the widely spread incidence of violence in the twentieth century, Arendt suggests that it is a reaction born of political frustration. It emerges from the obstructions that deny peoples the ability to participate in the public forum. In the absence of evident access to power, violence, because of its seeming capacity to get things done, is a strong temptation and may be, mistakenly, glorified.

I suggest that violence is mistakenly glorified because violence, given its inner meaning and "deep structure"[3] does not do and cannot do what it pretends to do. In its pretense, it is an expression of power; in its reality, at least as played out in the long term, it is self-destructive. In ordinary usage, violence is present where an agent causes injury—usually to an Other—through the use of physical force. But upon further reflection, that usage only touches the surface expressions of violence in human affairs.

As a beginning of that further reflection, we must recognize that to do violence to an Other means to violate the Other, to run counter to the Other's dignity. Such violation may occur in many ways, blatant and subtle. Physical violence is usually blatant. It attracts our immediate attention. Whether between persons (as in crime in the streets) or among groups (as in war), it is dramatic. It terrifies, yet it fascinates. It makes us shudder, but it also excites us, interrupting the humdrum routines of life and providing a common focus of concern. That is part of the reason for the attractiveness of physical violence.

Yet the violation of an Other through physical force is more than matched in its virulence by the violation of an Other through psychological means where the instruments are often less ostentatious, the results less obvious, but the damage just as, if not more, profound and long lasting. Through words and gestures, tone of voice, and subtlety of suggestion we manipulate each other, subdue each other, instill self-doubts in each other. Memories of such moments haunt us throughout the remainder of our lives.

Psychological violence on the personal level—in relations, for example, between parent and child, employer and employee, teacher and student—has its counterpart on the social level in institutional violence. Institutions of all kinds, political and economic, may appear smooth running and highly creative on the surface, but, in their day-to-day routines and in their long-range effects, perpetuate dominative and destructive relationships throughout a community.

Twenty-five years ago, Dom Helder Camara, giving voice to conditions of institutional violence in a Latin American context, admonished:

> Look closely at the injustices in the underdeveloped countries, in the relations between the developed world and the underdeveloped world. You will find that everywhere the injustices are a form of violence. One can and must say that they are everywhere the basic violence, violence No. 1.[4]

At critical moments in human history, Camara observed, basic violence provokes a "spiral of violence": violence No. 1 (the institutional violence of structural injustice) gives rise to violence No. 2 (revolutionary resistance by the oppressed) which, in turn, provokes violence No. 3 (repressive reaction by the authorities in an effort to sustain the status quo). Too often in such circumstances we attend so exclusively to the violent expressions of revolt and repression given their immediacy and their flair, we neglect the longer lasting, sometimes hidden violence of institutional injustice.

But what is it that specifies the kind of violation accomplished by violence? Following Robert Litke's effort to trace the "deep structure" of violence, I would, as an initial suggestion, propose that violence in human intercourse is an attack on basic human rights, particularly on the right to participate creatively and effectively in those forms of interaction that constitute the matrix of our lives. The concept of violence is used, Litke asserts, "to censure the fact that some or all of a person's power to act, and to interact, in bodily and decision-making ways has been nullified by someone else. That is the heart of violence: the nullification or disempowerment of persons."[5]

At this point, we must take sharp notice of a curiosity that resides at the heart of violence; namely, that in doing violence to the Other presumably for the sake of some benefit to the Self, the agent impoverishes that matrix out of which the Self itself finds nurturance.

In puzzling over this curiosity, Litke proposes that the Self turns to violence because of a fundamental mistake, which he dubs "epistemic nullification," namely, the assumption "that we have nothing to learn from the other"[6] and that, therefore, whenever Self and Other are at odds, one's gain is another's loss and that, in such circumstances, the Other is, simply put, an enemy not to be trusted or respected but to be done in. However that is an error. In the field of interaction, we belong together even under conditions of radical alienation—which means that as we violate the Other, we deprive the Self, however blind we may be to that side of the dynamic.

That proposition, that we belong together whatever the conditions of our interaction, is a supposition that underlies Sergio Cotta's understanding of the "specific character and existential meaning" of violence which, in summary definition, he renders as "activity-contra, unruly, nondialogical, and noncoexistential."[7] It is activity-contra: it refuses to consider the consent of the Other as it imposes its Self upon the Other. It is unruly: it breaks the bonds of restraint and measure, requisites of any kind of creative interaction. It is nondialogical: it fails to listen to the Other, its form of intercommunication is narrowly Self-serving. It is noncoexistential: it entails a loss of awareness of the fundamental character of our lived experience as always and everywhere being-with-the-Other, it is a denial of that intertwining of our lives through which Self and Other belong together. Violence, so understood, is reflexive in its effects: as it degrades the Other, so also it diminishes the Self. Its apparent victories are a sham.

That conclusion may seem extreme, particularly where a principled distinction is drawn between illegitimate and legitimate violence. The use of violent means, it has often been alleged, is legitimate in a range of cases, for example, in the defense of a nation against a threat to its people or to its territory; where vital national interests are at stake; sometimes in instances of revolutionary war (Camara's violence no. 2); and as an instrument of legal enforcement, particularly in response to violent criminal activity, actual or potential. Arguments on behalf of the use of violence in such cases are tantalizing. They seem persuasive. Surely, in such cases, it would seem, the Self is protected, not diminished, through the use of violent means to control or to subdue the Other. However, in each case, we need to ask what it is that is really at stake in the encounter that seems to call for violence; what the conditions are that brought about the encounter; what the full effects of the use of violence are likely to be; and whether there are alternative ways of approaching the conflict that, from a moral perspective, might be no less effective. We need, among other things, to pursue the dynamics of nonviolence as an alternative.

THE DYNAMICS OF NONVIOLENCE

Nonviolence, I mean to suggest, is more than a possible technique of effective social action in cases of conflict, although it is that. From the perspective of the principle of relationality, nonviolence, in its expanded meaning, is an expression of the process of creative interaction through which, in intent, all participants gain in insight and growth. In the phrasing of Joan Bondurant, nonviolence is a matter of "creative conflict"[8]—which is her felicitous rephrasing of Mohandas Gandhi's concept of *satyagraha*.

Conflict, in the sense of encounter among incompatible paths of thought and action, is an inevitable part of life, whether that encounter is among individuals or associations. In the dialectic of life—between participation and individuation—each of us brings to that process a unique perspective that constitutes our particular aim and character. While we belong together, each individual contributes something sui generis to that togetherness. Given that dynamic, differences, including differences of a radical character—differences that in themselves may be irreconcilable—are to be expected. But, depending on how conflict is handled, they are also to be celebrated, for out of the intensity of conflict where the parties are at odds with each other, new insights and new possibilities can emerge.

Margaret Fisher, acknowledging a range of alternative approaches to social conflict, contrasts two fundamentally different methods in an effort to demonstrate the moral significance of pursuing one or the other as a means of moving forward toward conflict resolution. She labels the two methods: "*satyagraha*" and "agonology." *Satyagraha*, she avers, "asserts the relevance of moral values, defines ends in terms of engaging the adversary in a search for 'truth', insists upon nonviolent means, and stresses the bonds of common humanity linking the opposing sides." In contrast, agonology "elevates efficiency above all other values, takes no account of any ethical, moral, or emotional aspects of conflict except insofar as they may affect efficiency, seeks either victory or the denial of victory to the opponent, restricts means only by criteria based on expediency, and assumes a basic need to guard at all times against human depravity."[9] Most significantly, the two methods differ in the objectives that govern them. In the case of *satyagraha*, or creative conflict, the objective is "to achieve an agreement with the opponent acceptable to both sides, by engaging [the opponent] in a search for 'truth', using only nonviolent means." In the case of agonology, the objective is "to defeat the opponent, or at least to avoid being defeated, using whatever means may be expedient."[10]

Bondurant casts the objective of *satyagraha* somewhat more precisely, appropriating the language of the dialectical tradition, as "a restructuring of the opposing elements to achieve a situation which is satisfactory to both the original opposing antagonists, but in such a way as to present an entirely new total circumstance."[11] That is, the aim of creative conflict is to give rise to a synthesis out of a head-on encounter between thesis and antithesis. Those committed to the method of creative conflict do all they can to convince the opponent of the wisdom of their perspective but, at the same time, they invite the Other to do the same, with the anticipation that, in time, although not necessarily without suffering and loss, even loss of life, a new form of relationship between Self and Other may emerge. At its best, that new form of relationship is not merely a *modus vivendi*, a grudging accommodation or compromise, but rather the effectuation of a kind of reciprocity through which the lives of each are deepened in intensity. That is the objective of *satyagraha*—which, I would propose, can be understood as an expression of a koinonological form of ethics, a form of ethics whose primary concern is with the quality of interrelationships among participants in the ongoing community of life.

Three concepts are prominent in Gandhi's rendition of *satyagraha*—truth (*satya*), nonviolence (*ahimsa*), and self-suffering (*tapasya*)—concepts which I would reconfigure given the principle of relationality.

At times, Gandhi suggests that truth (*satya*) is an end for which nonviolence (*ahimsa*) is the appropriate means. But the separation between ends and means that that suggestion seems to entail is deceptive unless it is understood that means are not ultimately distinguishable from ends. They are the ends in the process of realization. That is why a commensurability of means and ends must be sustained. Perhaps in the sphere of human interaction, we should consider ends not so much a final state to be achieved in some future time, as a quality of interrelationship to be instantiated so far as possible at each moment in the unfolding of our lives together. From this perspective, means and ends are fused in each event of life—although in the continuing adventure of life we may look on each event from different angles. Each event (in itself of some intrinsic value, positive or negative) constitutes at the same time a condition (an instrumental value, or means in this sense) out of which may emerge new possibilities of growth in value (that is, ends). The question posed by the nonviolent tradition is whether it is possible to realize a nonviolent end (genuine peace) through the use of violent means? Given the fusion of ends and means, that possibility would seem unlikely. That is why, in the logic of *satyagraha*, truth (*satya*) and nonviolence (*ahimsa*) are inseparable.

Devotion to truth (*satya*), according to Gandhi, is the ultimate justification for our lives. But, he recognizes, no one of us in the course of history has or can have a complete grasp of truth. Each one of has, rather, a perspective on what is true. We may speak of what is true for us—which embraces what we have projected as the meaningfulness (or, for that matter, the meaninglessness) of life and how we may go about creating conditions for the living of that life. Each cultural form, each political system, each economic structure is the expression of what some class of people has determined is sensible and important for them. In this way, they live out their truth through the institutions they have formed. To Gandhi, that was as applicable to British imperialism as it was to Indian nationalism. But, if we are truthful about the status of our truth, we must recognize the partiality of our perspective, the limitations of our comprehension, the possible flaws in our understanding. And we must recognize the plausibility of the Other from the perspective of the Other, including those who stand firmly opposed to us. In our devotion to truth, while we must cling vigorously to our own perspective (our own truth), especially to its core principles, we must learn to listen creatively to that Other given the prospect that out of the encounter between Self and Other, a deeper, richer, more sophisticated understanding and way of life may emerge through what Henry Nelson Wieman has called a "process of creative transformation"—which, in his rendition, is an expansive energy enhancing the complexity of one's powers of understanding, appreciation, action, and integration:

> Creativity is an expanding of the range and diversity of what the individual can know, evaluate, and control. Creativity is an increasing of [one's] ability to understand appreciatively other persons and peoples across greater barriers of estrangement and hostility. Creativity is an increasing of the freedom of the individual when freedom means one's ability to absorb any cause acting on oneself in such a way that the consequences resulting from it express the character and fulfil the purpose of the individual.... [Creativity is an] increasing [of] the capacity of the individual to integrate into the uniqueness of [one's] own individuality a greater diversity of experiences so that more of all that [one] encounters becomes a source of enrichment and strength rather than impoverishing and weakening one.[12]

In the dynamics of this process, devotion to truth (*satya*) entails nonviolence (*ahimsa*). Violence, aggressive or defensive, in its destructiveness of the Other and its denial of essential connectedness with the

Other, runs counter to the prospect that out of conflictual encounter possibilities of advancement in understanding and in value may emerge. As an alternative to violence, the principle of nonviolence (*ahimsa*) does not dictate sheer passivity or capitulation to the Other in cases of conflict. Rather it prescribes a range of vigorous, even at times coercive, actions.

Coercion, it should be noted, in the sense of acting contrary to the will of the Other in an effort to stifle or to transform the will of the Other, is not necessarily violent, although, it must be admitted, coercion employed in the interest of creative transformation always runs of risk of an inversion into its antithesis. To restrain a child acting out of a blind rage is to coerce, but not, necessarily, to do violence to the child. To launch a protest demonstration in contravention to the orders of a sheriff is similarly coercive, but not therefore violent if conducted in the way of *satyagraha*.

Ahimsa, in its narrowest usage, means merely nonharming. But, as Nathaniel Altman construes it, *ahimsa*, in its broadest usage, means "dynamic compassion"[13]—which I would define as the deliberate cultivation and practice of appreciative consciousness. Through appreciative consciousness, the Self, sensitive to the full depth of relations that sustains the life of each individual and responsive to the need to nurture those relations providing for the release of energies of healing and growth, is brought to respect the Other and to do what seems most likely to bring Self and Other together in forms of mutuality and friendship, however antagonistic their momentarily prevailing relationship.

Self-suffering (*tapasya*) is a possible implication of nonviolence, for there is no assurance that an antagonistic Other will be responsive in a constructive manner to the nonviolent assertiveness of a Self in cases of serious conflict. The Other may, on the contrary, press forward employing methods that are violent. For the Self, committed to the full meaning of nonviolence, to respond to such methods with violence or even the threat of violence simply compounds the potential destructiveness of the conflict and denies what is of greatest importance, namely, the development of relations of reciprocity and friendship throughout the community of life. This is why Martin Luther King, Jr., in his promotion of nonviolence affirms that such an approach to conflict and contention "does not seek to defeat or humiliate the opponent, but to win [the opponent's] friendship and understanding." Nonviolence manifests "a willingness to accept suffering without retaliation." Repeatedly, King affirms that nonviolence is based on "the realization that unearned suffering is redemptive," that is, unearned suffering initiates a dynamic that contains within itself significant transformative possibilities for the future.[14]

THE DISCIPLINE OF PEACEMAKING

The relative efficacy of these transformative possibilities, however, is contingent on the development of a rigorous discipline of peacemaking. Throughout most social systems we have devoted massive resources to disciplines of conflict resolution whose *ultima ratio* is violence—disciplines of warmaking and law enforcement—resulting in untold suffering and degradation throughout both the human world and the ecosphere. If the concrete historical ideal that I have adumbrated above (the ideal of genuine reciprocity throughout the entire community of life) is to become a genuine prospect, we shall have to redirect such resources—technological, organizational, and cultural—toward the deliberate making of peace.

We should, in this connection, recall Martin Luther King, Jr.'s distinction between negative peace ("the absence of tension") and positive peace ("the presence of justice").[15] Often, in peace-seeking, we intend the former: a cessation of armed conflict, a truce among warring parties, an agreement to accept mediation. However, without a determined move toward positive peace, negative peace may conceal deep injustices and thereby constitute not genuine peace at all, but a form of institutional violence. And yet we have been, again and again, comforted with the trappings of a negative peace on the assumption that merely the reduction of tension is a good to be cherished. That is not, in King's moral lexicon, always and everywhere the case. The making of genuine peace, in King's vision, entails nothing less that a move toward radical social transformation, directing the energies of our common life toward the creation of a "beloved community" throughout the world. And that move may, on occasion, mandate an increase in tension.

In a variation on that same theme, Betty Reardon, sketching the outlines of a feminist understanding of global security, construes the distinction between negative and positive peace as indicative of two complementary movements toward global peace that should be undertaken: first, a reversal in the full continuum of violence that pervades our common life (ranging from domestic violence to military violence—which are not, she insists, unconnected) and, second, a concerted move toward the fulfillment of the basic needs of all peoples (which is the foundation of a doctrine of human or, more inclusively, natural rights). Against that backdrop, she declares, if global security is our concern, we need to construct a social policy devoid of reliance on methods of violence and oriented toward a sustainable earth and equitable human relations.

To announce that such a move is possible is to declare that structures of violence and alienation are not inherent in the human condition.[16] They are constructions of human history and, as such, susceptible to deconstruction and change. Since every type of social life consists of two interactive dimensions—it is a form of social consciousness and it is a type of social order—social change may be initiated in either or both of these dimensions. The discipline of peacemaking must embrace both dimensions, seeking, as aspects of a concrete historical ideal for our times, to effect a new kind of mentality and a new kind of social policy.

As a proposal directed toward the former—developing a new kind of mentality—Reardon suggests that, as an important beginning in the move toward genuine global peace, we attend to "the demilitarization of the mind" because, in her judgment, "the way we think, and the way we teach the young to think, about the world and others will be the main determinant of the future security of the world."[17] More generally, the way we think about Self and the Self's relation to the Other is a vital dimension in the discipline of peacemaking.

At this point, I suggest that the meditative instruction of Thich Nhat Hanh might prove fruitful. Nhat Hanh, out of the Zen Buddhist tradition, promotes the idea of "being peace"— of embodying peace directly in the immediacy of one's life. That is a possibility open to anyone and everyone at all times. "Being peace" entails right mindfulness, a kind of understanding that is, given its inner character, conjoined with compassion. With right mindfulness, one awakens to the realization that "there is no such thing as an individual."[18] We do not because we cannot, Nhat Hanh explains, exist solely by ourselves, for ourselves, with ourselves alone. We are, in a sense, composites of an untold network of relationships, ultimately encompassing the entire adventure of life.

To be sure, our mentality is often that of a "small self"—we identify ourselves in a relatively narrow manner as a sole individual or as simply a member of some delineable group—nation, race, class, family, corporation. But when we are comfortable with our small self, we act in ways, advertently or inadvertently, destructive of our "large self." Nhat Hanh has coined the term *interbeing* to convey the notion of our "large self," a term that, in its own way, bears with it the idea of the dialectic between participation and individuation.[19] While, from the perspective I am here promoting, we must not detract from the creativity and character of the individual, we must, in extending our awareness of the full depth of the Self—its beginning, its living, its ending—acknowledge that none of us, in any simple way, lives alone. Our identity is an identity of mutuality, of interrelatedness with all that is. To gain that insight, which I would term a form of appreciative consciousness, is to initiate an extension of understanding and compassion whose implication is that Self and Other belong together. Any diminishment of the Other is *ipso facto* a diminishment of the Self.[20] In Nhat Hanh's direct, somewhat elementary, formula: "If we see deeply into the nature of interbeing, that all things 'inter-are', we will stop blaming, arguing, and killing, and we will become friends with everyone."[21]

Such a transformation of mentality, through the increased sensitization of the human spirit to the extensiveness and complexities of the Self-Other relationship and to the larger identity of the Self, is one side of the discipline of making peace. The other side bears on the formation of fundamental social practices—including defense policies and institutions in the criminal justice system, but extending, in the aspect of positive peace, to basic economic and political structures.

We have become accustomed, over the years, to associate defense policies with the development of militia—organizationally (in the form of armed forces) and technologically (in the form of advanced weapons of destruction and techniques of subduing the enemy). However, out of the tradition of nonviolence, an alternative has long been proposed and is worthy of consideration as we confront the challenge of the next century: the formation of a civilian-based defense system, trained particularly in the methods and techniques of noncooperation. As Gene Sharp puts this possibility: "Civilian defense aims to defeat military aggression by using resistance by the civilian population as a whole to make it impossible for the enemy to establish and maintain political control over the country.... The citizens would prevent enemy control of the country by massive and selective refusal to cooperate and to obey, supporting instead the legal government and its call to resist."[22] Police would refuse to do the bidding of the invaders; teachers would refuse to introduce the enemy's propaganda in schools; workers would use delays and strikes to impede production; journalists and lecturers would publicize, through open or clandestine channels, critiques of events and happenings and would persist in keeping before the public the principles and concepts of a peaceable and just cosmopolis.

On one level, the principle of noncooperation derives from a relational understanding of power according to which persons in positions of presumed power are effective only insofar as their subjects are at least acquiescent, if not supportive, in adhering to their dictates. Noncooperation is a method of reducing their power to naught. To be sure, those who engage in methods of noncooperation must be prepared to suffer painful consequences, even death. That is but a clear example of *tapasya* (self-suffering) which, as indicated above, is integral to the full meaning of nonviolence. On another level, the principle of noncooperation is, somewhat ironically, expressive of an authentic and embracing cooperative spirit infused with the most basic understanding of politics whose governing purpose is incorporated in the concept of positive peace. From this perspective, a morally acceptable form of defense policy must totally reconstruct concepts of "national security" and "vital national interest" which, in their conventional meanings, are dysfunctional[23] since, in sustaining the prevailing nation-state system, they run counter to the genuine interests of the community of life given current historical conditions.

Institutions of the criminal justice system are in similar need of radical reconstruction. The prevailing criminal justice system, in its presumed effort to mitigate the incidence of violence throughout the social order, in fact does violence to those ensnared in its network. Racism and classism are rampant throughout the system. In addition, the entire institution is constructed as a means of ostracism and degradation. In the judgment of M. Kay Harris, "We all want to be protected from those who would violate our houses, our persons, and our general welfare and safety; but the protections we are offered tend to reinforce the divisions and distorted relations in society and to exacerbate the conditions that create much of the need for such protections."[24]

The alternative is a criminology of peacemaking, aimed at the creation of methods of societal reconciliation and dispute resolution. The agenda of a criminology of peacemaking is threefold. Its first task is conceptual: to redefine crime in accordance with the concrete historical ideal sketched above. Its second task is preventative: to transform those conditions and institutions that tend to stimulate criminal behavior. Its third task is restorative: to do what can be done to initiate moves toward reconciliation among persons (and, I would add, other forms of life) where injury has been done.

In its full transformative implications, the discipline of peacemaking would touch on virtually all aspects of social consciousness and social practice—political and economic, religious and cultural. Nothing less is required of us if we would pursue the concrete historical ideal that, in my judgment, is appropriate at this moment in our history. That we may, even most likely will, fail in that pursuit—such is the tragic irony of human life, that we act contrary to our own good—does not detract from the urgency of the task or from the possibility that we can, at the very least, make the effort to display the eloquence and strength of the principle of nonviolence in the immediate circles of our lives together.

One final comment. With Thich Nhat Hanh[25] and Martin Luther King, Jr.,[26] I would declare that the principle of nonviolence, in its expanded meaning, is rooted in an understanding of love as that creative force pervading the universe whose inspiration draws us toward each other, even amidst our radical differences, into communities of mutual sustenance and intensity. The discipline of peacemaking is engendered and energized by the driving impulse of love if only we would open our hearts and minds to its subtle but powerful presence.

13

Interlude: Criminality and Community

> Let those without sin among you
> be the first to throw a stone at her.
> —*John 8:7*

Twenty years ago, Norval Morris and Gordon Hawkins, both well known in the field of criminal justice at the time, published a *Letter to the President on Crime Control*. In that letter, they announced that crime "is our major domestic problem and, although other nations in recent years have experienced alarming crime growth rates, it remains vastly more extensive and more virulent here than anywhere else in the world. All Americans are victims of crime, for in the latter half of this century it has massively eroded the quality of life in this country."[1] Over the intervening period, the matter of crime has remained a national obsession, commanding overwhelming attention in the media and in electoral politics and commandeering enormous proportions of our public funds.

We are, I suggest, so consumed by this obsession, which is provoked and sustained by a pervasive sense of fear, we too often fail to remember that those whom we identify as criminals are our companions in the ongoing adventure of life and, whatever they have (or have not) done, they deserve the respect of companionship. Moreover, criminality, as we customarily identify it nowadays, may not be in itself our "major domestic problem," but rather may be symptomatic of a deeper disorder that permeates our common life, a disorder that promotes criminality of various kinds.

First of all, we should note, the predominant form of crime control in the United States—incarceration—constitutes one of the grand ironies of our common life. We pride ourselves as a free country. Freedom of opinion, freedom of speech, freedom of association, freedom of mobility are all central features in the credo of our national self-understanding. The citizens of this nation, we like to claim, enjoy a more generous range of freedoms than citizens of any other land.

247

But, at the same time, we lock up, proportionately, more of our fellow citizens in jails, prisons, and penitentiaries than any other country in the world. According to a 1991 report, where the rate of incarcerated persons per 100,000 was 426 in the United States, it was only 333 in South Africa, 268 in the (then) Soviet Union, and but a measly 100 in the United Kingdom and 45 in Japan.[2] In 1994, the number of persons behind bars in the United States surpassed a sum of one million. In 1996, the reported total was 1.6 million. Prison facilities are so crowded, some prisoners who have already served most of their assigned time behind bars, have been—with grave reluctance—released early to make room for the newly convicted. We anticipate, at the present time, an appreciable rise in the numbers to be committed, and many political leaders and citizens are clamoring for longer sentences. In August 1994, the United States Congress adopted a 30 billion dollar omnibus anticrime bill, almost one-third of which was designated for the construction of new prisons and boot camps for the convicted.

Whatever else imprisonment signifies and however else it functions, it severely constricts the scope of possibilities open for personal determination by inmates and, in ways both official and unofficial, it constitutes a radical intrusion into a prisoner's everyday life. The prison, in short, is, by intention, the epitome of totalitarian control. As such, it is the very antithesis of a genuinely free society—although perhaps, as Michel Foucault has proposed, it is not uncharacteristic of other forms of modern organization despite pompous pretenses to the contrary.[3] When it comes to the particulars of our life together, given the peculiar character and extensive influence of corporate capitalism, we may not be quite as free as we like to proclaim.

In large part, the penal system is sustained, despite its enormous costs (in excess of $25,000 annually for each inmate in operating costs alone) and its social implications, because of a pervasive sense of fear and insecurity. And the fear of crime is sustained by what appears—through personal anecdotes, sensational news stories, dramatic courtroom cases, gripping TV series, and some ways of construing statistical reports—to be an ever accelerating increase in the extent and viciousness of criminal activity throughout the country.

According to the Federal Bureau of Investigation's Uniform Crime Reports, the degree of violent crime in the United States increased by a rate of 19 percent during the four year period from 1988 through 1992. (It has subsequently decreased significantly: the 1995 rate was 10 percent lower than the 1991 rate—although, even with that decrease, 1995 registered a rate 11 percent higher than 1986.) In 1992, the FBI estimated 758 violent crimes per 100,000 citizens, a grand total of nearly two million such cases; in 1995, the estimate had slackened to 685 per 100,000. Violent crime in the FBI's calculus consists of four kinds of offenses: murder and nonnegligent manslaughter; forcible rape; robbery; and aggravated assault. During the period from 1988–1992, incidentally, the rate of (nonviolent) property crimes (ranging from burglary to arson) decreased by 2 percent and the rate has continued to decline in subsequent years. Curiously, the FBI attends only to violent crimes and property crimes in its annual reports. That limitation is perhaps understandable, for these are the kinds of activities that have, it seems, a dramatic and immediate impact on our personal lives, if not by direct experience, then by a pervasive sense of expectation—that is, a sense of what *might* happen to us at any time—induced by the media and by a "commonsense" state of mind. Consider, for instance, that, on average, a rape occurs in the United States about every five minutes, day and night, but no one knows, in advance, where or to whom. "Common sense," we like to think, informs us to be constantly on the alert wherever we might be, to be wary of strangers, to fortify our persons and homes with secure protective devices.

Intriguingly, however, we often become so fixated on the types of criminal activity indicated above—murder, rape, robbery—we are blinded to another category of crime that has, perhaps in even greater measure, "massively eroded the quality of life in this country." Over fifty years ago, Edwin H. Sutherland labelled this category, "white-collar crime."[4] More recently, Gilbert Geis called it "upperworld crime."[5] Stuart Hills calls it more pointedly "corporate violence," which he defines broadly as "actual harm and risk of harm inflicted on consumers, workers, and the general public as a result of decisions by corporate executives or managers, [whether] from corporate negligence, the quest for profits at any cost, [or] willful violations of health, safety, and environmental laws."[6]

Statistics in the area of white-collar/upperworld crime are not easily compiled. Take, for instance, the widespread collapse of savings and loan associations in the eighties, whose final bail-out, according to one estimate, will eventually cost over $1 trillion. A study by the Resolution Trust Corporation concluded that fraud and insider abuse contributed to the failure of over 40 percent of the associations taken over by the RTC. The financial costs of such criminal activity are obviously enormous, although the exact amount is virtually impossible to calculate. Take, as another instance, occupational health crimes, ranging from severed limbs and acute chemical poisoning to loss of hand function given repetitive motions and the gradual onset of stress-related diseases often resulting in death. The Occupational Safety and Health Administration (OSHA) was created in 1970 to establish standards and to monitor industries in an effort to protect workers from harm, but OSHA has been constantly obstructed in its work in many ways, by cutbacks in personnel and by pressure to favor voluntary compliance. It is virtually impossible to ascertain the full extent of death and injuries resulting from violations of the health and safety standards promulgated by OSHA, but according to a calculation by a President's Commission a few years ago, "Deaths caused by occupational health and safety hazards number over 100,000 annually, and even with a more efficient and responsive OSHA, this number may increase as the number of lethal chemicals used in the work place increases beyond the limits of regulatory control."[7]

However, granting the difficulty of securing highly reliable statistics respecting the incidence of white-collar crime (or, as some put it, "crime in the suites") it may not be unreasonable to surmise that its physical, financial, and social costs most likely surpass the impact of crime in the streets. Ponder the startling estimate of the National Safe Workplace Institute "that 1 of 6 workers dies from an occupationally related disease."[8] Of whom should we be more afraid: the ghetto gang or the corporate board?

Reflecting about all these forms of criminal activity—the violent crime in the streets and the (seemingly) more subtle, but no less injurious, crime in the suites—which, taken altogether, have "massively eroded the quality of life in this country," we should pause for a time to ask what it is, in the final analysis, that constitutes "crime." The category "crime" is, after all, a human construction. An activity is dubbed a crime only by our determination, although once so designated, that activity is (presumably) stigmatized, marked with infamy and disgrace (except by those, who, out of defiance, take it as a matter of pride or, in the case of upperworld crime, justify it as "business necessity"). But what is it that informs, or should inform, the determination of an activity as criminal?

Crime is a legal category (albeit often tinged with a high degree of moral connotation) and, as such, its meaning is contingent on how the idea of law is construed. Among diverse possibilities (the field of jurisprudence is rife with alternatives these days), I would distinguish three, each of which conveys some insight about the dynamics of criminality, but the most telling of which is, I believe, the third.

First, from a positivist perspective, crime consists of actions (or nonactions) that violate criminal laws but only as those laws are actually applied by public authorities—police officers, prosecuting attorneys, judges and juries, administrative agencies. This definition honors the eminently worthy maxim that we are all innocent until proven guilty and it accounts for the wide range of discretionary power at the command of public officials. However, it bypasses the issue of how certain forms of activity are or should be designated by law as crimes in the first place and it, in effect, suggests that wherever the laws are silent and public officials are ineffective or corrupt, no crime has occurred—which, from the standpoint of public judgment, would seem utterly bizarre.

Second, from a more sociological standpoint, crime consists of actions (or nonactions) that are deeply offensive to the most central sensibilities of the dominant culture in a political community. This understanding indicates why, at times, specific criminal laws are ineffective (e.g., prohibition). Moreover, it is a possible explanation of why, given the cultural hegemony of the business mind in our political society, corporate violence, despite its massive impact on the lives of individuals and communities, seems to provoke less indignation than street violence. However, it tends to favor whatever sensibilities are held by persons in positions of cultural and political power and it begs the normative question of what *should* be deeply offensive to us in our common life.

For a third perspective, I invoke an emerging "criminology of peacemaking," which, in my judgment, is, in its basic understanding and principles, congruent with the concerns of a politics of relationality.[9] The criminology of peacemaking bears the influences of several strains of reflection: religious, feminist, and critical. In a synthesis of all these influences, crime might be understood as any action (or nonaction) that is seriously antagonistic to or disruptive of an all-inclusive and mutually supportive "peacemaking community." Peace, in this context, is not to be rendered negatively as merely an absence of violence, however important that may be. Peace is more amply to be interpreted as the fulfillment of justice—justice in all realms of our common life: political, social, economic, even, we must surely now add, ecological. From this perspective, crime in the suites is no less important, and may be even more significant, than crime in the streets, for corporate violence, in its extent and its ordinariness, is indicative of something fundamentally gone awry in the structural conditions of our life together.

I must add that, from a peacemaking perspective, prisons—at least as they are currently constructed and administered—are terribly perverse in their effects. So concludes Fay Honey Knopp, a distinguished activist in criminal justice:

> Prisons *do not work*. They do not reduce crimes; they do not rehabilitate people; they rarely deter; and they fail to protect the public in any enduring way. Imprisonment punishes deeply and expensively in both human and fiscal costs, with damaging effects to both the individual and the community. Prisons punish mainly the poor, the minorities, the powerless, the "losers," the young. Increasingly, prisons are being used to punish women, and to punish them more harshly than ever before.[10]

As presently existing, prisons do nothing to restore the community; they do nothing to heal the rupture created by criminal activity; they do nothing to promote a just peace. At best, they may serve a temporary custodial function in cases where some persons seem to be of such a disposition that the lives of others are seriously threatened.

From a peacemaking perspective, we are in dire need of exploring alternative ways of organizing our lives together in response to all levels of criminal activity, from murder and rape to corporate fraud and chemical poisoning. But, in the process, we need to remember that the criminal—the person or association responsible for criminal activity in any given case—is never *merely* a criminal. (There may be, let us confess, a bit of the criminal in all of us—particularly as defined from the third perspective.) But the criminal is also a participant in that interactive process on which we all depend for our several pursuits. The criminal is our companion. The issue we confront is how, effectively, once criminal activity has been identified, to effect, so far as possible, a restoration, how to draw all parties together in some constructive manner for the advancement of a peacemaking community, how to engage in a reconciling form of corrective justice.

Part V

Ecological Community

The earth is the Lord's
and the fulness thereof,
the world
and those that dwell therein.
—*Psalm 24:1*

Despite our usage, now and then, of well-known metaphors expressing a kinship between the human community and the more encompassing ecological sphere—mother earth, father sky, brother sun, sister moon—we tend, in our everyday life, to treat the latter as radically distinct from the former. Given the clamor of the ecological movement, of course, the current generation seems—at least in some circles—somewhat more sensitive to the suffering of animals and of land than previous generations have been. But the dominant economic and social systems throughout the world, especially in the industrialized world, are overwhelmingly bent to treat that which is nonhuman as, at best, an instrumental value, a resource to be exploited for the satisfaction of human desires. From the perspective of the principle of relationality that I have been promoting throughout all the preceding essays, that understanding of the ecological sphere is short-sighted.

To be sure, however we refine our self-understanding as a distinct species, humans are different in significant respects from granite and humus, daisies and oak trees, giraffes and pelicans. But we are all embedded in a process of constant interaction whereby the existence of any (relatively) distinguishable entity is caught up with the existence of all others more or less directly. Our destinies are intertwined; the condition and character of the life of any subject depend in large measure on the condition and character of the life of those others. In an effort to convey this sense, Aldo Leopold constructs the metaphor of a "biotic pyramid" through which energy flows in an elaborate process from soil through insects and vegetation, small animals and large, to humankind and so on around in a continuous circuit. The metaphor of a "pyramid" is, in fact, too static an image to convey the flow and the manner of our interconnection.

The significance of that complex interconnection among the entities of this world is twofold. It informs us about who we are and it instructs us about what we ought to do. It indicates that we are participants in a dynamic and inclusive ecological system. It demonstrates that, as participants, we bear some responsibility for the quality and welfare of that entire system. What we think and how we act make a difference in the ongoing adventure of the world. That is the underlying theme of the chapters that follow.

The first chapter addresses the connection between ecological consciousness and social justice, drawing on the insights of both deep ecology and social ecology and demonstrating the relevance of faith (understood as appreciative consciousness) to ecological responsibility. The final brief chapter in the form of a postlude points to a convergence between ecology (as a way of understanding the conjunction between nature and humanity) and koinonology (as a form of moral reflection).

14
Ecology and Social Justice: Shattering the Boundaries of Moral Community

> In his hands are the depths of the earth;
> the heights of the mountains are his also.
> The sea is his, for he made it;
> for his hands formed the dry land.
> —*Psalm 95:4–5*

Beginning in the final third of the nineteenth century, progressive social theorists gave widespread voice to the "social question." Reacting to the exploitative character of a rapidly developing industrial capitalism and expressing solidarity with the laboring class, they provided an extensive critique of the capitalist system and envisioned, in variant versions, the possibility of a new, more humane and just civilization. Despite diverse efforts to mitigate the sufferings of the lower socioeconomic class, the social crisis—compounded with issues of race, gender, and ethnicity—persists.

Yet, during the final third of the twentieth century, the social question seems to have been overshadowed, at least in some circles, by the "ecological question," given the utterly destructive impact that modern industrialized society, whether in the form of corporate capitalism or state socialism, has had on the world of nature.

The social question (as a matter of social justice) and the ecological question (as a matter of the sustainability of the earth), although often separated from each other, if not held in antagonism with each other, belong together. At their roots, they converge. Each is a version of the question of Otherness and thus also a question of the character of the Self. Each is an expression of a paradox of Otherness: the Other, although distant from the Self and external to the Self, is nonetheless an intimate companion of the Self, indeed, participates in the Self. To state the paradox in that way is to indicate that both social crisis and ecological crisis are, in a profound sense,

255

forms of a crisis of the human spirit, manifesting a distorted sense of who we are and what we might become.

While I do not wish to detract from the institutional and techno-logical dimensions of the social crisis or the ecological crisis, I would assert that these crises, as versions of the question of Otherness, are expressions of a crisis of faith. However, faith, while reaching beyond the strictures and delimitations of institutional forms, is not wholly independent of them.

Institutions and technologies are, after all, creations of humankind. They may be, at any given time and place, part of our destiny. But they are not, in their beginnings or in their continuance, matters of necessity. Their durability is a function, sometimes of outright commitment, sometimes of fear and intimidation, but sometimes of sheer routine and inability to envision alternatives. Institutions constrain us and empower us. But whatever their strength or whatever their character, they are symbols of the condition of the human spirit, susceptible there-fore to transformation as the sensitivity of the spirit is quickened. That is the import of faith.

In pursuing my dominant theme—that social crisis and ecological crisis are convergent as versions of a crisis of the human spirit or, oth-erwise stated, a crisis of faith—I shall, in what follows, initiate four lines of inquiry:

- that the development of faith, understood as appreciative aware-ness, is a means of expanding the reach of the human spirit, thereby responding to the question of Otherness;

- that despite the overt antagonism between deep ecology and social ecology, they converge on a principle of nondominative comple-mentarity as responsive to the ecological and social questions;

- that, in contrast to those who propose the restoration of localized forms of moral community to sustain us through our troubled times, we need instead to shatter the boundaries of customary moral communities to embrace the entire creaturely sphere, to cre-ate, in effect, a cosmopolitan community; and

- that in considering the demands of social justice in an inclusive moral community, we should turn our attention from the prevail-ing distributive model of justice to its structural significance and to reconceive justice as a form of mutuality or solidarity.

All four lines of inquiry have been shaped by a metaphysics of relationality with its correlative ethic. From this perspective, we are born of a dynamic matrix of interrelationships whose depth and extent elude our ordinary consciousness even though they are constitutive of our most profound identity. How fully we are receptive to the intricacies of that matrix within which, in its ultimate reach, all life is lived, is demonstrated in those moments that call upon our resources for empathy. A metaphysics of relationality is, I would propose, the philosophical persuasion most apt in approaching a comprehension of both the social question and the ecological question. Moreover, in its contribution to the art of life, a metaphysics of relationality moves us beyond traditional limitations of utilitarianism and deontologism, both of which, in their popular forms, tend toward an individualist view of selfhood. In this sense at least, a metaphysics of relationality betokens a move toward a postmodern world, more so than alternatives that have made that claim.

FAITH AS APPRECIATIVE AWARENESS

First line of inquiry:
The development of faith,
understood as appreciative awareness,
is a means of expanding the reach of the human spirit,
thereby responding to the question of Otherness.

Nowadays, to have faith tends to signify credulity. That is, subjectively, faith means the acceptance of a set of beliefs which, taken altogether, constitute a world of meaning.[1] To the faithful, that world of meaning is all-consuming, providing a source of self-identity and a vision of importance. Shared with others, it results in a community of faith which, over time, eventuates in a rich and complex tradition of faith with all the trappings of doctrine and liturgy, architecture and sociology we associate with the religions of humankind. Thus we speak of the faith of various forms of Christians, Buddhists, Muslims, Jews, Parsees. What bearing such forms of faith have on contemporary social and ecological crises depends on the character of the classic beliefs of the tradition and how they are interpreted by prevailing hermeneutical trends.

However, Bernard Meland, following a tradition of deep empiricism in American thought,[2] has proposed an alternative understanding of the function of faith in human life. Faith is not, in the first instance, a matter of credulity so much as it is a matter of sensitivity. It is not an effort to explain the otherwise inexplicable so much as it is a deepening of the human spirit. It is less a matter of commitment, intellectual or emotional, to a set of beliefs than it is an open receptiveness to dimensions of meaning resident within the full context of one's existence and an intention to give embodied expression to those dimensions in the structures of life.

From the perspective of Meland's empirical realism, existence is two-sided:

> On its subjective side, I see existence as a stream of experience; in its objective side, as a Creative Passage. I use the term "Creative Passage" as an ultimate reference in the way traditional metaphysics employed the term "Being" or "Ground of Being.". . . I have come to think of the Creative Passage as being the most basic characterization of existence as it applies to all life, to all people, to all cultures.[3]

Lived experience, as Meland modifies a concept appropriated from the phenomenological tradition, is more than the intentional participation of the self in the flow of events. In its "holistic character," it implies the "full, ongoing context" of life.[4] It includes the inherited legacy of times past and the anticipated possibility of times future. It encompasses the immediacies of the moment, but also the subtle yet nonetheless powerful presence of ultimacy, that is, the primordial goodness that constitutes the Ultimate Efficacy of the Creative Passage.[5] Experience so understood "is the primal source of all awareness. It is not so much an interplay of explicit sensory responses as a bodily event which conveys to the living organism, in a holistic way, its rapport [with] and participation in the nexus of relationships which constitutes its existence."[6] As Meland affirms repeatedly, "we live more deeply than we can think."[7]

However, while lived experience embraces this amplitude of life's context at any moment, it attains a particularized focus in the relative singularity of the individual at that moment. From the standpoint of empirical realism, Individuality-in-Community is a persistent theme: "No creature is singular or wholly individuated; yet none is assimilable without remainder to the communal life of culture, nature, or, for that matter, to the depth of the Creative Passage as expressed in the reality of God."[8] While acknowledging the relative uniqueness of each individual, yet in the depths of our experience, however little we may discern this to be our circumstance, this theme insists we live in solidarity with all life: "To emerge in the world of the concrete...is to take on instantaneously relations with every other event. The full implication of this doctrine of prehension is that community is a constituent of the individual."[9]

The communal matrix of one's life includes the social and cultural history of humankind. But it includes as well the entire biotic community. We are, as Meland, asserts, the "creation in miniature."

> The sea water flows through our veins. The minerals of the earth lie embedded in our bodies. The rhythms of the tides move within us in the rise and fall of passion, in the alternation of moods, and in the varying secretions of the endocrine glands. All of these identify the individual event with all events in the sense that they represent existence in its constituent parts.[10]

Yet, although our experience, in its full depth, connects us as unique individuals with all that is through the broad sweep of social and natural history as the communal ground of our being, our lives are also marked with what Meland has named the "surd of insensitivity." The paradox of insensitivity, whether in the social or ecological arena, is its destructive effects on the very sources of the goodness of life. "The peril of existing derives in large measure from the surd of insensitivity that intrudes upon all relationships with varying degrees of defeat and destructiveness, ranging from the anguish and evil of isolated existences among individuals to explosive encounters between individuals and groups."[11] Within the modern world, the surd of insensitivity has become pervasively embedded in the institutionalized systems of our common life—industrialism, capitalism, nationalism, sexism, racism— in which and through which we have, perversely, designed as a matter of realism and practical wisdom policies that result in the death and degradation of whole forms of life. Through this surd of insensitivity, we have become agents of "creation-in-reverse."[12] The virulence and massiveness of this surd of insensitivity has led Meland to affirm that "Existence...is sustained in most instances by a perilously slight margin of sensitivity."[13]

But herein lies the power of and need for faith. That slight margin of sensitivity might be extended through the reach of faith understood as appreciative awareness. In Meland's judgment, "it is the function of the response of faith to open the creature, elementally as well as critically, to its resources, and thus to avail it of a good not its own inherent in the Creative Passage which cradles and recreates all existent events."[14] Appreciative awareness in Meland's lexicon signifies an "orientation of mind which makes for a maximum degree of receptivity to the datum under consideration on the principle that what is given may be more than what is immediately perceived, or more than one can think."[15] It entails a process of deep empathy. It is an act of identification with the Other, a readiness to be freshly informed, if not transformed, by what is apprehended. It is a kind of perceptiveness open to the flow of events. Faith as appreciative awareness breaks through pregiven expectations, habitual routines, institutionalized frameworks to encounter the particularities of existence whatever their condition and complexity. As receptive, it means openness "to the full datum of experience." As interactive, it entails a flexibility of spirit, a willingness to be transformed through the encounter. As creative, it is committed to bend the structures of life, personal and social, toward a fuller release of the powers of goodness.[16] Through the sensitivity of faith, the richness of lived experience is restored and the estrangement between Self and Other is overcome.

Thus faith as appreciative awareness is not primarily a matter of credulity. Faith is not the same as belief. It is rather a psychic energy, a cultural and social energy, breaking through those routinized structures, psychological and societal, that deaden the spirit and delimit the full goodness of life. In its response to forces of political domination and ecological degradation, faith is the restless urge to reach out for new forms of common life out of commitment to the creative and redemptive good that, despite those forces, continues to sustain us. In this sense, faith is active in the cause of justice.

ECOLOGY AS NONDOMINATIVE COMPLEMENTARITY

Second line of inquiry:
Despite the overt antagonism between deep ecology
and social ecology, they converge in proposing a principle
of nondominative complementarity
as responsive to the ecological and social questions.

Deep ecology (Arne Naess) and social ecology (Murray Bookchin) are at odds over the precise status and role of humankind in the biosphere. But despite that antagonism, they converge in important respects. They are joined in their opposition to ordinary forms of environmentalism (or "shallow ecology") which, however intensely they struggle to resolve problems of air and water pollution, species extinction, and resource depletion, are fundamentally anthropocentric, sustaining a dichotomous, if not segmentalized, understanding of the world. In contrast, deep ecology and social ecology are grounded, although each in its own way, in a metaphysics of relationality. Moreover, each derives from that metaphysics, in defiance of the presumed naturalistic fallacy, an ethic of nondominative complementarity intended to govern humankind's relations not only with each other, but also with all creaturely entities and communities. Finally, both deep ecology and social ecology contain a hint, at least, of something akin to faith as appreciative awareness as a necessary dynamic to ecological theory and practice.

Arne Naess introduced the concept of deep ecology to designate a movement whose understanding of the condition of the world assumed a metaphysics and an ethic radically at odds with the cultural sensibilities of industrial society.[17] Metaphysically, deep ecology entails the "rejection of the man-in-environment image in favor of the relational, total-field image." Naess's expression of the doctrine of relationality seems closer at times to the monism of Spinoza (whose philosophical influence he acknowledges) than to the pluralism of Meland. He sketches the metaphysics roughly as follows:

> Organisms as knots in the biospherical net or field of intrinsic relations. An intrinsic relation between two things A and B is such that the relation belongs to the definitions or basic constitutions of A and B, so that without the relation, A and B are no longer the same things. The total-field model dissolves not only the man-in-environment concept, but every thing-in-milieu concept—except when talking at a superficial or preliminary level of communication.[18]

In deep ecology, this total-field image is conjoined with a concept of "biospherical egalitarianism—in principle." Naess intends the phrase *in principle* to acknowledge that predation to some degree is a tragic necessity of life, but, granting that constraint, he affirms, among all life forms, "the equal right to live and blossom."[19] Alternatively stated, biospherical egalitarianism means that "The flourishing of human and nonhuman life on Earth has intrinsic value. The value of nonhuman life forms is independent of the usefulness these may have for narrow human purposes."[20] The term *life forms,* is construed to include systems of interdependency such as watersheds, landscapes, ecocommunities, even the entire living earth. Biospherical egalitarianism is not without implications for systems of human life. It stands at odds with Western culture's propensity toward structures of dominance, "dominance of humans over nonhuman Nature, masculine over the feminine, wealthy and powerful over the poor, [as well as] ... the West over non-Western cultures."[21] Paradoxically, dominative structures, intended to benefit the powerful, in fact, diminish the quality of life for all. The flourishing of any organism, deep ecology contends, is contingent on the correlative flourishing of its milieu.

This understanding of the complementarity of all things for their respective flourishing underlies a fundamental norm in the ethic of deep ecology, namely, self-realization. To be sure, in modern Western culture, self-realization is ordinarily defined in a narrowly humanistic, if not individualistic, even hedonistic manner. Thus, Naess distinguishes ego-realization (signifying this modern Western propensity) from self-realization in a more comprehensive sense as embracing, ultimately, all reality. An advance in maturity is accompanied with a continuous widening of the Self. The unfolding of the potentialities of the Self is linked with the unfolding of new possibility among all life forms.[22] In the summary phrasing of Bill Devall and George Sessions, "'No one is saved until we are all saved,' where the phrase 'one' includes not only me, an individual human, but all humans, whales, grizzly bears, whole rain forest ecosystems, mountains and rivers, the tiniest microbes in the soil, and so on."[23] Yet, although Naess sometimes invokes the radically monist language of Vedanta in his expansion of the idea of Self, he does not mean to suggest "the dissolution of individual selves into a nondiversified supreme whole," insisting instead that "Both from cultural and ecological point[s] of view diversity and individuality are essential."[24]

The process of widening the Self—thereby overcoming structures of alienation and attaining to a more mature and realistic apprehension of the full character of one's true Self—Naess calls, "identification": "Identification is a spontaneous, non-rational, but not irrational, process through which the ... interests of another being are reacted to as our own ... interests. Intense identification obliterates the experience of a distinction between ego and alter, between me and sufferer."[25] Through identification, Naess claims, we transcend the presumed conflict between egoism and altruism and, therefore, the presumed conflict between the advancement of human life and the enhancement of the biosphere. Identification is a move toward a mature apprehension of the actual character of the conditions and possibilities of life and its fulfillment.

The potential congruence between Naess's concept of identification in its fullest sense and Meland's notion of faith as appreciative awareness is striking. From both standpoints, we are called to move beyond the narrow strictures and destructive implications of prevailing cultural and social forms by an opening of the human spirit to deeper dimensions of experience, extending beyond the immediacies of existence, yet without any loss of their genuine meanings. In both cases, we are called to an empathetic participation in the Creative Passage in which all life is lived through processes of interaction and structures of interdependency.

Naess is keenly aware of the inescapability of conflict among life forms and the need, among humankind, to establish priorities. For that purpose, he develops two indeterminate but useful criteria: vitalness and nearness. "The more vital interest has priority over the less vital. The nearer has priority over the more remote—in space, time, culture, species."[26] But the general principle, namely, to maximize self-realization, while of necessity colored in such cases, retains its regulative power. The ethic of deep ecology, it might be argued, entails, in cases of conflict among life forms, a certain kind of teleological calculus, but, in contrast to modern utilitarianism, a kind that is holistic and contextual, bent, over the course of time, on qualitative attainment not just for each entity taken by itself, but for the texture of the entire creaturely community.

Murray Bookchin, an exponent of social ecology, has issued several broadsides against deep ecology primarily as misanthropic (in its denigration of the human species) and simplistic (in its neglect of the specifically social dimensions of the ecological question). Central to social ecology is the thesis that the degradation of the ecosphere originates in the social system and, obversely, that "No ecological society, however communal or benign in its ideals, can ever remove the 'goal' of dominating the natural world until it has radically eliminated the domination of human by human, or, in essence, the entire hierarchical structure within society in which the very notion of domination rests."[27] The root cause of the ecological crisis is not, in any simple way, the arrogance of humanity in general; it is, more complexly, the development over the course of human evolution of hierarchical and dominative social systems.

The background of Bookchin's understanding of the intertwining of natural and social history is a metaphysics of dialectical naturalism according to which we are participants in an ages-long evolutionary process governed not deterministically, but by the lure of new possibility. The aim of the process is not stability, but creativity, a creativity through which life forms complement each other in the construction of ever richer wholes. Thus nature is "a constellation of communities...neither 'blind' nor 'mute,' 'cruel' nor 'competitive,' 'stingy' nor 'necessitarian' but...a participatory realm of interactive life-forms whose most outstanding attributes are fecundity, creativity, and directiveness, marked by complementarity."[28]

Adopting Cicero's language, Bookchin, understanding nature as the evolution of constantly differentiating and increasingly complex life forms, distinguishes, without separating, "second nature" (the development of specifically human culture) from "first nature" (the development of nonhuman forms of life). The distinction—which constitutes a key point of contention between deep ecology and social ecology—is Bookchin's acknowledgment that in the emergence of the human species, a relatively unique stage of complexity, self-awareness, even subjectivity, was attained in the course of evolution: "By second nature, I mean humanity's development of a uniquely human culture, a wide variety of institutionalized human communities, an effective human technics, a richly symbolic language, and a carefully managed source of nutriment."[29] In human culture, the evolutionary process was brought to a new level of self-awareness, but ironically, at that very point, to a new level of potential self-destruction.

Throughout social history, Bookchin argues, we have confronted critical moments of decision—"turning points"[30]—in the formation and reformation of the structures of our common life, at which points a hierarchical direction has tended to prevail. From gerontocracy to patriarchy, military autocracy to class hegemony, hierarchical domination has permeated all social spheres—family, workplace, politics, schools. The culminating form of hierarchical domination, whose effects extend into the furthest reach of first nature, is capitalism—"the most pernicious social order to emerge in the course of human history."[31] At this point, we encounter another turning point, given our enormous powers: "We can contribute to the diversity, fecundity, and richness of the natural world—what I call 'first nature'—more consciously, perhaps, than any other animal. Or our societies—'second nature'—can exploit the whole web of life and tear down the planet in a rapacious, cancerous manner."[32]

To create an "ecological society"[33] would entail a profoundly revolutionary project, the replacement of current institutional forms, especially the global economic system bent on unending economic growth, with a social order "based on nonhierarchical relationships, decentralized communities, eco-technologies like solar power, organic agriculture, and humanly scaled industries—in short, face-to-face democratic forms of settlement economically and structurally tailored to the ecosystems in which they were located."[34] Understood as such, the revolutionary project of social ecology is responsive to both the social question and the ecological question.[35] It is expressive of what Bookchin sometimes calls an "ethics of complementarity,"[36] and sometimes an "ethics of freedom"[37]—in both cases promoting the precepts of symbiosis: participation and differentiation.

> Social ecology is, first of all, a *sensibility* that includes not only a critique of hierarchy and domination, but a reconstructive outlook that advances a participatory concept of "otherness" and a new appreciation of differentiation as a social and biological desideratum.... [I]t is also guided by an ethics that emphasizes variety without structuring differences into a hierarchical order. If I were to single out the precepts for such an ethics, I would be obliged to use two words that give it meaning: participation and differentiation.[38]

Participation and differentiation are indicative of the development of ecocommunities throughout the course of natural evolution, but also of that form of political society which, by intention, would exist in harmony with first nature and through which principles of mutuality and individuality would wholly displace hierarchy and domination.

Despite Bookchin's acrimonious dismissal of some forms of deep ecology as "mystical" given their invocation of explicitly religious themes, he nonetheless himself calls for a "new spirituality" or "new ecological sensibility" as a central feature of social ecology—but a spirituality that is naturalist in its orientation.[39] Spirituality, in this context, means a "sensitivity to nature and its subtle interconnections." In a sense, given Bookchin's appropriation of Diderot's notion of "sensibilité" (sensitivity) as that crucial dimension of the natural process that constitutes its nisus for development, its creativity, its entelechy, then spirituality might well be taken to signify the sensitivity of the human spirit for the Ultimate Sensitivity whose creative and redemptive working, in Meland's construction, is foundational in the Creative Passage.[40] The constant aim of that sensitivity is for wholeness, which Bookchin defines as "the unity that finally gives order to the particularity of each of these phenomena [a newly planted seed, a newly born infant, a newly formed community, a newly emerging society]; it is what has emerged from the process, what integrates the particularities into a unified form, what renders the unity an operable reality... an order as the actualized unity of its diversity from the flowing and emergent process that yields its self-realization, the fixing of its directiveness into a clearly contoured form, and the creation in a dim sense of a 'self' that is identifiable with respect to the 'others' with which it interacts."[41]

Bookchin's concept of wholeness sounds very much like Naess's principle of self-realization. Moreover, Bookchin's concept of spirituality seems congruent with Naess's process of identification and has a character very much akin to Meland's understanding of faith as appreciative awareness. While differences between deep ecology and social ecology should not be ignored, they converge in their radical critique of prevailing forms of our common life and in their aspiration for new forms of association constructed in accord with a principle of mutual enhancement. Moreover, assuming the plausibility of my rendition of Naess's process of identification and Bookchin's notion of sensibilité, they stand with Meland on the need for faith as appreciative awareness if the cultural and social revolution they espouse is to become effective.

COMMUNITY AS COSMOPOLIS

Third line of inquiry:
In contrast to those who propose the restoration of localized forms
of moral community to sustain us through our troubled times,
we need instead to shatter the boundaries
of customary moral communities to embrace the entire creaturely sphere,
to create, in effect, a cosmopolitan community.

Slightly over a decade ago, Alasdair MacIntyre, in a provocative study of the state of moral understanding in the West, asserted that "What matters at this stage is the construction of local forms of community within which civility and the intellectual and moral life can be sustained through the dark ages which are already among us."[42] In a time of sharp moral disagreement if not moral antipathy, we are left to find moral comfort and direction in our respective traditional communities. However, MacIntyre warns, we should under no condition universalize the precepts of such communities or pretend that we might escape their parochialism in a realm of absolute maxims, for when men and women engage in such practices, "they usually behave worse than they would otherwise do."[43]

MacIntyre's counsel has merit. We are, in a sense, creatures of history. In Meland's language, our life always "partakes of a regional character."[44] Granting that, MacIntyre calls us, in a time of moral uncertainty and social crisis, to become more sensitive to what Meland has called the "structure of experience"—that is, "the persisting valuations of the culture which carry the net result of the cultural history into the present"[45]—out of the conviction that only through the profound myths of cultural inheritance might we attain some reservoir of meaning in our lives and some direction for invigorating those forms of interaction that constitute the setting, even the basic cultural identity of our lives.

But MacIntyre's counsel clashes with the moral direction of both deep ecology and social ecology which, precisely because of the social and ecological crises of our times, calls us to shatter the boundaries of traditional moral communities and to extend our moral embrace to include nothing less than the entire biosphere, even though, in significant respects, our lives may be lived in the immediate context of regionalized and local structures. The character of this move toward a biospheric moral community is discernible in Aldo Leopold's bold proposal for a land ethic, although Leopold's attention is directed almost exclusively to the ecological question to the neglect of the social question. Even with that grave limitation, a (critical) appreciation of the underlying ontology of Leopold's land ethic demonstrates the inadequacy, in our time, of MacIntyre's prescription for the "construction of local forms of community" particularly with its seeming strictures against any kind of universal responsibility. We are, willy nilly, members of a cosmopolis of sorts. The question is whether and how we might, given that condition, move toward the creation of cosmopolitan moral community within the context of which regional communities might find their proper place. Is it possible, we must now inquire, for regional communities to sustain their own unique cultures and specific identities, but as a means of contributing to the flourishing of the entire cosmopolitan community?

Every ethic, Leopold declares, is a function of membership in an interdependent community. Over the course of history, as the shape and size of communities have varied, so have their correlative ethics. A land ethic, which Leopold formulated originally in the late forties,[46] "simply enlarges the boundaries of the community to include soils, waters, plants, or collectively, the land."[47]

In proposing a land ethic, Leopold is asserting that humans are *in fact* members of a community of moral subjects that includes both humans and nonhumans whose welfare is contingent on a conscious acknowledgment by humans as moral agents of that community and on the development of forms of cooperative interaction that will enhance the community and all its members. That is the function of ethics.

> An ethic, ecologically, is a limitation on freedom of action in the struggle for existence. An ethic, philosophically, is a differentiation of social from antisocial conduct. These are two definitions of one thing. The thing has its origin in the tendency of interdependent individuals or groups to evolve modes of cooperation. The ecologist calls these symbioses.[48]

Most forms of ethic throughout social history have dealt strictly with human relations. We are now at a moment when we must affirm our participation in a more complex and inclusive community composed of humans and nonhumans. To convey the character of this community, Leopold constructs the image of a "biotic pyramid," although more often he speaks of it as simply the "land." Land, in this context, is not merely soil; it is the continuous flow of energy throughout the multiple beings that constitute the earth, even the universe:

> It is a fountain of energy flowing through a circuit of soils, plants, and animals. Food chains are the living channels which conduct energy upward; death and decay return it to the soil. The circuit is not closed...; but it is a sustained circuit, like a slowly augmented revolving fund of life.[49]

Over the course of evolution, the circuit has increased in complexity and diversity, progressing, pyramidlike, from layer to layer through various biota, ranging from soil, through plants, insects and birds, to larger carnivores. Once one comprehends land as an evolving community, then the identity of humankind relative to the nonhuman world is transformed. Humans are not, in their proper identity, "conquerors of the land-community"; they are, rather, plain members of it; they are biotic citizens, participants in an inclusive system of interaction. As such, they are obliged to treat their fellows never as means only, but always also as ends. A land ethic implies respect for one's fellow members "and also respect for the community as such."[50]

The latter mandate—that we are obliged to have respect for "the community as such"—has provoked some interpreters to charge that Leopold's land ethic is "holistic with a vengeance"[51] or, more harshly, a form of "environmental fascism,"[52] a kind of charge which, *mutatis mutandis*, might well be levelled against any form of ethics derived from a metaphysics of relationality. Leopold's maxim seems to give credence to such judgments: "A thing is right when it tends to preserve the integrity, stability, and beauty of the biotic community. It is wrong when it tends otherwise."[53] Again, he asserts, "an ethical relation to land" entails "love, respect, and admiration for land and a high regard to its value," meaning by value "something far broader than mere economic value; I mean value in the philosophical sense."[54]

Whether that moral declaration necessarily implies "environmental fascism" depends on the kind of holism Leopold intends. We may distinguish two versions of ethical holism.[55] In an organismic version, parts are wholly subsumed by the whole; with that version, the charge of environmental fascism would seem apt. In a communitarian version (which, in my judgment, is akin to Meland's empirical realism), parts and whole are dialectically related; to have respect for the whole, composed as it is of interacting agents, one must have respect for each participant and its potentialities. The latter, more pluralistic, version of ethical holism seems the more congenial to Leopold's land ethic,[56] even though intimations of both are interspersed throughout Leopold's writings.

Thus, according to a land ethic, the biotic pyramid as a whole throughout its continuing evolutionary unfolding as well as all particular creatures, species, and ecocommunities that constitute that pyramid are "morally considerable."[57] They are not to be treated merely as resources to satisfy the interests of humankind. Rather, out of moral concern, even if the language of rights is too stringent, their life and their welfare warrant our special consideration. In this sense at least, contra Alasdair MacIntyre, the moral community in which we participate and whose concerns should direct our lives, embraces the whole panorama of creaturely existence. Charles Birch and John Cobb have captured this understanding in their affirmation that "We are subjects in a wider community of subjects as well as objects in a wider community of objects. If we, as subjects, are of value, and we are, there is every reason to think that other subjects are of value, too. If our value is not only our usefulness to others but also our immediate enjoyment of our existence, this is true for other creatures as well."[58] As Scott Buchanan framed this same insight in the early sixties, we are all members of a "cosmopolis of nature," in which each creature is properly viewed "reciprocally with the others as means and ends."[59] Within the context of the evolving cosmopolis, humankind occupies a special role in two respects. First, given their specific powers of action, their impact on the entire biotic pyramid—for good or for ill—surpasses that of all other creatures.[60] Second, given the degree of creative freedom they possess, they bear special responsibility as moral agents for "the health of the land."[61]

But an effective moral agency responsive to the needs of the cosmopolitan biotic community is contingent on the emergence of an "ecological conscience": "Obligations have no meaning without conscience, and the problem we face is the extension of the social conscience from people to land." No shattering of the boundaries of traditional moral communities will occur "without an internal change in our intellectual emphasis, loyalties, affections, and convictions."[62] And such an "internal change," I would contend, is linked to the development of faith as appreciative awareness.

We live in regional communities. On this score, Alasdair MacIntyre's insistence that we engage in the construction of local forms of moral community makes sense. We are informed, more or less profoundly, by the subtle expectations and valuational mythos of cultural history. But, as Aldo Leopold reminds us, supplementing the empirical realism of Bernard Meland, that mythos, to be instructive in the midst of the ecological and social crises of our times, must so deepen our sensibilities and extend our bodily energies that we are brought to some apprehension, however dim, of our most elemental condition as participants in an interactive community consisting of all life and grounded in an Ultimate Sensitivity upon whose subtle workings we all depend. Perhaps, however, even Leopold's land ethic, illuminating as it is, is too simple in its conception, ignoring, as it tends to do, the sufferings and excruciations of the social question and neglecting the ultimate reach of faith.

JUSTICE AS MUTUALITY

Fourth line of inquiry:
In considering the demands of social justice
in an inclusive moral community,
we need to turn our attention from the prevailing
distributive model of justice to its structural significance
and to reconceive justice as a form of mutuality.

The social question and the ecological question belong together. At their most basic level, they are versions of the question of Otherness: Who is the Other and what is the Other's relation to the Self? The alternatives are many—friend or enemy, companion or servant, equal or subordinate, comrade or stranger. At the heart of the social and the ecological crises, as understood from the perspective of a metaphysics of relationality, is what I have called the paradox of Otherness, another name for which is alienation. Under conditions of alienation, the Other—human or otherwise—belongs, in some constitutive sense, to the Self, yet is estranged from the Self. Whether through antagonism or indifference, exploitation or rejection, destructive action or sheer ignorance, alienation is a form of relation in which the Self externalizes that which, nonetheless, participates in the communal context of the Self's own existence. In Alfred North Whitehead's language, alienation is that kind of negative prehension which, in its effects, eventuates in diminishing the qualitative attainment of Self and Other in their distinctiveness and in their conjunction.

The reversal of alienation is social justice, which John Rawls has reminded us is the first virtue of our basic political and economic institutions.[63] However, I would contend, Rawls's concept of social justice is, though useful in some respects, much too narrow. In keeping with a dominant trend in Anglo-American moral discourse, Rawls identifies justice as a specifically distributive concept. Within his framework, the subject matter of social justice consists of the principles and criteria according to which the benefits and burdens of a community are allocated. In this sense, contentions over taxation and the use of natural resources, housing and educational opportunity, civil rights and affirmative action are all expressions of the topic of social justice. The intent of any theory of social justice is to shift the consideration of such contentions from a stage of immediate and narrowly construed self-interest to a stage of justifiable principle. For that purpose, Rawls proposes replacing the modern Western tendency to employ a utilitarian calculus with an intricate doctrine of qualified equality.

Iris Marion Young, however, granting the importance of distributive principles in our social institutions, suggests that such principles are secondary to a more profound, more encompassing, more structural concern of social justice, namely, the character of our lives together. Underlying the distributive model of social justice, taken by itself, is an individualist metaphysics that tends to ignore the constitutive importance of the communal matrix of life and to elevate the possession of things over the quality of relationships.[64] Underlying the more encompassing, contextual model of social justice, on the other hand, is a metaphysics whose central theme is Individuality-in-Community. As Carol C. Gould delineates this alternative: "Individuals act fundamentally in and through social relations. The individuals are therefore ontologically primary, but the relations among them are also essential aspects of their being. However, these relations do not exist independently or apart from the individuals who are related. Rather they are relational properties of these individuals."[65] In somewhat more felicitous, albeit more simplistic, phrasing, Robert Johann takes this to mean that "life is essentially a shared undertaking in a shared world."[66] From this perspective, more important than the quantity of what one possesses (a distributive concern) is the quality of one's interactions (a structural concern).

Social justice, on this structural level, is less a matter of principles of distribution than a matter of the patterns of interaction, institutional and cultural, through which life is lived. The test of justice is mutuality (or solidarity), the sense in which and the degree to which the life of each enhances the life of all others, but through that very process redounds to the enrichment of one's own experience.[67] The elementary maxim of social justice is: So act within the circumstances at hand that the life of the entire community and each of its participants might, so far as possible, flourish. Given this maxim and its underlying metaphysics, our common life, with its constant process of giving and receiving, is not (necessarily) a zero-sum game. Rather, under conditions of mutuality, in giving, because of the character of Otherness, one also receives. This assumes that Self and Other, though different in subjectivity, nonetheless belong together. They are, if you will, participants in each other's life.

In their development of this form of understanding social justice, Young, Gould, and Johann do not address the ecological question explicitly, but I suggest that, through an extension of the moral community to embrace the biosphere (as proposed by Aldo Leopold), the same maxim applies, *mutatis mutandis,* to relations between human and nonhuman life forms. All life forms, human and nonhuman, are moral subjects, even if, it appears, only humans are specifically moral agents. Perhaps only humans, because of their relatively unique capacities of perceptual awareness and purposeful action, can be conceived to have moral responsibility, but all creatures are of moral concern as individuals,[68] and as participants in communities of reciprocal interaction.[69] The moral responsibility of humans thus extends to the entire cosmopolis of creaturely life. Although the maxim of justice is addressed to us as human agents, it is intended in its focus to be responsive to both the social question and the ecological question.

Granting the complexities of its application, the maxim of justice as mutuality or solidarity enjoins us in a revolutionary struggle against forms of systemic domination and institutionalized oppression[70] whether exercised over fellow humans or other creatures. From the perspective of the ordinary world of social practice and historical expectation such a struggle may seem utterly unrealistic. The social question and the ecological question have seemed, over the course of history, to defy resolution. I would contend to the contrary however that, given the sensitivities of faith as appreciative awareness, the promotion of justice as mutuality is a profoundly realistic venture, deriving from an apprehension of the deeper impulses of the Creative Passage within which all life is lived. Justice is the expression of the communal ground of our existence; it is indicative of the deepest meaning of our life; it is the structural articulation of that capacity for empathy by which we are enabled to recognize our solidarity with the ongoing complex of creaturely life. Social justice as mutuality is the creative unfolding in patterns of interaction of the apprehension of faith.

In sum, through faith as appreciative awareness, we are awakened to the communal ground of all life, we discern the workings of complementarity central in the understandings of both deep ecology and social ecology, we discover our identity as participant members of an inclusive cosmopolis, we are encouraged in a constant striving for social justice. In this sense at least, we might say that, respecting the social question and the ecological question as they converge in the question of Otherness, we are, as the old-fashioned phrasing would have it, saved by faith.

15

Postlude:
Koinonology and the Ecological Principle

Our ecology should be
a deep ecology—not only deep,
but universal.
—*Thich Nhat Hanh*[1]

We do not live in solitude. We cannot live in solitude. We may, at times, yearn for a certain kind of solitude, seeking to escape the intrusions of unwanted associations. We may, at other times, be fearful of solitude, needing the comfort and encouragement of intimate association. But, if we are at all aware of the fundamental condition of our lives, from their beginnings to their ends, we know that they consist of a flow of ever-changing relationships. And these relationships are extensive and complex. We most certainly will never comprehend them in every detail. In a sense, the entire evolutionary process is brought to focus in each event of our lives. Yet, within that vast matrix of our lives, each of us is unique and each of us is afforded the possibility of making a difference in the ongoing process. That's the singular importance of our individual lives in the world. And that's the importance of how we understand our selves and what we do with our selves.

Against that backdrop, I mean to suggest, as a postlude to these chapters, a convergence between ecology (which customarily betokens a way of understanding nature) and koinonology (which designates a form of moral reflection). Ecology and koinonology both place dominant focus on the quality of relationships. On their descriptive side, they are alert to the manner in which alterations in a pattern of interaction bear on the vitality of each participant in a biotic community and the vibrancy of the community as a whole. On their prescriptive side, they are both concerned to resist those kinds of interaction that have a deadening effect on the biotic community and to promote those that alleviate suffering and advance solidarity. In their realism, ecology and koinonology are tinged with a tragic sense of life, aware of the inescapability of destructive conflict and the inevitability of loss. But they are

275

also buoyed with a redemptive sense of life, aware of the presence of profound powers of possibility and creativity, reconciliation and restoration that sustain hope in the midst of tragedy.

FORMS OF CONJUNCTION
BETWEEN HUMAN AND NONHUMAN

To comprehend the import of ecology as a principle of understanding and action, I would distinguish it from two other, not unrelated principles, conservationism and environmentalism. All three principles, associated with movements that have emerged in strength over the past century, concentrate on the conjunction between the worlds of the human and the nonhuman. All three are, by intention, protective of the nonhuman world and critical of the manner in which our economic and cultural systems have had a deleterious effect on it. Yet—if I may treat them as ideal types, caricaturing their differences to accentuate the distinctiveness of the ecological alternative—they tend to diverge as principles of interpretation and evaluation. Consider the following comparative tabulation of characteristics indicating the kind of transformation that transpires in the move from the conservationist principle to the ecological principle, locating the environmentalist principle as a middle way between them.

Conservationist Principle—Environmentalist Principle—Ecological Principle

anthropocentric orientation	biocentric orientation
directive/manipulative process	interactive/cooperative process
centralized planning	federal collaboration
segmental analysis	holistic understanding
instrumental/utilitarian values	intrinsic/sacramental values

Conservationist Principle. As human populations expanded by leaps and bounds in the modern age and the industrial revolution accelerated the pace of economic production, giving rise to methods and instruments of modern technology, the strain on the natural resources of the earth became increasingly evident. In the nineteenth century, vast herds of wild animals were hunted and killed to the point of extinction or near extinction. Grasslands were destroyed through overgrazing. Top soils were badly eroded and lost, given thoughtless agricultural practices and resultant dust storms. Indiscriminate logging devastated forested areas. Water supplies were subjected to pollution and overuse. Land was mined indiscriminately for its minerals and ores.

The principle of the conservation movement that emerged in response to these developments was protective—protective of natural resources and of future generations of humankind. The conservation movement pressed for legislation to take deliberate care of the resources of the earth, to guard them against harm and waste, to manage them in such a way to assure, so far as possible, that succeeding generations of humankind might have some share in them.

But the fundamental orientation of the movement was anthropocentric. Land, air, water, plants, animals were considered resources for the enjoyment and use of the human species. As resources, these features of the world of nature had instrumental value, that is, they were valuable only insofar as they might contribute to human interests—economic, recreational, or aesthetic. They had no value in themselves.

From the perspective of conservationism, these natural resources should be subjected to deliberate control and manipulation according to principles and techniques of scientific management. Conservationism promoted agricultural practices delimiting soil erosion, the protection of watershed areas, methods of mineral extraction minimizing waste, the establishment of wilderness areas and national parks, the development of fisheries and wildlife preserves, and many other similar programs—all designed to counter the reckless exploitation of resources for short-term profit or one-time enjoyment.

But, however admirable these programs were in their resistance to the onslaught of a burgeoning human population with its expanding industrialization, conservationism tended to sustain a bifurcated worldview, setting the spheres of the human and the nonhuman apart from each other—if not over against each other. Nature was to be subdued and controlled, subjected to manipulation (albeit prudent manipulation) through human governance for the sake of long-term human gain.

Environmentalist Principle. Given my purpose—to suggest a convergence between ecology and koinonology—I have identified the environmentalist principle as an intermediate way, vacillating in its various expressions between the two sets of characteristics outlined above.

The environmentalist movement has tended to move beyond the more segmental approach of conservationism to the preservation of natural resources and toward the more holistic understanding of ecology in its appreciation of the links that connect problems of population explosion, air and water pollution, soil erosion, famine, the depletion of sources of energy, and the like. As those committed to the environmentalist principle discerned these connections and became increasingly aware of the synergistic effects these developments had on each other, they approached the public forum with a sense of urgency and alarm, calling for radical regulatory action. They pressed for the development of major pieces of environmental legislation: a clean air act, clean water legislation, mandatory recycling programs, auto emission standards, logging limitations, an endangered species act. They promoted movements designed to slow (if not reverse) the rate of population growth within the human community. They protested against industries and enterprises (e.g., nuclear power, whaling, toxic waste disposal) whose practices were deemed particularly vile given a concern for the health of the environment.

Such developments have been admirable, even, in some cases (e.g., Greenpeace), courageous. Nevertheless those associated with the environmentalist principle as a middle way have tended to argue the case for these actions on anthropocentric grounds. The policies and practices were deemed desirable because they redounded to the benefit of humankind. An "environment," from this perspective, is the aggregate of surrounding things providing an infrastructure favorable to the life of human beings. Environmental conditions are important only as means; human beings, their desires and needs, constitute the ends. That is the reason environmentalism, as I am circumscribing the type, is so often prepared to compromise with the immediate demands of the prevailing economic system in its drive to exploit the resources of the earth and in its willingness to tolerate various forms of pollution as a presumably inevitable by-product of its provision of goods and services.

Environmentalism, although imbued with a strong sense of alarm about the future, given current social and economic trends, has not taken the radical turn of theory and practice represented by the ecological principle.

Ecological Principle. The term *ecology* was fabricated in the nineteenth century by Ernst Haeckel, a zoologist, to designate the interrelation of an animal with its environment, organic and inorganic. In its Greek origins, the term is a synthesis of two words: *oikos* (household/habitat) and *logos* (study/structure). Ecology is the study of that place within which one lives and of which one is a part—presumably for the sake of caring for that place as a whole. As the science of ecology developed, it attended to the investigation of ecosystems, the interactions of individuals and populations within a delineable territory in their interdependence with each other for sustenance and development. For a time, plant and animal ecology evolved separately; they converged in the early part of the twentieth century in a focus on the interconnections between animals and plants as a whole biotic community.

In the mid-twentieth century, modern ecology moved to a new stage with the emergence of such concepts as food chain and energy flow, processes that permeate an entire ecosystem, drawing together whole aggregates—human and nonhuman, organic and inorganic—in an intricate and intimate connection with each other. Attention was focused not on separate and distinct individuals within the system (or even species), but on the field that brings these individuals—human and nonhuman—together in an interactive process. From this perspective, individual entities (or species) are important, but less as distinct individuals than as nodes within a network of internal relations—from which the individuals (and species) benefit and to which they contribute.

The adoption of an ecological principle results in a radical shift in orientation. It is holistic; it is biocentric; it locates human life with all of its institutions and associations within a more embracing context. Human beings, to be sure, are not the same as oak trees, grizzly bears, or crystals. But all these entities, humans included, are coparticipants—partners—in a "circle of life": "In the Circle of Life every being is no more, or less, than any other. We are all Sisters and Brothers. Life is shared with the bird, bear, insects, plants, mountains, clouds, stars, sun. To be in harmony with the natural world, one must live within the cycles of life."[2]

John Cobb, in his move toward a "theology of ecology," suggests that an "ecological attitude" approaches the problems of life not in isolation but in context. It assesses individual actions not simply in relation to the immediate objectives of those actions (as, for instance, in the methodology of "Management by Objectives") but more broadly in relation to the full array of effects that will result from them. And, in turn, these effects are evaluated in a twofold way: as important in themselves and as having further effects beyond themselves. Where a more "technological attitude" isolates problems to solve them efficiently and quickly, an ecological attitude is more patient and hesitant, concerned with indirect consequences, less easily detectable results, and the impact of actions throughout the entire flow of life.[3]

In its fullest import, the ecological attitude, Cobb argues, moves us toward a certain kind of fundamental commitment—as active participants "in a process of healing and growth." Such a commitment gives us responsibilities, but not as "masters" in control of an external world, rather as members of a community, as coagents with many other coagents, human and nonhuman, engaged in a sequence of interactive procedures all of which we do not fully comprehend. With this commitment, our primary concern is to "develop sensitivity to that process and by restraint and openness assist its working." Cobb speaks of this as the "Creative Process," which "makes for life and the enrichment of life, variety of forms, intensity of experience, consciousness and love." The Creative Process is at work conjunctively throughout all dimensions of the world, human and nonhuman.[4]

As André Gorz—distinguishing "two kinds of ecology"—acknowledges, "the ecological movement is not an end in itself, but a stage in a larger struggle."[5] That is, if ecology is construed too narrowly as exploiting the earth's resources with some restraint but without fundamentally transforming the world's economic system with its prevailing ideology of economic expansion, it will exacerbate the misery of millions of peoples across the globe. In Gorz's judgment, the ecological principle, understood in its most embracing significance, mandates the adoption of a radically new criterion of social formation in which "The only things worthy of each are those which are worthy for all; the only things worthy of being produced are those which neither privilege nor diminish anyone; it is possible to be happier with less affluence, for in a society without privilege no one will be poor."[6]

From within a Latin American context, Tony Brun appropriates the concept of "social ecology" to display a similar concern, to draw together environmental and social issues in a new paradigm for the future: "Social ecology has emerged to challenge the dualism between the human sciences and the natural sciences in recognition of their connectedness.... Social ecology offers us one of the most timely paradigms for the search to reorganize society from a human and ecological perspective, starting with the interests of the impoverished majorities."[7] In Brun's estimation, the ecological crisis is inextricably linked with the social and economic crisis. The massive deterioration of the earth's ecosphere and the conditions of indigent and marginalized peoples on all continents of the world taken together constitute a call for the kind of holistic/relational understanding signified in the ecological principle and, I mean to suggest, the kind of moral reflection and moral response indicated by what I have proposed as koinonology.

TYPES OF MORAL REASONING

I have asserted that ecology (as a movement originating in the study of nature) and koinonology (as a method of moral reflection) converge in their respective concerns for the quality of relationships. They are attentive to patterns of interaction on the supposition that things can be understood only within the context of their interactive engagement with other things. That is the genius of Martin Buber's dialogic philosophy. We always exist, Buber claims, in active relation with someone or something else. The moral question is, What is the character of that relation? In Buber's simplified, but insightful, typology, only two possibilities are given to us: I-Thou and I-It. Where I-Thou is dominant, both parties flourish; where I-It prevails, both parties are diminished. But in either case, we are social selves and it is in the quality of our relationships with each other that we find our fulfillment or our degeneration. Buber applied his typology, we should take note, not only to relations between persons. It was designed to embrace relations of the Self with any kind of Other—in the world of natural entities and in the world of cultural possibilities as well as in the world of human encounter. Buber's dialogic philosophy is a version of what I intend to convey through the concept of koinonology.

To develop the meaning of koinonology further, I would distinguish it as a form of moral reflection from other possibilities. H. Richard Niebuhr, in a set of lectures published posthumously, contrasted three forms of moral reflection, each centered in a different understanding of the Self—Self as Maker, as Citizen, and as Respondent.[8] Each understanding articulates something of importance in human life; each of them is instructive in the effort to consider how life ought to be conducted; each of them is expressive of a long-standing tradition of ethical theory. Yet of the three, Niebuhr claims—and I would concur—that the last is the most comprehensive and, given current historical conditions, perhaps the most adequate in addressing the kinds of moral issues and challenges confronting us in the framing of our future.

Self as Maker (teleology). From the perspective of Self as Maker, we are purposive beings, guided toward the realization of envisioned

ends. Those envisioned ends may be, in some fashion, inner potentialities whose impetus drives us toward their unfolding—as in a self-
realization ethic. Those envisioned ends may be, instead, understood
as self-defined, drawing upon our energies toward their refinement
and actualization—as in a utilitarian ethic. In either case, we are
engaged in the shaping of ourselves and our environment to conform
to an objective whose importance to us justifies whatever we may do
in that process so long as it moves us along the way expeditiously and
effectively.

That is the point of the practical arts and disciplines: to inform us
how best to act if we would be true to our ends, whatever they may
be. In a self-realization ethic, training in the virtues makes us more
genuinely human. In a capitalist ethic, training in the ways of the market enables us to increase the wealth of nations. In a hedonist ethic,
training in the subtleties of the aesthetic life elevates our sensibilities
to ever more sophisticated pleasures. In a nationalist ethic, training in
the heritage of the nation's history and principles of the national character makes us acutely aware of what we must do to represent and to
defend that tradition. In each case, the arts and disciplines assume
that we are self-determinative, but in need of instruction as we pursue our ends.

Given the standpoint of Self as Maker, everything that surrounds
us is interpreted and assessed in relation to our ends: as hindrance or as
help, as resistance or as resource. Our moral interest is to appropriate
what will contribute toward our vision and to suppress what will deter
us from its fulfillment. Our moral success is measured by how amply
we realize our purposes.

Self as Citizen (deontology). When we construe our Self as Citizen as
our most fundamental identity, we imagine ourselves engaged in a
public forum whose inner workings are governed by rules. From one
angle, the rules inform us about our duties and obligations to each
other. From another angle, they list our rights and privileges as agents.
Within this scheme, many of our most basic duties and rights are correlative. So, for instance, if, according to the terms of our constitutional
order, I have a right to trial by jury, then the officials of the regime have
a duty to do what is needed to provide that trial. If, according to the
terms of our contractual arrangement, you are obligated to compensate
me for my work, then I have a right to that compensation. If parents
have a duty to provide food and clothing to their children, then those
children have a right to hold parents to that standard. If each of us

holds a right to freedom of speech, then others are obliged not to stifle our exercise of that freedom.

The rights and duties that define the appropriate structure of our relationships with each other may be rooted in legislation or custom, divine commands or natural law. But in any case, the principles incorporated in that structure inform us about what we must do and what we may be if we are to be good citizens. In assessing our conduct, consequences are of less importance than conformity. As long as we abide by the rules, our actions are warranted and we may proceed with our lives, acting as we will. On some levels, we may seek to transform the rules—to broaden the scope of individual rights (e.g., to secure women's right to vote) or to increase the burden of obligations (e.g., to protect endangered species)—but, customarily, there are rules for that process as well.

Given this perspective, fundamental rules constitute a standard for the interpretation and assessment of human conduct. Our moral interest is to advance, through instruction or, if need be, through negative sanctions, conformity with the rules. Our moral success is determined by how effectively our obligations are met and how amply our rights and liberties are respected.

Self as Respondent (koinonology). The concepts of Self as Maker and Self as Citizen encapsulate significant dimensions of our moral experience. We do pursue purposes whose lure is compelling and whose elusiveness may prove devastating. We do live within the framework of rules whose expectation is assertive and whose transgression is condemnable. But these concepts by themselves, I suggest, do not capture a more primordial dimension of our lives together, a dimension that has an immediacy about it neglected in the concepts of Self as Maker and Self as Citizen.

Niebuhr casts this alternative in the concept of Self as Answerer or Self as Respondent, derived from a universal experience of humankind, namely, that we live in the thick of communities of continuous give-and-take. We live in milieux in which we are acted upon and we respond: "To be engaged in dialogue, to answer questions addressed to us, to defend ourselves against attacks, to reply to injunctions, to meet challenges—this is a common experience."[9] Our lives are pervasively interactional. On many levels—consciously and subconsciously—we are sensitized by multiple forces that impinge upon us and we react to those forces. We are, in this sense, responsive beings. We belong to a vast network of dynamic intercommunication.

Our basic disposition consists of the depth of sensitivity through which we apprehend the intricacies of that network and the pattern of our responses to possibilities that emerge from our participation in it. Our identity as a Self derives from this process as much as—if not more than—from the ideals we reach after or the principles and laws by which we are measured. From this interactional perspective, the central moral question we must ask of an action is, Was it fitting? How sensitively did it take into account the complexity of its circumstance? How appropriate was it as a response to what was happening? How well did the action fit within the full context that induced it? As Niebuhr dramatizes this approach: "We seek to have them [our actions] fit into the whole as a sentence fits into a paragraph in a book, a note into a chord in a movement in a symphony, as the act of eating a common meal fits into the lifelong companionship of a family, as the decision of a statesman fits into the ongoing movement of his nation's life with other nations, or as the discovery of a scientific verifact fits into the history of science."[10]

Where Niebuhr calls this form of moral reflection "cathekontics" (an ethics of the fitting), I propose an alternative, "koinonology" (an ethics of solidarity), in order to convey the general quality of the kind of action that is fitting, namely, an action of conviviality, an action which, in its context, enhances the life of the community as a whole—including the agent (the Self as Participant)—so far as that is possible given the constraints and opportunities that are borne by that context. But, with Niebuhr, I would insist that we not define the context of our action and reactions too constrictedly. The ultimate context relevant to our actions embraces "the total community of being"—human and nonhuman.[11]

"Koinonia," a concept prominent in the lexicon of primitive Christianity, means community, a kind of association through which participants find their identity in the give-and-take of their connectedness with each other. In community, each participant benefits from the association; each participant contributes to the association; the identity of each participant is contingent on one's location within the association. In that interplay, the association is not merely a means to the gain of each party; it is itself a source of delight. Its ongoing life is a goodness to be cherished for itself and for its participants. Nicolas Berdyaev appropriated the Russian word *sobornost* to express the full meaning of community. In its narrowest sense, sobornost is an ecclesiological term, designating the inner meaning of the church, a specifically religious association; but in its most encompassing sense, *sobornost* is an escha-tological term, designating the ultimate meaning and final destiny of all creation. *Sobornost*, as community, includes not only humankind; it encompasses all life. It is intended as the quality that permeates—or should permeate—all the particularities of our lives together.

We are, to be sure, as individuals and in our associations with each other, Makers with purposes and pursuits. Creative advance in all our endeavors is impossible with the driving impulse of purpose. This is as true of the inner purposiveness that directs our development from infancy to maturity as it is of the kind of purposiveness that motivates innovation in our cultural constructions and political policies. The his-torical process is ever generated and regenerated with prospective vision and the play of imagination about what might be and should be in the movement toward the future. Without such vision and without such play, our life would languish. But in and through all the purposes that quicken our energies and enliven our spirits, one question should resound: What is likely to be their impress on the continuing commu-nity of life and all its participants? In a sense that question is projective of the purpose of purposes, but a kind of purpose that does not desig-nate a desirable end-state. Rather it designates a quality of living together whose configuration is ever a matter for redetermination and reconstruction, given the creative passage of time. That, I would like to think, is what Martin Luther King, Jr., intended by his image of the "beloved community."

While we are Makers with purposes and pursuits, we are, in addi-tion, Citizens with rights and obligations. We are, as such, governed by rules of many kinds. Some rules direct us, others constrain us; some rules provide means of collaboration, others protect us from each other; some rules provide us with space and time to do as we will; oth-ers inform us how we are to employ our resources for the common good. All told, the rules we define in various forms—legal and moral, administrative and customary—create a basic structure of social expec-tations guiding us in our interactions with each other. At their worst, as we often recognize, rules are cumbersome and awkward; they can be obstructive and demeaning. As those who appeal beyond rules of law to courts of equity acknowledge, rules are too often lacking in subtlety and refinement to do justice in particular cases. Moreover, as recog-nized by legal realists decades ago, the efficacy and meaning of rules depend on the determination of those with the power to interpret and to apply them. However, at their best, rules are useful. In more stressful circumstances, they coercively control the behavior of people who, for whatever reason, intentionally or through negligence, would do harm to others. In less menacing circumstances, they instruct us about our dependency on each other and remind us of our responsibilities and possibilities. But the overarching point of rules is to direct us in the ways of justice—which, in its ultimate form, names that quality of living together in which each of us, in seeking some kind of fulfillment for ourselves contributes to the flourishing of the whole community of life. In short, the "higher law" that governs and guides all other laws is the law of justice as solidarity.[12]

Hence, while we are Makers and Citizens, we are most fundamentally Participants in a vast commonwealth with responsibility for the sustenance and advancement of the community of life. That commonwealth undergirds and its concerns should infuse all our other activities. That's the moral interest of koinonology and the measure of our moral success or failure. That's the ultimate test of all our purposes and the final ground for all our rules. That's the perspective from which we must maintain a critical distance to ponder our projects, local and global, and to assess our laws, domestic and international.

At this point, the practical concerns of koinonology and ecology are clearly discernible as convergent. Both, acknowledging the thoroughgoing relational character of life, are committed to symbiosis, that kind of coexistence which, within the limitations that accompany all finite existence, promotes the qualitative attainment of each participant in the creative process.

But the limitations cannot be ignored. We do, literally, draw on each other for sustenance. More crudely, we feed on each other. The intimate relationship between parent and child is emblematic of the condition of all life. Parenthood (particularly, if we consider the aspect of breastfeeding during the earliest years, Motherhood), understood as an indispensable function in the development of a child from infancy to maturity, entails a giving of Self for the sake of the Other, but a giving through which a highly significant form of fulfillment is a consequence.

Moreover, even as life is interactive, so also it is conflictual. A koinonological ethic is not antithetical to conflict and dissent, struggle and opposition. But it would have us distinguish between creative conflict and destructive conflict. The former, at least by intent, seeks to minimize loss and is respectful to all participants in the clash of life, even those considered deadly enemies. Moreover, with Mohandas

Gandhi, I would propose that, in creative conflict, a koinonological ethic prepares us for *yajna* (sacrifice)—prepares us, that is, to suffer if that is the necessary result of an action that, in our best judgment, is most apt for the ongoing life of the community. As Gandhi remarks, "The world cannot subsist for a single moment without *yajna* in this sense."[13] Destructive conflict may be inescapable in the encounter of life with life, but a koinonological ethic would prod us to do what we can to transform such moments into an opportunity for reconciliation out of the conviction that through solidarity the life of each participant flourishes.

Under conditions of destructive conflict in the course of history, the immediate impulse of a koinonological ethic is to seek out the most vulnerable of peoples or living creatures—the poor, the deprived, the marginalized, the endangered—and to do what can be done working in identity with them to restore their place in the ongoing adventure of our common life. As such, the perspective of koinonology is neither simply altruistic nor simply self-serving. It is rather an effort to revivify that process of creative intercommunication through which the life of the entire community, including both Self and Other, is quickened and enhanced.

In theological language, the inner compulsion of koinonology may be cast in a summary phrase: We are to love one another even as God has loved us. That is the overriding purpose and the overarching law of our life. That is the imperative that is drawn from our most primordial experience and that articulates our most endearing hope. That is, I believe, the ultimate intent of the ecological principle. That is the spirit, I would claim, that underlies each of the preceding chapters in this text on the interplay between solidarity and suffering.

NOTES

CHAPTER 1. PRELUDE
TOWARD A POLITICS OF RELATIONALITY

1. Bernard E. Meland, *The Realities of Faith* (New York: Oxford University Press, 1962), p. 280.

2. See, e.g., Norman Furniss and Timothy Tilton, *The Case for the Welfare State: From Social Security to Social Equality* (Bloomington: Indiana University Press, 1977); T. H. Marshall and Tom Bottomore, *Citizenship and Social Class* (London & Concord, Mass.: Pluto Press, 1992); and John Rawls, *A Theory of Justice* (Cambridge: Harvard University Press, 1971).

3. See, e.g., Robert Nozick, *Anarchy, State, and Utopia* (New York: Basic Books, 1974); and Milton and Rose Friedman, *Free to Choose: A Personal Statement* (New York: Harcourt Brace Jovanovich, 1980).

4. See, e.g., Ralph Reed, *Active Faith: How Christians Are Changing the Face of American Politics* (New York: Free Press, 1996).

5. See, e.g., Amitai Etzioni, *The New Golden Rule: Community and Morality in a Democratic Society* (New York: Basic Books, 1996).

6. See, e.g, Iris Marion Young, *Justice and the Politics of Difference* (Princeton, N.J.: Princeton University Press, 1990); Amy Gutman, editor, *Multiculturalism: Examining the Politics of Recognition* (Princeton, N.J.: Princeton University Press, 1994); and John Anner, editor, *Beyond Identity Politics: Emerging Social Justice Movements in Communities of Color* (Boston: South End Press, 1996).

7. See, e.g., George Sessions, editor, *Deep Ecology for the Twenty-First Century* (Boston & London: Shambhala, 1995); and Roy Morrison, *Ecological Democracy* (Boston: South End Press, 1995).

8. Amos 5:21, 24.

9. Derrick Bell, *Faces at the Bottom of the Well: The Permanence of Racism* (New York: Basic Books, 1992), p. 12.

10. James Baldwin, *The Fire Next Time* (New York: Dial Press, 1963), pp. 22–24.

11.   Richard A. Epstein, *Simple Rules for a Complex World* (Cambridge: Harvard University Press, 1995).

12.   Carol C. Gould, "Private Rights and Public Virtues: Women, Family, and Democracy," in Carol C. Gould, ed., *Beyond Domination: New Perspectives on Women and Philosophy* (Totowa, N.J.: Rowman & Allanheld, 1983), p. 5. See also Carol C. Gould, *Rethinking Democracy: Freedom and Social Cooperation in Politics, Economy, and Society* (Cambridge: Cambridge University Press, 1988).

13.   Patricia A. Cain, "Feminist Jurisprudence: Grounding the Theories," in Katherine T. Bartlett and Rosanne Kennedy, eds., *Feminist Legal Theory: Readings in Law and Gender* (Boulder, Colo.: Westview Press, 1991), p. 268.

14.   Ibid., p. 274.

15.   Exodus 22:21.

16.   Henry James Young, *Hope in Process: A Theology of Social Process* (Minneapolis: Fortress Press, 1990), p. 45.

17.   Bernard E. Meland, *Realities of Faith*, p. 233.

PART I.
HUMAN RIGHTS

1.   Thomas Paine, *Common Sense*, in *The Complete Writings of Thomas Paine*, edited by Philip S. Foner, vol. 1 (New York: Citadel, 1945), p. 45.

CHAPTER 2.
THE IDEA OF HUMAN RIGHTS:
A COMMUNITARIAN PERSPECTIVE

1.   As quoted in Carl Becker, *The Declaration of Independence: A Study in the History of Political Ideas* (New York: Vintage Books, 1958), p. 186.

2.   John Locke, *Second Treatise of Government* (originally published, 1690), edited by C. B. MacPherson (Indianapolis: Hackett, 1980), § 4.

3.   Ibid., § 124.

4.   Ibid., § 5 and 6.

5.   Ibid., § 77.

6.   Richard Tuck, *Natural Rights Theories: Their Origin and Development* (Cambridge: Cambridge University Press), p. 72.

7.   Alfred North Whitehead, *Adventures of Ideas* (New York: Free Press, 1967), p. 34.

8.   Bernard Eugene Meland, *Essays in Constructive Theology: A Process Perspective*, edited by Perry LeFevre (Chicago: Exploration Press, 1988), p. 129.

9.   Whitehead, *Adventures of Ideas*, p. 27.

10.   Hannah Arendt, *The Origins of Totalitarianism* (New York: Harcourt Brace, 1951), p. 294.

11.   Ibid., pp. 293–95.

12.   Maurice Cranston, *What Are Human Rights?* (New York: Taplinger, 1973).

13.   Ibid., p. 68.

14.   Whitehead, *Adventures of Ideas*, p. 66.

15.   Ibid., italics added.

16.   Carol Gould, *Rethinking Democracy* (Cambridge: Cambridge University Press, 1990), p. 198.

17.   Ibid., p. 199.

18.   Ronald Dworkin, *Taking Rights Seriously* (Cambridge: Harvard University Press, 1978), p. xi.

19.   Robert Nozick, *Anarchy, State, and Utopia* (New York: Basic Books, 1974), p. 29.

20.   Ibid., pp. 30–31.

21.   Ibid., pp. 32–33.

22.   Gould, *Rethinking Democracy*, p. 201.

23.   Albert Schweitzer, *Reverence for Life: The Words of Albert Schweitzer*, compiled by Harold E. Robles (San Francisco: Harper, 1993), p. 67.

CHAPTER 3.
ON THE SUFFERING AND RIGHTS OF CHILDREN:
TOWARD A THEOLOGY OF CHILDHOOD LIBERATION

1.   Marjorie Hewitt Suchocki, *The End of Evil: Process Eschatology in Historical Context* (Albany: State University of New York Press, 1988), p. 123.

2.   Within the United States, this judgment is supported by the final

report of the National Commission on Children, *Beyond Rhetoric: A New American Agenda for Children and Families* (Washington: U.S. Printing Office, 1991). The Commission was chaired by John D. Rockefeller IV, Senator from West Virginia.

3.   David Bakan, *Slaughter of Innocents: A Study of the Battered Child Phenomenon* (San Francisco: Jossey-Bass, 1971), pp. 1, 4.

4.   This has been a constant theme in the annual reports of UNICEF. See, e.g., James P. Grant, *The State of the World's Children 1990* (Oxford: Oxford University Press, 1989), pp. 1–15.

5.   Stanley Hauerwas, *Naming the Silences: God, Medicine, and the Problem of Suffering* (Grand Rapids, Mich.: William B. Eerdmans, 1990), passim.

6.   See Beverly Harrison's stirring essay, "The Power of Anger in the Work of Love," in her *Making the Connections: Essays in Feminist Social Ethics*, edited by Carol S. Robb (Boston: Beacon Press, 1985), pp. 3–21.

7.   Compare, in this connection, the opposing perspectives of Joseph Woodward and Rebecca S. Chopp. In "The End of Suffering: Who's Right: Ancients, Moderns, or Christians?" (*Crisis*, 9/1 [January 1991]: 22–30), Woodward argues that we must be reconciled to a life that is inevitably permeated with suffering. But in *The Praxis of Suffering: An Interpretation of Liberation and Political Theologies* (Maryknoll: Orbis Books, 1986), Chopp proposes that suffering, as a condition of historical constructions, should provoke political transformation. Dorothee Soelle's nuanced study of *Suffering* (Philadelphia: Fortress Press, 1975) embraces both perspectives, but sides predominantly with Chopp.

8.   See Edmond Cahn, *The Sense of Injustice* (Bloomington,: Indiana University Press, 1964), p. 186. Cahn's work was first published in 1946, fifteen years preceding the emergence of liberation theology, but expresses something of the same dynamic within the framework of a jurisprudence deeply influenced by Jewish tradition.

9.   Schubert Ogden, *Faith and Freedom: Toward a Theology of Liberation* (Nashville, Tenn.: Abingdon, 1979), pp. 63–64.

10.   See Isaiah Berlin's classic essay on "Two Concepts of Liberty" in his *Four Essays on Liberty* (Oxford: Oxford University Press, 1970). Where, however, he argues for negative freedom, I am presenting the opposite case. See Carol C. Gould, *Rethinking Democracy* (Cambridge: Cambridge University Press, 1988), especially chapter 1. Erich Fromm developed the same distinction in his *Escape from Freedom* (New York: Holt, Rinehart & Winston, 1941).

11.   Gould, *Rethinking Democracy*, pp. 40–41.

12.   Within the framework of process philosophy, the mandate of love, I would affirm, extends beyond the human to the entire biotic community.

13. Philippe Aries, *Centuries of Childhood: A Social History of the Family*, translated by Robert Baldick (New York: Alfred A. Knopf, 1962), originally published in French in 1960. See also Richard Farson's declaration in *Birthrights* (New York: Macmillan, 1974) that "childhood is not a natural state. It is a myth" (p.18).

14. M. D. A. Freeman, *The Rights and Wrongs of Children* (London & Dover: Frances Pinter, 1983), p. 11. In the same text, Freeman asserts that "childhood, like adulthood and old age, is to a large extent a social construct" (p. 6). Virtually the same phrasing appears in Jo Boyden and Andy Hudson, *Children: Rights and Responsibilities*, Report No. 69 (London: Minority Rights Group, 1985), p. 4.

15. Valerie Polakow Suransky, *The Erosion of Childhood* (Chicago: University of Chicago Press, 1982), p. 8.

16. Lloyd deMause, "The Evolution of Childhood," in *The History of Childhood*, edited by Lloyd deMause (New York: Psychohistory Press, 1974), p. 54.

17. Linda A. Pollack, *Forgotten Children: Parent-Child Relations from 1500 to 1900* (Cambridge: Cambridge University Press, 1983), pp. 270–71.

18. Suransky, *The Erosion of Childhood*, p. 36 (italics in original). Suransky's affirmations result from her interpretive study of various child-care centers in the United States. A similar statement about the meaning of childhood is presented in Myra Bluebond-Langner, *The Private World of Dying Children* (Princeton, N.J.: Princeton University Press, 1978). Through an intensive anthropological study of terminally ill children, mostly between the ages of three and nine, Bluebond-Langner was driven to conclude that even the youngest children are creative agents engaged in an intricate network of symbolic interactions.

19. Ibid., p. 172.

20. See, for instance, Brazelton's contributions to *The Growing Child in Family and Society: An Interdisciplinary Study in Parent-Infant Bonding*, edited by Noboru Kobayashi and T. Berry Brazelton (Tokyo: University of Tokyo Press, 1984); and *The Cultural Context of Infancy: Biology, Culture and Infant Development*, edited by J. Kevin Nugent, Barry M. Lester, and T. Berry Brazelton (Norwood, N.J.: Ablex, 1989).

21. Chopp, *The Praxis of Suffering*, p. 151.

22. See J. Christaan Beker, *Suffering and Hope* (Philadelphia: Fortress Press, 1987).

23. See, e.g., Ruth S. Kempe and C. Henry Kempe, *Child Abuse* (Cam-

bridge: Harvard University Press, 1978) and Nigel Parton, *The Politics of Child Abuse* (London: Macmillan, 1985). In 1961, C. Henry Kempe, a pediatrician, coined the phrase "battered baby syndrome"—now considered passé—to focus public attention on the widely spread presence of brutal maltreatment of children by caretakers. But the reality of childhood suffering long predates the language of child abuse. See, e.g., John Spargo, *The Bitter Cry of Children* (New York & London: Johnson Reprint, 1969), originally published in 1906.

24.   Boyden and Hudson, *Children: Their Rights and Responsibilities*, p. 4. See also David Gil's construal of child abuse, quoted in Parton, *The Politics of Child Abuse*, p. 167, as "inflicted gaps or deficits between circumstances of living which would facilitate the optimum development of children, to which they should be entitled, and their actual circumstances, irrespective of the sources or agents of the deficit."

25.   Freeman, *The Rights and Wrongs of Children*, pp. 115–24. Note Freeman's comment, respecting a cultural explanation, that "The whole ethos of our society, though often described as 'child-centered,' is geared to seeing children as objects, rather than human beings in their own right. . . . We have not got far from the point when a child was regarded as one of his parent's possessions, rather like the television set or refrigerator. Many of us are inclined to kick them when they go wrong. Is it surprising that we should treat children differently?" (p. 124).

26.   The issue of defining child abuse and neglect has become increasingly important and difficult as the number of cross-cultural studies of the maltreatment of children has multiplied. See, e.g., Richard J. Gelles, "What to Learn from Cross-Cultural and Historical Research on Child Abuse and Neglect"; and Jill E. Korbin, "Child Maltreatment in Cross-Cultural Perspective: Vulnerable Children and Circumstances," in *Child Abuse and Neglect: Biosocial Dimensions*, edited by Richard J. Gelles and Jane B. Lancaster (New York: Aldine de Gruyter, 1987), pp. 15–53.

27.   Kempe and Kempe, *Child Abuse*, p. 32.

28.   Kenneth Keniston and the Carnegie Council on Children, *All Our Children: The American Family under Stress* (New York & London: Harcourt Brace Jovanovich, 1977), p. 33.

29.   James P. Grant, *The State of the World's Children 1989* (Oxford: Oxford University Press, 1989), p. 30. See also Anuradha Vittachi, *Stolen Childhood: In Search of the Rights of the Child* (Cambridge: Polity Press, 1989), especially chapter 4, "Wolf at the Door." The UNICEF yearbooks provide a rich array of statistical data respecting the condition of children in each country throughout the globe, covering such matters as health, education, nutrition, the condition of women as well as general economic indicators. During the

past few years, UNICEF has proposed replacing the Gross National Product (GNP) as the key index of economic development with a measure combining two poverty-related factors: (i) under five mortality rate (U5MR) and (ii) illiteracy rate.

30. James P. Grant, *The State of the World's Children 1990*, p. 7. On this principle and its implications for governmental policy, see pp. 1–15 and 55–68.

31. *Beyond Rhetoric*, p. 24. See also Marian Wright Edelman, *Families in Peril: An Agenda for Social Change* (Cambridge: Harvard University Press, 1987). Edelman is the longtime president of the Children's Defense Fund whose annual report, *The Health of America's Children*, is a rich resource of current statistics on the status of children in the United States.

32. *Beyond Rhetoric*, p. 29. See also Jonathan Kozol, *Rachel and Her Children: Homeless Families in America* (New York: Fawcett Columbine, 1988).

33. Boyden and Hudson, *Children: Rights and Responsibilities*, p. 5.

34. Ibid., p. 7.

35. *Betrayal: A Report on Violence toward Children in Today's World*, edited by Carolyn Moorehead (New York: Doubleday, 1990), p. 57.

36. Ibid., p. 32. See also Vittachi, *Stolen Childhood*, chapter 2.

37. Boyden and Hudson, *Children: Rights and Responsibilities*, p. 8.

38. Keniston, *All Our Children*, p. 70.

39. *Beyond Rhetoric*, op. cit., p. 344.

40. The specific problems of African American children, for instance, assume their own particular form. See *Children of Color*, edited by Jewelle Taylor Gibbs (San Francisco: Jossey-Bass, 1989). Stanley Hauerwas intimates that the basic meaning of suffering may be radically divergent among cultures (*Naming the Silences*, pp. 69–71). The position I have presented, on the contrary, suggests that the basic meaning of childhood suffering is constant, although it has many causes and forms. I am here taking seriously both of two seemingly divergent (but actually interdependent) meanings of the concept of "historical consciousness": first, that it allows us to discern and to appreciate cultural differences, but, second, that it implies "that to be fully human is to be an active *subject* of historical change, not merely its passive *object*" (Schubert Ogden, *Faith and Freedom*, p. 22).

41. Freeman, *The Rights and Wrongs of Children*, chapter 1.

42. The Declaration (also known as the Declaration of Geneva) appears in the *League of Nations Official Journal Special Supplement No. 21*, October 1924, p. 43.

43.   *Yearbook of the United Nations 1959* (New York: Columbia University Press, 1959), pp. 198–99.

44.   United Nations General Assembly: A/RES/44/25 (5 December 1989), Forty-fourth session, Agenda item 108 (24 pages plus one page correction dated 26 January 1990).

45.   Several states complied shortly thereafter. However, despite supportive resolutions by both House of Representatives and Senate, the United States government has refused to sign the convention. See Kenneth J. Herrmann, "Challenge to Help the Children," *Christian Social Action* 4/3 (March 1991): 32–34.

46.   See C. R. Margolin, "Salvation versus Liberation: The Movement for Children's Rights in a Historical Context," *Social Problems* 25 (1978): 441–52; and Carl M. Rogers and Lawrence S. Wrightsman, "Attitudes toward Children's Rights: Nurturance or Self-Determination?" *Journal of Social Issues* 34/2 (1978): 59–68.

47.   Bernard J. Coughlin, S.J., "The Rights of Children," in *The Rights of Children: Emergent Concepts in Law and Society*, edited by Albert E. Wilkerson (Philadelphia: Temple University, 1973), p. 11.

48.   Colin Wringe, *Children's Rights* (London: Routledge & Kegan Paul, 1981), p. 89. See Diana Baumrind, "Reciprocal Rights and Responsibilities in Parent-Child Relationships," *Journal for Social Issues* 34/2 (1978): 179–96. Baumrind argues against liberationists on both scientific and moral grounds. Her basic argument is that children necessarily live in a condition of dependency, lacking in the competencies and maturity for self-determination.

49.   Coughlin, *The Rights of Children*, p. 8.

50.   Richard Farson, *Birthrights: A Bill of Rights for Children* (New York: Macmillan, 1974), p. 213.

51.   Ibid., p. 12.

52.   Ibid., chapter 4.

53.   Ibid., chapter 6.

54.   Ibid., chapter 10.

55.   Altogether, Farson enunciates nine rights of children, including a "right to responsive design," taking note that, although children compose a significant proportion of the population, virtually all facilities are designed for adult-sized people. In this connection, cf. Kate Douglas Wiggin, *Children's Rights: A Book of Nursery Logic* (Boston: Houghton, Mifflin, 1892), pp. 1–25. Farson's "right to political power" (chapter 11) was echoed in a proposal by

Vita Wallace, a sixteen year old, that all children be given the right to vote in "Give Children the Vote," *The Nation* 253/12 (October 14, 1991): 439–40, 442.

56. Freeman, *The Rights and Wrongs of Children.*

57. See the provocative and compelling article by Joel Feinberg, "The Child's Right to an Open Future," in *Whose Child? Children's Rights, Parental Authority, and State Power,* edited by William Aiken and Hugh LaFollette (Totowa, N.J.: Littlefield Adams, 1980), pp. 124–53. I am indebted to Dena Davis for this reference.

58. Suchocki, *The End of Evil,* p. 123.

59. As I have remarked, given the focus of this chapter, I am concentrating on the human community. But, given the perspective of process philosophy, a similar kind of argument can be made, *mutatis mutandis,* for members of the entire biotic community.

60. Maxine Greene, "An Overview of Children's Rights: A Moral and Ethical Perspective," in *Children's Rights: Contemporary Perspectives,* edited by Patricia A. Vardin and Ilene N. Brody (New York: Teachers College Press, 1979), p. 79.

61. Ibid., pp. 6–7.

CHAPTER 4.   INTERLUDE
AFFIRMATIVE ACTION AND THE DEPRIVATIONS OF RACISM

1. See Cornel West, *Race Matters* (Boston: Beacon Press, 1993).

2. W. E. B. DuBois, *The Souls of Black Folk* (Greenwich: Fawcett, 1961), originally published 1903.

3. Robert Miles, *Racism* (London & New York: Routledge, 1989), p. 10.

4. See Ben A. Franklin, "Affirmative Action Is under Election Year Attack," *Washington Spectator,* July 1, 1995, p. 2.

5. See Peter Gabel's article, "Affirmative Action and Racial Harmony, in *Tikkun* (May/June 1995, vol. 10, no. 3, pp. 33–36), which develops a similar thought.

6. See Henry James Young, *Hope in Process: A Theology of Social Pluralism* (Minneapolis: Fortress Press, 1990).

7. See, e.g., H. N. Wieman, *Man's Ultimate Commitment* (Carbondale: Southern Illinois University Press, 1958).

8.   James Baldwin, *The Fire Next Time* (New York: Dial Press, 1963), pp. 22–23.

CHAPTER 5.
THE MEANING AND USE OF PROPERTY

1.   John Locke, *Two Treatises of Government,* edited by Peter Laslett (Cambridge: Cambridge University Press, 1966) II 124.

2.   Karl Marx, *Capital* (Chicago: Encyclopedia Brittanica, Great Books, vol. 50, 1952) I, p. xxxii.

3.   C. B. Macpherson, "The Meaning of Property," in *Property*, edited by C. B. MacPherson (Toronto: University of Toronto Press, 1978), p. 1. Italics added.

4.   An illuminating distinction has been drawn between two forms of liberalism in Anglo-American history: (i) established and (ii) reformed. See, e.g., Franklin I. Gamwell, *Beyond Preference: Liberal Theories of Independent Associations* (Chicago: University of Chicago Press, 1984). By classical liberalism, I am referring to the former, which is prevalent in the political rhetoric, although less so in the political practice of the United States. The constructive position I am unfolding is closer in spirit to the latter.

5.   See Frederick G. Whelan, "Property as Artifice: Hume and Blackstone" in *Property*, edited by J. Roland Pennock and John W. Chapman (New York: New York University Press, 1980), pp. 114–25.

6.   Blackstone, *Commentaries* II 2, quoted in ibid., p. 118.

7.   Quoted by James McClellan, *Joseph Story and the American Constitution* (Norman: University of Oklahoma Press, 1971), p. 214.

8.   Gottfried Dietze, *In Defense of Property* (Baltimore, Md.: Johns Hopkins Press, 1971), p. 93.

9.   Ibid., p. 39.

10.   Ibid., pp. 126–27.

11.   Friedrich A. Hayek, *The Mirage of Social Justice* (Chicago: University of Chicago Press, 1976).

12.   See Thomas C. Grey, "The Disintegration of Property," in *Property*, edited by Pennock and Chapman, pp. 69–85.

13.   Richard Schlatter, *Private Property: The History of the Idea* (New York: Russell & Russell, 1973), p. 278.

14.   Karl Marx and Friedrich Engels, *Manifesto of the Communist Party* (Chicago: Encyclopedia Brittanica, Great Books, vol. 50, 1952), pp. 425–26.

15.   94 U.S. 113, 126.

16.   Walter Lippman, *The Public Philosophy* (New York: New American Library, 1956), p. 93.

17.   George Cabot Lodge, *The New American Ideology* (New York: Alfred A. Knopf, 1976), p. 198.

18.   Ibid., pp. 17–18. See all of chapter 7.

19.   At the present, this controversy is vividly present in struggles over the interpretation of the "takings" clause of the United States Constitution. Richard A. Epstein, for instance, in *Takings: Private Property and the Power of Eminent Domain* (Cambridge: Harvard University Press, 1985), argues that any legislation that delimits or imposes on anyone's use of property requires commensurate compensation out of public funds. Zoning regulations, environmental protection laws, rent control, and workers' compensation are among the kinds of legal actions that Epstein has in mind. Bills reflecting this perspective have been initiated in several states.

20.   J. H. Bogart, "Lockean Proviso and State of Nature Theories," *Ethics* 94/4 (July 1985): 832.

21.   See John H. Chapman, "Justice, Freedom and Property," in *Property*, edited by Pennock and Chapman, pp. 289–324 for a detailed spectrum of fundamental positions of economic justice.

22.   John Locke, *Two Treatises*, II 25.

23.   Quoted in Macpherson, *Property*, p. 110.

24.   Ibid., pp. 3–4, 6–9.

25.   A. M. Honoré, "Ownership" in *Oxford Essays in Jurisprudence*, edited by A. G. Guest (London: Oxford University Press, 1961), p. 137.

26.   Ewart Lewis, *Medieval Political Ideas*, vol. 1 (New York: Cooper Square Publishers, 1974), p. 89.

27.   See William B. Scott, *In Pursuit of Happiness: American Conceptions of Property from the Seventeenth to the Twentieth Century* (Bloomington: Indiana University Press, 1977), pp. 137–47.

28.   James Gwartney, "Private Property, Freedom and the West," *The Intercollegiate Review* 20/3 (Spring/Summer 1985): 48.

29.   Macpherson, *Property*, p. 11; see also pp. 4–6, 9–11.

30.   Ibid., p. 206.

31. Charles Donahue, Jr., "The Future of the Concept of Property Predicted from Its Past," in *Property*, edited by Pennock and Chapman, p. 56.

32. Kenneth R. Minogue, "The Concept of Property and Its Contemporary Significance," in ibid., pp. 14–15.

33. Hastings Rashdall, "The Philosophical Theory of Property," in Charles Gore, et al., *Property: Its Duties and Rights* (New York: Macmillan, 1922), p. 66.

34. Ibid., pp. 66–67.

35. Quoted in Macpherson, *Property*, pp. 98–99.

36. Charles Reich, "The New Property," *Yale Law Journal* 73/5 (April 1964): 733.

37. Ibid., p. 786.

38. A. M. Honoré, "Ownership," p. 123.

39. Charles Gore, *Property: Its Rights and Duties*, p. xxiii.

40. Ibid., p. xv.

41. Quoted in Macpherson, *Property*, p. 159.

42. Ibid., p. 172.

43. Ibid., p. 175.

44. Aldo Leopold, *A Sand County Almanac* (London: Oxford University Press, 1968), p. viii.

45. John B. Cobb, Jr., *Is It Too Late?* (revised edition, Denton, Tex.: Environmental Ethics Books, 1995), p. 35.

46. Thomas Hobbes, *Leviathan*, II 18.

47. Alan Ryan, *Property and Political Theory* (Oxford: Basil Blackwell, 1984).

48. Charles Donahue, Jr., in *Property*, edited by Pennock and Chapman, p. 58.

49. Dietze, *In Defense of Property*, p. 16.

50. E. K. Hunt, *Property and Prophets* (New York: Harper & Row, 1972), p. 11.

51. Anthony Parel, "Aquinas's Theory of Property," in *Theories of Property: Aquinas to the Present*, edited by Anthony Parel and Thomas Flanagan (Waterloo, Ontario: Wilfrid Laurier University Press, 1979), p. 89.

52. Ibid., p. 92. See Thomas Aquinas, *Summa Theologica* I–II Q. 2.

53. *Summa Theologica* I–II Q. 4 Art. 7.

54. Parel, *Theories of Property*, p. 89.

55. *Summa Theologica* I–II Q. 94 art. 5 ad. 3; see also II–II Q. 57 art. 3.

56. Parel, *Theories of Property*, p. 97.

57. *Summa Theologica* II–II Q. 66 art. 7.

58. Ibid., II–II Q. 118 art. 1 ad. 2.

59. *St. Thomas Aquinas, Summa Theologiae,* vol. 41 *Virtues of Justice in the Human Community,* edited by T. C. O'Brien, II–II 101–102 (New York: Blackfriars & McGraw Hill, 1972), p. 243, footnote b.

60. *Summa Theologica* II–II Q. 66 art. 7

61. Ibid.

62. Ibid., I Q. 63 art. 2 ad. 2.

63. See ibid., II–II Q. 118 art 1.

64. Ibid., II–II Q. 118 art 8.

65. See Immanuel Wallerstein, *Historical Capitalism* (London: Verso, 1983), chapter 13, "The Commodification of Everything."

66. See *Summa Theologica* II–II Q. 117 (on liberality) and Q. 58 (on justice).

67. Ibid., II–II Q. 58 art. 2.

68. See ibid., II–II Q. 66 art. 8.

69. Schlatter, *Private Property*, p. 55.

70. Henry Kariel, *Beyond Liberalism* (New York: Harper & Row, 1977), p. 5.

71. Schlatter, *Private Property*, p. 252.

72. See James Tully, "The Framework of Natural Rights in Locke's Analysis of Property," in *Theories of Property,* edited by Parel and Flanagan, p. 115; and Ryan, *Property and Political Theory,* pp. 18–24.

73. John Dunn, *The Political Thought of John Locke* (Cambridge: Cambridge University Press, 1982), p. 214; see generally pp. 214–41.

74. C. B. Macpherson, *The Political Theory of Possessive Individualism* (London: Oxford University Press, 1972), p. 199.

75. Ibid., p. 221.

76. See John Dunn, *Political Thought of John Locke*; James Tully, *A Discourse on Property: John Locke and His Adversaries* (Cambridge: Cambridge University Press, 1980); Alan Ryan, *Property and Political Theory*; Eldon J. Eisenach, *Two Worlds of Liberalism* (Chicago: University of Chicago Press, 1981).

77. Locke, *Two Treatises*, II 6.

78. Dunn, *Political Thought of John Locke*, p. 87.

79. Locke, *Two Treatises*, II 6.

80. Ibid., II 57.

81. Ibid., II 135.

82. Tully, in *Theories of Property*, edited by Parel and Flanagan, pp. 127–29; also Tully, *A Discourse on Property*, pp. 43–50, 62, 163.

83. Locke, *Two Treatises*, II 25.

84. Ibid., II 60.

85. Ibid., II 25.

86. Ibid., II 123.

87. Ibid., II 25.

88. Ibid., II 27.

89. Rashdall, in Gore, *Property*, pp. 47–50; see also Robert Nozick, *Anarchy, State, and Utopia* (New York: Basic Books, 1974), pp. 174–82.

90. Ryan, *Property and Political Theory*, pp. 31–32.

91. Dunn, *Political Thought of John Locke*, p. 217.

92. Tully, *Discourse on Property*, p. 110.

93. Locke, *Two Treatises*, II 27.

94. Ibid., II 31.

95. Ibid., II 32.

96. Ibid., II 36.

97. Ibid., II 50.

98. Macpherson, *Possessive Individualism*, p. 208.

99. Tully, *Discourse on Property*, p. 150; see Dunn, *Political Thought of John Locke*, p. 248.

100. Tully, ibid., p. 166; see Locke, *Two Treatises*, II 50 & 123.

101. Tully, ibid., p.170.

102. J. M. Winter, "Introduction: Tawney the Historian," in *History and Society: Essays by R. H. Tawney*, edited by J. M. Winter (London: Routledge and Kegan Paul, 1978), p. 8. See also J. M. Winter and D. M. Joslin, "Introduction," in *R. H. Tawney's Commonplace Book*, edited by Winter and Joslin (Cambridge: Cambridge University Press, 1972), p. xx.

103. R. H. Tawney, "The Study of Economic History (1933)," in Winter, ibid., pp. 54–55. See also R. H. Tawney, *Social History and Literature* (London: Leicester University Press, 1958), p. 6.

104. Winter, *History and Society*, p. 2.

105. W. H. Nelson, "R. H. Tawney," in *Some Modern Historians of Britain* (New York: Dryden Press, 1951), p. 334.

106. R. H. Tawney, *Religion and the Rise of Capitalism* (New York: Penguin Books, 1947), p. 235.

107. Nelson, "R. H. Tawney," p. 326.

108. Winter, *History and Society*, p.15.

109. See Alasdair MacIntyre, *Against the Self-Images of the Age* (New York: Schocken, 1971), pp. 38–42.

110. Tawney, *Commonplace Books*, pp. 45–46.

111. Ibid., p. 56.

112. R. H. Tawney, "The Sickness of Acquisitive Society," *The Hibbert Journal* 17/3 (1919): 353.

113. R. H. Tawney, *The Acquisitive Society* (New York: Harcourt Brace, 1920), p. 26.

114. Tawney, "The Sickness of Acquisitive Society," pp. 356–57. See also Tawney, *Acquisitive Society*, pp. 29–30.

115. Tawney, *Acquisitive Society*, p. 24.

116. Tawney, "The Sickness of Acquisitive Society," p. 356; *Acquisitive Society*, pp. 28–29.

117. Tawney, *Acquisitive Society*, p. 8.

118. Ibid., p. 85.

119. Ibid., p. 45.

120. Tawney, *Equality* (New York: Harcourt, Brace & Co., 1931), p. 271.

121. Tawney, *Acquisitive Society*, pp. 53–54.

122. Tawney, "The Sickness of Acquisitive Society," p. 370.

123. Tawney, *The Attack and Other Papers* (New York: Harcourt Brace, 1953), p. 188.

124. Tawney, *Acquisitive Society*, p. 56.

125. Ibid., p. 59.

126. Ibid., pp. 61–62.

127. Ibid., pp. 71–72. See also *Equality*, chapter 2, "The Religion of Inequality," pp. 12–49.

128. Tawney, "The Sickness of Acquisitive Society," p. 368.

129. Tawney, *Equality*, p. 50.

130. Ibid., pp. 130–31.

131. Tawney, *The Attack*, pp. 190–91 and *Equality*, pp. 119–36.

132. Tawney, *Acquisitive Society*, p. 84.

133. Tawney, *Equality*, 153; see the whole of chapter 5, The Strategy of Equality," pp. 149–208.

134. Ibid., p. 220.

135. Ibid., pp. 246, 62. See also *Acquisitive Society*, pp. 139–60; and *Religion and the Rise of Capitalism*, p. 232. On the other hand, see Tawney's comment in his *Commonplace Book*, pp. 70–71: "If industry could be so organized that the mass of workers would feel convinced that the social order was just, a decrease in efficiency wld [sic] be cheap at the price."

136. Lois Gehr Livezey, *Whitehead's Conception of the Public World*, unpublished doctoral dissertation (Chicago, 1983).

137. Alfred North Whitehead, *Science and the Modern World* (New York: Macmillan, 1939), p. 281.

138. Alfred North Whitehead, *Process and Reality: Corrected Edition* (New York: Free Press, 1979), p. 290.

139. Ibid., p. 289. Italics added.

140. Whitehead, *Science and the Modern World*, p. 288.

141. Ibid., pp. 281–82.

142. Ibid., pp. 291–92.

143. Alfred North Whitehead, *Adventures of Ideas* (New York: Free Press, 1967), p. 13.

144. Ibid., pp. 15, 13.

145. Ibid., p. 143.

146. Ibid., p. 62.

147. Ibid., pp. 62–63.

148. Ibid., see also p. 67.

149. Whitehead, *Process and Reality*, p. 18.

150. Ibid., p. 23.

151. Ibid., p. 21.

152. Ibid., p. 22.

153. This is the character of Lois Livezey's argument in *Whitehead's Conception of the Public World.*

154. Livezey, ibid., p. 324.

155. Whitehead, *Adventures of Ideas*, pp. 28, 56.

156. Ibid., p. 43.

157. Ibid., p. 62.

CHAPTER 6.
CORPORATE GOVERNANCE AND DEMOCRACY

1. Quoted in *Democracy in a World of Tensions: A Symposium Prepared by UNESCO*, edited by Richard P. McKeon (Chicago: University of Chicago Press, 1951), p. 40.

2. *Democracy in a World of Tensions*, edited by McKeon.

3. See Douglas Sturm, "Winstanley, Seventeenth-Century Radical: From the Mystery of God to the Law of Freedom," in *The Weightier Things of the Law*, edited by John Witte and Frank Alexander (Atlanta: Scholars Press, 1988), pp. 99–122.

4. Tom Baumgartner, Tom Burns, and Philippe DeVille, "Work, Politics, and Social Structuring under Capitalism," in *Work and Power*, edited by Tom R. Burns, Lars Erik Karlsson, and Veljko Rus (London & Beverly Hills: Sage, 1979), p. 182.

5. James Burnham, *The Managerial Revolution* (Bloomington: Indiana University Press, 1960), original publication in 1941.

6. Kenneth Boulding, *The Organizational Revolution* (New York: Harpers, 1953), p. 202.

7. Peter Drucker, *Management: Tasks, Responsibilities, Practices* (New York: Harper & Row, 1973/1974), p. ix.

8. Robert L. Heilbroner, *Business Civilization in Decline* (New York: W. W. Norton, 1976).

9. See, e.g., Robert L. Heilbroner, *An Inquiry into the Human Prospect: Updated and Reconsidered for the 1980s* (New York: W. W. Norton, 1980); *Twenty-First Century Capitalism* (New York: W. W. Norton, 1993); *Visions of the Future* (New York: Oxford University Press, 1995).

10. Roberto Mangabeira Unger, *Knowledge and Politics* (New York: Free Press, 1975), p. 188. In a subsequent series of books under the theme of *Politics: A Work in Constructive Social Theory*, Unger pressed these understandings further, arguing for the development of a future society of "radical democracy": *False Necessity* (Cambridge: Cambridge University Press, 1987); *Plasticity into Power* (Cambridge: Cambridge University Press, 1987); and *Social Theory: Its Situation and Its Task* (Cambridge: Cambridge University Press, 1987).

11. Bernard E. Meland, *The Realities of Faith* (New York: Oxford University Press, 1962), p. 201.

12. Daniel Day Williams, *Essays in Process Theology*, edited by Perry LeFevre (Chicago: Exploration Press, 1985), p. 15.

13. Ibid., p. 15.

14. Ibid., p. 16.

15. Ibid., pp. 16–17.

16. Ibid., p. 16.

17. Ibid., p. 17.

18. John Hallowell, *The Moral Foundation of Democracy* (Chicago: University of Chicago Press, 1954), p. 48.

19. *Democracy in a World of Tensions*, edited by McKeon, pp. 516, 393–94.

20. Carl Cohen, *Four Systems* (New York: Random House, 1982), p. 67.

21. John Stuart Mill, *On Liberty* (Library of Liberal Arts, Indianapolis & New York: Bobbs-Merrill, 1956), p. 13. Original publication date: 1859.

22. John Stuart Mill, *Considerations on Representative Government* (Library of Liberal Arts, Indianapolis & New York: Bobbs-Merrill, 1958), p. 25. Original publication date: 1861.

23. Ibid., pp. 102–47.

24. See, e.g., Yves R. Simon, *Philosophy of Democratic Government* (Chicago: University of Chicago Press, 1951); Jacques Maritain, *Man and the State* (Chicago: University of Chicago Press, 1951); and John Hallowell, *The Moral Foundation of Democracy*.

25. See, e.g., David B. Truman, *The Governmental Process* (New York: Alfred A. Knopf, 1951); and Bertram Gross, *The Legislative Struggle* (New York: McGraw Hill, 1953).

26. Truman, ibid., pp. 514, 520.

27. Michael Margolis, *Viable Democracy* (New York: Penguin Press, 1979), pp. 125–54.

28. Seymour Martin Lipset, "Introduction," in Robert Michels, *Political Parties*, translated by Eden and Cedar Paul (New York: Collier Books, 1962), p. 33.

29. Joseph A. Schumpeter, *Capitalism, Socialist, and Democracy* (New York: Harper & Bros., 1947), p. 167. Original publication date 1942.

30. Ibid., p. 250.

31. Ibid., p. 242. See also Peter Bachrach, *The Theory of Democratic Elitism* (Lanham, Md.: University Press of America, 1980), pp. 18–21. Original publication date 1967.

32. Schumpeter, ibid., p.269.

33. Ibid., p. 285.

34. Lipset, "Introduction," p. 36.

35. Robert A. Dahl, *A Preface to Democratic Theory* (Chicago: University of Chicago Press, 1956); *Polyarchy* (New Haven, Conn.: Yale University Press, 1970); and "Further Reflections on 'The Elite Theory of Democracy,'" *American Political Science Review* 60/2 (June 1966): 296–305.

36. Lipset, "Introduction," pp. 36–37. See also Reinhold Niebuhr, *The Children of Light and the Children of Darkness* (New York: Charles Scribner's Sons, 1944).

37. Carole Pateman, *Participation and Democratic Theory* (Cambridge: Cambridge University Press, 1970).

38.   Jack L. Walker, "A Critique of Elitist Theory of Democracy," *American Political Science Review* 60/2 (June 1966): 285–95.

39.   Bachrach, *The Theory of Democratic Elitism*.

40.   Benjamin Barber, *Strong Democracy: Participatory Politics for a New Age* (Berkeley: University of California Press, 1984).

41.   Philip Green, *Retrieving Democracy: In Search of Civic Equality* (Totawa, N.J.: Rowman & Allanheld, 1985).

42.   Barber, *Strong Democracy,* pp. 34–35. See also Carol Gould, *Rethinking Democracy: Freedom and Social Cooperation in Politics, Economy, and Society* (Cambridge: Cambridge University Press, 1988).

43.   Barber, ibid., p. 215.

44.   Ibid., p. 261.

45.   Jane J. Mansbridge, *Beyond Adversarial Democracy* (Chicago: University of Chicago Press, 1983).

46.   Green, *Retrieving Democracy,* p. 5.

47.   Ibid., p. 269.

48.   See, e.g., Joshua Cohen and Joel Rogers, *On Democracy: Toward a Transformation of American Society* (New York: Penguin Books, 1983); Keith Graham, *The Battle of Democracy* (Totawa, N.J.: Barnes and Noble, 1986); Carol Gould, *Rethinking Democracy*.

49.   Martin Carnoy and Derek Shearer, *Economic Democracy: The Challenge of the 1980s* (Armonk: M. E. Sharpe, 1980), pp. 3–4.

50.   Peter Bachrach, "Interest, Participation, and Democratic Theory," in *Participation in Politics,* edited by J. Roland Pennock and John W. Chapman (New York: Lieber-Atherton, 1975), p. 47. See also Peter Bachrach, "Corporate Authority and Democratic Theory," in *Political Theory and Social Change,* edited by David Spitz (New York: Atherton Press, 1967).

51.   Bachrach, "Corporate Authority and Democratic Theory," pp. 264–67.

52.   Robert Dahl, *After the Revolution?* (New Haven, Conn.: Yale University Press, 1970), p. 120.

53.   Ibid., p. 116.

54.   Ibid., p. 64.

55.   Ibid., p. 123.

56. Robert Dahl, *A Preface to Economic Democracy* (Berkeley: University of California Press, 1985), p. 135.

57. Bachrach, *Theory of Democratic Elitism*, p. 38.

58. Bachrach, "Interest, Participation, and Democratic Theory," pp. 49–52. See also Henry Nelson Wieman, *Man's Ultimate Commitment* (Carbondale: Southern Illinois University Press, 1958), in which the concept of "creative intercommunication" is a central normative concept.

59. Samuel Bowles, David M. Gordon, and Thomas E. Weisskopf, *Beyond the Wasteland: A Democratic Alternative to Economic Decline* (Garden City. N.Y.: Anchor-Doubleday, 1984).

60. Sidney and Beatrice Webb, *Industrial Democracy* (New York: A. M. Kelley, 1965). Original publication date 1897.

61. Quoted in Milton Derber, *The American Idea of Industrial Democracy, 1865–1965* (Urbana: University of Illinois Press, 1970), p.7.

62. Quoted in ibid., p. 151.

63. Quoted in Carnoy and Shearer, *Economic Democracy*, p. 375.

64. Quoted in Paul Blumberg, *Industrial Democracy: The Sociology of Participation* (London: Constable, 1968), p. 8

65. See, e.g., Peter Brannen, *Authority and Participation in Industry* (New York: St. Martin's Press, 1983), pp. 13–14; Tom Schuller, *Democracy at Work* (Oxford: Oxford University Press, 1985), pp. 7–10; and Michael Poole, *Toward a New Industrial Democracy* (London: Routledge & Kegan Paul, 1986), p. 176.

66. Derber, *The American Idea of Industrial Democracy*, p. 104.

67. H. A. Clegg, *A New Approach to Industrial Democracy* (Oxford: Basil Blackwell, 1960), p. 131.

68. See Blumberg, *Industrial Democracy*, pp. 139–67, and Ronald Mason, *Participatory and Workplace Democracy* (Carbondale: Southern Illinois University Press, 1982), p. 151.

69. Poole, *Towards a New Industrial Democracy*, pp. 131–34.

70. Paul Bernstein, "Necessary Elements for Effective Worker Participation in Decision Making" in *Workplace Democracy and Social Change*, edited by Frank Lindenfield and Joyce Rothschild-Whitt (Boston: Porter Sargent, 1982), pp. 56–60.

71. Poole, *Towards a New Industrial Democracy*, pp. 47–81.

72. Douglas MacGregor, *The Human Side of Enterprise* (New York: McGraw Hill, 1960), pp. 33–57.

73. Douglas MacGregor, *The Professional Manager* (New York: McGraw Hill, 1967), pp. 84–96; and Rensis Likert, *The Human Organization* (New York: McGraw Hill, 1967), pp. 47–67.

74. Schuller, *Democracy at Work*, pp. 42, 58–62.

75. MacGregor, *The Human Side of Enterprise*, pp. 110–23; Douglas MacGregor, *Leadership and Motivation* (Cambridge: MIT Press, 1966), pp. 114–41; Likert, *The Human Organization*, pp. 40–41.

76. Rensis Likert, *New Patterns of Management* (New York: McGraw Hill, 1961), pp. 178–91.

77. Drucker, *Management*, pp. 231–45.

78. Blumberg, *Industrial Democracy*, pp. 44–46.

79. David Ewing, *Freedom Inside the Organization* (New York: E. P. Dutton, 1977).

80. Patricia H. Werhane, *Persons, Rights, and Corporations* (Engelwood Cliffs, N.J.: Prentice-Hall, 1985).

81. Bowles, Gordon, and Weisskopf, *Beyond the Wasteland*, pp. 323–51.

82. Schuller, *Democracy at Work*, p. 151.

83. Ibid., pp. 117–31; Peter Brannen, *Authority and Participation in Industry*, pp. 98–115; Poole, *Towards a New Industrial Democracy*, pp. 158–65.

84. Bowles, Gordon, and Weisskopf, *Beyond the Wasteland*, pp. 316–17. See also Gary Dorrien, "Beyond State and Market: Christianity and the Future of Economic Democracy," *Cross Currents* 45/2 (Summer 1995): 197–98.

85. Schuller, *Democracy at Work*, p. 72.

86. Daniel Zwerdling, *Workplace Democracy* (New York: Harper & Row, 1984).

87. Schuller, *Democracy at Work*, p. 62.

88. Brannen, *Authority and Participation in Industry*, pp. 129–45.

89. Schuller, *Democracy at Work*, p. 71. See also Dorrien, "Beyond State and Market," pp. 191–96.

90. Peter Abell, "Hierarchy and Democratic Authority" in *Work and Power*, edited by Burns, Karlsson, and Rus, pp. 141–71; Joyce Rothschild-Whitt, "The Collectivist Organization: An Alternative to Bureaucratic Mod-

els" in *Workplace Democracy and Social Change*, edited by Lindenfeld and Rothschild-Whitt, pp. 26–27.

CHAPTER 7.   INTERLUDE
THE SOCIALIST VISION REVISITED

1.   Norman Rush, "What Was Socialism . . . And Why We Will All Miss It So Much," *The Nation* (January 24, 1994): 90, 92.

2.   Robert N. Bellah, *The Broken Covenant* (New York: Seabury Press, 1975), chap. 5.

3.   Bernard Crick, *Socialism* (Minneapolis: University of Minnesota Press, 1987), p. 29.

4.   Robert A. Dahl, *A Preface to Economic Democracy* (Berkeley: University of California Press, 1985), p. 61. Cf. Carol C. Gould, *Rethinking Democracy: Freedom and Social Cooperation in Politics, Economy, and Society* (Cambridge: Cambridge University Press, 1988).

CHAPTER 8.
RELIGION AS CRITIQUE AND THE CRITIQUE OF RELIGION:
THE PROBLEM OF THE SELF IN THE MODERN WORLD

1.   Aloysius Pieris, "The Place of Non-Christian Cultures in the Evolution of Third World Theology," in *Irruption of the Third World*, edited by V. Fabella and S. Torres (Maryknoll: Orbis, 1983), p. 134.

2.   Albert Camus, *The Plague*, trans. by Stuart Gilbert (New York: Modern Library, 1948), pp. 192–93.

3.   Johann Baptist Metz, *Faith in History and Society*, translated by David Smith (New York: Seabury Press, 1980), p. 124.

4.   Richard Rubenstein, *The Age of Triage* (Boston: Beacon Press, 1983), p. 222.

5.   Ibid., p. 240.

6.   Tzvetan Todorov, *The Conquest of America*, translated by Richard Howard (New York: Harper & Row, 1984), pp. 185–86.

7.   Friedrich Nietzsche, *Twilight of the Idols and the Anti-Christ*, translated by R. J. Hollingdale (New York: Penguin Books, 1968), pp. 117–18.

8. Sigmund Freud, *The Future of an Illusion*, translated by W. D. Robson-Scott, revised by James Strachey (Garden City, N.Y.: Anchor Books, 1964), pp. 47–48.

9. Karl Marx, *The Marx-Engels Reader*, edited by Robert C. Tucker (New York: W. W. Norton, 1978), p. 54. Italics in the original.

10. Robert Ackerman, *Religion as Critique* (Amherst: University of Massachusetts Press, 1985), p. ix.

11. Ibid., p. 1.

12. Ibid., p. 3.

13. Ibid., p. 5.

14. *Womanspirit Rising: A Feminist Reader in Religion*, edited by Carol Christ and Judith Plaskow (New York: Harper & Row, 1979), p. 1. See also *Weaving the Visions: New Pattern of Feminist Spirituality*, edited by Judith Plaskow and Carol Christ (San Francisco: Harper & Row, 1989).

15. Riffat Hassan, "Women in the Context of Change and Confrontation within Muslim Communities," in *Women of Faith in Dialogue*, edited by Virginia Mollenkott (New York: Crossroad, 1987), p. 97.

16. Ibid., p. 98.

17. Ibid., p. 107.

18. Ibid., p. 198.

19. Ibid., p. 109.

20. Rubenstein, *Age of Triage*, p. 240.

21. Marjorie Hewitt Suchocki, "In Search of Justice: Religious Pluralism from a Feminist Perspective," in *The Myth of Christian Uniqueness*, edited by John Hick and Paul Knitter (Maryknoll: Orbis, 1987), p. 158.

22. Alan Race, *Christians and Religious Pluralism* (Maryknoll: Orbis, 1982). A decade later, Schubert Ogden developed what he considers to be a fourth possibility in *Is There Only One True Religion or Are There Many?* (Dallas, Tex.: Southern Methodist University Press, 1992).

23. Suchocki, "In Search of Justice," p. 149.

24. Ibid., p. 159.

25. Ibid., p. 157.

26. Ibid., p. 159.

27. Paul Knitter, "Toward a Liberation Theology of Religions," in *The Myth of Christian Uniqueness*, edited by Hick and Knitter, p. 182.

28. Ibid., p. 185.

29. Paul Knitter, "Making Sense of the Many," *Religious Studies Review* 15/3 (1989): 207.

30. Richard J. Bernstein, *Beyond Objectivism and Relativism* (Philadelphia: University of Pennsylvania Press, 1983), p. 8.

31. Quoted in Bernstein, ibid., pp. 223–24.

32. Caroline Whitbeck, "A Different Reality: Feminist Ontology," in *Beyond Domination: New Perspectives on Women and Philosophy*, edited by Carol Gould (Totowa, N.J.: Rowman & Allanheld, 1983), p. 82.

33. Pieris, "The Place of Non-Christian Cultures in the Evolution of Third World Theology," p. 134.

34. Alfred North Whitehead, *Religion in the Making* (New York: Meridian Books, 1960), pp. 58–59.

CHAPTER 9.
CROSSING THE BOUNDARIES:
INTERRELIGIOUS DIALOGUE AND THE POLITICAL QUESTION

1. On this tripartite typology (exclusivism, inclusivism, pluralism), see Alan Race, *Christians and Religious Plurality* (Maryknoll: Orbis, 1985). For alternative typologies, see Paul F. Knitter, *No Other Name? A Critical Survey of Christian Attitudes toward the World Religions* (Maryknoll: Orbis, 1985); and Glyn Richards, *Towards a Theology of Religions* (London & New York: Routledge, 1989). See also Schubert Ogden's construction of a fourth option in his *Is There Only One True Religion or Are There Many?* (Dallas, Tex.: SMU Press, 1992).

2. Leonard Swidler, John B. Cobb, Jr., Paul F. Knitter, Monika K. Hellwig, *Death or Dialogue? From the Age of Monologue to the Age of Dialogue* (Philadelphia: Trinity Press International, 1990).

3. Cf., e.g., David Lochhead, *The Dialogical Imperative* (Maryknoll: Orbis, 1988); and Maura O'Neill, *Women Speaking, Women Listening: Women in Interreligious Dialogue* (Maryknoll: Orbis, 1990), especially Part I.

4. Lochhead, *The Dialogical Imperative*, p. 79.

5. This definition is broader than Leonard Swidler's rendition: "dialogue is a two-way communication between persons who hold significantly differing views on a subject with the purpose of learning more truth about the

subject from the other" ("A Dialogue on Dialogue" in Swidler, et al., *Death or Dialogue,* p. 57).

6. See, e.g., Catherine Keller, *From a Broken Web: Separation, Sex, and Self* (Boston: Beacon Press, 1986).

7. Lochhead, *Dialogical Imperative,* p. 79.

8. Leonard Swidler, *After the Absolute: The Dialogical Future of Religious Reflection* (Minneapolis: Fortress Press, 1990), p. 6.

9. John B. Cobb, Jr., *Beyond Dialogue: Toward a Mutual Transformation of Christianity and Buddhism* (Philadelphia: Fortress Press, 1982), pp. 47–52. Cf. John B. Cobb, Jr., "Responses to Relativism: Common Ground, Deconstruction and Reconstruction," *Soundings* 73/4 (Winter 1990): 614.

10. Cobb cites Henry Nelson Wieman as his source for the concept of creative transformation. Cf. *Man's Ultimate Commitment* (Carbondale: University of Southern Illinois Press, 1958), p. 4.

11. John S. Dunne, *The Way of All the Earth: Experiments in Truth and Religion* (New York: Macmillan, 1972), p. ix.

12. Raimundo Panikkar, "The Invisible Harmony: A Universal Theory of Religion or a Cosmic Confidence in Reality," in *Toward a Universal Theology of Religion,* edited by Leonard Swidler (Maryknoll: Orbis, 1987), p. 141. See also Pannikar's *The Intra-Religious Dialogue* (New York: Paulist Press, 1978); and *Myth, Faith and Hermeneutics* (New York: Paulist Press, 1979).

13. Pannikar, "The Invisible Harmony," p. 143.

14. Ibid., p. 142.

15. Ibid., p. 145.

16. Cobb, "Responses to Relativism," p. 609.

17. Ibid., p. 615.

18. Ibid., p. 614.

19. Ibid., p. 616.

20. Iris Marion Young, *Justice and the Politics of Difference* (Princeton, N.J.: Princeton University Press, 1990), p. 40.

21. David Krieger, *The New Universalism* (Maryknoll: Orbis, 1991), p. 151, italics removed.

22. Krieger, it should be noted, draws heavily on the thought of Panikkar. In this connection, note Panikkar's essay, "The Myth of Pluralism:

The Tower of Babel—A Meditation on Non-Violence," *Cross Currents* 29/2 (Summer 1979:197–230.

23. Kreiger, *New Universalism*, pp. 15–16.

24. Ibid., p. 139.

25. Robert McAfee Brown, *Religion and Violence* (Philadelphia: Westminster Press, 1973), pp. 6–7. See also William Robert Miller, *Nonviolence: A Christian Interpretation* (New York: Association Press, 1964), pp. 33–45.

26. Young, *Justice and the Politics of Difference*, p. 241.

27. Krieger, *The New Universalism*, p. 150.

28. In *Conflict: Violence and Nonviolence*, edited by Joan Bondurant (New York: Lieber-Atherton, 1973), see Bondurant's articles, "The Search for a Theory of Conflict," p. 15, and "Creative Conflict and the Limits of Symbolic Violence," pp. 124, 128.

29. See Arne Naess, *Gandhi and Group Conflict* (Oslo: Universietsforlaget, 1974), pp. 28–34.

30. Joan Bondurant, *Conquest of Violence: The Gandhian Philosophy of Conflict*, new revised edition (Princeton, N.J.: Princeton University Press, 1965; original publication 1958), p. 231.

31. Marjorie Hewitt Suchocki, "In Search of Justice: Religious Pluralism from a Feminist Perspective," in *The Myth of Christian Uniqueness: Towards a Pluralistic Theology of Religions*, edited by John Hick and Paul Knitter (Maryknoll: Orbis, 1987), p. 149.

32. Ibid., p. 151.

33. Ibid., p. 153.

34. Ibid., p. 149.

35. Ibid., p. 155.

36. Paul Knitter, "Toward a Liberation Theology of Religions," *The Myth of Christian Uniqueness*, op. cit., p. 181, italics removed. On the presence of liberation themes in a wide range of the world's religions, see *World Religions and Human Liberation*, edited by Dan Cohn-Sherbok (Maryknoll: Orbis, 1992).

37. Young, *Justice and the Politics of Difference*, pp. 39–65.

38. Paul Knitter, "Dialogue and Liberation: Foundations for a Pluralist Theology of Religion," *Drew Gateway* 58/1 (1988), p. 18.

39. Knitter, "Toward a Liberation Theology of Religions," op. cit., pp. 181–90.

40.   Aloysius Pieris, "The Place of Non-Christian Religions and Cultures in the Evolution of Third World Theology," in *Irruption of the Third World: Challenge to Theology*, edited by V. Fabella and S. Torres (Maryknoll: Orbis, 1983), pp. 113–39.

41.   Knitter, "Toward a Liberation Theology of Religions," p. 183. Italics removed.

42.   Ibid., p. 185. Italics removed.

43.   Ibid., p. 190.

44.   Knitter, "Dialogue and Liberation," p. 26. Italics in the original.

45.   Ibid., p. 29.

46.   Ibid., p. 32. Italics in the original.

47.   Paula M. Cooey, "The Redemption of the Body: Post-Patriarchal Reconstruction of Inherited Christian Doctrine," in *After Patriarchy: Feminist Transformations of the World's Religions*, edited by Paula M. Cooey, William R. Eakin, Jay B. McDaniel (Maryknoll: Orbis, 1991), p. 111.

48.   See, e.g., ibid., pp. xi–xii. This collection, it should be noted, includes essays by women from a wide range of religious communities: Christian, Hindu, Jewish, Buddhist, Islamic, Native American, concluding with one by a "freethinker."

49.   Beverly Wildung Harrison, *Making the Connections: Essays in Feminist Social Ethics*, edited by Carol S. Robb (Boston: Beacon Press, 1985), p. 16.

50.   Cooey, Eakin, and McDaniel, *After Patriarchy*, p. xii, italics in the original.

51.   See, e.g., *Women of Faith in Dialogue*, edited by Virginia Mollenkott (New York: Crossroad, 1987); *Womanspirit Rising*, edited by Carol P. Christ and Judith Plaskow (New York : Harper & Row, 1979); *Weaving the Visions*, edited by Judith Plaskow and Carol P. Christ (San Francisco: Harper & Row, 1989); *After Patriarchy*, edited by Paula M. Cooey, et al.

52.   O'Neill, op. cit., pp. 57–59. In this connection, see Sheila Greeve Davaney's radical historicist critique of appeals to women's experience by feminist theologians—as if that experience were the same the world over—in her article, "The Limits of Appeal to Women's Experience," in *Shaping New Visions: Gender and Values in American Culture*, edited by Clarissa W. Atkinson, Con-

stance H. Buchanan, and Margaret R. Miles (Ann Arbor, Mich.: UMI Research Press, 1987), pp. 31–49. Yet, despite her strong historicist thesis, Davaney is supportive of a critical pragmatics promoting full participation by women in their respective communities. See also Wendy Doniger's critique of David Tracy's "radical pluralism" as insufficiently radical in "Pluralism and Intolerance in Hinduism," in *Radical Pluralism and Truth*, edited by Werner G. Jeanrond and Jennifer L. Rike (New York: Crossroad, 1991), pp. 215–33. In addition, see John Millbank's attack on the "universalism" inherent in the idea of interreligious dialogue (especially in the "praxis" approach of Knitter and Suchocki) as a form of imperialism in his "The End of Dialogue," in *Christian Uniqueness Reconsidered*, edited by Gavin D'Costa (Maryknoll: Orbis, 1990), pp. 174–91. Dialogue, Millbank concludes, should be replaced with "mutual suspicion." Finally, see Kay A. Read's article on the "familiar and the strange" in cross-cultural interpretation, "Negotiating the Familiar and the Strange in Aztec Ethics," *The Journal of Religious Ethics* 15/1 (Spring 1987): 1–13. Read is responding to the critical reaction of Charles Reynolds and Ronald Green to an earlier article of hers, both of which appear in *The Journal of Religious Ethics* 14/1 (Spring 1986): 113–56.

53. O'Neill, *Women Speaking*, p. 60. Italics in original.

54. Ibid., p. 64.

55. Ibid., pp. 3–20. In this connection, she cites the work of Caroline Whitbeck who asserts, as a key to her feminist ontology, that "The model of the person that I propose is a relational and historical model but, unlike the relational and historical models of patriarchy, one that takes seriously *everyone's* creativity and moral integrity" ("A Different Reality: Feminist Ontology," in *Beyond Domination: Perspectives on Women and Philosophy*, edited by Carol C. Gould [Totawa, N.J.: Rowman & Allanheld, 1983], p. 77, italics added). From the perspective of "goddess consciousness," Winnie Tomm has developed a similar model of the person in her paradigm of a "permeable self." See "Goddess Consciousness and Social Realities: The 'Permeable Self,'" in *The Annual Review of Women in World Religions*, vol. I, edited by Arvind Sharma and Katherine K. Young (Albany: State University of New York Press, 1991), pp. 71–104.

56. On the concept of the "axial age," see Karl Jaspers, *The Origin and Goal of History*, trans. Michael Bullock (New Haven, Conn.: Yale University Press, 1953). According to Jaspers, during a period ranging, roughly, from 800 to 200 B.C.E., a radical transformation of human understanding emerged in many cultures across the world, shifting from a narrow parochialism to an inclusive universalism.

CHAPTER 10.   INTERLUDE
WISDOM AND COMPASSION—
THE DEEPER DIMENSIONS OF UNDERSTANDING

1.   Alfred North Whitehead, *The Aims of Education and Other Essays* (New York: Free Press, 1929, 1957; first Free Press paperback 1967), p. 30.

2.   Beverly Harrison, "The Power of Anger in the Work of Love: Christian Ethics for Women and Other Strangers," in Harrison, *Making the Connections*, edited by Carol S. Robb (Boston: Beacon Press, 1985), pp. 3–21.

3.   Exodus 23:9.

4.   I Corinthians 12:26.

5.   I John 3:16.

6.   From Shantideva's *Compendium of Doctrine*, excerpts included in *Sources of Indian Tradition* I, edited by Theodore deBary, et al. (New York: Columbia University Press, 1958), p. 161.

7.   Excerpts from *Black Elk Speaks* contained in *Religious Worlds: Primary Readings in Comparative Perspective*, edited by John Dominic Crossan, et al. (Dubuque, Iowa: Kendall/Hunt, 1991), p. 569.

8.   Ibid., p. 571.

9.   Bernard Eugene Meland, *The Reawakening of the Christian Faith* (New York: Macmillan, 1949), p. 120.

10.   Isaiah 11:6–9.

11.   Matthew 25:37–40.

CHAPTER 11.
THE POLITICS OF ANNIHILATION
AND THE MISSION OF HIGHER EDUCATION

1.   Walker Knight, "The Peacemaker," in *Peace is Our Profession*, edited by Jan Barry (Montclair, N.J.: East River Anthology, 1981), pp. 172–73.

2.   John Rawls, *A Theory of Justice* (Cambridge: Harvard University Press, 1971). Within Anglo-American discourse over moral matters, Rawls's reflection in this text stimulated a widespread debate over the meaning of justice and the pertinence of justice to our common life. Even though Rawls him-

self has refined and modified his position over the past quarter of a century, the debate over the matter of justice initiated by him continues even yet.

3. Robert Cumming Neville, *Behind the Masks of God: An Essay toward Comparative Theology* (Albany: State University of New York Press, 1991), pp. 25–26: "Tillich's preoccupation with the intellectual fortunes of the European theological community prevented him from seeing an even greater change in religious context. Our problem now, it can be argued, is the challenge of distributive justice. This problem subordinates, without removing, the subjective problems of personal anxiety and the search for immortality, forgiveness, and meaning, to the more objective problems of structural and attitudinal social change."

4. Paul Tillich, *The Courage to Be* (New Haven & London: Yale University Press, 1952), pp. 40–63.

5. Tzvetan Todorov, *The Conquest of America: The Question of the Other*, translated by Richard Howard (New York: Harper & Row, 1985).

6. Ibid., p. 3, italics in the original.

7. Ibid., p. 5.

8. Ibid., pp. 42–43.

9. Ibid., p. 143.

10. Ibid., p. 145.

11. Gil Elliot, *Twentieth-Century Book of the Dead* (London: Allen Lane, Penguin Press, 1972).

12. Edith Wyschogrod, *Spirit in Ashes: Hegel, Heidegger, and Man-Made Mass Death* (New Haven & London: Yale University Press, 1985).

13. Ibid., p. 15.

14. *Beyond Rhetoric—A New American Agenda for Children and Families: Final Report of the National Commission on Children* (Washington, D.C.: National Commission on Children, 1991), p. 24. The National Commission was chaired by Senator John D. Rockefeller IV. The paragraph preceding the datum in the text above announces: "Today, children are the poorest Americans. One in five lives in a family with an income below the federal poverty level. One in four infants and toddlers under the age of three is poor. Nearly 13 million children live in poverty, more than 2 million more than a decade ago. Many of these children are desperately poor; nearly 5 million live in families with incomes less than half the federal poverty level."

15. Robert O. Johann, "Rationality, Justice, and Dominant Ends," in *The Value of Justice: Essays on the Theory and Practice of Social Virtue* (New York: Fordham University Press, 1979), pp. 20–21.

16. Iris Marion Young, *Justice and the Politics of Difference* (Princeton, N.J.: Princeton University Press, 1990), p. 159.

17. Henry Shue, *Basic Rights: Subsistence, Affluence, and U.S. Foreign Policy* (Princeton, N.J.: Princeton University Press, 1980), p. 23.

18. On "cultural imperialism," see Young, *Justice and the Politics of Difference*, pp. 58–61, 123–24.

19. Tillich, *The Courage to Be*.

20. Bruce Wilshire, *The Moral Collapse of the University: Professionalism, Purity, and Alienation* (Albany: State University of New York, 1990), p. 217.

21. Ibid., p. 190.

22. Ibid., pp. 211–12.

23. Jürgen Habermas, *Knowledge and Human Interests*, translated by Jeremy J. Shapiro (Boston: Beacon Press, 1971).

24. William James, *The Varieties of Religious Experience: A Study in Human Nature* (New York: Modern Library, 1902), p. 35; cited in Wilshire, *Moral Collapse of the University*, p. 108.

25. Marjorie Hewitt Suchocki, "In Search of Justice: Religious Pluralism from a Feminist Perspective," in *The Myth of Christian Uniqueness*, edited by John Hick and Paul Knitter (Maryknoll: Orbis Books, 1987), p. 149.

26. Young, *Justice and the Politics of Difference*, pp. 39–65.

27. See, e.g., *Women of Faith in Dialogue*, edited by Virginia Mollenkott (New York: Crossroad, 1987); Maura O'Neill, *Women Speaking, Women Listening: Women in Interreligious Dialogue*, Faith Meets Faith Series (Maryknoll: Orbis Books, 1990); *Womanspirit Rising*, edited by Carol P. Christ and Judith Plaskow (New York: Harper & Row, 1979); *Weaving the Visions*, edited by Judith Plaskow and Carol P. Christ (San Francisco: Harper & Row, 1989); *After Patriarchy: Feminist Transformations of the World's Religions*, edited by Paula M. Cooey, William R. Eakin, Jay B. McDaniel (Maryknoll: Orbis, 1991).

28. David Tracy, *Plurality and Ambiguity: Hermeneutics, Religion, Hope* (San Francisco: Harper & Row, 1987), chapter 5 "Resistance and Hope: The Question of Religion," pp. 82–114.

29. Micah 6:8.

CHAPTER 12.
ON MAKING PEACE:
NONVIOLENCE AND THE PRINCIPLE OF RELATIONALITY

1. Jacques Maritain, *Integral Humanism*, translated by Joseph W. Evans (New York: Scribners, 1968), pp. 127–28.

2. Hannah Arendt, *On Violence* (New York: Harcourt, Brace & World, 1970), see especially section 2, pp. 35–56.

3. Robert Litke, "On the Deep Structure of Violence," in *In the Interest of Peace: A Spectrum of Philosophical Views*, edited by Kenneth H. Klein and Joseph C. Kunkel (Wakefield, N.H.: Longwood Academic, 1990), pp. 33–43.

4. Dom Helder Camara, *Spiral of Violence*, translated by Della Couling (Denville, N.J.: Dimension Books, 1971), pp. 29–30.

5. Litke, "Deep Structure of Violence," pp. 36–37.

6. Ibid., pp. 39, 42.

7. Sergio Cotta, *Why Violence? A Philosophical Interpretation*, translated by Giovanni Gullace (Gainesville: University of Florida Press, 1985), p. 66.

8. Joan Bondurant, "Creative Conflict and the Limits of Symbolic Violence," in *Conflict: Violence and Nonviolence*, edited by Joan Bondurant (New York: Lieber-Atherton, 1971), pp. 122–23.

9. Margaret Fisher, "Contrasting Approaches to Conflict," in *Conflict*, edited by Bondurant, pp. 183–84.

10. Ibid., p. 190.

11. Joan V. Bondurant, *Conquest of Violence: The Gandhian Philosophy of Conflict* (new rev. ed., Princeton, N.J.: Princeton University Press, 1988, original edition 1958), p. 195.

12. Henry Nelson Wieman, *Man's Ultimate Commitment* (Carbondale: Southern Illinois University Press, 1958), pp. 3–4.

13. Nathaniel Altman, *The Nonviolent Revolution* (Longmead, Shaftesbury, Dorset: Element Books, 1988), p. 9.

14. Martin Luther King, Jr., *Stride toward Freedom: The Montgomery Story* (San Francisco: Harper & Row, 1958), pp. 102–103.

15. Martin Luther King, Jr., "Letter from Birmingham City Jail (1963)," in *A Testament of Hope: The Essential Writings of Martin Luther King, Jr.*, edited by James M. Washington (San Francisco: Harper & Row, 1986), p. 295.

16.   Betty A. Reardon, *Women and Peace: Feminist Visions of Global Security* (Albany: State University of New York Press, 1993), pp. 45–47.

17.   Ibid., p. 159.

18.   Thich Nhat Hanh, *Being Peace* (Berkeley: Parallax Press, 1987), p. 45.

19.   Ibid., pp. 85–87.

20.   See Mary Roodkowsky, "Feminism, Peace, and Power," in *Nonviolent Action and Social Change*, edited by Severyn T. Bruyn and Paula M. Rayman (New York: Irvington, 1979), pp. 254–66.

21.   Thich Nhat Hanh, *Love in Action: Writings on Nonviolent Social Change* (Berkeley: Parallax Press, 1993), p. 68.

22.   Gene Sharp, *Exploring Nonviolent Alternatives* (Boston: Porter Sargent, 1970), pp. 50–51.

23.   See Paul Joseph, *Peace Politics: The United States Between the Old and New World Orders* (Philadelphia: Temple University Press, 1993), chapter 1, "National Security in the Old and New World Orders," pp. 1–21.

24.   M. Kay Harris, "Moving into the New Millennium: Toward a Feminist Vision of Justice," in *Criminology as Peacemaking*, edited by Harold E. Pepinski and Richard Quinney (Bloomington: Indiana University Press, 1991), p. 91.

25.   Nhat Hanh, *Love in Action*, p. 39.

26.   King, *Stride toward Freedom*, pp. 103–106.

CHAPTER 13.   INTERLUDE
CRIMINALITY AND COMMUNITY

1.   Norval Morris and Gordon Hawkins, *Letter to the President on Crime Control* (Chicago: University of Chicago Press, 1977), p. 3.

2.   Patricia Horn, "Caging America: The U.S. Imprisonment Binge," *Dollars and Sense* (September 1991): 14.

3.   Michel Foucault, *Discipline and Punish: The Birth of the Prison*, translated by Alan Sheridan (New York: Pantheon Books, 1977).

4.   See Edwin H. Sutherland, *White Collar Crime: The Uncut Version* (New Haven, Conn.: Yale University Press, 1983). In its original publication in 1949, Sutherland's study was radically edited by the publisher, removing specific identities and altering case studies to "protect" the perpetrators of the ille-

gal activity. Sutherland had introduced the concept of "white-collar crime" at a meeting of the American Sociological Association in 1939. A more recent set of essays honoring Sutherland's work reexamines the concept, *White-Collar Crime Reconsidered*, edited by Kip Schlegel and David Weisburd (Boston: Northeastern University Press, 1992).

5. See, e.g., Gilbert Geis, "Upperworld Crime" in *Current Perspectives on Criminal Behavior*, edited by Abraham Blumberg (New York: Alfred A. Knopf, 1974/1981), pp. 179–98.

6. *Corporate Violence: Injury and Death for Profit*, edited by Stuart L. Hills (Totowa, N.J.: Rowman & Littlefield, 1987), p. vii.

7. Richard Guarasci, "Death by Cotton Dust," in *Corporate Violence*, edited by Hills, p. 89. Studies of a range of kinds of white-collar crimes have been published in *The Annals of the American Academy of Political and Social Science*, volume 525 (January 1993), *White-Collar Crime*, edited by Gilbert Geis and Paul Jesilow.

8. Nancy Frank, "Maiming and Killing: Occupational Health Crimes," in *White-Collar Crime*, edited by Geis and Jesilow, p. 108.

9. See *Criminology as Peacemaking*, edited by Harold E. Pepinsky and Richard Quinney (Bloomington: Indiana University Press, 1991); and Richard Quinney and John Wildeman, *The Problem of Crime: A Peace and Social Justice Perspective*, 3d ed. (Mountain View, Calif.: Mayfield, 1991).

10. Fay Honey Knopp, "Community Solutions to Sexual Violence," in *Criminology as Peacemaking*, edited by Pepinsky and Quinney, p. 182.

CHAPTER 14.
ECOLOGY AND SOCIAL JUSTICE:
SHATTERING THE BOUNDARIES OF MORAL COMMUNITY

1. See Gordon D. Kaufman, *An Essay in Theological Method* (Missoula, Mont.: Scholars Press, 1975); and George Lindbeck, *The Nature of Doctrine* (Philadelphia: Westminster Press, 1984).

2. Meland was strongly influenced by the kind of experiential turn signalled in William James's radical empiricism and in Alfred North Whitehead's reformed subjectivist principle.

3. Bernard Eugene Meland, *Fallible Forms and Symbols* (Philadelphia: Fortress Press, 1976), 150–51. See also Meland, *Faith and Culture* (New York: Oxford University Press, 1953), 142–43.

4. Meland, *Fallible Forms*, p. 54.

5. Ibid., p. 152.

6. Bernard Eugene Meland, *Realities of Faith* (New York: Oxford University Press, 1962), p. 262.

7. E.g., Meland, *Fallible Forms*, pp. 24, 28.

8. Ibid., p. 108.

9. Meland, *Faith and Culture*, p. 133.

10. Ibid., p. 140. See also p. 181 and Meland, *The Secularization of Modern Cultures* (New York: Oxford University Press, 1966), p. 119.

11. Meland, *Fallible Forms*, p. 45.

12. Meland, *Faith and Culture*, p. 161.

13. Ibid., p. 169.

14. Meland, *Fallible Forms*, pp. xiii–xiv; see also Meland, *Faith and Culture*, p. 120.

15. Meland, *Higher Education and the Human Spirit* (Chicago: University of Chicago Press, 1953), p. 63; see all of chap. 5.

16. Meland, *Faith and Culture*, pp. 172–75.

17. Arne Naess, "The Shallow and the Deep, Long-Range Ecology Movement," *Inquiry* 16 (1973):95–100. See also Naess, *Ecology, Community, and Lifestyle*, translated by David Rothenberg (Cambridge: Cambridge University Press, 1989), p. 68.

18. Naess, "Shallow and Deep Ecology," p. 96.

19. Ibid.

20. Naess, *Ecology, Community, and Lifestyle*, p. 29; see also Bill Devall and George Sessions, *Deep Ecology* (Salt Lake City: Peregrine Smith Books, 1985), p. 70.

21. Devall and Sessions, *Deep Ecology*, p. 66.

22. Arne Naess, "Identification as a Source of Deep Ecological Attitudes," in *Deep Ecology*, edited by Michael Tobias (San Marcos, Calif.: Avant Books, 1984), pp. 259–61; see also Naess, *Ecology, Community, and Lifestyle*, pp. 84–86.

23. Devall and Sessions, *Deep Ecology*, p. 67.

24. Naess, "Identification," p. 261; see also "Self-Realization in Mixed Communities of Humans, Bears, Sheep, and Wolves," in *Inquiry* 22 (1979):234.

25. Naess, "Identification," 261. Italics removed.

26. Ibid., p. 266; see also Naess, "Self-Realization in Mixed Communities," pp. 231–41 and *Ecology, Community,, and Lifestyle*, pp. 170–71, 174.

27. Murray Bookchin, *Remaking Society* (Boston: South End Press, 1990), p. 60.

28. Murray Bookchin, *The Modern Crisis*, 2d rev. ed. (Montreal: Black Rose Books, 1987), p. 55; see also Murray Bookchin, *The Ecology of Freedom*, rev. ed. (Montreal: Black Rose Books, 1991), pp. 20–27.

29. Murray Bookchin, *The Philosophy of Social Ecology* (Montreal: Black Rose Books, 1990), p. 162.

30. Bookchin, *Remaking Society*, pp. 75–94.

31. Ibid., pp. 46, 94.

32. Murray Bookchin and Dave Foreman, *Defending the Earth* (Boston: South End Press, 1991), p. 33.

33. Bookchin, The *Ecology of Freedom*, ch. 12.

34. Bookchin, *Remaking Society*, p. 155.

35. Bookchin, *The Ecology of Freedom*, p. 217.

36. E.g., Murray Bookchin, "Toward a Philosophy of Nature: The Bases for an Ecological Ethics," in *Deep Ecology*, edited by Michael Tobias, p. 235.

37. E.g., Bookchin, *The Modern Crisis*, p. 72.

38. Ibid., p, 25, italics in the original.

39. Bookchin and Foreman, *Defending the Earth*, pp. 35–36.

40. Bookchin, "Toward a Philosophy of Nature," pp. 228–31.

41. Bookchin, *The Modern Crisis*, p. 61.

42. Alasdair MacIntyre, *After Virtue*, 2d ed. (Notre Dame, Ind.: University of Notre Dame Press, 1984), p. 263.

43. Ibid., 221.

44. Meland, *Faith and Culture*, p. 85.

45. Ibid., p. 102.

46.   Susan Flader, *Thinking Like a Mountain* (Columbia: University of Missouri Press, 1974), p. 34.

47.   Aldo Leopold, *Sand County Almanac* (London: Oxford University Press, 1968), p. 204.

48.   Ibid., p. 202.

49.   Ibid., p. 216.

50.   Ibid., p. 204.

51.   J. Baird Callicott, *In Defense of the Land Ethic* (Albany: State University of New York Press, 1989), p. 84; see also Jon M. Moline, "Aldo Leopold and the Moral Community," *Environmental Ethics* 8 (1986):99–120; and Peter S. Wenz, *Environmental Justice* (Albany: State University of New York Press, 1988), section 13.8.

52.   Tom Regan, *The Case for Animal Rights* (Berkeley: University of California Press, 1983), p. 362.

53.   Leopold, *Sand County Almanac*, pp. 224–25; see also quotes in Flader, *Thinking Like a Mountain*, pp. 18, 31.

54.   Leopold, *Sand County Almanac*, p. 223.

55.   Callicott, *In Defense of the Land Ethic*, p. 87.

56.   See Leopold, *Sand County Almanac*, pp. 204, 210, 211.

57.   The term *morally considerable*, coined by Kenneth Goodpaster, is applied in this manner by Callicott, *In Defense of the Land Ethic*, pp. 262–64.

58.   Charles Birch and John B. Cobb, Jr., *The Liberation of Life* (Cambridge: Cambridge University Press, 1981), p. 151.

59.   Scott Buchanan, "Natural Law and Teleology," in John Cogley, et al., *Natural Law and Modern Society* (Cleveland: World Publishing, 1963), pp. 140, 150.

60.   Leopold, *Sand County Almanac*, p. 218.

61.   Ibid., p. 221.

62.   Ibid., pp. 209–10; see also 225.

63.   John Rawls, *A Theory of Justice* (Cambridge: Harvard University Press, 1971).

64.   Iris Marion Young, *Justice and the Politics of Difference* (Princeton, N.J.: Princeton University Press, 1990), pp. 18, 25, 27.

65. Carol C. Gould, *Rethinking Democracy* (Cambridge: Cambridge University Press, 1990), p. 105.

66. Robert O. Johann, "Rationality, Justice, and Dominant Ends," in *The Value of Justice*, edited by Charles A. Kelbley (New York: Fordham University Press, 1979), p. 21.

67. See Gould, *Rethinking Democracy*, p. 77.

68. This is the point of the argument by Paul W. Taylor in his *Respect for Nature* (Princeton, N.J.: Princeton University Press, 1986).

69. This is the perspective of Aldo Leopold in his *Sand County Almanac*, see also Wenz, *Environmental Justice*, ch. 13.

70. Young, *Justice and the Politics of Difference*, chapters 1 and 2.

CHAPTER 15.   POSTLUDE
KOINONOLOGY AND THE ECOLOGICAL PRINCIPLE

1. Thich Nhat Hanh, *Love in Action: Writings on Nonviolent Social Change* (Berkeley: Parallax Press, 1993), p. 132.

2. Stan Steiner, quoted in George Sessions, "Ecological Consciousness and Paradigm Change," in *Deep Ecology*, edited by Michael Tobias (San Marcos, Calif.: Avant Books, 1984/1988), p. 35.

3. John B. Cobb, Jr., *Is It Too Late? A Theology of Ecology* (Beverly Hills, Calif.: Bruce, 1972), p. 28.

4. Ibid., pp. 124–25.

5. André Gorz, *Ecology as Politics*, translated by Patsy Vigderman and Jonathan Cloud (Boston: South End Press, 1980), p. 3.

6. Ibid., p. 8.

7. Tony Brun, "Social Ecology: A Timely Paradigm for Reflection and Praxis for Life in Latin America," in *Ecotheology: Voices from South and North*, edited by David G. Hallman (Maryknoll: Orbis, 1994), p. 82.

8. H. Richard Niebuhr, *The Responsible Self: An Essay in Christian Moral Philosophy* (San Francisco: Harper & Row, 1978).

9. Ibid., p. 56.

10. Ibid., p. 97.

11. Ibid., p. 87.

12.   See Paul Tillich, *Morality and Beyond* (Louisville, Ky.: Westminster John Knox Press, 1995). Originally published in 1963.

13.   M. K. Gandhi, *Non-Violent Resistance* (New York: Schocken Books, 1961), p. 48.

INDEX